The Civil War Letters of Joseph Hopkins Twichell

The Civil War Letters of

Edited by Peter Messent
and Steve Courtney

The University of Georgia Press   *Athens and London*

To Joanne —
and Scott —
with all best wishes +
appreciation for your
interest —
Steve Courtney

Joseph Hopkins Twichell

A CHAPLAIN'S STORY

The paper in

this book meets

the guidelines

for permanence

and durability

of the Committee

on Production

Guidelines for

Book Longevity

of the

Council on Library

Resources.

© 2006 by the University of Georgia Press
Athens, Georgia 30602
Set in 10 on 14 Carter and Cone Galiard by BookComp
Printed and bound by Maple-Vail
Printed in the United States of America
10 09 08 07 06 C 5 4 3 2 1

Library of Congress Cataloging-in-Publication Data
Twichell, Joseph Hopkins, 1838–1918.
The Civil War letters of Joseph Hopkins Twichell :
a chaplain's story / edited by Peter Messent and
Steve Courtney.
      p. cm.
Includes bibliographical references and index.
ISBN-13: 978-0-8203-2693-1 (hardcover : alk. paper)
ISBN-10: 0-8203-2693-3 (hardcover : alk. paper)
1. Twichell, Joseph Hopkins, 1838–1918—Correspondence.
2. United States—History—Civil War, 1861–1865—Personal
narratives. 3. United States—History—Civil War, 1861–1865
—Religious aspects. 4. United States—History—Civil War,
1861–1865—Chaplains. 5. Chaplains, Military—United
States—Correspondence. I. Messent, Peter B. II. Courtney,
Steve, 1948–   III. Title.
E605.T85 2006
973.7'78'092—dc22   2005020764
British Library Cataloging-in-Publication Data available

For Carin and Lisa

CONTENTS

ILLUSTRATIONS

ACKNOWLEDGMENTS

The Civil War letters of Joseph Hopkins Twichell—nearly nine hundred pages are held by the Yale Collection of American Literature in the Beinecke Rare Book and Manuscript Library—provide the basis for the selection that follows. We thank the Library, and especially Steve Jones, for access to the letters and for help in having them copied. We also thank Joseph Twichell's descendants, Margaret Mowbray Jones, Chase Twichell, David C. Twichell, and Charles Ives Tyler for their help and encouragement. Our thanks, too, to Jacqui Clay, who did a first-class job of transcribing these letters from photocopy to word-processed form; to our editor at Georgia University Press, Nancy Grayson, a very supportive presence in the project; to Jon Davies, project editor, for his quietly thorough supervision of the publication process; to Gay Gragson, copy editor, for her attention to detail and substantive suggestions; to John McLeod, marketing and sales manager, and to Sandra Hudson, designer. Peter Messent wishes to thank the British Academy for its generous support that enabled him to do his share of the research for this project, and the University of Nottingham, which gave financial support for some of the costs involved. Steve Courtney would like to thank Asylum Hill Congregational Church, its senior minister, Gary Miller, its senior associate minister, Peter Grandy, and its Webmaster, Gery Krewson. Others who helped both of us enormously are Tess Allard, John W. Brinsfield, Janet Burkitt, Robert E. L. Crick, Diane Depew, Kerry Driscoll, Ellen Hollister, Jim Kuykendall, Thomas P. Lowry, Susan C. Martin, John Reazer, Wayne Rollins, Andrew H. Walsh, Thomas Adrian Wheat, and librarians at the Connecticut State Library, the Harriet Beecher Stowe Center, Andover Newton Theological Seminary, the College of the Holy Cross, the Indiana State Library, the Library of Congress, and the Mark Twain Papers and Project at the University of California. And, of course, we wish to acknowledge the sacrifice and support of our beloved wives, Carin Messent and Lisa Bower Courtney.

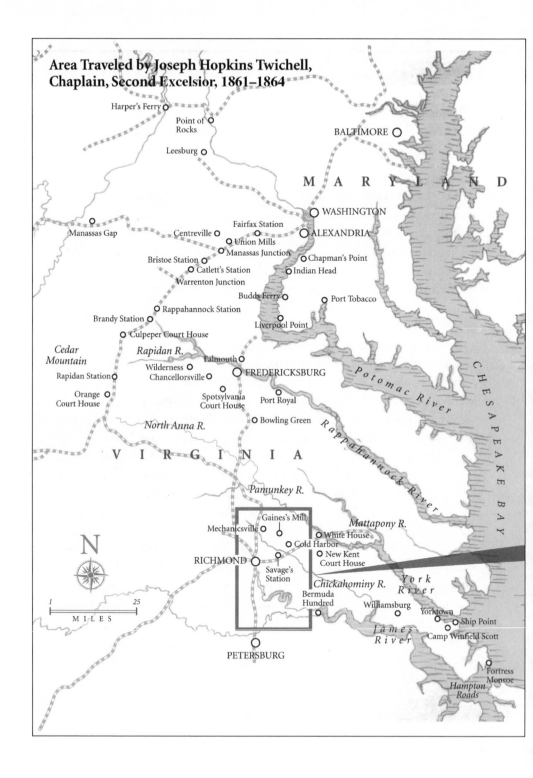

Area Traveled by Joseph Hopkins Twichell, Chaplain, Second Excelsior, 1861–1864

Harper's Ferry

Point of Rocks

Leesburg

BALTIMORE

M A R Y L A N D

WASHINGTON

Manassas Gap

Fairfax Station

Centreville

ALEXANDRIA

Union Mills

Manassas Junction

Bristoe Station

Chapman's Point

Catlett's Station

Indian Head

Warrenton Junction

Budds Ferry

Port Tobacco

Rappahannock Station

Brandy Station

Liverpool Point

Culpeper Court House

Cedar Mountain

Rapidan R.

Falmouth

Wilderness

FREDERICKSBURG

Rapidan Station

Chancellorsville

Orange Court House

Spotsylvania Court House

Port Royal

North Anna R.

Bowling Green

V I R G I N I A

P o t o m a c   R i v e r

R a p p a h a n n o c k   R i v e r

C H E S A P E A K E   B A Y

Pamunkey R.

Gaines's Mill

Mattapony R.

Mechanicsville

White House

Cold Harbor

N

RICHMOND

New Kent Court House

Savage's Station

Chickahominy R.

York River

Bermuda Hundred

Williamsburg

Yorktown

Ship Point

J a m e s   R i v e r

Camp Winfield Scott

1   25

M I L E S

PETERSBURG

Fortress Monroe

Hampton Roads

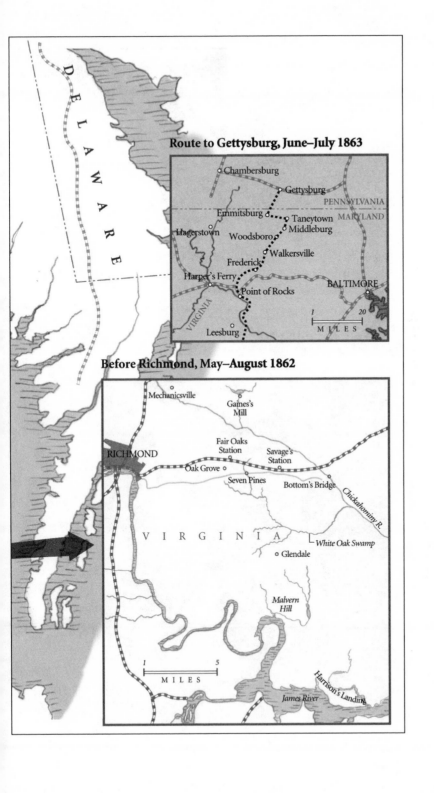

Route to Gettysburg, June–July 1863

Chambersburg
Gettysburg
PENNSYLVANIA
Emmitsburg
Taneytown
MARYLAND
Hagerstown
Middleburg
Woodsboro
Walkersville
Frederick
Harper's Ferry
Point of Rocks
BALTIMORE
Leesburg
VIRGINIA

1   20
M I L E S

DELAWARE

Before Richmond, May–August 1862

Mechanicsville
Gaines's Mill
Fair Oaks Station
Savage's Station
RICHMOND
Oak Grove
Seven Pines
Bottom's Bridge
Chickahominy R.

V I R G I N I A
White Oak Swamp
Glendale

Malvern Hill

1   5
M I L E S

Harrison's Landing
James River

The Civil War Letters of Joseph Hopkins Twichell

Joseph Hopkins Twichell was just two years out of Yale and studying for the clergy when he enlisted as chaplain of the Jackson Regiment of Daniel Sickles's Excelsior Brigade in Lower Manhattan. The irony of a small-town New England Congregationalist minister-in-training shepherding the souls of tough Irish Catholics from the brickyards and tanneries of this neighborhood was not lost on Twichell. He wrote to his father on 22 April 1861: "If you ask why I fixed upon this particular regiment, composed as it is of rough, wicked men, I answer, that was the very reason. I saw that the companies of the better class of citizens were all attended by Chaplains, but nothing was said about these. *There*, I thought, is a place for me. . . . I should not expect a revival, but I should expect to make some good impressions, by treating with kindness a class of men who are little used to it."

Twichell consequently accompanied the regiment through three years of war—through the Peninsula Campaign, the Second Bull Run Campaign, Fredericksburg, Chancellorsville, Gettysburg, Spotsylvania, and the Wilderness. Almost 150 years after the event, the letters he wrote back home describing the three years of his wartime experience are both powerful and emotive, carrying the present-day reader back to the actions, thoughts, and feelings of that troubled but momentous time. Twichell's letters, unlike those of many soldiers (and indeed of a good number of chaplains), are written in the style of an educated young man of the era and describe battles, hospitals, the religious life of the troops, internal regimental politics, national politics, and issues of slavery and race. They are highly literate and descriptively vivid. But they also use a variety of other devices to convey their meaning and message effectively, including plain speaking ("so far as slavery is concerned, nothing could deepen my hatred of it"), homely but striking simile ("regiments . . . as plenty as blackberries"), and forceful vernacular expressions ("the Army is boss of this job"; "I can no more supply advice . . . than I could teach a horse to knit"). If at times Twichell gives way to the overrhetorical verbal flourish, at others his use of heightened language works to genuine emotional effect, as when he looks down from a raised position on a battle below to describe how "I . . . felt all free America beating in my one heart, as I saw our standards plunged in the smoke of battle, rising and falling, advancing and borne backward with its mighty tide." Similarly, near Williamsburg on 9 May 1862, he writes of his first encounter with the aftermath of fight:

> By-and-by we encountered a dead horse with a hideous wound in his side, then another, then four or five lying together, all mangled by shot or shell. . . . A rod or two further on, and our horses shied at a rebel corpse, lying stark and stiff, the hands clutched above the head, while the open bosom showed a ghastly wound— then another and another. It was horrible and my brain almost reeled. . . . [T]here I saw sights that can never fade from my memory. "Sin entered into the world and death through sin" kept ringing through my brain as I wandered among the slain unburied.

Although his descriptions of battle have been partially quoted in several published sources—Carl Sandburg's *Abraham Lincoln: The War Years*, Harry W. Pfanz's *Gettysburg: The Second Day*, and Kenneth M. Andrews's *Nook Farm: Mark Twain's Hartford Circle*—the vast bulk of the letters have remained unknown until now. It is the present volume's task, and the editors' pleasure, to bring them before a wider audience.

The Reverend Joseph Hopkins Twichell was one of Mark Twain's closest friends. He was also a well-known figure in the religious and cultural life of New England and New York in the late nineteenth century. The frequency of his participation in public debates of various types, the wide range of his interests, and his status in the late Victorian public world belie his present obscurity. Twichell both served in the Civil War and participated in the postbellum public commemoration and memorializing of that event. He is, thus, a noteworthy figure in the social dialogue described by Nina Silber in *The Romance of Reunion* and David W. Blight in *Race and Reunion: The Civil War in American Memory.*

Born in Southington Corners, Connecticut, on 27 May 1838, Joseph Twichell was the son of Edward Twichell, a tanner—see the 30 June 1863 letter— and deacon in the local Congregationalist church who later became a partner in a hardware manufacturing firm. Joseph's mother, Selina Carter Twichell, died in 1849, and his father married Jane Walkley in 1850. Joseph had three siblings: two brothers, Edward William, born in 1839, and Upson Carter, who was born in 1841 but who only lived to 1843; and a sister, Sarah Jane, born in 1843, the "Sis" of these letters. Joseph also had four half-sisters and a half-brother by Edward Twichell's second marriage. The early death of his mother may have had considerable bearing on the deep affection Twichell felt for his

Joseph Hopkins Twichell was a twenty-two-year-old divinity school student in New York City and not yet ordained when he signed up as chaplain of the Jackson Regiment of Daniel E. Sickles's Excelsior Brigade. (Asylum Hill Congregational Church)

father and the dependent nature of his relationship to him—as the letters that follow reveal.

After attending Lewis Academy in Southington, Joseph entered Yale in 1855. There, he had a standard classical education, though his religious thought was influenced by the revivalism of the period. He suffered some temporary disgrace—and suspension from his college—through his participation in a famous town-gown riot in February 1858, when a local fireman was killed (probably by one of his friends, Edward Carrington, who figures in these letters). Yet he distinguished himself on the Yale crew in its early years of interscholastic competition with Harvard, and physical energy and athleticism would continue to be one of his defining qualities, when, for instance, he walked with Mark Twain in the Alps or summered in the Adirondacks with his large family.

After Twichell graduated from Yale in 1859, he entered Union Theological Seminary in New York City. When the Civil War broke out, his strong abolitionist sympathies led him to volunteer as chaplain to the Jackson Regiment. To conform with army chaplaincy rules, Twichell was ordained at his home church in Southington in 1863 (see his letter of 7 December 1862 and letters of 15 February 1863 and immediately following). Soon after Twichell joined the Jackson Regiment, it was renamed the Second Excelsior Regiment, and later it received the state designation of Seventy-first Regiment, New York State Volunteers. It was part of the Excelsior Brigade, raised by Daniel Edgar Sickles, an attorney and politician who had served as a Democratic U.S. representative from New York from 1857 to 1861. Twichell's regiment spent the early part of the war performing various guard and construction duties in Washington and Maryland. It moved to the offensive with McClellan's Peninsula Campaign of March to July 1862, first distinguishing itself at the Battle of Fair Oaks on June 1. It also fought at Bristoe Station in the Second Bull Run Campaign, at Fredericksburg and Chancellorsville, and, after Sickles's departure, in Grant's Overland or Wilderness Campaign, as well as in many other smaller engagements, before Twichell was mustered out in July 1864.

Perhaps Twichell's most significant experience in these years, however, was his participation in the famous events surrounding the Third Corps on the second day at Gettysburg, which included the wounding of General Sickles, by now the corps commander. The unauthorized advance Sickles made during that battle is still the subject of debate today.

After leaving the army, Twichell returned to his studies, this time at Andover Theological Seminary in Massachusetts. During the war he had become a protégé of the Reverend Horace Bushnell of Hartford, a leading theological

Chaplain Joseph Hopkins Twichell poses in officer's regalia for a studio photograph. The rank of chaplain was considered equal to that of a cavalry captain, which Twichell, in his riding boots, here resembles. The sword was purely decorative. (Asylum Hill Congregational Church)

and civic reformer. The latter's influence helped him become, in 1865, pastor of the Asylum Hill Congregational Church immediately upon its construction in the western suburbs of Hartford, Connecticut (the wealthiest town in America during the Gilded Age). He married Julia Harmony Cushman of New Jersey the same year. They eventually had nine children. With an ironic appropriateness, their daughter Harmony married the composer Charles Ives. Twichell served as pastor at Asylum Hill for the whole of his career—a forty-seven-year period. Under his guidance, the church (which served such a wealthy congregation that Mark Twain dubbed it "The Church of the Holy Speculators") grew from a few hundred to about a thousand members and developed a considerable number of what we would now call "outreach programs" to serve the poor of the growing industrial city.

Twichell met Mark Twain—Samuel L. Clemens—in October 1868 when Twain was visiting his publisher in Hartford. The two men struck up an immediate friendship that included autumnal walks in the hills near Hartford, long conversations, and a shared family intimacy following Twain's marriage in February 1870. Twichell provided much-welcomed and necessary spiritual guidance to the humorist in the lead-up to this marriage, and Twain remained for the rest of his Hartford years, despite a growing religious skepticism, an active participant in church events. Mark—as Twichell would always address him—attended Asylum Hill to hear his friend's "sane and beautiful" sermons (the words are from William Dean Howells). The two men later traveled together to Bermuda and to Germany and Switzerland. The latter trip in 1878 was the basis for the most successful sections of Twain's second European travel book, *A Tramp Abroad* (1880), in which Twichell appears in fictional guise as the character "Harris." A version of Twichell also appears as a minor character in other Twain works (among them, "Some Rambling Notes of an Idle Excursion," "Luck," "Punch, Brothers, Punch," and "Wapping Alice"). Twichell joined Twain and other Connecticut Republicans in a letter of public protest against the GOP presidential candidate in 1884, the corrupt James G. Blaine—an act of courage for a minister in a Republican enclave.

In 1871, Twichell became a backer of the Chinese Educational Mission, a program initiated by his close friend Yung Wing. Headquartered in Hartford, this effort was an attempt by the Chinese government to educate 120 young Chinese men in Western technology and science, although the attempt lasted only nine years before being ended by Chinese-U.S. tensions over cultural differences and immigration issues. Yung Wing later became a Chinese diplomat in Washington and a reformer in China. Twichell played a significant public role in defending the mission during its various difficulties, going to New York with Twain to plead its cause (successfully for a time) before his old command-ing officer, the former president Ulysses S. Grant.

Twichell was generally aware of the important social and intellectual issues of his day—and took an active part in the Hartford Monday Evening Club, a forum for male discussion of such matters. His Civil War years, and the partic-ular group of men that he served, had broadened his view of life. So, later, did the lively intellectual life of Nook Farm, the Hartford literary community he pastored and mentored after the war. His intellect was alive to the new strains of Protestantism and modern thought in his era, and he was quick to respond to the international influence of Spencer and Darwin. He could not, however, be called the deepest or most original of thinkers, and he tended to respond to issues such as evolution, social Darwinism, and theological change with a general Christian optimism. In later life he became increasingly conservative, exhorting Twain, for instance, not to speak out strongly against the U.S. inter-vention in the Philippines. Twain answered this attempt with friendly venom.

Apart from his temporary 1884 defection, Twichell was a member and ac-tivist in the dominant Republican Party all of his adult life. He also played a major role in the governing body of his alma mater, Yale. He took his pastoral duties at the Asylum Hill church seriously, overseeing a large number of orga-nizations for charitable work and taking a special interest in youth education. Generally, indeed, he was held in the greatest esteem by his parishioners, and he was made the church's pastor emeritus after his retirement. Like all other minis-ters in the 1865–1914 era, he had to come to terms with rapid change in a mod-ernizing America: massive new accumulations of wealth, labor-management strife, the racial bitterness of the postwar South, and the massive inflow of immigrants that, in Hartford's case, helped triple its population between 1860 and 1910.

Twichell only rarely recaptured in his later public writings the intimate tone, easy narrative fluency and force, and frequent rhetorical power of his Civil War letters. He published two books, a biography of John Winthrop, the early Pu-ritan governor of Massachusetts, and a collection of Winthrop's and his wife's correspondence. He also published two widely circulated pamphlets, lauda-tory biographies of missionaries in Arabia and Micronesia. He wrote essays in journals such as *Harper's* and the *North American Review* on such various Nook Farm literary characters as Harriet Beecher Stowe and Charles Dudley Warner; on a London pilgrimage in the footsteps of Charles Lamb; and on Chinese-American affairs. In religious journals he wrote about the education of African Americans in the South (he was a trustee of Atlanta University, one of the first post–Civil War colleges for African Americans), the composition of sermons, the spiritual development of young people, and evolution from a religious perspective.

From 1874 to 1913 he was a member of Yale's governing corporation, a conservative force at a time when Harvard, by contrast, was becoming a modern university. Increasing deafness led to his retirement from the church in 1912. After a debilitating illness in his last years, he died in Hartford on 20 December 1918.

The range of Twichell's activities and friendships, his reputation as a public speaker, his role in a Congregationalist church in the process of rapid and significant change, and the number of significant public causes with which he was involved—even before the relationship with Twain is taken into account—make him a figure of real historical interest. His Civil War letters both confirm and extend that interest.

Twichell's letters are a major historical resource that provide an extraordinary perspective on the war. They are unusually literate and detailed. They were written regularly—usually at weekly intervals—over the first two years of the war, and continued until July 1864 (the letters become generally more sporadic and thinner after his father's death in 1863). Twichell's material ranges widely as he describes the key events of his war experience and as he reveals both his own social, racial, religious, and political attitudes and those of his fellow combatants.

The letters speak to, and engage, an increasing contemporary interest in the place of chaplains in the Civil War and the multiple roles they assumed. Until recently (see particularly John W. Brinsfield, William C. Davis, Benedict Maryniak, and James I. Robertson Jr.'s *Faith in the Fight: Civil War Chaplains* [2003]), the lives of chaplains and the extent of their participation in the war have been a neglected subject. Brinsfield, chaplain corps historian for the U.S. Army, reminds us, however, that for "the overwhelming number of Union and Confederate soldiers, religion was the greatest sustainer of morale in the Civil War"—an understanding that Twichell's letters tend to confirm. But the chaplain was more than a religious authority and practitioner. Twichell wrote dozens of accounts of tending to the spiritual needs of the living and to the physical and spiritual needs of the wounded and dying, and of conducting burial services. But he also describes a range of other activities, such as taking part in "whisky hunting" expeditions to keep hard liquor (a particular demon in his eyes) from the soldiers, arranging a complimentary supply of newspapers for the regiment, and escorting a girl fallen into prostitution back to Washington to settle her with the Catholic Sisters of Charity. He had a role as a banker, too, carrying soldiers' pay to Washington to be formally deposited for withdrawal by their families. In the course of this work, he encountered Theodore Roosevelt, father of the future president, sent by the Sanitary Commission to set up a more systematic method of dealing with the pay problem.

The part Twichell played in the war extended further than this, though. When the Peninsula Campaign fizzled out and the Army of the Potomac withdrew from the Richmond front, a vast field hospital at Savage's Station was abandoned to the enemy. Twichell was detailed to lead a crowd of the ambulatory wounded south to the James River, a distance of about twenty miles, an odyssey he describes in harrowing detail. He also describes, at intervals, his work among the Confederate wounded. His response to these "poor creatures" speaks of a humanitarian sympathy that crosses all battle lines.

More generally, Twichell's role as an observer of events and army movements was facilitated by the relative freedom a chaplain within the lines enjoyed, his life at war lived at a slight remove from conventional army discipline and routine. Even though Twichell could not perceive all that occurred around him with total clarity—caught, as he expresses it, "inside the wheel"—nevertheless his descriptions of regimental and national politics and of military campaigns come from a wider and more thoughtful perspective than might be expected.

Another reason for the importance of Twichell's letters lies in his unique access, both during and after the war, to General Sickles, a controversial figure whose career has been subject to recent and highly publicized reconsideration. Twichell was initially wary of Sickles on moral grounds. In 1859, before the war, Sickles had gained notoriety by killing his wife's lover, only to be acquitted on the basis of temporary insanity (the first use of such a plea). When Twichell was invited to join Sickles's wife and her mother in their carriage in New York shortly after he had joined the regiment, he demurred, confiding to his father that he preferred not to share the conveyance with an adulteress ("I did not want to look the woman in the face"). He quickly became fiercely loyal to the general, however, even despite Charles Francis Adams Jr.'s famous description of the Army of the Potomac headquarters as "a combination of bar-room and a brothel" while under the authority of generals Joseph Hooker and Sickles. It was Sickles's bravery that won Twichell over. Indeed he is a key figure in two of the very best sections of Twichell's correspondence. On 26 March 1862, Twichell vividly describes a slave hunt in his army camp—something almost unbelievable to the contemporary reader. It was Sickles who ended this obscenity, defying the Maryland slaveholders in their (probably legal) attempts to recover their escaped "property."

Sickles, subject of a recent biography by novelist Thomas Keneally, needed his defenders in a more famous act of insubordination. His advance to the Peach Orchard at Gettysburg, without orders from General George Meade, ultimately caused major controversy concerning the wisdom or foolishness of the act. Most recent scholarship has come down on the side of foolishness, and lethal foolishness at that. Twichell, however, was among those who backed Sickles, and he continued to do so for the next half century. When Sickles's leg was crushed by a cannonball during the battle (see the Gettysburg letter of 5 July 1863), Twichell rode in the ambulance with him and held the chloroform for the amputation, recording what he thought might be the general's last words. In old age, Sickles asked Twichell to speak at his funeral, partly to read out documentation supporting the part he played at Gettysburg. Sickles's Gettysburg role has usually been condemned, partly because of a record of underhanded behavior and devious self-aggrandizement throughout his long life. William Robertson's essay, "The Peach Orchard Revisited," does, however, provide a qualified defense of his action. In his letters, Twichell provides us with close-up views of this larger-than-life character.

Further reasons for the importance of Twichell's correspondence have to do with the type of narrative the letters form, the journey of personal development they describe, and the representative quality they come to possess as a story of both personal and national catastrophe. For the letters chart what amounts to Twichell's rite of passage as he develops from a well-intentioned but inexperienced and somewhat narrow-minded young minister to an impressive and generous-spirited maturity—confident in his opinions; devoted to his own men, to abolitionism, and to the Union cause; willing to give up even his own life should that sacrifice be required. The further one reads into these letters, the more one's estimation of Twichell is likely to rise.

Twichell's lack of confidence in his own spiritual vocation surfaces at the time of his ordination (and would indeed remain an issue throughout his long career). Clearly, however, he gained confidence as the war progressed in his ability to counsel and comfort the spiritually troubled among his men and to minister effectively to them. Though he retained his suspicion of Catholicism and the "conscience-lulling errors of Rome," and his preference for "the simple forms of Congregationalism," he was increasingly tolerant of religious difference and less dogmatic in his views as his time in the army progressed. His close friendship (which continued beyond the war) with the Catholic chaplain, Father Joseph B. O'Hagan, S.J., was one sign of this. His willingness to serve the spiritual needs of the Catholics in his regiment in whatever way he could was another. Indeed, Twichell's attitude to those around him came to foreshadow a type of muscular Christianity more readily associated with a later period—and one which placed more emphasis on personal action and morality than on doctrinal orthodoxy. His stress on one-to-one interconnection (as he writes in part of a letter not reproduced here, "the faculty of making these poor boys like me, not only as chaplain, but as a person") and his belief in "manliness" as a core virtue suggests that, in wartime at any rate, honesty, uprightness, integrity, and the simple expression of faith counted more to him than any theological distinction or difference. Twichell's sharing of "family prayers" with his "boys" speaks of a comradeship, inclusiveness, and emotional warmth that, in the last analysis, seems fundamental to his personal sense of Christian mission.

Twichell's political allegiances and his sense of social justice also assert themselves with increasing vigor as his letters continue. His loyalty to Lincoln and to abolitionism form a consistent strand of belief. His 9 July 1862 description of Lincoln's visit to the lines notes the ludicrousness of the president's horsemanship, but also his popularity with both African Americans and with the general soldiery, and it is clear that he has Twichell's entire support. Similarly his view of slavery—as a moral abomination—is plainly spoken. An abolitionist and evangelist, he was politically knowledgeable and racially radical. The Copperhead threat to Lincoln's political authority is met with absolute scorn: their party is described as "a mighty mean set of fellows . . . a stench in all our nostrils." The strength of Twichell's Unionist convictions carry with them, too, a certain rhetorical eloquence: "The greater our reverses, the more tenacious should we be of the grand principle with which we started. While we have men for an army, and bread for their mouths, we should not abate one jot or tittle of our original claim for an undivided Union. Much blood has been shed and not in vain. All that is behind urges us forward, and what is before beckons us on." Twichell returns from the war a battle-hardened veteran but one whose endurance, integrity, courage and intelligence, love for his men and his country, and sympathy for his enemy are impressive in their scope.

Twichell's account of his wartime experiences also conveys, somewhat more nebulously, a sense of change and trauma which reflects his larger culture. Twichell's life (almost symbolically) formed a bridge between the premodern and the modern. He was very much a Victorian American, but he was raised in an antebellum world, and the small New England town of his birth was still considerably influenced by its Puritan heritage. He notes the army's "unsettled style of living," the constant possibility of breaking camp and moving on at just a moment's notice, and remarks that this should act as good training for his future life, "preparing me for that roving, changing, career that many ministers are doomed to. I shall learn the art of moving to perfection." Ironically, his postbellum career in the Hartford ministry could not have been more settled, and he remained attached to the one congregation until his death—a month after the Armistice—in 1918.

The Civil War was, of course, a traumatic event—perhaps *the* traumatic event—in American history. Twichell's life spanned the period from the premodern (1830s) to the modern (post–World War I). But the Civil War stood for him as a defining and extended moment of rupture in both the personal and national record. In F. Scott Fitzgerald's *Tender is the Night* (1933), the death of Dick Diver's father, a clergyman in upstate New York, is associatively linked with the loss of stable Victorian values. Dick traces this loss to the world war, represented by the battlefields that he visits. His words, "Good-by, my father—good-by, all my fathers," reverberate as a cry of both personal and public loss, of a world forever changed as a result of that war. As if to endorse an argument about historical repetition, the Civil War sounds in Twichell's mind a half-century earlier in a similar way. Personal and public trauma peculiarly combine and produce an analogous sense of the loss of an older, simpler, and better world.

Indeed, it is the death of Twichell's own father, his primary correspondent for the majority of his army career and a deeply loved figure in his life, that triggers this sense of rupture. Twichell received an unexpected visit from his father in camp in March 1863 and was clearly delighted by this "rare treat." Less than a month later, his father was dead. Exactly a month before his father's visit, Twichell wrote to him describing the previous night's snowstorm. He tells how, the next day, wading in the drifts, he is overtaken by "sensations of boyhood" and tempted by "the juvenile instinct of snow bathing." Resisting this impulse, he nonetheless recollects that prior boyhood time: "My early life was so exceeding happy that my visions of memory are always sweet, and I sigh when they vanish. Occasionally I get back so far that I happen upon Innocence, and then a pang of regret closes the retrospect." The sense of personal loss that he felt on learning of his father's death was overwhelming. The 26 April letter to his stepmother expressed the full depth of his feelings: "O, my Father! My Father, where art thou? Is it I, or is it he that is lost? I'm very lonesome here to-night. . . . Now with unutterable yearning I grope round the shadowed world after him, and find nothing but the fresh grave. Mother; it's trouble, trouble, trouble—empty dreariness. . . . Oh God! Blankness gathers about the future. . . . I shall never write 'Dear Father' again—never."

Twichell's reports of the war, the "lacerated bodies" it produced, and its "months of battle and toil" ("months that drank our blood, consumed our treasure and filled our land with mourning, and where are we, what is left of us?") were set against his past memories. The sense of personal and domestic loss felt with his father's death echoed the question prompted by the larger historical event—"where are we, what is left of us?" Meeting an old Yale colleague on 19 June 1862, Twichell wrote that "My thoughts . . . wander back to the peace and happiness of our golden life at Yale. The present seemed like a dream. 'Can it be', I mentally exclaimed, 'that these things are real? Here I am going to my tent pitched among the bloody graves of countrymen slain in civil war. . . . Which is the dream, this or that?'" The shift between the personal and the historical that we find here, the shift from sweet and idyllic personal memory to present public horror—the death of his father somehow putting the seal on this bloody transition—gives a sense of symbolic structure to Twichell's narrative (for this is what the very full sequence of letters forms). A similar sense of profound rupture is played out over and over again in the minds and writings of his contemporaries. It suffuses, what is more, the work of his friend, Mark Twain, even though Twain scarcely wrote directly about the war. And one cannot help but think of a later period too, wondering whether in their talk together Twichell ever brought up his "Which is the dream?" question. If he did, he may possibly have helped stimulate Twain's own late fictional turn (following personal and career traumas of his own) in which he explored exactly the scenario of existing between two worlds, reality and dream, with borderlines impossible to fix.

A NOTE ON THE TEXT

In editing the Twichell letters we have taken the liberty of amending his more common spelling mistakes and tidying up some of the punctuation. We have also necessarily cut a good deal of material from the letters. These cuts are signalled as individual sections of a letter are introduced or marked by ellipses. Where accounts are given of Twichell's conduct of religious affairs, his ministrations among the sick, and the relationships he thereby built up with individual soldiers, both Union and Confederate, we give pertinent illustration, rather than often-repeated example. Necessarily constrained by space, our intention in carrying out such editing has been to remain true to the larger spirit and tone of the correspondence while omitting repetitive material and personal details with little interest to a larger audience. Our working principle has been to use Twichell's correspondence selectively, in no way to misrepresent the larger whole, but to give the fairest and most effective illustration of the overlap between his family commitments, his religious duties, his observations of army and national life, and his participation in military conflict. Perhaps of necessity, it is the latter element that forms both the center and the climax of much of the larger movement of this narrative. Annotation has been kept to a minimum. Our intention has been to give as much knowledge of personal and historical background as the reader will need to understand both the individual references in, and historical background to, the letters. Our primary intention has always been to give Twichell's own words and responses center stage.

Joseph Twichell is at present something of a forgotten historical figure. However, there are indications of a burgeoning interest in his life and achievements. Peter Messent, one of the present editors, has written an essay on "Mark Twain, Joseph Twichell, and Religion," and is also working on a monograph on *Mark Twain and Male Friendship in the Victorian Era*, which features the Twain-Twichell relationship as one of its core strands. Steve Courtney, his coeditor, is completing a new biography. (A 1966 biography by Leah Strong was written with only limited reference to primary sources, as Twichell's descendants limited access to these at the time.) Others, including Harold K. Bush of the University of St. Louis and independent scholar Dwayne Eutsey, have focused on Twichell's religious influence on Twain: Bush in the provisionally titled *Mark Twain and the Spiritual Crisis of His Age*, forthcoming from the University of Alabama Press, and Eutsey in his studies of the links between Twain and Unitarianism. Twichell, as these letters confirm, is certainly deserving of such attention.

PETER MESSENT AND STEVE COURTNEY

April–July 1861

Joseph Hopkins Twichell graduated from Yale College in 1859 and entered Union Theological Seminary in New York City that fall. There, he roomed with his closest college friend, Edward Carrington, a student at the Columbia School of Law. Other classmates from Yale College living in New York included Eugene Smith, always known by his college nickname "Mons"; Henry "Billy" Boies; and Robert Stiles, whose Southern background and political sympathies contrasted with that of his abolitionist friends.

Twichell's tenure at Union was set against a background of gathering violence. Sectional feeling between North and South had become increasingly bitter in the late 1850s as abolitionists and slaveholders debated and fought—often literally fought, as in the battles of "Bleeding Kansas." In October 1859 the messianic abolitionist John Brown seized the arsenal at Harper's Ferry, Virginia, hoping to spark a slave uprising. After a short battle Brown was captured and hanged. Twichell called him a "glorious martyr."

Observing these and other sectional events kept Twichell and his friends engaged in debate over what their own roles should be in the coming struggle. Twichell supported the 1860 Republican presidential candidate, Abraham Lincoln of Illinois. However, Lincoln's election started an exodus of Southern states from the Union with the goal of establishing their own Confederacy. On 6 April 1861 Twichell and Stiles together watched as ships at the docks of lower Manhattan were loaded with arms and soldiers on a mission to supply and strengthen federal forts in the South. Six days later Southerners, provoked by this defiance of their secession, fired on one of these forts—Fort Sumter in Charleston Harbor. The fort was surrendered, Lincoln called for 75,000 volunteers to keep the Southern states in the Union, and the Civil War had begun.

Twichell had corresponded weekly with his father, Edward Twichell, all during college, and he kept this up after his move to New York. The elder Twichell, a deacon of Southington's First Congregational Church, was deeply religious and strongly antislavery. Twichell's first letter to his father on his role in the war is dated 22 April 1861.

I have now something to say concerning my personal proceedings with reference to the war. I have before mentioned that I had some thoughts of becoming individually involved in it. I found myself an able bodied young citizen, without a family of my own, or such business as renders absence perilous to its interests. Moreover, I thought, that outside the strong current of excitement I had some just appreciation of the real point at issue, the dire necessity which alone should make the idea of civil strife tolerable—such an appreciation that I could pray and weep over it, yet contemplate with firmness the dreadful path, by which America is to struggle up to better days. What should I do? My prospective profession was to be regarded and receive due influence. I had thus far been fitting for a life not yet lived—to confer upon society benefits not yet conferred. It was plainly not my duty to risk that life until it was more unquestionably called for. Such has always been the theory and generally the practice. Besides this, the ranks are full. More than can be equipped have already presented themselves. The recruiting stations are daily thronged. Nevertheless I felt uneasy, I wanted to do something. The blood of the Twichells was emphatically up. After some reflection I conceived a project. For three days I turned it over in my mind. This morning I went to see Prof. [Roswell D.] Hitchcock° [of Union Theological Seminary] and laid it before him. After asking a few questions, he said, Go! and gave me his blessing. I went at once, and offered my services as Chaplain to the New York Firemans Zouave Regiment, which has been organized and will be commanded by Col. [Elmer E.] Ellsworth late of the Chicago Zouaves.° I say I *offered* my services. I do not yet know the result. I had a letter of recommendation from Billy Boies, and owing to the Col.'s great absorption in business, I presented the letter and the tender of my services through Lieut. [Stephen W.] Stryker of the same command, to whom Boies introduced me last Friday. If I am invited, I shall go. I do not feel any need of vindicating this step in your eyes. I am sure that you would *send* me to any post where you thought I could be of real use. If you ask why I fixed upon this particular regiment, composed as it is of rough,

I have now something to say concerning my personal proceedings with reference to the war. I have before mentioned that I had some thoughts of becoming individually involved in it. I found myself an able bodied young citizen, without a family of my own, or such business as renders absence perilous to its interests, moreover I thought, that outside the strong current of excitement I had some just appreciation of the real point at issue, the dire necessity which alone should make the idea of civil strife tolerable—such an appreciation that I could pray and weep over it, yet contemplate with firmness, the dreadful path by which America is to struggle up to better days. What should I do? My prospective profession was to be regarded and recieve due influence. I had thus far been fitting for a life not yet lived—to confer upon society benefits not yet conferred. It was plainly not my duty to risk that life until it was more unquestionably called for. Such has always been the theory and generally the practice. Besides this, the ranks are full. More than can be equipped have already presented themselves. The recruiting stations are daily thronged. Nevertheless I felt uneasy, I wanted to do something. The blood of the Twichell was emphatically up. After some reflection I concieved a project. For three days I turned it over in my mind. This morning I went to see Prof. Hitchcock and laid it before him. After asking a few questions, he said "Go!" and gave me his blessing. I went at once, and offered my services as chaplain to the New York Firemans Zouave Regiment which has been organized and will be commanded by Col. Ellsworth late of the Chicago Zouaves. I say I offered my services. I do not yet know the result. I had a letter of recommendation from Billy Boies, and owing to Lt. Col.

The 22 April 1861 letter in which Twichell informed his father, Edward Twichell of Plantsville, Connecticut, of his intention to sign up as a chaplain. This was the first of the letters Twichell wrote almost every Sunday night, and other times as needed, during the three years of his service. His original plan to serve with the Zouave regiment mentioned here did not work out. (Beinecke Rare Book and Manuscript Library) wicked men, I answer, that was the very reason. I saw that the companies of the better class of citizens were all attended by Chaplains, but nothing was said about these. *There*, I thought, is a place for me. My objects are not personal conflicts, but the discharge of duties entirely consonant with my profession and such as will fill up my coming long vacation° to advantage with reference to future life. So far as I can find out, my risk of physical injury, in any event, will be slight. If my life is lost, it will be given just where it could not be refused in caring for the sick, in maintaining discipline not by violence and in the pursuit of peaceful ministrations, such as may soften in some degree the asperities of war. My Bible, tracts and a few books will constitute my weapons. You know how I have often thought myself fitted by nature to influence this class of men. If I may judge by a little experience, I shall expect by a cautious study of ways and means, to gain confidence, then influence and so do good. I should not expect a revival, but I should expect to make some good impressions, by treating with kindness a class of men who are little used to it. Another thing. Nothing is more repugnant to a civilized sense than the burial of a man as though he were a dog. This it is the privilege of the Chaplain to prevent. Where the Regiment is going I know not. It will likely see tough times. Then I am the more needed. As soon as I know anything, I will write. If I should go suddenly Ed [Carrington] will attend to my affairs. God bless you all at home, and deliver us all from all evil. God save the Union and grant civilization and Christianity to sit unmolested and fearless under the wide-spreading branches of *Constitutional Law.*

Good night. Your aff. Son—Joseph.

I went to see Prof. [Roswell D.] Hitchcock: The Reverend Roswell Dwight Hitchcock taught church history at Union, a seminary known for its relative ecumenism for the period and its interest in historical criticism of the Bible. Hitchcock, who traveled in Palestine and wrote on Biblical archaeology, later served as Union's president.

Col. [Elmer] Ellsworth late of the Chicago Zouaves: Ellsworth, twenty-four and a protégé of Lincoln's in Illinois, had organized this military unit that affected the red pantaloons, vests, and fezzes of French African troops. He had come to New York to organize a similar unit from city fire departments.

my coming long vacation: The Union Theological Seminary's long vacation ran from the third week in May to the last week in August. At the outset of the war, many believed subduing the South would be a matter of a few weeks.

Twichell next wrote to his father from New York on 5 May 1861.

Now for my news. I told you when you were here, that Mr [Daniel E.] Sickles had promised to recommend me° to a friend of his who was raising a

General Daniel E. Sickles had been an attorney, Tammany Hall politician, diplomat, and congressman before the war. In 1859 he was arrested and tried for shooting to death his wife's lover, but he was judged not guilty due to temporary insanity. After initial doubts, Twichell accepted him as a hero and remained a steadfast friend until Sickles's death in 1914. (Library of Congress)

regiment. Well, that friend was spoken to, I was introduced to him, and he appointed me his Chaplain. So I am booked for a campaign at least. I can say very little about the matter now, for I know very little. In the course of the coming week I shall become fully posted, and you shall know all. From the enclosed document, you will learn that there is an Excelsior Brigade° composed of two Regiments—the "Jackson" and the "Excelsior." Mr Sickles is Brig. General of the whole: Col. [George B.] Hall commands the "Jackson" and Col. Montgomery the "Excelsior."° Col. Hall is my superior officer. The Brigade is not yet fully recruited and will probably occupy its present quarters for nearly two weeks. The "Excelsior" also has a chaplain, whom I have not yet seen. Until I have seen and conferred with him, I shall not know our programme. I am told that he is a man in middle life, hence, I presume that for the present he will do most of the preaching. I am informed by the officers that the Brigade will be placed under orders just as soon as it is full and equipped, also that it will be transferred as soon as may be to some neighboring fort, for more secure and uninterrupted drill.

The state order for volunteers does not authorize Chaplains.° Col. Hall informed me of this yesterday, stating that such being the case, my pay might not be forthcoming. I asked him if I should be allowed rations. He said "Yes, certainly." I then told him that the pay was the least part of my business, my only indispensables being bed and board. "Very well," said he, "then I retain you." I don't know how it will be about the outfit. At any-rate it will not be very expensive. I am very anxious to see my companion Chaplain. Upon him will depend in a great measure my enjoyment, for, elsewhere I shall look for very little Christian sympathy.

Of the officers and men I will say more when I have had opportunity to investigate. . . .

Mr [Daniel E.] Sickles had promised to recommend me: Daniel E. Sickles is one of the most colorful and controversial characters of the Civil War. He was a Democrat and active in Tammany Hall, the party's New York organization. As a diplomat in London in 1853, he had introduced a New York City prostitute to Queen Victoria at a royal reception. A generally pro-Southern congressman, in 1859 he had shot to death the district attorney of the District of Columbia, Philip Barton Key, who was carrying on an affair with Sickles's wife. Sickles was acquitted on the grounds of temporary insanity, and he was the first American to plead the defense successfully. He won favor with Lincoln for bringing the city's Democrats to support the war effort.

there is an Excelsior Brigade: "Excelsior"—"Ever Upward"—is the motto of New York State. The designations "Excelsior" and "Jackson" for these regiments was temporary; ultimately they became known as the First and Second Excelsior. A Third, Fourth, and Fifth

were soon added to the brigade, and later in the year these regiments received state designation as the Seventieth to Seventy-fourth New York State Volunteer Infantry. However,
they retained their original numbering in veterans' memories and hearts. The Jackson Light
Infantry, or Second—Twichell's regiment—had been recruited by city politicians George B.
Hall and Henry L. Potter beginning 25 April, but by the time Twichell enlisted it was part of
the Excelsior Brigade.

Col. Montgomery [commands] the "Excelsior": In the regimental roster, Sickles himself is
listed as the first colonel of the First Excelsior.

The state order . . . does not authorize Chaplains: The status of chaplains in the U.S. military was governed by custom and constrained by the constitutional separation of church
and state. While detailed standards for chaplains were not enacted by Congress until 1864,
the War Department's General Orders 15 and 16 of May 1861 provided for regimental commanders to appoint chaplains. They were generally expected to conduct public worship,
distribute tracts and Testaments, and counsel individual soldiers. Eventually, duties became
broader: Chaplains—as Twichell did—took on increasing duties as aides in field hospitals.
Twichell later (10 September 1861) reported his salary as about $125 a month including rations
and forage for his horse. But in 1863, when chaplains' pay was decreased (see letter, 5 April
1863), he reported it had been $145. In general, early in the war a chaplain earned $145.50 a
month plus three daily rations and forage.

On 8 May, Twichell tells his father news of his fellow chaplain:

I wrote to you Sunday night concerning my affairs military. Among other
things I mentioned that the other Regiment of our Brigade had a Chaplain,
whom I had not then seen. Gen. Sickles had told me that he was an old college friend of his and denominated him Rev. Dr. ———(I had not caught the
name). Upon this unknown individual, I felt that a good measure of my usefulness and enjoyment depended. I wanted to see him, although I had serious
doubts about our congeniality. I expected nothing less than an Episcopalian,°
and the intimate friendship of Gen. Sickles, I did not regard as a promise of
extraordinary piety. I wanted, yet rather feared, to confront and talk with him.

Yesterday afternoon, as I sat in the mess room of the Staff, Gen. Sickles
informed me that my Senior was present and conducted me to him. I was
introduced. One glance relieved me. He was not an Episcopalian at any rate I
knew from his dress—a man, I judged of about 35 years of age—medium size,
rather slim—open faced and pleasant. I liked him at once. His name, after a
little difficulty, I got hold of. It was [Charles H.] Bulkley. By way of an introductory remark, I observed that I had known of a Rev. Bulkley once minister
at Winsted, Ct. "I am that same," was his immediate reply. I don't know what
Mr. B. thought of me. I fear I was rather demonstrative, but I was overjoyed.
Only think of it! My highest hopes were more than realized. A Congregation-

alist and an anti-slavery man, moreover a man who had breathed Connecticut air for many years. We dined with the officers and had a long, sweet talk together. My liking for him waxed stronger every moment. He knew many of my friends intimately among others Russel and Ed. Carrington's folks [who lived in nearby Colebrook, Connecticut]. Almost his first remark was "I was afraid you would be an Episcopalian." I had consulted Dr. Hitchcock about the propriety of using the Prayer Book in case my associate were a churchman. He advised me to do it by all means rather than try to mix the service. I told Mr. B. this. He said that he had resolved on the same. But now we both felt like men set free. You may rely upon it, the simple forms of Congregationalism will not be hampered or hindered by any foreign methods. . . . I am happy to say that the matter of the Chaplains' pay has been provided for by the State Government. The question "where we are going" is a matter of interest, although we do not much care. Mr. B. told me that he had great confidence in Gen. Sickles far-sightedness and so had asked his opinion. The General said that he now thought our first destination would be Richmond, Va. I like that. Mr. B. says that he wants to preach from a Richmond pulpit, especially that one, whose occupant not long since announced, "I accept American Slavery, as it is." I hope he will have a chance. . . .

I expected nothing less than an Episcopalian: To Twichell and his father, this would have been bad news indeed. Sickles was an Episcopalian. The trappings and ceremony of Episcopalianism, the American branch of the Church of England, and particularly its Book of Common Prayer were considered by New England Congregationalists to be too close to the practices of Rome for comfort.

New York, Sunday Evening, May 12th 1861.

Dear Father,

I have taken this large sheet of paper not because I am about to write an unusually large letter, but for the simple reason that our stationery is low and I am forced to use what we have. However I have to record the proceedings of one of the most interesting and I hope important days of my life and it may be this sheet will not prove too large after all. Mr. Bulkley and myself have been introduced this afternoon for the first time officially to our respective regiments in a public service. During the week we had caused about 1500 Testaments, the gift of the Bible Society,° to be conveyed to the barracks, and we thought best to make their presentation to the men as much an event as possible in order that more impression might be made than if they were more quietly distributed. In pursuance of this idea we invited in about 20 citizens and theologues with a sprinkling of clergymen, to officiate in the matter of dispensing them, so that all appearance of authority might be absent as would not have been the case had the officers done it. At about 3½ o'clock the men were formed in a hollow square and the exercises opened by music from a full band of music in one of the galleries—The piece performed was wonderfully like Hail Columbia, in fact, I think it *was* Hail Columbia, but we had no control over that. Then followed an address by Gen. Sickles introducing Mr. Bulkley and myself. . . . Had you heard this address, blindfolded, I am sure you would never have recognized the speaker as Danl. E. Sickles, i.e., if you had formed the opinion of him which the recorded events of his public life seem to [have] induced in most cases. His opening words concerning the power of God and the accountability of men and nations, might well have emanated from any pulpit in the land. His idea of the Christian ministry and its offices indicated that he had thought on the subject. In short, I could see no reason why Gen. Sickles, in theory at least, was not himself admirably fitted to undertake the Chaplaincy of his own regiments. Notwithstanding Mr. Bulkley's faith in the man and his evident high estimation of him, I was surprised and delighted. It was worth a great deal to have him *talk* so, at any rate, the General's address was quite lengthy and after it we sang one verse—"Praise God etc."—the usual Doxology. Then I read a Psalm—then Mr. Bulkley offered prayer—then I spoke introducing the Testaments, which were at once distributed. In speaking I announced that they were free-gifts and that no one was compelled to accept. Only one man so far as I knew declined to receive one. The officers were also presented with a Testament and Psalms each, handsomely bound. Then Mr. Bulkley spoke—very well indeed and wound up by formally bestowing upon Gen. Sickles a copy of the Testament and Psalms aforesaid, enjoining upon him its use and observance. Then the General made another speech, better and more pious if possible than the last. Then we sang, "Lord dismiss us with thy blessing"—one verse, accompanying the band. Then—the benediction by Rev. Mr. Bush of the Boston Tract Society. While the band played "Star Spangled banner" the men were marched off and dismissed. I think that the whole thing went off very well and tended to accomplish the result aimed at. I saw some of the boys engaged in carefully covering their Testaments with strong brown paper, after it was over and I marked them for future reference. We had 50 German copies which were exhausted and more called for. . . .

Quite a number of spectators were present, in one of the galleries, among the rest Mrs. Sickles. It was enjoined upon me by Mr. Bulkley not [to] mention the fact lest it might get into the papers. At about 12 o'clock Mr. B. drove around to my room in a carriage and we went together up to the Seminary to get Hymn books from the Chapel. He then asked me to accompany him to Gen. Sickles house and ride down with Mrs. Sickles and her mother. I declined. Some how or other I had not the courage. I did not want to look the woman in the face. I have no doubt she has paid dearly in bitter repentance for her past dark sin, but without much reflection I preferred not to see her in so close proximity as the same carriage. I expect to learn much more from Mr. B. concerning this sadly notorious family. So far as I can now judge, I shall be led to better thoughts of them. Mr. B. is strangely inclined toward them. . . . Love to all.

Your aff. Son—Joseph.

the gift of the Bible Society: The American Bible Society had been founded by New England Congregationalists in 1816 with the goal of distributing Bibles "without note or comment" to any home that did not possess one.

New York, Tuesday Evening, May 14th 1861.

Dear Father,

I write to tell you that it is doubtful whether I come home this week. The Brigade is to be transferred tomorrow to the Fashion Race Course—Long Island,° where it will quarter for a few days until other barracks are assigned. This step is rendered necessary by the utter insufficiency of the present quarters to accommodate so many in such warm weather. . . . The Jackson Regiment had a parade on Broadway this afternoon and was reviewed by Gen. Sickles. Prominent among the staff officers might have been seen the venerable form of the Rev. Dr. Twichell—our men now look rather rough, but uniforms and arms will transform them into a fine body of soldiers.

Your letter came yesterday and was welcome for its advice as was the last before it. To some of your sentiments in the latter I intended to make some response, but news crowded it out. You spoke of the probable existence of a religious element in my regiment. . . . It would be the joy of my soul if a few good men were found. I was told that last night a great many were reading their Testaments. That augurs well. My reliance is mostly on the youth of the larger number. A boy of 20 years is generally approachable. Every day reveals new data, upon which I form an opinion of what the work is to be. I can easily discern that it is to be accompanied by peculiar hindrances and can be prosecuted only at intervals. Much of the time, for weeks at least will be consumed in drill. Nevertheless, we count upon every aid from the General which military necessity will allow. If I were asked whether I anticipated a revival,° I could not say, yes. Such a result could hardly be hoped. Still, I do not mean to withhold my hand, on every available occasion. A good deal of seed may be sown. God only knows when it will spring up. One of the first things will be to preach true patriotism. An intelligent idea of the cause of the war will be a great advance with most. You ask whether I am to be licensed.° I thought of it somewhat and took counsel with others. At best it could only be provisional and irregular and the presence of Mr. Bulkley rendered it less desirable than if I had been alone. On the whole, I have concluded not to. Moreover, I look to my experience in this service for a solution of some things which have troubled me concerning the whole matter of the ministry. That was not the least of my reasons for engaging in it. Other advice I thank you for. Much obliged to Grandfather for his letter. I was near losing it entirely in trying to open it. The mucilage used, was evidently of the best quality. I have procured the medicine he sent for.

Love to all—Your aff. Son, Joseph.

the Fashion Race Course—Long Island: Twichell's regiment did not end up moving to this course, named for a popular racehorse, in what is now Corona, Queens.

If I were asked whether I anticipated a revival: Religious revivals were an important part of antebellum American life. Twichell's father had entered the church through a revival in 1834, and Twichell himself was greatly influenced by a revival in early 1858 that was generally considered a reaction to the financial panic of the year before.

You ask whether I am to be licensed: Edward Twichell seems to be concerned with the issue of how his son, an unordained divinity student, could act as a chaplain. Only later in the war did the adjutant general require that chaplains be ordained, leading to Twichell's own ordination in Southington in 1863. Educational training among chaplains in 1861 ranged from none to postgraduate degrees. "Many drifters, misfits and ne'er-do-wells among the clergy wormed their way into the chaplaincy," writes Army historian Herman A. Norton.

New York, Wednesday Evening, May 15th 1861.

Perhaps, Father, you will think that my bulletins are rather frequent and I hope you do not tire of them, but I find that in my leisure, home is the never failing centre of mental gravitation, and I am seized with a desire to *do* something consonant with my thoughts. If I have news to tell, I count myself fortunate. If not, I write for the sake of doing something agreeable. . . .

You have learned from the papers that the Brigade has been accepted by the Government at Washington,° which is a surety that it will soon be in the field. Gen. Sickles adopted this course rather than the ordinary one—through the state Gov't, in order to avoid the delays of red-tapeism to a certain extent, and to thwart some plans supposed to be set on foot by political opponents to hamper his movements. . . . I am pleased to observe that the General is flat-footed on the matter of temperance among officers—I do not say that he insists on total abstinence, but anything like getting tight he frowns upon. Mr B. tells me that some changes are about to take place in pursuance of that idea. I am glad of it. Every man suspected of having a facile elbow was warned in the beginning, and if any suffers military decapitation, it is his own fault. I learn that the quarters I rented yesterday proved unsatisfactory to our men, although they had been used for that purpose recently, and this morning there were some signs of mutiny. We must get into new barracks at once or there will be loss through desertion. . . .

Amid the hurry . . . I find that my thoughts are for hours together narrowed down, from general reflections on our country's great grief to the interests of the Excelsior Brigade. Still at the season of quiet and prayer the subject grows whole again and I pray that God will so rule that the Excelsior may disperse without experience of war, with joyful shouts for the Union, and devout thanks that the nation is delivered without blood. But, it is not for man to know the Eternal Plan. Love to all.

Your aff. Son—Joseph.

P.S. I observe with a measure of disgust that the pronoun "I" recurs very frequently in my letters. I hardly know how to avoid it and yet give intelligence, supposed to interest the family. Nevertheless we will try to rule the gentleman off the floor occasionally.

the Brigade has been accepted by the Government at Washington: After authorizing Sickles and his friend William Wiley to form a brigade, Edwin Morgan, governor of New York State, gave in to pressure from upstate politicians who believed too many regiments were being drawn from the city. Sickles's spotty political and personal career had gained him many enemies. Sickles traveled to Washington and convinced Lincoln to appoint the brigade directly as United States Volunteers. Sickles's helpful role as a prounion, prowar Democrat may have helped convince the Republican Lincoln.

New York, May 20th 1861. Monday morning.

Dear Father,

On Thursday about 500 of our men were transferred from 446 Broadway to "The Red House"—a place about 5 miles up 3rd Avenue, in Harlem. Mr B—— and I went with them but did not remain overnight. We embarked on board a steamboat at the foot of Grand St. and had a splendid sail up the river—all along the shore of the city islands. Every passing boat saluted us, every public building dipped its flag—even the striped convicts on Blackwell's° ranged along the shore and gave three cheers. I cannot tell you how much the men enjoyed it. They had been pent up—more than a thousand of them—for three weeks in the city Assembly Rooms, where dirt and noisome smells reigned supreme, and to be let out into the clean light, with rations of fresh air, almost turned their heads. They sang and howled and, when landed on shore and marched to a green field, they frisked like colts. The accommodations there were partial and for two nights, some of them were stowed away rather uncomfortably but they stood it well. Yesterday the last of the Brigade was taken up there, where all will remain till about the middle of this week, when they will be transferred to Fort Tompkins on Staten Island. No service was held yesterday, because it was too windy for the open air. Mr. B. and I were up there and arrived at this conclusion after due consideration. At the fort we shall always be able to do Sunday work. I was disappointed yesterday, for I am anxious to begin to *do* something; as it was, we visited the sick and distributed some tracts. I shall be glad when the chaotic state is past and the Brigade organised thoroughly. Mr. B. says "wait"! The General has not yet returned from Washington. When he does, under the fresh stimulus of administration smiles, we expect to see things put through with new energy. He himself is worth any ten of his officers to make things move. . . .

Love to all.

Your aff. Son, Joseph.

striped convicts on Blackwell's: Blackwell's Island, now Roosevelt Island, in the East River, was a repository for the social ills of New York City, containing the city penitentiary as well as an almshouse, workhouse, lunatic asylum, and charity hospital.

> Several letters follow, reporting on conditions in the barracks, the upcoming transfer to Staten Island, on visiting the sick in the brigade hospital, and the prospect of a visit home. On 24 May, Twichell notes that:

Your letter contains several remarks on public affairs. I am sorry that the dark side seems so present to you. The terrible news of Col. Ellsworth's assassination° has just reached us. The event will make New York foam again, and the element of *revenge* will enter more than ever into the popular heart—a fact to be deplored.

news of Col. Ellsworth's assassination: Ellsworth was killed by a rebel innkeeper in Alexandria, Virginia, while trying to remove a Confederate flag from the hotel's roof. His death, sometimes called the war's first combat casualty, was mourned by Lincoln and throughout the North.

Dear Father,

In the event of my not coming home on my birth-day,° I promised myself at least the luxury of taking a large sheet of paper and writing you a long letter to-night, but it is quite late, Ed has gone to bed and wants the gas put out,° besides, I am very tired myself and favorably inclined to slumber.

It is as I feared. I shall not come home to-morrow. The Jackson Regiment was not moved yesterday or to-day. I am now of the impression that Tuesday night will mark the limit of my patience, but I really think that by that time we shall have seen our quarters on the Island. A Captain told me to-day that the next four weeks at least, will be consumed in preparations, so that I feel perfectly sure of seeing you all. That point being settled beyond a doubt, it makes little difference when the visit comes, only I liked the idea of the birth-day.

I remarked that I am tired and so I am. I have done a days work. The same cause which hindered a service last Sunday, together with the absence of Mr. Bulkley, rendered it not feasible to-day, but I had made up my mind not to let Sunday slip by unnoticed. So I took care yesterday to furnish myself with a supply of soldier tracts and publications of all sorts and thus armed I spent several hours in distributing them among the men, seasoning the operation by such conversation or admonition as chance suggested or allowed. It proved harder work and consumed more time than I had anticipated. Beginning at 11 o'clock, the end was reached at 2 leaving the Rev. Dr. Twichell a jaded and hungry mortal as ever longed for food. I was very well satisfied withal, for I gleaned much encouragement for the future. A few refused to accept my offers, but not one offered me any personal disrespect and the most thanked me very heartily. This was better than I expected. I was prepared for rude repulses if not abuse. I told some of the officers how I was received and they seemed surprised. I think I shall be able to make friends of a good many of these fellows yet. God grant it. I have visited the hospital every day of the week with one exception, and I find that my coming is welcomed. Those who have been discharged from the sick list never fail to salute me when we meet, and that right pleasantly. I would not regret it if every man in the Regiment were on the sick list for a day or two with some slight ailment, so that I could prove my love by appreciable kindness. After my work was over to-day, the officer in command passed me through the guard and I came down town just in time to see the funeral procession of Col. Ellsworth—the most imposing I ever witnessed. Poor fellow! It seems but yesterday since Billy Boies introduced me to him and I took his hand and met his bright eye. Let his untimely fate pass for a mystery. Why was it? I know a great deal about him which I will tell when we talk. . . . I have so much else to talk about, that my own thoughts and opinions on general topics find no place. I am glad you give me yours. Can I not have a birth-day letter? Love to all—Joseph.

my not coming home on my birth-day: Twichell's birthday was 27 May.

Ed . . . wants the gas put out: That is, Twichell's roommate, Edward Carrington; Twichell still lived in his Waverly Place rooms at this point.

New York, June 7th 1861.

Dear Father,

I came up to the city yesterday for the double purpose of drying myself and getting tracts for Sunday. The incomplete condition of the encampment rendered it very disagreeable staying there in the rain, I had nothing in particular to do, everybody was cold and cross, so, with [Assistant] Surgeon [Harvey E.] Brown I journeyed hither, having, as I state above a cause beside. Mr. B. fled before the rain began.

When Camp Scott is fully organized° and finished it will be a magnificent sight and a pleasant place to dwell in. The tent I inhabited for the first three days has been removed together with those about it and pitched elsewhere. At present I am living with one of the Captains until the Colonel's marquee is put up and the quarters of the staff assigned about it. Then, with the furniture I now have, I shall be able to begin housekeeping in fair style.

The damp weather has swelled the sick list considerably, still, as a whole the men are in fine condition and seem to enjoy it. I sat up part of night before last with a poor fellow whose limbs were inflamed and very painful. He got asleep at last and felt easier in the morning. Many incidents of great interest to me have transpired since I left home. I cannot tell them on paper to any advantage, moreover I am writing in haste. It is enough to say that I am hopeful of doing the men some good and that this is a daily increasing conviction. God's help is all I want.

On Wednesday a private came to me as I was walking about, and after several awkward attempts to say something which I could not comprehend, on my encouraging him by speaking kindly, burst into tears and in a broken voice said that he had once thought he loved Christ (these were his words) but had fallen from his hope, that he came into the camp a hard-hearted man but was aroused by the Sunday service. I was not prepared for anything of the kind and felt very much agitated. On inquiring I found that he belonged to Mr. Bulkley's regiment, so after a few words of sympathy and encouragement I commended him to his own chaplain, promising to pray for him.

We have procured a grant of 100 daily papers for each regiment—which argues that the several proprietors regard themselves as beholden to the war-makers. I hope the gift will tend to make the men intelligent and appreciative of the causes of war. . . .

Your aff. Son, Joseph.

When Camp Scott is fully organized: At the end of May the brigade had moved from the Red House in Harlem to Staten Island, south of Manhattan, to establish this camp, named for the general in chief of the army, Winfield Scott. The move marked Twichell's entry into camp life.

Camp Scott, June 9th 1861. Sunday afternoon.

My dear Father,

The uncivilized character of the men who to-day control the affairs of this encampment places the afternoon at my disposal. I feel grieved and indignant; so does Mr. Bulkley. He being very tired, consoles himself with a nap; I write to you, seeking relief by confiding my troubles to one of whose sympathy I am sure.

The three thousand men here assembled are on this Christian Sabbath day passing their time as if there were no holy time, no day of rest, no risen Lord, no sacred cause. Here is a willing audience, I am sure, and there are certainly two anxious Chaplains who count it a hardship that they are not called to minister, yet, under as fair a sky as ever shone, the men are not summoned to hear the word of Life, or in any way acknowledge the existence of Almighty God. And why? Because, forsooth, it is a fine day for shows and a grand parade has been ordered.° Even while I write the tramp of regiments, the roll of drums, the resonant brass, the shrill fife, rise upon the air, inspiring, even grand at the proper time, but when intruding upon the hours demanded by God for better purposes, a profanation, and a shame. It hurts my Puritan ears to listen. I don't know but I state the case rather strongly, but I feel disappointed. The Sabbath of Camp Scott must of necessity be unlike the sweet, calm Sabbath of Plantsville, still I did expect beyond a doubt that at least one hour of the day would be reclaimed from active worldliness. Last Sunday, service was provided for in the General Order issued in the morning. We took no thought but that such would always be the case and this morning went to the Episcopal church in a village about a mile distant to indulge in the luxury of hearing a sermon, not doubting but that all would be right. On returning we learned for the first time that service had not been provided for, and that the Colonel wanted to see us.° I may here observe that the Colonel in command of the post to-day is not the same man who was chief last Sunday and one who cared much less for the thing on his own account. Amid the confusion of the camp we had not noticed this fact or we might have been forewarned to some extent and been more active ourselves. On finding the Colonel, he told us that he wanted service early and short on account of the parade and instructed us to prepare and post the order, which we did, appointing it at 2 o'clock. Here occurred a snarl. The order was not properly included in the General Order of the day and the officers were not acquainted with the fact, consequently 2 o'clock came and no move toward assembling was made. . . . Just here, Col. [Dow] Williamson of the Excelsior . . . returned and on learning the state of the case averred that religious services must take place. The Col. is a good man and I am sure was anxious to honor the day, but he had just arrived on the grounds, the skein was too tangled to unravel easily and, while he was trying, the hour for parade overtook him. That, you know, could not be delayed, for a full band had been imported, the camp was full of visitors and an impression was to be made. The plan of divine service on the Lord's day was abandoned. You are not to suppose that during all this time Mr. B. and I were racing about anxiously, as if we had wares of some kind to sell. I staid in my tent, while he quietly observed what was moving, neither did we appear on parade, having concluded that it was not our duty under the circumstances and considering the day, unless specifically ordered to do so. After all we are persuaded that the event is not without its value as an item of experience. Hereafter we shall see to it that service is included in the general order, and we shall refrain from wandering away Sunday morning to neighboring churches. So far as we are accountable for the failure, we have received instruction. We learn anew that we must *assert* ourselves. I think we shall do it, God helping us. Mr. B. does not seem so much exercised about it as I am and says he is not much surprised. Everything here is jumbled and there is probably the secret of it, but forewarned is forearmed, and we shall see whether or no the thing is done again. The worst of it is that there were very many men among the privates who felt very bad about it. It was an outrage on every Christian or moral man.

I have given so much room to what I was most thinking about, that little is left for other things. . . . I feel a great temptation to slip up to New Haven Tuesday night to Wooden Spoon and my Senior Soc[iety] initiation.° No telling when I shall see the fellows or Yale again. . . . Give my love to all the neighbors. Pray for us at the blessed little Saturday night prayer meeting. God bless us all.

Your aff. Son, Joseph.

The Excelsior Brigade stands for review. Regimental officers enjoyed such displays of
military pomp, to which, in the early part of the war, prominent local citizens would
be invited. While the regiment was camped at Staten Island, New York, early in the
war, Twichell became infuriated over one such review because it was held on the
Sabbath. He called the display, "when intruding upon the hours demanded by God
for better purposes, a profanation, and a shame" (letter of 9 June 1861). (Library
of Congress)

P.S. Your letter came to Camp Scott all right, but I would prefer not to risk valuables. I must get a pair of marching shoes at $5½ and in view of the multitude of similar demands I suggest $50.00 as necessary—none of which will be lightly dispensed. I am surprised that I need so much. If you have the willingness to regard all money I have now as only advances to be returned from my pay hereafter, I shall be glad. I have anew canvassed the matter of Ordination° and am again satisfied that I need not trouble about it. Surgeon Brown, of experience in the army, says that I *shall never be asked*.

a grand parade has been ordered: With few guidelines for the duties of a chaplain, Twichell and Bulkley were at the mercy of whichever officer was in charge and his interest or lack of interest in preserving the Sabbath and encouraging attendance at services.

the Colonel wanted to see us: Apparently not necessarily Hall but one of the regimental colonels in charge of the camp for that day.

Wooden Spoon and my Senior Soc[iety] initiation: The Wooden Spoon Presentation and Promenade was a Yale custom that had arisen in the 1840s as a lampoon reversal of the Junior Exhibition, which honored the best in the class. The Wooden Spoon honored the worst. By the 1860s it had become an elective popularity contest for the role of Spoon Man, carried on with pageantry and humor; Twichell made the presentation to Boies in his class. "Senior Soc. initiation" refers to the initiation of juniors into Scroll and Key, Twichell's senior society.

the matter of Ordination: Twichell seems to hope the matter of his ordination will never come up.

In his 16 June letter to his father in which he speaks of matters of personal and local interest, Twichell briefly refers to an exceptional camp activity:

Yesterday morning I passed among my men talking and distributing tracts and papers. The after-noon was devoted to a grand parade and flag raising. A magnificent pole 150 feet high had been raised during the week and the hoisting of the colors was made as great an event as possible. The whole brigade turned out in full dress, the General hauled up the "stars and stripes" and a salute of 34 guns was fired. Then followed a religious exercise . . . [including] address of ten minutes by myself. . . . A full band was in attendance, the camp was swarmed with visitors and everything was very gay and un-Sunday like as possible.

I never addressed so vast a concourse before and I confess that I felt no slight trepidation, still, between you and I, I think I did not make a fool of myself.

Twichell writes to his brother, Edward William Twichell, from Camp Scott on 22 June:

My dear Brother,

Although my letters are all designed for the family, I have generally directed them to Father because he is our head, because I am full of grateful affection for him and lastly because he writes so often himself. I was glad to get your short note. . . . You intimated that the present dearth of business leaves considerable time on your hands for fancy investment, now what's to hinder you, when you find an empty hour before your nose, from giving me a page or two of Plantsville gossip. I don't care what it is, it will be a delight to me. . . . [N]ow, to me, in these strange circumstances, the hundred miles or so between here and happy Plantsville become a lens of intense power. Anything, from the cluck of a hen to an earthquake, will be a pleasant food to my thoughts. . . . I have been to see Sis—found her in prime condition.° You *must* go and visit her. She complained bitterly of your neglect to do so. The effort would pay you well. Outside of the brotherly duty and pleasure of doing so, you will find an extensive crop of girls of all descriptions to feast your eyes on—a regular harem of them. You ought to go, Ed, for Sis' sake at any rate. I tell you what, we have got a sister to be proud of and grateful for. To all appearances she is growing up into a noble, intelligent, accomplished, and Christian womanhood. We must cherish her for her own self, and for the memory of our Mother. . . .

With regard to my peculiar work in this camp, my ideas have undergone some change, not a change of essentials, but a change of form. As I gain knowledge of the material with which I have to deal, I find myself compelled to study a problem whose terms are somewhat different from what I anticipated and for whose solution I must wait—I know not how long—I try to fortify myself with patience and faith. I am satisfied that my labor is in the main to consist of sowing—the reaping I leave to God. The Grace of Heaven is Almighty, I have no right to set limits to it, but I look forward to the last great Day for the seals of my ministry here. At least half, I might say two thirds, of my men are Irish Catholics.° Of course I cannot, it is not best that I should, approach them as a Protestant clergyman. I shall try to make the term Chaplain synonymous with Friend, and while I wrestle in prayer for their salvation now, my aim must be, first, in a legitimate way to secure their confidence and respect toward me as a man and to allay all suspicion, or rather to show that there is no ground for suspicion of me as a proselyter. Thank God! There is some precious common ground between us. As a man said to me last Sunday "we are all looking for the same little place," meaning Heaven.

Pray for and with me, my Brother, that my faith may not fail and that my consecration may grow complete.

Yours affectionately—Joe.

two thirds . . . are Irish Catholics: Chaplains dealt in a variety of ways with the religious
differences among the men in a regiment. In Twichell's case, his eventual friendship with
the Jesuit chaplain of another regiment, Father Joseph O'Hagan, enabled him to provide
his Catholic charges with sacraments he could not—and would not—perform himself. In
general, Protestant chaplains provided services that included scripture reading, songs, and a
sermon without much emphasis on liturgy.

On 23 June, Twichell wrote to his father about the success of the religious services that day: "Today has been a complete success—a glorious time for me—and I think for all religious persons in the encampment." The letter continues:

This morning at 10 o'clock the regiments were paraded for service. The Adjutant of my Regiment, after the line was formed, announced the object of the parade at the same time granting permission to all who felt conscientious scruples against it to advance four paces from the ranks. About 75 Irish Catholics responded, which considering the fact that nearly three quarters of the entire body are of that religion I considered a small number. The "conscientious" men were then ordered to drill an hour under the hot sun and the rest were marched to the monster tent where Mr. Bulkley's regiment was already assembled. I should state that nearly a hundred men had before been taken to the Catholic church in the neighborhood, at their own request. This step, of course, I highly approved. In the big tent (once used for a circus) an extempore pulpit had been erected and draped in the American flag. The men were scattered in companies upon the ground filling the whole enclosure. After opening exercises, I preached a short sermon from Heb XIII—17, first clause.° The whole service was very interesting and made I think a good impression. The singing was excellent, conducted by a chorister from my regiment and calling out some very fine verses. Everything was made short, and after it was over, Mr. B. and I went to our tent in a grateful frame. In the afternoon, we held another service—of 15 minutes—just before the grand dress parade. . . . But the religious delights of the day did not end here. A splendid large marquee has been erected for the General [Sickles], but not yet furnished for his occupation. In this we secured permission to hold a meeting at 8 o'clock. At that hour the "assembly" drum was beat in front of the tent aforesaid. This signal . . . was responded to in a way we could not anticipate. The marquee was crowded—at least 60 men were there and all evidently for good purposes. It was a glorious meeting and I believe the spirit of God was there. Mr. Bulkley opened the exercises very appropriately and on invitation to participate, there was found no lack of Christian brethren. Nay, better, a sergeant, a fine young fellow rose, and in a voice broken by emotion asked prayers for his soul. I can assure you that his request was granted on the spot. A captain—not a professedly pious man—rose and declared his belief in God and religion. The Methodists (and there were many of them) betrayed themselves by their fervor. Prayers abounded and we sang a great deal. I never saw the like. It was glorious. My heart was almost too full for utterance. . . . We shall, by the blessing of God, have more of these meetings. I hope, nay even have confidence, that they will prove a great means of usefulness—perhaps the chief means. . . .

Love to all. Your Son. J. H. Twichell.

Heb[rews] XIII—17, first clause: "Obey them that have the rule over you, and submit yourselves."

Camp Scott, June 27th 1861.

Dear Father,

I despatched to you on Monday . . . a very hastily written letter, which was chiefly devoted to an account of the religious matters of the Brigade, to the exclusion of other things concerning which you had inquired. . . .

You asked about the success of our call for books. I am happy to say that it was abundantly successful, so far as quantity was concerned and in the main acceptable as to quality. Some of the contributions were beneath and some above the calibre of the men for whom they were designed. I should hesitate long before giving out the "Confessions" of a notorious villain,° and I should anticipate that very little edification to most of my flock would result from the perusal of an Edinburgh Review. From the mass collected, however, we shall be able to glean very valuable material; the residue we can turn over to some other regiment. . . .

I have a servant, Tim [Gleason] by name°—a slim, large-eyed, hungry looking boy—18 years old. He was in the ranks, but could not pass the Doctor on account of deafness. Moreover he was not hardy enough to be a soldier, indeed, I fear he has the seeds of consumption in him. A companion of his spoke to me about him and asked permission to present him for inspection. He passed a good examination in mental and moral branches, but was decidedly lacking in the physical. I wanted a stout man, for the sake of my baggage, library etc., but Tim's pleading looks and sad story carried the day. I found on questioning him, that in case he left the Brigade, he had no place on earth to go to, his parents having died, and a brother with whom he has lived being just at the point of death with consumption and miserably poor. Work was not to be had for book-binders and Tim was hard up enough. I thought the Lord had sent him, and so I took him in. He proves to be handy, honest and very intelligent and has the virtue of being quiet. While over in New York yesterday, I went with him to see his brother. After climbing up several stories through the dark and sloppy passage-way of a cheap tenement house, I found him in a dingy little room apparently in the last stages of consumption. He spoke cheerfully of death, said he felt secure with Christ, and thanked me for taking Tim. He was evidently an Irishman of the better class. . . . I received the impression that although a Catholic, his confidence was rightly placed in the atonement alone.° I hope to see him again before he dies. The pay of my servant is allowed me by the Government—being the same with that of private in the ranks.°

My visit to Sis was a very delightful one and, to me at least, perfectly satisfactory. She appears to be everything I could wish her to be. I found that she had been in quite low spirits for a good part of the term, induced by a sort of vague idea that the family at home was living on bread and water for the sake of keeping her at school. Really, Father, I don't see what is the use of vexing the girl, with her feeble apprehensions of financial matters, with a businessman's lament over the deplorable state of our commerce. She knows nothing of it, takes it for granted that everything is going to the dogs and allows herself to become very miserable. I consoled her, so far as I was able, by telling her that our Father was better off than the great majority of his craft, in that he had not been compelled to suspend payments or impair his credit by forced operations in cash—that he was fortunately able to stop without falling over his horses' head and that although he was temporarily drawing more from the top of the cistern than flowed in, still there was no frightful "2 per cent a month" hole at the bottom etc. etc. Wasn't that about right? Now while we are upon the edge of the family purse, peering down into its vacuity, let us retain our perch awhile, till I unfold a tale as distasteful to me as the moral of a story to reading children.

You have been sending me money lately, which I know has come hard. I try to be proportionately grateful for it, yet console myself that it is but an advance which my coming pay will enable me to refund, at least for safe keeping. That pay I have expected to receive soon, and hence have hoped that each draft on you would be the last, a consummation which you cannot more devoutly wish than I. Until it comes, it is certain that I must call on you to supply my needs. No other way is open. I am compelled now in proportion as I long for the day when Government cash will chink in my pocket, by so much does it seem to recede. I cannot say when I expect to get the first installment. My confidence in rumors is entirely gone and I am convinced that no one *knows* about it with any certainty. The commonest complaint of the camp is the utter dearth of money. A dime is as big as a dollar. Borrowers are numerous—lenders few. I lent a Captain $3.00, under a solemn promise that it should be paid the next day. That is the last I have heard of it. I lend no more. Our greatest day of rejoicing will be when Uncle Sam's cashier takes up his abode with us. I suppose that this will surely not be till after Congress meets.

Moral. I must notify you of all my wants and look for supplies from home, until that auspicious event. Now for my present wants. The officers are now dividing up into messes—the mode prescribed by military regulations, after mustering in. Mr. Bulkley, a Lieut. [George F.] Young and myself have formed one. We make a requisition on the Commissary every morning for the days rations and our servants prepare the meals. This step necessitates the purchase of a Camp chest, stove and other tools for housekeeping or rather *tent*keeping. Moreover the Commissariat is poorly supplied—furnishing only the three grand staples, bread, meat and potatoes, so that we have to do a great deal of foraging, which requires money. As Mr. Bulkley says it "costs" to go to war. . . . I had no idea of it and regarded 7th Regt. accounts as the record of reckless expenditure.° Come down and see me. You will be able to become an eyewitness. It were well if nothing dearer than money were poured out in this sad war, it were well if families lost nothing more valued than property. The cost is least of all to be reckoned numerically in dollars. There are many men in this Brigade (I am proud to say it) who have left all to fight in patriotic love and honesty. With many officers the entire neglect and loss of business interests has been met cheerfully. . . .

Everything has been moving on successfully to completion ever since we came here. The US mustering officer has been at work among us for nearly a week.° Three regiments at least have been sworn in. Some unfruitful limbs have been lopped off.° That is what you read in the papers—the expiring whine. Today I distributed a large number of Irish newspapers among my Catholics. I had procured them from their respective officers. I think the effect was good. Good night. Your aff. Son, Joseph.

"Confessions" of a notorious villain: Twichell is speaking in general terms of the popular genre of lurid criminal memoirs.

I have a servant, Tim [Gleason] by name: Servants were provided for army officers at government expense. A chaplain's rank was equal to that of captain.

although a Catholic . . . placed in the atonement alone: Twichell is reassuring his father that he has not been involved in what he would regard as illusory Catholic sacraments: the anointment of oil and the reading of the last rites. Congregationalists believed in only two sacraments, baptism and communion, and that they were wholly symbolic, not directly conferring God's grace. Gleason's dying brother put his faith in Christ's voluntary sacrifice for the sins of mankind, so, Twichell believes, he qualified for salvation despite his Catholicism.

pay . . . being the same with that of private in the ranks: That is, thirteen dollars per month.

regarded 7th Regt. accounts . . . reckless expenditure: This may be a reference to the New York Seventh Regiment, the silk-stocking militia group that had proceeded to Washington on the outbreak of war with velvet-covered camp stools and sandwiches prepared at Delmonico's.

The US mustering officer . . . among us for nearly a week: After the brigade was accepted as United States Volunteers, its members had to be officially mustered in for three years by the War Department.

Some unfruitful limbs have been lopped off: The *New York Times* reported on 1 July 1861 that captains of at least two Excelsior companies had registered grievances against Sickles in the state supreme court: one, that his command "were induced to join the Brigade by promises that had not been fully realized"; the other that Sickles had "attempted to place over the men officers from among his own City friends." The latter charge was brought by the Pittsburgh company whose case Twichell describes in the following letter.

Camp Scott, July 3rd 1861

Dear Father, . . .

Sunday was a pleasant day. It would have been hot but for the kindly shelter of clouds which remained nearly all day. The morning service was well attended, and Mr. B. preached from "wherefore, seeing we are compassed about by so great a cloud of witnesses etc."° Our chapel tent was dedicated at two o'clock. . . . In the afternoon we had Brigade Service, as usual, just before parade, all being formed into a hollow square and the square being crowded with visitors, which latter was not wholly agreeable to the Chaplains. Every thing went well, I think, and the fact that we had a temporary pulpit, rendered the proximity of the lookers on and the remoteness of our real audience less annoying. We had a fair shot over the curious rabble. I had the sermonizing, of 5 minutes only, to do, and found my subject in Philippians 3, 13 &14.° A portion of the crowd seemed to think that courtesy demanded the most violent applause when I was through, but Mr. Bulkley squelched them immediately. In some respects the most interesting event since my connection with the Brigade took place immediately after. You perhaps remember noticing in the paper an account of the desertion and recapture of an insubordinate Pittsburgh Company—how the General rode down to the Ferry, and pistol in hand, forced them back—how they were thrust into a guard house and fed like swine—how a writ of habeas corpus was served on the General and a session of the Superior court held on the grounds etc. etc. I believe it was all in the papers. Well, the guard house is hard by the big tent where we hold morning service and many of the prisoners were at the windows. After benediction the Adjutant of my regiment came to me saying that some of the jail-birds had expressed a desire to have religious exercises held with them, adding that he had spoken to the officer of the day, who wholly consented. So, after Brigade service in the afternoon when it was the quiet part of the day about the guard house, all the soldiers being on parade, we went in. They assembled at one end of the building, about 70 of them, and we both of us preached to them. No minister ever received better attention than they gave us and I think we were gifted with peculiar unction in speaking. I have omitted to mention that during the day we had distributed 1000 Soldiers Hymn books, several of which were handed in to these men at morning service. We found that many of them could sing which added much to the enjoyment of the meeting. Altogether it was a most gratifying circumstance. We had some talk with them after we were through and found them very intelligent—in fact as intelligent as any Company in the Brigade. As soon as they are released they purpose joining some Pennsylvania Regiment. I am sorry for it. Of course we avoided all discussion of the merits of their case, because it was out of our province and because the fault is understood to rest with their officers, whom it would not do to criticize with their command. The evening meeting was a glorious one. The new tent was crowded and all the exercises were very fervent. . . .

Again I am writing on a gallop. Since I sat down, I have been interrupted to write two letters for uneducated privates, and also by a notification from the General that I am to deliver the oration tomorrow. Short notice, in all conscience. I hardly know what to do. Now, Mr. Bulkley is urging me to leave this and help him about his tent. The next hour of quiet I get shall be devoted to you. To be busy has some comforts, but is not wanting in discomfort. God bless you all.

Your aff. Son, Joseph.

"Wherefore, seeing we are encompassed about . . .": Bulkley's text is from St. Paul's Epistle to the Hebrews, 12:1–2: "Wherefore seeing we also are encompassed about with so great a cloud of witnesses . . . let us run with patience the race that is set before us, looking unto Jesus the author and finisher of our faith."

Philippians 3, 13 &14: "Brethren, I count not myself to have apprehended: but this one thing I do, forgetting those things which are behind, and reaching forth unto those things which are before, I press toward the mark for the prize of the high calling of God in Christ Jesus."

Twichell next writes to his father on 5 July.

Fourth of July is over and done—it was done well throughout the loyal parts of this country, I hope. The accounts so far as they have come in seem to indicate it. Camp Scott was as gay and magnificent as parades, music, salutes and a few thousand visitors could make it. From sunrise till midnight all was commotion and noise. You have probably seen the program in the papers as previously announced in the general order for the day. It all came off duly, including the Oration by Chaplain Twichell. By reason of an outrageously short notice my travail was brief but violent, resulting in an effort of about 15 minutes, which thus possessed at least the merit of brevity—a thing not always true of 4th of July doses. It was long enough however for the broiling soldiers, who had been marched about all day, and had just been regaled by the reading of the Declaration to say nothing of Mr. Bulkley's prayer, which by the way was a grand one. It was long enough for me also, who would have been compelled, by proceeding much further, to enter the region of old platitudes and worn out splurges, which I forswore to start with. I feel no delicacy, in writing to you, in saying that I was able to discern that my performance was not unsatisfactory to my audience. . . .

The only unanticipated incident of the day was a powerful one. A man was killed, for trying to break guard.° He was a desperate fellow and had before been insubordinate. The guard ran him through with a bayonet, or rather, he rushed upon the point of one. A court of inquiry held this morning unanimously approved the act and recommended the faithful guard—of the dead man's own regiment—for promotion. To me this seems dreadful, but I suppose it was right and best, and that I shall grow less sensitive on such matters. I have been enough already in this camp to show me that I shall get used to things which before have been night-mares. The dead will be buried tomorrow morning at sunrise without military honors. Perhaps a Catholic priest will be here to perform the solitary religious rites, if not myself (Mr. Bulkley has gone home with his wife who spent the 4th with us). . . .

I could write a great deal about the Brigade, but it is not necessary and would not be very interesting to you. Everything is going on well. The general health is excellent—extraordinary—and the men are for the most part contented. The drill is every day improving—if I mistake not the Brigade will be put in splendid shape and condition before long. . . .

Love! Love! Love to all, Joseph.

A man was killed, for trying to break guard: Military justice was harsh during the war. Cowardice, desertion, theft, sleeping on guard duty could bring execution by firing squad or hanging. "Breaking guard" was the practice of leaving the camp illegally.

Dear Father,

It is quite late, but I am unwilling to turn in until I have exercised myself home-wards a little. The day has been a most uncomfortable one for encamped soldiers. Ever since morning a drizzling rain, varying somewhat in intensity, has fallen and our gayest day of all the week converted into a season of muddy discomfort. Every thing is dripping and the sole consolation afforded is the fact, grateful only to a few, that holy time has been less openly and noisily desecrated than usual. Most of the men have kept their tents and very few visitors have appeared. . . . The evening prayer meeting was full, on account of the interest felt in it and a cessation of the rain. Like the others it was fervently participated and evidently enjoyed. It is there that we look for the blessing to appear. . . . An impression had gone abroad among the Catholics that mass was to be celebrated at our tent, as on last Sabbath, and on going there at about 10 o'clock I found it full of expectant Irishmen. I took occasion in informing them of their mistake to express some very liberal views concerning the worship of a common Father in Heaven, which I could see pleased many of them. On approaching the scene of their service, when ours was finished, I was most cordially invited to a seat within, which from motives prudential I accepted. If I can only get my Catholic parishioners to feel that there is some precious common ground between us, a great point will be gained. Not that I expect to gather them all under my public Sabbath ministrations, but that it will lead them to receive me with more confidence and pleasure and profit into their private tents and to their sick couches, where much of my labor is to lie. I long for their good-will as an instrument to their salvation, moreover you know my weakness for a hearty, generous Irishman and I want them to like me. I trust in time to show them that I preach piety and not Protestantism. . . .

The idea of going up to Commencement [at Yale] and coming home has violent hold on me at present. Unless we go before or are on the point of starting, I am disposed to regard the movement as highly probable. Commencement comes on the last Thursday of the month. I could leave here Monday or Tuesday and return via N. Haven, reaching Camp Scott Friday night, and include a great deal in the trip.

Everything here goes on well. Yesterday and to-day arms have been distributed to parts of three regiments. Success seems certain, at least a large measure of it. The splendid successes of our arms at the seat of war° calls for devout thanksgiving, likewise the noble zeal displayed in Congress. . . . God bless you all abundantly. Affectionately, Joseph.

The splendid successes . . . the seat of war: Probably a reference to General George B. Mc-Clellan's successes in western Virginia during this period.

Camp Scott, July 18th 1861.

Dear Father,

Both yesterday and to-day have I enjoyed that most delectable dessert for my plain rations, viz—a letter from home. . . . The information that Ed and Sis will probably be my guests shortly fills me with the most pleasurable antic-ipations, although I have indulged such emotions before. . . . Our mess table will accommodate two visitors quite comfortably. Mr. B., Dr Brown, a Lieut. Young (attached to the Generals staff) and myself break bread together and form a very congenial party. Dr B. is "caterer" of the mess, i.e. makes all the requisitions for rations and bears the purse—the expense to be equally divided. If you at home feel anxious to contribute to our larder, I would suggest dried beef, pickles, and cheese (particularly dried beef) as a list to choose from.

Mr. B. and myself no longer tent together. After being my honoured guest for 5 weeks he has procured a tent in his own line, with another tent attached for mess accommodations. I really regretted the change, although we were very much crowded under the same canvas. Now, I have room enough for my luggage and servant;—which word "servant" brings me to my latest grief. I fear that I must lose the boy Tim Gleeson [sic] to whom I am attached. He was mustered in as a soldier and the edict has gone forth, "No officer can have a soldier for a servant." His Captain will detail him for duty at my tent, the greater part of each day for a few weeks, but ultimately we must part, much to my own dissatisfaction and I think to Tim's. I must be on the look out for another. . . .

Mr Otis (Otis & Upson) and Lavinia Buck° were here to-day. Who next? Every body but those I long for comes to see me. I am sometimes slightly bored. This has been the busiest week I have seen as well as the hottest. Mr. B. went home this afternoon—much love—J. H. T.

Mr [William Y.] Otis (Otis & Upson) and Lavinia Buck: Otis was a clock manufacturer and brickyard owner from Southington; the Bucks were a family in the town.

Camp Scott, July 23rd 1861.

Good bye! Pa! I fear that I am not to see you before we go° and my dis-appointment is bitter. Yet, perhaps it is as well so. Both of us have said all we want to, and the rest would be very sober if not sad. I shrank from it.

My things, what I have, are packed and I am prepared to take an early start. It is anticipated that we start at 5 o'clock in the morning. The 1st went this morning. Mr. Bulkley left me a note saying that he had provided for the packing and forwarding of our books. Of course, I have not been able to equip myself as I wished. A sword and belt which I chanced upon is all I have got. The rest I must either get at the seat of war or have them sent. I drew $65.00 from Mr. Beadle°—all that they had. As soon as I get a chance, I shall write. I find that I have enough of everything for present needs, so that you may not think I have gone off at all destitute. My only fears are for the men, who will not be equipped as they should be. They are very jubilant at the prospect of departure and the camp was never so merry. Poor fellows. I can't help thinking of Bull's Run. Arms have been distributed this evening and everything needful is promised on the arrival at Washington.

Give my hearty love to all Plantsville.° Next time I tread her sod, I hope it will be part of a whole country. We go for God and sweet Liberty which He loves and which He surely must favour. Good-bye! Good-bye. Let our prayers for each other abound, my very dear Father, that in all things we may fight the good fight and at last wear the beautiful, immortal garment—even Christ's righteousness. Good-bye.

Your affectionate Son. Joseph.

I am not to see you before we go: After the Union disaster at Bull Run, reinforcements were summoned from the North—including the Excelsior Brigade.

I drew $65.00 from Mr. Beadle: Beadle appears to have been a business agent for the Twichells in New York and later employed Edward William Twichell.

Give my hearty love to all Plantsville: Twichell's birthplace, Southington Corners, a section of the town of Southington, had changed its name to Plantsville in the 1850s.

July 1861–March 1862

The knowledge that the war would not just be a matter of a long vacation had struck the United States government cruelly on 21 July 1861. Thirty miles from Washington, General Irvin McDowell moved his thirty thousand men to attack twenty thousand Confederates defending the crucial railroad junction at Manassas, Virginia. Despite Union gains early in the battle, lack of coordination and officers' and men's inexperience in war turned Bull Run (named for a nearby stream) into a disaster. Demoralized soldiers fled back to the capital. Fresh troops— including the Second Excelsior—were quickly summoned from the North. The First Excelsior was the first regiment that came "to the rescue" of the capital, as a brigade historian put it.

Washington, July 26th 1861.

My dear Father,

After a long (i.e. slow) but quite comfortable journey we set feet on the soil of the capital at about 10 o'clock last night. The men on the whole behaved finely the whole way. We found no quarters provided for us and the entire Regiment bivouacked on the low damp ground adjoining the railroad. I lay right down without covering of any kind save the clothes I had on—not even a blanket—and slept like a log till the sun was up. . . . Although wet with dew and dirty from head to foot, I never felt better in my life than I did after shaking myself a little, and all the boys are in the best of spirits. They were too tired last night to grumble and this morning they are merry. Mr. Bulkley met us last night at the cars, but went up to a hotel to sleep, returning early, when we took a stroll about town, which I am concluding by writing this. Washington is a scene of motley confusion. Soldiers everywhere, in every imaginable uniform—baggage wagons ambulances and stores throng the streets. About half an hour since our Regiment was started for its quarters—I know not exactly where, but mean to find out as soon as I finish this. . . . I got a servant in Baltimore—a colored boy about 20 years old—and he will attend to my baggage. We met large numbers of 3 months' men° going back, but all declaring their intention to return.

The picket of the enemy is said to be within 4 miles of this city, but I hardly believe it.

The day promises to be a hot one and I am glad our fellows got so early a start. By night we shall be comfortably pitched and at the first opportunity I shall write you a long letter. I should not write at all now, so great is my hurry, if I did not think you would be anxious. I thought much of you all the way here. May God spare us all to meet in His good time. With much love. I remain etc., Joseph.

[P.S.] . . . The state of the public mind here seems very bitter with regard to the stampede from Bulls Run. A flank movement over the upper Potomac for the capture of the city is talked about, but very little believed I guess.

We met large numbers of 3 months' men: The initial volunteers summoned by Lincoln in April had enlisted for ninety days on the assumption that they would not be needed longer.

Camp—July 27th 1861.

My dear Father,

Yesterday morning I dispatched to you a very hastily written note, announcing our arrival here in good condition. Well, after I had done writing, with Mr. Bulkley who was with me, I went back to where the Regiment had bivouacked in the mud the night before and found it gone with all the baggage. The direction it had taken was pointed out and we deliberated whether we had better pursue immediately or go back to the city again and report ourselves at leisure. Feeling no uneasiness about my baggage, on account of having previously instructed my servant with reference to it, we decided upon the latter. After another stroll and a peep in at both the House and Senate, we took a hearty lunch, and set out for our regimental quarters. I had heard the General's orderly that morning reading instructions to our Lieut. Col. to the effect that the 2nd was to be located near the 1st, so we mounted a vehicle and went up to the 1st, about 2½ miles from the city on 14th street. To my astonishment, no one there knew anything of the whereabouts of the 2nd. It was certainly not in their immediate vicinity. Mr. B. had a bundle of letters brought to him by his men to be mailed and he proposed that we should turn our faces again toward the city, inquiring on the way at the numerous camps all along the road. . . .

The whole country on that side the city (I don't know which side it is, for my head is wrong) is white with tents. Regiments are as plenty as blackberries. We visited several and among others the 2nd Connecticut, where Mr. B. found a number of his old Winsted friends. At length, after much dust and sweat and a protracted wandering, we found the glorious 2nd pitching its tents in the most beautiful grove you ever saw at least a mile from the 1st and about 1½ miles from the city, on 7th St, near a humble establishment called Park Hotel. The men were tired but delighted with the charming location and worked with a will to get things in shape. I found my boy sitting on my trunk and all my effects safe. . . . At Mr. Bulkley's request I went on with him to the city, returning before dark to a quiet pipe . . . and as early a bed as weariness suggested. This morning found me in prime condition. To the refreshment of sleep I added that of a thorough sponge bath; breakfasted . . . on milkless tea, uncooked ham and plain bread, forming a hearty wholesome but not very luxurious meal. . . .

Our journey here, as I wrote yesterday, was a slow one but without serious discomfort, save the shelterless night with which it ended. From [the] time our friends waved us adieu from the shores of Staten Island, all along the route by the Camden & Amboy R.R., we met enthusiastic receptions—the stridulous notes of small boys mingling with the deeper shouts of men who knew wherefore they hailed us. The women especially favoured us with clouds of fluttering handkerchiefs at every station. Everybody on board was in high spirits, save now and then a lengthened face betrayed that the dark side of our errand was not wholly lost sight of, nor the lonesome folks left at home forgotten. We arrived in Philadelphia at about dark, or rather, at Camden. The unloading and transfer of men and baggage over the river occupied some two hours. Once over, we were conducted to a large, long edifice temporarily erected for the purpose and substantially feasted, by the hospitable citizens, who have extended a like kindness to every Regiment that has passed through there. We met hosts of vociferous friends, and if a guard had not been posted at the door of every neighbouring rum-hole, the regiment would have been made a drunken one by mistaken liberality. As it was bottles were circulated somewhat. Just as we were leaving a man was seriously wounded in the face by a cannon fired in our honor. He was left in the hospital. Although it was half past one o'clock when our train started for Baltimore, thousands of people thronged the streets and we went off in a tumult of God-speeds. Frequent halts were made on the road to wait for due trains—the necessities of 2000 soldiers not seeming to be regarded of sufficient importance to infringe upon the customary time-table.

At some of these places men were left behind, not-withstanding orders had been issued that none should leave the cars. Lack of strict discipline is the great fault and danger of this Regiment. The men who were left have been joining us since by twos and threes, having come on by other trains. At about noon we reached Baltimore and had to march a mile and a half to the Balt. & Ohio R.R. depot—the same road which the 6th Mass. found so hard a one.° Baltimore being passed we whirled on to our destination. Soon signs of the war began to appear. Pickets were stationed all along the track at intervals of half a mile or so and at every bridge—fine looking fellows from Massachusetts, most of them. They all cheered us on. I omitted to say that at Baltimore we were received in silence. Not an American flag was displayed, not a cheer was raised, not a hiss was heard. It was a rather solemn march. I cannot tell you of the emotions I experienced by the way. They were most profound especially through Maryland, and so they have been ever since I got here.

A most affecting thing was to see the black slaves cheer us from the fields as we passed and here every moment brings some reminder that battlefields are not far off. There is an endless procession of troops pouring along the streets and the heavy roll of baggage wagons never ceases. Drill in musket firing is going on every where and one has only to shut his eyes to imagine himself in the midst of a battle. On one side of us, so near that the sentinels can touch bayonets, is the 3rd Pennsylvania Reg. and on the other side is a troop of regular cavalry, equally near. Washington is the place for rumors. You can't walk a rod° without meeting one. The most important I have heard are that Gen. Scott was hardly prevented from resigning after the great battle, and, 2nd, that a large part of the regular army has been ordered here at once both of which seem probable. I give these because I was impressed with their probability. Soldiers who were at the battle are everywhere to be seen surrounded by small knots of listeners, detailing each his own account of the events. In many cases of this kind, as you might easily imagine, a strict regard for truth would materially alter the tales thus unfolded.

This morning some of our fellows fixed suspicion on a poor half-intoxicated vagabond, who was loafing about, as a secession spy, and haled him before some officers, who enjoyed the joke better than the subject of it did. He was cheated out of the "drunk" of at least his last three drinks by fright. The boys thought he was reconnoitering and drawing a plan of our camp, for [Confederate Gen. Pierre G. T.] Beauregard's benefit and that he was a dangerous visitor. I think they claimed to have seen him swallow a paper, on being closely stared at. They would have hung him with little urging. He was probably some Washington loafer and too drunk to explain himself. . . .

How long we shall stay here I know not. The Colonel told me yesterday, that twelve hours might find us on the march to the other side of the river, to receive the instruction that throwing up intrenchments and being in enemy's country affords. Such being the case, you must not wonder if quite a long break in my correspondence occurs before a great while. . . .

I think of home a great deal and though I do not expect to see it in months at least, have yet begun to anticipate the time. God bless all of us as He has heretofore with love and harmony. I shall expect long letters from as many of you as can write.

Your aff. Son, Joseph.

the same road which the 6th Mass. found so hard a one: On 19 April, as the war commenced, the Sixth Massachusetts Regiment headed for Washington and had to make this same Baltimore transit along several city blocks. Maryland was a slaveholding state bordering Washington, and many of its citizens favored secession. Rioters attacked the soldiers, who opened fire; nine civilians and four soldiers were killed. Turmoil continued in the city until Lincoln took draconian measures to maintain control of the state.

You can't walk a rod: A rod is 5.5 yards.

In Camp—Washington July 29th 1861.

Dear Folks at Home

It is so hot this forenoon that I can do nothing else but sit as still as possible in my tent. Even the exertion necessary to writing makes me stream with perspiration and any out door work would be burning torture. We have left the cool oak grove where we first pitched and moved about a mile to the neighbourhood of the 1st. . . . Our present camp is on a bare hill, with nothing to break the full force of the sun, at least for the men. The officers quarters are a little shielded by an occasional tree, but nothing compared with the thick shade of our first abode, which we all covet back. . . .

Saturday night about 10 o'clock we had quite a refreshing alarm. The stillness was first cracked by an explosion of muskets and the whizzing of several bullets through the trees, cutting off twigs etc. over our heads. One passed within a rod of my tent, with a sound like a humming bee in rapid motion, perhaps a little sharper. This, as I said, cracked the silence, and the men soon accomplished a perfect breakage. A Pennsylvania Regiment near us first set the drums rolling, then it spread to us and the others around. What with the drums, and the bawling of officers, and running of soldiers, the din was enough to have won a considerable battle without firing. Of course, every sensible [man] knew it could be no enemy, or we should have been advised hours before, so I kept on writing a letter, although I felt a glow of excitement. In half an hour everything subsided into quiet again. So ended our first call to arms. The racket was all out of place, provided there were any danger, but everybody was green and went on the panic principle. It was probably the accident (i.e. the firing was) of some imprudent fools who deserved 48 hours guard house on bread and water for their blunder. Still, the fact that the hostile army is within 30 miles, that their pickets are within 7 miles—and that Washington is considered threatened—any thing that suggests an attack will quicken the blood. These false alarms are common, I am told, and we shall get used to them. I don't like the idea of *friendly* bullets though. I want to be shot at by the enemy, if at all. The sentry whose beat was near my tent, as soon as he heard the lead, dropped on his face and lay prone for some time. It was funny. The men in their ignorance most of them thought a fight was coming surely, and showed good pluck for the anticipated encounter, nay even, some rejoiced at the prospect. One sick fellow jumped from his bed, saying "Give me a gun, boys! I had rather die fighting, than under the Doctor". . . .

The smoke from secession camps is almost visible and might be blown across the Potomac by a fair wind. All men have their eyes turned that way. We shall soon know what God designs for us. Till then let us give ourselves to watchfulness and prayer and humiliation. I think of you all the while. The hundreds of miles between us are no bar to our affections, thank God. Write me long letters. With much love—Joseph.

In Camp—Washington, Sunday Aug 4th '61.

My dear Father,

We have moved twice since I wrote to you. Now moving a camp of 1000 men is no slight job. What with the accompanying march and other collateral labours, it takes the best part of a day. The first time we pitched, you remember, was in a grove. We staid there two nights, then removed to a bare hill and staid till Friday. New orders then led us to another change. After the hottest march I ever imagined of about 5 miles we came to a stop in a beautiful clover field bordered by a wood which screened the officers quarters—on the magnificent ornamental estate of Corcoran the celebrated banker, who is regarded a Secessionist.° There we reposed overnight congratulating ourselves on having found at last a tarrying place and a pleasant one. But it seems that there was some misunderstanding somewhere, for down came old Corcoran himself with one of Gen. Scott's staff and ordered us off. So about noon we packed up and marched a couple of miles more to our present quarters the location of which I could hardly describe, not having had a chance to look about. . . . Although we only came here last night and everything was in confusion I determined to make an effort for a service, as last Sunday it was impossible. . . . At the beating of the assembly, quite a respectable little congregation collected under the shade of 3 or 4 cherry trees near my tent, and we had a very agreeable season of worship. For a pulpit I had draped a dry-goods box in the flag and it answered every purpose. The singing was hearty and as congregational as any one could wish. I was pleased and thankful to see a larger representative from the officers than ever before. . . . Under the circumstances I have every reason to be grateful and encouraged. If I once get the officers and especially the Col. into my audience, service will grow popular. I expect that it will often be impossible to attempt preaching, but whenever hereafter there is the least chance, I shall try. . . . As I remarked, the march of Friday was a hot one. I never witnessed such a sweltering, burning sun. Had not a drenching rain two days before laid the dust, there would have been considerable suffering. I made it the hardest working day, I believe, of my whole life. In the first place, my own baggage had to [be] attended to, although I committed the most of that business to my very efficient colored servant Joe. Then there were about 30 sick men to be cared for—some of them very sick. Much legitimate labor here devolved upon me, by reason of the absence of the Asst. Surgeon. They had to be nursed while lying on the ground and then stowed away in the Ambulances. Among the rest two of the officers were flat on their backs with fever and ague. On the march I took the rear and we had not gone a mile before I had a load of knapsacks and muskets which I took from men who fainted and fell out of the ranks. Notwithstanding frequent halts, a great many were forced to step from the lines and lie down by the road-side. Most of these were men who had been weakened by recent diarrhea or touches of chills and fever. Just here my muscle came in excellent play for I found that I could shoulder two or three men's burdens and march without much discomfort, although I perspired like rain, as my Father's son should. So I worked it all along the route, never carrying a less load than two muskets, cheering up the fellows that lagged, giving now one and now another a lift. I saw that I had fallen upon an advantage for myself, and I really think I improved it. "That's the sort of a Chaplain to have!" I heard a great many say—and I do not think it was intended for my ears in every instance. We made the weary rear rank the merriest part of the Regiment after all, for I don't believe any others sang Star Spangled banner as they went along, and we did until the woods rang and the heat was forgotten. The way to mitigate the oppression of heat or weariness is to divert the attention to something else. That much at least I have found out here. A song, a joke, an arousing of interest in something outside the present, will slip a quarter mile from under the feet wonderfully. After we arrived at our destination—and the last part of the march was over gravelled walks and through splendid grounds, which the heavy baggage wagons cut up terribly—there were the sick to be unloaded and tucked up and my own tent to be pitched. At bed-time I was thoroughly tired out and found my cot and blanket delicious beyond description. I had a double purpose to spur me up all day—the present comfort of the men in particular and the desire to work my way into their confidence in general. From this and other similar operations I hope to reap much fruit hereafter. . . . The war we hear very little about. Forty or fifty poor fellows from Bull Run, whom I saw in . . . hospital, stopped my joking for a while I assure you. Gen. McClellan seems to be very energetic° and has introduced some valuable reforms among the volunteers. I have a thousand things to write but there is no use in trying to tell all, besides, I have to use my knees for a table and my pen is a poor, borrowed one. Mine is strayed or stolen. Shall get more tomorrow at Washington. . . .

Corcoran . . . is regarded a Secessionist: W. W. Corcoran's mansion on H Street contained a huge collection of paintings and sculpture, which eventually went to the nation as what is now the Corcoran Museum of Art. Corcoran's pro-Southern sympathies led him to move to Europe in 1862 for the duration of the war. He turned the Excelsior Brigade away from Glenwood, his estate two miles north of Washington.

Gen. McClellan seems . . . energetic: McClellan's success in keeping Kentucky and western Virginia in the Union led to Lincoln's appointing him on 27 July as commander of the Federal Division of the Potomac—essentially, in charge of Union forces in the East. His energy in organization and improving morale was not often accompanied by success in battle.

Camp Clendenen.° Monday morning. August 5th 1861.

Dear Father, . . .

Day before yesterday the Col. said to me "Doctor! I wish to have my staff mounted as soon as possible." I instantly replied, "I will attend to it sir," meaning, of course, I will write to Father about it. The Surgeon, Quartermaster and Adjutant have all furnished themselves, so that, in a sort, I *stand* alone. I seem to be compelled to possess the body of a horse, or, at least, to have one subject to my control. . . . Of course, I wish to be as economical in this respect as possible. . . . If the horse is lost in any natural or military way, the Government pays me for him. If nothing happens of ill fortune, we have the horse in the family, and can, in all probability, make a little money by his sale. If you send me the money, a draft on Washington would be more easily handled than anything else, except cash, but good New York paper would do nearly as well—quite as well if I was handy at business.

That is, I believe, the whole story. It is a source of great regret to me to have to call on you to help me so considerably. I have . . . tried to find out whether pay-day was not so near at hand that I need call on you for only part of the money. Here, I can get no satisfaction. The probability is that we shall not see the color of U.S. gold before the 1st of September, which I regret more on account of our poor fellows whose families are hungry at home, than on my own. Whenever the time does come, I shall immediately send my share home to you, to do what you like with. . . .

My colored servant Joseph gives me great satisfaction. He is ignorant, reading and writing being not in the list of his accomplishments—talks the real Uncle Toms Cabin negro dialect to perfection, and has many negro ways which I have read of but never saw before, but he knows exactly how to take care of himself and his master. I should have no fears to my property, either that it would be lost or broken, if I could not be present at all while the regiment was breaking up camp and moving. Of his honesty I have no doubt, for he is a Christian—at least a praying man. Although brought up in Maryland he has always been free, but betrays his association with slaves by rather servile manners. In addition to his other virtues he is rather good looking—cooks admirably and is a scientific forager—having a peculiar faculty of moving the sympathies of neighboring farmers in the interest of our mess. His only fault is his name which sometimes makes confusion. So much for Joe. With much love to all. I remain. Joseph.

Camp Clendenen: This was apparently a name given in honor of the more hospitable owner of the land to which the regiment moved after being ejected by Corcoran.

Camp Clendenen. Washington. Aug 7th 1861.

Dear Father,

Certain rumors of another move are rife in camp today. . . . When we shall pull up stakes I have a very inaccurate idea. "In a short time," is as near as . . . can be arrived at officially. Where we are going is another generally undetermined thing. Many say that our next March will not end this side of the Potomac. The most reliable information I have been able to gain is from the Adjutant, who says that we are ordered to guard duty on the Balt. and Ohio R.R. I am sure that I don't much care where it is, although my scales of preference incline toward the adventures of a hostile country, rather than to the dry routine of mounting and relieving guard at stations scattered along for several miles of a public highway—service involving very little danger, none in fact, and affording very little excitement. Still it ought to make very little difference with me in my peculiar sphere of action. This fact, however, does not wholly prevent my leanings of choice, and I don't know that it should altogether. One consideration presents itself forcibly in case we take to railroading. My need of a horse will be well-nigh imperative. My parish will be a scattered people, and I shall have to ride a circuit whose proportions would dismay a western Methodist. Since I wrote, I have continued to prosecute my investigations of the process of buying a horse. The last idea is from the Colonel—an idea which carried out will secure a good animal and save money. He says that he will introduce me to a friend of his at Washington, who in consideration of $5 or $10 commission will for $100 put me in possession of a captured remnant of the Black Horse Cavalry,° some similar beast. . . . I can't say that I found any very bright hopes on this project, but we shall see.

The General was here this morning. . . . With regard to Sickles' commission as Brig. General:° We are informed that the President sent in his name for confirmation, but that the Senate adjourned without doing it. Whether it was actually voted down I don't know. He still signs himself, Col. of 1st Regt. & Acting Brig. Gen. I have no doubt he will be virtual commander of his regiments for some time at least. Among other things he visited our hospital and played the Napoleon Bonaparte among our sick . . . very successfully—ordering soup and beef-tea and all manner of comfort for them, besides speaking a kind word to many. . . . To tell the truth, between ourselves, the sick of the regiment do not receive proper care. In saying so I state a fact that is a daily burden and grief to me as well as to those more immediately concerned. Notwithstanding the superior accommodations we have secured, many a poor fellow fails entirely to have his necessary wants supplied. There is no one to blame that I know of. Our Surgeon [John J. McGowan] works hard° and is not seriously wanting in medical skill, so far as I can judge, but he is fat, slow, rather unsympathetic, tenacious of dignity and does not inspire that confidence with his patients which is worth more than doses. Besides this, he has no adequate assistance in his arduous labours. With about a hundred sick on his hands, and some of them very sick, he has no Assistant Surgeon (ours having been detailed to the 1st) and the attendants are all inefficient not to say worthless. One of them was sent to the guard house yesterday, and another was returned to the company from which he was detailed—both for disobedience of orders. The remaining ones are the Hospital steward—a mere boy—and another lad, who is worth nothing except to bring water etc. Some fresh ones have been detailed to assist in nursing, but I doubt whether they are fit for the place, however willing and industrious. Until lately there has been a great lack of proper medical stores. These have at length been procured, but even now none but the sickest have any couch but a blanket on a hard floor, with perhaps a little straw to soften it.

There is inefficiency somewhere. We have a right to as many comfortable beds as we need, but somebody does not see to it that we have them. All these things have aroused my deepest sympathy, both with the sick and with the Doctor, and I am doing all I can to mitigate the evils. Here, in fact, do I regard the best part of my efforts as legitimately belonging. Several hours of each day I spend at the hospital, bathing sores, laying wet cloths on burning foreheads—encouraging the despondent—writing letters home for the home-sick—in fact, tucking them up generally both in body and mind. I always act under the Doctor's permission, at least. For the most part he is grateful for my efforts, but occasionally being as I intimated a little irascible and jealous of his position, as well as a Roman Catholic, he gently snubs me. I do not mind that at all, but keep on, carefully avoiding the breakage of any rule, or any act which might weaken or excite the patient, and my visit generally winds up with the Doctor's thanks and a pressing request to continue. If a patient asks me to write a letter for him, I go at once to the Doctor, and so in all cases of requests. There are many interesting things in this connection which I could tell you, but another time will suffice. . . .

Love to all.

Joseph.

a captured remnant of the Black Horse Cavalry: The Black Horse Cavalry was an independent unit formed of patrician northern Virginia horsemen who had served as an escort during the hanging of John Brown in 1859. Going over to the Confederate side upon Virginia's secession in April, the unit made a famous charge on a New York Zouave regiment at Bull Run. Twichell's "captured remnant" comment may have been wishful thinking.

With regard to Sickles' commission as Brig. General: Sickles was still only provisionally brigadier general, commanding the brigade he had raised. He used his presence in Washington to further ingratiate himself with the Lincolns and his friend Edwin M. Stanton, his defense counsel in the murder trial and now counsel to the secretary of war. But powerful opposition in the Senate to the Democratic Sickles's advancement delayed his commission.

Our Surgeon [John J. McGowan] works hard: Each regiment was assigned a surgeon and eventually assistant surgeons. Twichell later criticized McGowan for debauchery and called him a "political Surgeon."

On 10 August, Twichell gave his father more accurate information on his regiment's coming duties:

We have not moved yet, although we stand in hourly fear of it. The Lieut. Col. [Potter] yesterday explained to me our next position and its duties. It is to cut off communication between the Secession part of Maryland and Virginia, not to watch the R.R. as I wrote before.

My honored Father,

Another pleasant Sabbath—with the fierce rays of the sun broken by a kindly veil of clouds—another cooperation of officers, more hearty I think and surely more efficient than ever before, to bring out their men for worship—another service with singing of familiar hymns, and prayer to God, and spoken words designed through the Grace from above to be those of truth and soberness—all these I have again to record as the evidence of Divine Goodness toward me who am unworthy. If ever man had cause for gratitude, I am he. Never in all my mercy-marked life have I been so stirred within myself by views of Gods thankworthiness, as for the last few days, and it culminates today. I am strangely moved by it. Ever since I dated this page, I have put down my pen to wipe the tears that would rise. I hardly know why this is, or what it is. I hope it is the blessing of God on my half-consecrated soul. . . . I am aware that here, many things, which when encountered before—at Camp Scott for instance—have seemed shared by others, appear to be more personally bestowed. When I tell you that I receive daily fresh evidence of good-will from those about me—that I seem to be gaining the confidence of my men—that my opportunities of convincing them of my friendly designs are multiplied—that many of religious or moral principles have gathered more boldness and that one soul at least has been striving against sin—I have told you all. . . . If from what I have said you can infer what I mean it will be well, for I find it difficult to express accurately. Suffice it to declare, that the Lord has shown himself to me in this camp, as kind to the unthankful and unholy. Blessed be his holy name!

I have hinted above at a fact by far the most significant and interesting which has occurred to me as a Chaplain. A boy—George Hawkes—19 years old, fell sick soon after we reached Washington. He had a hard time of it in the first place with diarrhea, then followed a siege of intermittent fever, and lately as an after-clap he has suffered from a frightfully swollen head and face. . . . His youth, his excessive weakness and his great dejection coupled with a fine countenance, first called my attention to him. Since then I have visited him often, [and] as he grew sicker and his troubles complicated, so I increased my ministrations. He was so very weak that I seldom said much to him save to encourage and cheer. About a week ago he began to mend, and now that good news, or news not altogether bad, was possible, I offered to write to his folks, which offer he eagerly accepted. . . . The subsequent process of getting up our . . . letter revealed that he was a real tender-hearted boy. After that I occasionally spoke to him of the salvation of his soul. To everything I said he always assented, but made little reply otherwise. Yesterday morning he was much stronger and when I went to him, he said rather excitedly, "Chaplain I wish you would take me out on a little walk. I am strong enough, and I want to see you alone." I knew in a minute what he wanted. It seemed I could feel it. . . . Hawkes rose with difficulty to his feet, although with the air of one who had made up his mind to something. As we crept down stairs and out upon the lawn—my arm about him—I began to think of what was coming. To tell the truth I wished myself that moment a thousand miles away. I was glad, God knows that, but the words rose to my lips in a whisper, "I can't do this, oh, that Father or . . . Mr. Bulkley or somebody were here to do it for me!" I was oppressed beyond expression by a sense of incapacity, nay even, inexperience in my own soul. Thus, of little faith and narrow sight, I forgot that the Lord was my Helper—sure and sufficient, but it was only for a few minutes then. Before we found a seat, I found a better mood. It was as I thought. "I am a sinner" said George "and feel that I am lost." He . . . bowed his head and wept bitterly. I let him cry on, and when he became a little composed, tried to tell him what he was to do, enjoining upon him especially not to trust to any word of man for sole guidance, but to ask God in prayer and through the Bible for light. For a long time we talked. Every few minutes he fell sobbing. I never saw one so apparently heart broken. I feared that the violence of his emotions would endanger his weak health and, as soon as I had told him all I knew, I led him back to his bed and soon left him. In my tent I prayed for him as I never prayed for anything else, that God would take him in charge and deliver him from his sin. . . . Several times in the course of the afternoon I peeped into the door of his ward, but he lay with his face turned away and I feared to disturb him. You can imagine the anxiety I felt. As soon as I could get away to-day after service I hastened over to the hospital, full of hopes and fears for Hawkes. He was not there. With about a dozen others the Doctor had in the morning transferred him to a permanent Government hospital down in the city. . . . It was a great disappointment to me and I doubt not to him. If possible I shall go to see him and the rest of the boys tomorrow, when I really expect to find him enjoying the presence of a new-found Savior. . . . God grant it.

Late in the evening—and raining like blazes.

After I had finished the last page before this, I went again over to the Hospital. Although there has been a thinning of the ranks there, yet enough are left who greet me kindly to make it a pleasure to go. Here let me say—I do not wish you to think that I have my favourites among them in the matter of attention. Some, to be sure, are more approachable and responsive to kindness than others, and it is more agreeable to do something for such, but I try to allow that fact no influence in my external deportment toward them. . . . Indeed, I suppose the best course to pursue is to run up a heavier account of kindness with the crabbed rascals than with any others, but it goes rather against the grain to do so. . . . At about 6 o'clock the clouds, that had been a parasol for the benefit of morning service, began to exude. It poured a torrent for two whole hours. I was compelled to wait until an ambulance went over to camp for the hospital rations, in which I found tolerably dry transportation to the door of my tent. But there, the idea of anything dry had been abandoned an hour before. My premises were inundated. My trunk, valise, bed-clothes, boots, slippers . . . were without much mitigation subjected to the action of a rushing stream. I had permitted Joseph to go to Washington to church early in the afternoon, with the understanding that he would be back at 6 o'clock, and I had rested at the hospital under the idea that he had returned and would look after the things. But he was a little late, and had to take shelter under a wayside shed, so my property "came to grief."

Everything was wet and nasty, and under the influence of my perambulating feet the floor of the tent began to convert itself into the slipperiest, meanest kind of mud. I could not help laughing at the pickle I was in, and secretly exulted that everybody else was about as bad off. Just here, in all the rain, my parishioners began to drop in to a prayer meeting appointed for the evening. Once glance sufficed to convince them of the impossibility of attempting any such thing. They all said that their quarters were worse, and I more than half suspect that they ventured out partly with the hope that we could have a dry as well as a devotional time. . . . The loss of the meeting was a disappointment as we had reason to expect a good one.

This matter being disposed of and the baggage having been hoisted on various supports, so that it rested above the water mark, over came Mr. Clendenen with an invitation, to several of the officers including the Chaplain, to come over to his house. At this moment Joe came in soaked through, as to every inch of his black hide. I informed him on the spot that going down to Washington to church, as it was a luxury I could not myself afford, would hereafter be dispensed with by all members of my household, especially when it looked like rain. His next hour's work probably convinced him of the justice of my observations. Mr. C.'s invitation was accepted. We had some sacred music and ice cream, and returned about 10½ o'clock to our damp quarters. As a peace offering Joe had prepared a hot cup of tea. . . . Joe is snoring just outside under an extra awning I have laid hold of, and I am up alone finishing this too long letter to the people I love best. The rain has nearly ceased and millions of bugs of every species are celebrating the glad event by an assault on every exposed portion of my body. They are a feature of the country. My table is covered with them—at the farther end of it a couple of lightening bugs are regaling me with cheap fire-works. . . . Thank Heaven, few of them are mosquitoes. About a hundred (bless their folly) have met a greasy grave at the foot of my candle's wick, since I last lighted it. Tomorrow will probably be hot and cloudless, with more diarrhea and fevers. . . .

It is a comfortable thought to-night to think that those transferred sick men are between cool, white sheets, with a soft pillow and a woman's hand to smooth it. . . . We shall probably move to-morrow night. So says the Col. . . . The Regiment is doing as well as might be expected, perhaps, without pay. There are some faults of administration, besides this, however, which afford me some fears. I will say more of this sometime. Your letters and the papers have all reached me. . . . Thank you. I probably created a wrong impression about the papers in my first letter. We can get the N.Y. dailies the same night, if by chance some one is in Washington. Love to all. . . . God bless us—Good night. Joseph.

Camp Selkirk. Good Hope, Maryland—Aug 19th 1861.

Dear Father,

So long an interval as seven days between my letters home will I hope be of rare occurrence, yet I cannot prophesy. Circumstances compelling it may—probably will—occur. To night I am tired out, and my blanket is a sore temptation, but I think of your desire at home to know of my welfare, and the blanket must go unpressed until I have recorded some account of myself to send by tomorrow's mail. I shall make it succinct as possible. To begin—Wednesday morning we received orders to move again. By twelve o'clock the baggage was loaded, the regiment was in line—the drummers beat a lively march and we bade Good-bye to camp Clendenen. Owing to the previous receipt of new caps, overcoats and arms the boys presented a fine appearance. . . . The day was just fitted for a march. Rain had fallen in profuse showers the night before and the sky was still thickly overcast. . . . We touched the city at Capitol Hill, proceeded northward over Anacostia bridge, and came to a halt at about 5 o'clock in a sloping field some three miles further on. While we were still pitching our tents, the sun came out just in time to afford us the most gorgeous sunset I ever saw. The evening purple deepened on the hills, and our wearied soldiers settled to their slumbers. . . . Next morning a mist arose which has not yet cleared away. Rain has fallen at frequent intervals for three whole days.

This is a prime evil so far as the sick are concerned. Cases of intermittent fever have multiplied and yesterday a man very low with the typhoid was sent to the Govt. Hospital. The ground is saturated and spongy. The tents are all muddy-floored. I can hardly stand up in mine. Of course, it is not strange that many contract colds and fevers, while at the same time medical treatment is hampered and thwarted. . . .

I have been greatly blessed to-day in the means for conducting divine service, and in the service itself. The unfavorableness of the soaked ground concluded me not to call it out-of-doors, if it could be possibly avoided. . . . While making my petition [to Col. Hall to use a room in a nearby house], the Lt. Col. [Potter] spoke up, "Why not use my tent, Chaplain?" I could hardly believe my ears. Although we have been on good terms, he is a man who swears and drinks and I have heard him sneer at religious persons. Not only did he have his large marquee cleared out but, when service opened, he came in himself and took a seat beside me. The tent was filled, and more, and it seemed to me, as the prayers and hymns and preaching went on, that there was deep feeling manifested, at least, the *closest* attention was paid to everything. . . .

Col. Hall has received a severe injury, from the kick of a horse in the shin. He is at a house near by. After prayer meeting, the Dr. came in, saying that he had been sent for to go over again, as the Col. was suffering great pain. I went over with him. The leg is not broken, i.e. in two, but it is feared that some pieces of bone were cracked off and that inflammation with suppuration will ensue. In that case, he will be laid up several weeks and I don't know what we shall do, for he is our back-bone. . . .

We are in a secession country. Everybody but the vegetable peddlers refuses us any greeting. All look glum. The man on whose land we are pitched has a son—an officer in the Confederate Army—and he protested against our stopping here. In fact, our advance guard was warned off every place they fixed upon the first day and compelled to bivouac in the road for the night. Recruits and stores have been taken from this section over the river lately, and we are here to stop it. Our pickets extend along the road for about five miles. The 1st and 3rd Regts. are from a mile to two miles off. . . . If you wish to know exactly where we are, look on as minute a map as you have at home and find Marlboro. We are about half-way between that and Anacostia creek. . . .

I have a multitude of things to write but the time fails. You must pardon the chirography. The paper is so damp that the pen almost goes through it. I think of you all every hour of the day. God bring us together again in his good time. Love to all.

Your aff. Son. Joseph.

Camp Selkirk, Md. Sunday night, Aug 25th 1861.

Dear Father,

I don't know when I shall get time to sit down and write you a leisurely, unhurried letter. It certainly is not in my power to-night. I am as tired as fifteen hours of physical motion unremitted, and no small worry of mind added thereto, can make a man.

My Sabbath has passed very much as the last and preceding one did—the weather adding its favor also. Never was Chaplain so blessed as I. I should like to know how many swearing, moderate-drinking Lieut. Colonels in the Army give up their private tents willingly for divine service and attend themselves, as mine does. Not many, I think. God has supplied my seeming and my real wants in a way that leaves room for nothing but gratitude. The way is open before me and I am called upon irresistibly to press forward in it. . . .

Sickness still prevails among us to an alarming extent. The weather has been good now for several days, but the effect of the rain continues. Those aggravated intermittent fevers, protracted by untoward circumstances, are developing into the dreadful typhoid.° We have within two weeks taken about 50 men to Hospitals in or near Washington. Two of them—[George E.] Burham [Jr.] and [Thomas] McDevitt—have died. Poor fellows! Their soldiering is over. It has been a heavy hearted week with me on their account and a gloom has pervaded the whole regiment. I saw McDevitt the day before he died, but he was wandering in his mind and did not know me. Burham I did not see after he was carried away. . . . God comfort their mothers! . . . I could write a volume about our time of sickness, for it enlists all my sympathies and a great part of my time. There are some most affecting cases. Before going away today [helping transfer "four ambulance loads of sick men" to hospital] I went to see the Quartermasters Orderly—a boy 18 years old—who has just had two very profuse hemorrhages of the lungs and lies very low, probably near death. He is a most interesting youth and was a favorite. Although a Catholic he expressed a willingness that I should pray with him, and I did so, using the Episcopal form of "Visitation of the Sick."

My horse. After considerable looking about with Capt. [Eyre C.] Croker, I fixed at length upon a bay horse, 5 years old, gracefully and strongly built, elegant under the saddle—just the thing I wanted—for $135. . . . The horse pleases me perfectly so far° and I think he will prove a treasure. . . .

So far as Mother's offer of ointment and things for me is concerned, I thank her very much, but must decline. The Hospital stores embrace the best of everything medicinal, and the transportation of any thing for me would perhaps be expensive, besides spoiling on the way. As soon as I get time I will write much more. It seems as if I had said nothing. . . . Love. Love. Love. Your aff. Son—Joseph.

fevers . . . are developing into the dreadful typhoid: About half the deaths from disease during the war were caused by intestinal disorders: diarrhea, dysentery, and typhoid fever were caused by the consumption of food or water contaminated by salmonella bacteria.

The horse pleases me perfectly so far: Twichell's horse, dubbed "Garryowen" after a famous Irish dance tune, lived into the 1880s.

Camp Selkirk. Sept. 1st 1861

Dear Father,

Nothing but absolute want of time could have debarred me from writing to you at least once during the week and so it has been for some time past. A hurried, ill arranged, letter, late Sunday night when I am thoroughly tired, does not at all come up to my ideas of what a correspondence between a Father and a son away at the wars should be. I have no lack of subjects, no lack of news; but the time fails. I really never anticipated that I could be so wholly occupied. Every day of this past week I have been on the move without cessation save as I took my meat, from morn till bed-time. I sat up one night with two sick men, and purposed then to balance my epistolary account with you, but the dawn found me, before the leisure did. To-night I am fitter to be snoring in my bed, than writing here. . . .

Our sickness is still sore although abating, thank God. Since I wrote last, five more of our poor boys have been buried away from our sight, making seven within ten days. One of our dead is Lieut. Robinson of Co. K,° who was taken to the hospital before we left Camp Clendenen. He expired of weakness—debility—out of which he could not be lifted after the fever left him. He lay for a week scarcely able to move a finger yet free from actual disease as I am. . . . Every day, when I went to his bedside, he eagerly asked me how I thought he was, and his feeble but intense whisper was pitiful to hear. . . . Another of our sick, but two beds removed from him in the same ward, preceded him into the other world by but a few minutes. This latter was named [William O.] Fuller of Co. I—a fine, manly youth who won upon me greatly during his illness which began before we left our last quarters. I conceived a tender interest in him and when our extempore hospital at Camp Clendenen was broken up . . . and several . . . of the patients were deemed too sick to be taken to the new place, I had Fuller placed in the ambulance with more than usual care, drove myself with the utmost gentleness, and when arrived, took him out and bore him to his bed in my own arms unassisted save by his arms about my neck. . . . One of the men I took down last Sunday died of inflammation of the bowels Tuesday morning—another valuable man, [John] Fleming by name. . . . He left at home a wife and five small children; God be merciful to them! . . . [William R. Eckert] Acker [sic] of Co. K died at the City Hospital Tuesday Aug. 27th. He was attended during his last two days by one of our boys who was convalescent but not then discharged. Disease laid more violent hands on him than on any other of the sick. He was twenty four hours dying, amid writhings and groans and delirium and vomiting of blood—a sight that would have almost slain me a year ago. He was a stout, hearty youth and the son of a widow.

That is all at present. Do you wonder now, Father, that I have no time for writing letters?—That I go to bed every night in sorrow and wake with a heartache? That I am restless and hurried and anxious? That every day I am like the parched drunkard foiled of his dram, until I get my eyes on the sickest of my block? That I am as serious a man as is about Washington. My jokes are gone and much of my sociability. . . . My visits to those who are convalescent are some of them delightful. There is more than one boy whose eye I am sure to catch with my first step into a ward although twenty beds intervene, and more than one thin hand is slowly lifted to salute me with its feeble grasp. There are some who have been delivered by God from the very jaws of death, and if I mistake not, more than one of them is devoutly grateful. I thank God that we are mending somewhat. . . . The hospital tents have been floored—comfortable mattresses are on hand and the accommodations in every way bettered. A Sanitary Commission from Washington° examined one camp day before yesterday and found much fault. A thorough cleansing has resulted therefrom—I might say much concerning the management of our Hospital department i.e. my opinion of it, but what I should say would not all be pleasant, and I refrain. I am persuaded that our medical administration is improving. The Doctors are pretty well scared now, and with reason. Dr McGowan was yesterday required by special order to report the causes of our sickness, which he did to his own complete satisfaction, no doubt. You observe that I am doing much work—transporting to hospital etc.—that belongs elsewhere. Thereby hangs a tale. The boys must be cared for right off, and time wasted in waiting for heavy bodies to acquire motion, or in thrusting legal spurs into slow-bellies, is so much lost to the patients whose hours are of decisive importance. If you will believe me, I am accustomed to go around in the morning, at least, I often do it, and conclude with myself who of the sick ought to be taken away [to hospital], and report the same to the M.D.'s, and my counsel is seldom gainsayed or resisted. Of course I do this in a manner as little offensive as possible, in the way of suggestion or asking opinion etc. I am on excellent—most friendly—terms with both Doctors,° but I wonder how they keep so good-natured. Perhaps they think they had better. I have a dissatisfied regiment, from the Col. down, to back me in anything, and they know it. I verily believe that they fear me for the reason that I am in possession of ugly facts, which I have so far kept and will keep if the present "scare" lasts. My occupation renders it impossible that things should go far out the way without my observing it. That man Fleming who died of peritonitis or inflammation of the abdominal membrane—of which a post mortem examination revealed that had been progressing for more than a week . . . —this man was, up to the time I took him away, treated for bilious fever, and bilious fever was the disease ascribed to him on our Doctors "admit." If it were ignorance it would be more tolerable, but it is something worse. Again, what do you think of a man stricken with the typhoid fever, being compelled in the night alone to rise from his bed and reel out of the hospital tent to obey the call of nature and because he staggered being arrested by the guard for drunkenness and about to be taken to the guard house, before he could weakly explain his situation? I know this and they know that I know it, for I went to them the next morning and told them not very calmly that it must not happen again, or—I see that I have told much more than I intended. I trust you perceive that I indulge in no self complacency that I have a chance to aid the unfortunate. I have been too much troubled to be egotistical. All that I do, I am driven to. Sometimes I have been almost distracted to know what was my duty. I haven't told you a quarter or an eighth or a sixteenth of the things that have fired my indignation and pity by turns. Toward one of the Doctors at least I play the complete hypocrite. I make him think I admire him, whereas I despise him. None but the most friendly words ever pass between us, yet I ache to denounce him. I may do it yet. It is too late—too late to help some things now—but he had better look out. My boys must not be *killed* except in fair fight. Political Generals and Colonels are bad enough, but a political Surgeon who can bear? Pardon me Father, for running on so. I believe I shall go crazy over these sick fellows unless there is some change soon, of which thank Heaven there are indications—these beautiful days are doing the thing—thwarting the Doctors. I cannot get the matter out of my head. It burdens one day and night. I could not keep it out of my preaching today. Pray for us, Father, that we may be saved from further disaster and that God may give me his own wisdom. . . .

Events seem to be hastening. For three days we have been under orders to be ready to march at an hour notice. I don't much care how soon it comes. We are quite ready, but for the sickness. I am proud of the Regiment. It is developing well and will surely give a good account of itself. The Col. is fast recovering from his wound and will be on hand—a gallant a fellow as ever handled steel. We have tonight received intelligence of the success of Gen. Butler's naval expedition.° Very well. The rumor that an advance on [Gen. Nathaniel P.] Banks' division is imminent° prevails generally, with how much foundation I can't say. Fortifications and breastworks are being constructed near us—by the Government. We are about five miles from Bladensburg and with a good glass we can see troops—several regiments encamped near there—and the construction of a battery on the brow of a hill—covering the rail-road, I suppose. . . . I am glad after all that mother sent the ointment. I can tame men with it. Many little aches do not get to the Doctors ears at all and one of these days it may allay much suffering. I shall carry at least one box in my saddle bags. . . .

Our part of Maryland is filling with Union troops and some things make us think that we may soon be in for a scrimmage. Never were men more willing than our boys. Since paid they have been cheerful enough. A breastwork on a hill near Bladensburg in plain sight from our camp—about 4 miles off— received a few evenings since a delicate attention from some rebel battery over the river in the shape of a round shot. So the Chaplain of the Regiment there stationed told me.

The Hatteras success has restored whatever confidence was lacking in the might of our arms i.e. among the rank and file. Some thinking and observing men still shake their heads soberly, and I think with reason. I fear that our misfortunes are not all over. Some things are not yet right, and will not be made so, until bitter experience forces it. Gen McClellan makes things go with a snap. Nobody seems to doubt his fitness. Late last week he issued an order or suggestion for the better keeping of the Sabbath in the army. That to me seems a prophecy of the man's success. God bless him! . . .

About my money. I have concluded to hold on to it till we are paid again, which will be shortly, and then send to you. My chief reason is that I have lent quite an amount—all of it on good security I think—which will be paid me at that time. The most that I have parted with has gone to relieve hard-pressed families. My horse is a complete success. I have seen animals for which $200 was paid, which I would not take for him. . . . Your aff. Son. Joseph.

One of our dead is Lieut. Robinson of Co. K: Apparently an error. Second Lieutenant George Robinson of Company K, First Excelsior, remained in service until he was discharged for disability in March 1864.

A Sanitary Commission from Washington: In June 1861, philanthropists and reformers from New York City, headed by Louisa Lee Schuyler and Dr. Elizabeth Blackwell, established the United States Sanitary Commission. The same month, Lincoln and Stanton authorized the agency to minister to the health and welfare needs of the Union army.

terms with both Doctors: Dr. McGowan had obtained an assistant surgeon, Dr. James Ash.

the success of Gen. Butler's naval expedition: On 27 August, a Union force under Commodore Silas Stringham and General Benjamin F. Butler had captured forts Clark and Hatteras, important positions on the North Carolina coast.

The rumor that an advance . . . is imminent: Probably Twichell meant an advance "of" Union general Nathaniel Banks's division. Banks's command was at Harper's Ferry, Virginia.

Washington—Sept. 10th 1861.

Dear Father,

I have just taken breakfast though it is nearly noon, having been engaged all the morning in getting off quite a sum of money by express, and before I start on my hospital round I snatch time enough to assure you of my good health and tolerable spirits. . . . Last night was the third night within ten days which I have spent in Washington. The reason is this. With a confidence which under the circumstances is both a present qualification and a promise of good things to come, my parishioners, Catholics as well as others, have entrusted to my care their little pile of specie° lately received for transmission to their families or friends, in sums varying from $5.00 to $30.00. In the case of companies recruited from one town, it is the custom to have the Captain, if also a townsman, receive the various sums and, buying a draft for the whole amt., send it to some party in whom confidence is reposed, for personal distribution. E.g. Capt [Owen] Murphy (the big Paddy) sent the pay of his Company [E], nearly all of whom came from Orange N.J., to Dr. [William] Pierson° (by that same token—Capt M—not being thoroughly versed in the mysteries of letter writing, came to me one evening and desired me to write for him an expression of his views of "sojering" and of his gratitude to the people of Orange and Dr Pierson in particular. I did so, the Capt. holding the candle and approving the sentiments as I put them down. It was rather a high falutin' production, but as I signed the Captain's name I had no fears for my reputation. A day or two since he (the Capt.) handed me a paper in which the whole thing was published. If I can secure a copy I will send it to you for your amusement)—N.B. If you find it hard to distinguish the main letter now constructing from the parenthetical clauses or if the letter seem disproportionately long—please remember that I am in haste. To go on with the financial—My business as forwarder comes from those companies which are collected from places scattered and widely apart—permitting no one package for any considerable number of persons. I am generally detained till nearly noon at camp receiving money and directions for the same, which I am careful to make as particular as possible. Then I pack it safely in my saddle bags and mount for Washington—a ride of seven miles and five of it through thick woods, for which space I keep my revolver handy. As soon as I get down, I deposit my treasure in the safe of some hotel, and go at once to the hospitals to see my sick fellows. This takes till nearly dark. I do not wish to return to camp till I can carry the receipt from Adams & Co, consequently I have, as I said, staid down here three nights to perform my business. The first night I remained, it took me till long after midnight to get the packages ready. Having a large sum which I am responsible for, renders me of course uneasy till it is off my hands. . . .

Our sickness, thank God, is abating. . . . We are expecting marching orders soon. The 1st moved yesterday about 25 miles to a place where their pickets were fired on. A Mass. regiment has been placed near us and a company of Cavalry. One of our companies, under Lieut. Col. Potter, with a company from each of our other regiments, went away Sunday morning on some special duty and had not been heard from when I left yesterday noon. We were paid off yesterday, up to June 30th. The next two months pay is due and will soon be forthcoming. My own stipend, counting in rations and forage, is about $125 per month. I have now on hand a sum of money that is so large, I can hardly believe it my own. The boys take it well—better than I expected. The great majority are sending a large half home. No less than a hundred have asked me to-day to do it for them, and I have appointed to-morrow morning 8 o'clock as the time when I will entertain all such applications. Anticipating this, I have already investigated the matter and know how to proceed. It will probably be worth a man's while to waylay me next time I ride to town. This will be quite a job, but the happiness at the other end of the route makes me wish more—nay all would do it. A great part of the men entrust the matter to their Captains. After I have helped the boys I shall attend to the transmission of a portion of my own pile. I don't know how in the world, Father, we shall be able to stand the shock consequent upon the reversal of the current that has been flowing so steadily in one direction for 23 years. I shall probably send it by Adams Express. . . . Dea. [Henry] Upson has written to me asking my advice° about going as Chaplain. I can't get time to write to him just now, but, if you have facility of communication with him, you may tell him that I really do not think he could stand it. If he can endure going wet to the skin night and day for a week—at least, very damp—he may think about it. The labor he will find delightful—the pay good—the life stirring but, with his peculiar constitution and habits, he will run the chance of being on his back half the time. I haven't had a moment's physical irregularity since I came to Washington, but I am almost an exception in the Regiment. My present condition is beautiful—having lost some fat but no muscle. I own that it is by the blessing of God and perhaps he will bless the Dea. in the same way. . . . I have written long. It is 3 o'clock and past it. Good night. Your aff. Son. Joseph.

have entrusted to my care their little pile of specie: A perennial problem during the Civil War was getting soldiers' pay home to their families, who were often thrown into poverty by the absence of the chief breadwinner. Chaplains were often entrusted with getting these sums of money to the closest express office, as Twichell describes.

sent the pay of his Company [E] . . . to Dr. [William] Pierson: Pierson was a physician active in local government and politics in New Jersey.

Dea. [Henry] Upson . . . asking my advice: Upson, a classmate of Twichell's at Yale, was one of the deacons of the College Church at Yale chosen by the Class of 1859. Upson later served as chaplain in the Thirteenth Regiment, Connecticut Volunteers.

Washington. Sept. 14th '61

Dear Father,

You must not be surprised if I fail to write my usual letter tomorrow as I did last week. Capt. [Orville C.] Howard [of Company I] is dying and I shall stay with him till his last breath. . . . Day before yesterday I told him his danger and advised him to make all preparation both temporal and spiritual. He received the information calmly (in fact such is his state—a kind of deadness—not exactly torpor—that nothing can arouse much emotion in him). Slowly and with great difficulty he told me how to dispose of his pay received a few days since, remembering even such items as "quarters" owing to some of his men. . . . Poor Captain, he is a good-looking young man (about 30 years old), was a lawyer and man of influence in the town from which he came (Great Valley, Erie Co. N.Y.) [and] no doubt expected to make to himself a name by this war. He says that he believes in Sin and Redemption from it through Christ and promised me that he would try to give the care and cure of his soul into the hands of Him who is able. His company, for intelligence and character is by far the first in the regiment, but they have suffered grievously from sickness. . . .

I think I wrote to you that Col. Potter went off scouting last Sunday, in Command of 5 Companies—one from each regiment. He returned yesterday bringing several prisoners—one grey-haired old man—some rebel correspondence and a small quantity of arms. While he had been gone his wife had come and was at his tent to greet him. The 1st has moved down to Port Tobacco [Maryland] or thereabouts and expect stirring times. I hope you are all well at home. . . . Give my love to all our neighbours and tell them to pray that God will bless their unworthy friend, in his work among the soldiers. . . . Love to the family. Your aff. Son. Joseph.

Camp Selkirk. Prince George's Co. Md. Oct. 1st 1861.

My dear Father,

We are at length delivered from our grievous sickness. . . . Few remain in hospital and they are convalescing. Quite a number are under the Doctor's care here, and there are some serious cases of lung complaint, but all are more likely to live than die. For the first time in two weeks I am spending a quiet day in camp. All the morning has been occupied in giving out books. My library takes well and I wish it was better. Some German books I must have, if I buy them. It is refreshing to be relieved of anxiety for dying men and I thank God that our affliction is like to stop here. I was gratified by a larger attendance at service yesterday than ever before. . . .

I have bestowed not a little thought on the subject of temperance—how an efficient influence against drunkenness can be brought to bear upon the regiment. The use of rum is undoubtedly our worst evil among both officers and men. I have witnessed some disgraceful scenes of debauchery since I assumed my present place, and always with a heart-sick sense of shame. Are these men volunteers in a holy cause? Is it such as these that will save the republic? I desire to do something to counteract this wrong. What shall it be? Shall we try an organization? This has been somewhat discussed by the few who conscientiously abstain from drink. Organization, unity of effort, usually enlists power at the best advantage. The objection to it in this case is this. Probably not more than fifty men could be found to form a nucleus. Capt. [Thomas] Rafferty [of Company H] is the highest and almost only officer who would lend it his support. Now, a nucleus, to command respect must be at least of respectable dimensions, or ridicule will surely assail it on every side. Could I get my fifty men together, I not only fear that they would not keep a stiff upper lip when sneered at, but that, in case *they* stood firm, others who might be rightly inclined would shrink from going over from the crowd of laughers to the small company of the laughed at. An open step, in the face of ridicule, would have great terrors to men whose moral ideas are not of the most sublime order. I would not *fear* to call what retainers could be summoned, and take a bold stand, but would it be the means of the greatest good? For my own part, I always assert my teetotalism when with the officers, but I have been able so far, I think, to do it so as to command respect, at any rate no one has yet offered me an unpleasant remark on the subject. At present it appears to me advisable to work at this evil, without any flourish. I have used the temperance pledge to some extent, generally in cases where I have been solicited to help men out of scrapes begotten of whisky. With such, I have tried to make it a serious matter, the punishment only being suspended during good behaviour. And here I may say that the Col. has afforded me a great chance to gain importance with the men, by modifying severe sentences frequently at my request, and I thank him sincerely for it. In this temperance matter, to resume, is it not best to try to create quietly a state of sentiment on the subject, helping it to spread unostentatiously beneath the surface, before it shows its head above? Will you give me your advice on the difficulty. One would think that liquor might be kept out of camp altogether by an exercise of official vigilance. So far as that is concerned I will say this; that J.B. Gough himself° could not have advised more stringent or persistent measures than those which were employed before our last pay-day, to ferret out and seize all rum likely to be sold within miles of the regiment. Nearly a hundred gallons of rot-gut were in the Col.'s tent at one time, taken from houses and barns. Yet, two days after the money came, men would be found drunk. No family or store would dare to sell it. It was concealed in the woods, reached only by a secret path, and more trouble would be taken to get at it than a seeker after holiness ever employed. It does seem as if a love of inebriation, oblivion, forgetfulness is a more universal companion of a sinful heart than any other vice. There is a reason for it. I think the fear of punishment would put an end to the nuisance. Were *I* or *you* the Col., and the rest of the officers composed of such men as Dea. Higgins and Andrew Upson,° a few marked cases of severe discipline backed by examples of temperance in high places, and with the certainty established of no leniency, the thing might be violently and surely choked, but with us a mutiny would be likely to result from such measures.

Profanity is to be regarded very much in the same way with intemperance. "G——d d——m you, stop swearing, or I'll put you in the guard house," is breath wasted and worse. These things sometimes make me want to go home, but in the main I think I am taking root here. "*Yer Riverance*" is in more frequent demand than ever, now-a-days. From a sick baby at home, to the fears of a court martial here, everything is brought to me. I have almost hourly opportunities to comfort, admonish, reprove or encourage and I receive many hearty blessings—so far, no curses—not one disrespectful word. Mr Bulkley says, and truly, that I do not leave enough with God. May He help me to cast all my care on Him who is able to sustain it. . . .

We are again under orders to be ready to march at an hour's notice and yesterday afternoon the summons was momently expected. The Col. thinks that we are to form a part of a great *forward*!! Movement. God grant it! Yet, I do not see its probability just now. . . . The 1st Reg. has been recalled from

Port Tobacco and is now at its old quarters. I shall see our boys tomorrow. Good night. Love to all.

Joseph.

J.B. Gough himself: John B. Gough was an ex-alcoholic and ballad singer who, upon taking the temperance pledge in 1842, became the country's foremost orator against the evils of drink, making direct, personal appeals to his audiences.

such men as Dea. Higgins and Andrew Upson: Timothy Higgins and Andrew Upson were prominent citizens of Plantsville; Higgins was Edward Twichell's employer and later partner in his tannery and a fellow deacon in the First Congregational Church, Southington. Upson represented the town in the state legislature and served as a captain during the war.

Camp Selkirk. Sunday night. [7] Oct 1861

Dear Father, . . .

It was my design to write you a long letter to-day . . . but a call from Rev. Mr. [John W.] Alvord of the Boston Tract Society,° soon after morning service, and subsequent calls on the sick, render it necessary to . . . confine myself to only a short letter home.

My service last Sunday and to-day was held in the Colonel's tent—a high wind rendering it uncomfortable out of doors especially to several ladies who favored us with their presence. The attendance on the part of the regiment is a continual source of satisfaction and gratitude to me, and particularly the growing number of officers. The Col. has not yet taken his seat in my audience, not even when it has been convened in his tent. He generally remains till toward noon at a house adjoining which he makes his head quarters. Between ourselves, Col. Hall, although a most capable officer—a kind commander and a warm-hearted, manly person to deal with—is spoiling himself of the efficiency within his power and due to his place, by the habit of intemperance. If the thing goes on to its legitimate result, the man is lost. I grieve for this continually. He is never drunk i.e. staggering, but he lives on liquor. An iron constitution has kept him so far from yielding entirely to its effects, and he does not show it in his face, but his strength and snap, whenever he lays hold of business, are borrowed from the bottle. Early in the day before he is braced up, he is as one deprived of a back-bone, and this I can see is increasing on him. . . . His popularity with the men is great, but is the result of ignorance rather than knowledge on their part. Whenever he does appear, he bears himself graciously toward them, but he seldom appears at all, being like a king whose subjects like him because when they see him, once a year, he smiles and looks good. I learn from a reliable source that the General knows it all, and will

Father Joseph O'Hagan, S.J., joined the Fourth Regiment of the
Excelsior Brigade as chaplain in October 1861. He and the
Congregationalist Twichell struck up a firm friendship that bridged
theological differences. "We concluded a treaty of amity, peace, and
cooperation at our first introduction and I have no doubt we shall be
friends," Twichell wrote his father (letter of 7 October 1861). Their
friendship persisted after the war, when O'Hagan became president of
the College of the Holy Cross in Worcester, Massachusetts. Twichell
introduced O'Hagan to his close friend and Hartford neighbor,
Samuel L. Clemens (Mark Twain). (College of the Holy Cross Archives
and Special Collections)

not forbear to take measures demanded by prudence. The excellent condition of our regiment is in great part owing to the ceaseless energy of Lieut. Col. Potter, who drinks some himself, but not to excess. At-any-rate he is a famous worker. I did not mean to say so much about the Col. Let this be in some sort private, for I say it of a noble fellow by nature—a man whom, by his many splendid qualities, I am constrained to love, and to whom I am under great obligation for the kindest treatment a Chaplain ever knew. I never saw a man under whom, barring his one great defect, I had rather serve in this war. I shall always be grateful to Col. Hall, and would tonight give my right hand to save him from the breakers ahead. Pray for him. . . .

For the last three Sundays I have spent considerable time during the afternoon in the hospital tents, holding a sort of service, consisting of a chapter, a little talk and a prayer. I have evidence that it has proved acceptable to the patients both Catholic and Protestant. Day before yesterday a man sent for me to come and pray with him—the first summons of the kind I had ever received. Thank God for this.

Martin Gilmore of Co. E. died a week ago last Wednesday night of typhoid fever—our first death in camp. His funeral was attended by Father [Joseph B.] O'Hagan, chaplain of the 4th Reg. and another Catholic clergyman. I was present and rode between them to the cemetery, about two miles off—holding most pleasant converse by the way. I am pleased with this Father O'Hagan. He is appointed to the 4th, but officiates in turn throughout the brigade. He is a young man—very affable—and certainly a godly person. We concluded a treaty of amity, peace, and cooperation at our first introduction and I have no doubt we shall be friends. . . . Through O'H—I hope to get at the rum drinking although I observe he is not adverse to a little tipple on his own account. I wish he were a teetotaler. Love to all. . . . Your aff. Son. Joseph.

Rev. Mr. [John W.] Alvord of the Boston Tract Society: Alvord was an army representative for the American Tract Society, formed in 1825 to propagate the gospel by distributing Christian books and leaflets. After the war, Alvord served as superintendent of schools and finances for the postwar Freedmen's Bureau, and later he served as president of the Freedman's Savings and Trust Company.

Washington. Oct. 10th 1861.

Dear Father,

I have just returned from the most agreeable labor of paying my men in hospital, for which privilege (an unusual one, I believe) I am greatly indebted to the courtesy and confidence of our paymaster Major [John H.] McBlair

U.S.A.° The fellows took their money with the most evident satisfaction, although they have little use for it just now, except to look at it—an operation, however, in which the human race seems to find an unaccountable comfort. I have also drawn my own pay for two months, from the 30th of June to 30th of August. I enclose $125 of it to you, with this letter, by Adams Express. . . . Yesterday I dispatched a large number of packages, whose preparation had occupied me two whole days, working with all my might and main, on which I paid [Adams Express] the neat little sum of $52.00 although many were not prepaid. I have always tried to bring my freight to the office in as neat a shape as possible and have also saved some work to them by taking their blank receipt forms and filling them out myself, ready for the signature, arranging them in order so that they could compare the package and receipt, without hunting up either. My intercourse with the officials, generally so crusty, has been most kindly on all occasions and to-day they did the generous, to the extent of an offer to convey whatever bundles, packages etc. of my own I might desire to forward, free of all expense, to any part of the United States now loyal. They evidently meant it well and I think I shall accept their offer more for its own sake than for the cheapness of it. Although the work of receiving and preparing the men's money is one of responsibility and confinement, I find much pleasure in it, from the consideration of what it does for wives and babies at humble homes. I imagine the precious package on its arrival—the sensation it creates—the wondering eyes—the great event of its unsealing. Then, while the envelope is given to the children for a plaything, I follow the thankful and happy mother as she ties her bonnet strings and goes out with the means of comfort in her hand, to return laden to a household warmed and filled. I regret that I cannot send you a larger sum than I enclose. It is less than I intended. . . . The money that I lent first time has not yet been paid to me, and I have lent $20.00 more, under guarantee of the Col. That officer to whom I lent it, who is yet unattached and draws no pay, is surely to have a position in the regiment. The money went to a wife and two children suffering from poverty in New York City. In this matter of lending I try to be wise as may be, and so far I do not think I have lost anything, but I assure you that there are some cases among us which would excite the commiseration of a graven image. When a man, living along on promises yet unfulfilled (an evil in our Brigade) comes to me, and shows a letter from his wife imploring him to do something to save his family from want, and himself choking down the sobs, and I with money at command of which no one is in desperate need, I cannot long hesitate. What is money worth, anyway, but to help humanity with, and what if I do let part of mine go, at some risk of never seeing it again? I don't know that I can do better. . . . But, enough of that, I am writing this letter at the Ebbitt House. At my elbow sits my esteemed friend and seminary classmate Harry Hopkins.° You will rejoice with me when I tell you that he has come to Washington to spend the winter in laboring as Chaplain-at-large through the army and particularly in the Hospitals. Nothing has made me so glad for a long time as the note in which he informed me of his arrival and told me where to meet him. He is a young man of most pleasing address, excellent ability and high toned piety, in short—a Christian gentleman. I prized his companionship highly at the Seminary and here it will be a source of the greatest pleasure. He has made the best impression upon my boys in the Hospital, and they speak of his visits in warm terms. Although sent here under the patronage of some wealthy ladies of New York, he has received the additional confirmation of the President, conditional upon the approval of Congress. Gen. Scott has granted him a general pass throughout the army and he starts with great enthusiasm and no lack of encouragement, even in his first, inexperienced, effort. I shall spend the night with him here at his room. . . . We (Harry and I) find our sympathies quicker than ever and no want of things to talk about. . . . Your aff. Son. Joseph.

our paymaster Major [John H.] McBlair U.S.A.: McBlair, of the First Battalion, District of Columbia Infantry, had been a prominent grocer in Washington before the war—and Sickles's neighbor at the time he murdered Key. Twichell often stayed at his home during the war—perhaps partly because he had two attractive daughters—and for years afterward.

my esteemed friend and seminary classmate Harry Hopkins: Hopkins was in Twichell's class at Union and was chosen by Lincoln in September as one of seven military hospital chaplains in the Washington area.

In Camp. Saturday night. Oct. 26th 1861.

Dear Folks at Home,

I should make rather unintelligible work of it, were I to undertake to tell you just where I am now,° for I have only a faint idea myself. Oh! That I had pursued geography with more ardor while I was in jackets. Suffice it to say that my humble tent is pitched on a broad level plain . . . in Charles Co. Md., about 1½ miles from the Potomac river. We struck tents at Camp Selkirk early Thursday morning and after two and a half days march are here, a part of a comparatively large army comprising the Excelsior Brigade, the 1st Massachusetts, 26th Pennsylvania, 4th New Hampshire, 11th Mass., 1st Mich., which regiments (10 in all) compose the Division of General [Joseph] Hooker.° Just now while I am writing, the bed-time "tattoo" from camps on every side is vexing the air of night with multitudinous rattle and roll. We are located opposite some rebel batteries which have for some time been hindering navigation. Unless we get whipped their time is probably short, for I understand that they are the friends to visit whom we have come this long distance. All the afternoon, we have been regaled by occasional booms of secession shells as they are projected at some passing schooner or familiarly tossed across the river to try the range. The third Regiment met a sad accident with one of these secession projectiles. It was fired across and fell near the river bank not far from camp. Failing to explode, the guard picked it up and brought it to their quarters. It was inspected by the officers, the fuse extracted and it was laid away out of sight. Some of the men got hold of it, and like fools went to playing with it. After about a pint and a half of powder had been shaken out, water was poured in and it was supposed to [be] entirely harmless, but, subsequently on a cigar's being applied to the fuse hole, it exploded, killing two men dead and wounding several others, one of whom, at least, has since died. . . .

Our march here was not accomplished with as much credit to the Regt. as I could desire. By some great neglect a good part of the boys started without rations even for one day. The result may easily be imagined. They had to get something to eat as best they could. At one time not more than two hundred men were in line, the rest being scattered over at least five miles of the road cooking pigs, turkeys and geese etc. which they had shot. I never felt so bad for any state of affairs, in my life. The Col. [Hall] has been placed under arrest, for the condition we were in. . . . I have rarely seen so enraged a man as the General was. It was a thing worth a journey to witness. The Col. will probably be brought before a Court Martial, but will hardly be deprived of his command. On the Col.'s own account I regret the occurrence; on account of the Reg. I do not. It is hoped by the warmest friends of the Col. that this arrest will prove most salutary in its effects upon all parties concerned. Lieut. Col. Potter is now in command and things go with a snap.

Sunday morning.

I had appointed service in front of my own tent this morning, but, just as the time came, an order for inspection by the General arrived, which put the "church people" off till afternoon. . . . You asked about my servant. Joe is one among ten thousand. I would not part with him on any account. Watchful, industrious, rarely speaking a word beyond necessity, jealous of all my interests, honest as daylight, a good cook and a Christian, he is remarked by all the officers as a right man in a right place. I regard it as one of the best fortunes of my life that we fell together. I have serious thoughts of bringing him home, after the war, if he will come. My horse also serves me well. Exposure and irregular living have thinned him somewhat and he has had a cold, but he bids

General Joseph Hooker's first divisional command in late 1861 included the Excelsior Brigade. Like Sickles, he was controversial in his behavior, both military and personal. Charles Francis Adams described the Army of the Potomac headquarters under Hooker's leadership in the first half of 1863 as "a combination of bar-room and brothel." Nevertheless, Twichell greatly admired the general and named one of his sons after Hooker. (Library of Congress)

fair to carry me safely and spiritedly through the campaign. About the Adj. Gen's. order concerning Chaplains.° Probably it will [be] carried into effect only on formal *complaint*. If otherwise, Mr. Bulkley says that he, with the aid of some one clergyman beside, will ordain me. With the General I am on excellent terms. He always salutes me kindly. . . . Love to all. Your aff. Son. Joseph.

[P.S.] Some of the horrors of war begin to unfold among us now. Two men of one of the Massachusetts Regt's were shot yesterday for disobedience of orders and Gen. Sickles has proclaimed such rigid rules that I fear we may yet experience such tragedies in our camp. It is strange, but I do not *feel* about such things as I anticipated. We are to all intents and purposes in enemy's country and, very likely, shall be engaged in fighting to-morrow, yet I shall sleep to-night like a log.

just where I am now: Below Washington, the Potomac broadens as it flows between Virginia and Maryland, and the Confederates set up batteries on the Virginia side to harass shipping. McClellan desired to halt this activity and stop smuggling and recruitment in southern Maryland. The brigade had moved to the area of Indian Head, Maryland, on the Potomac shore facing Virginia.

compose the Division of General [Joseph] Hooker: Hooker was a career military man and Mexican War veteran who had risen from a hard-drinking, prewar civilian career in California to a brigadier generalship. On 11 October he was placed in command of the division of the Army of the Potomac, which comprised the ten regiments Twichell lists.

About the Adj. Gen's. order concerning Chaplains: In August the adjutant general, chief administrative officer of the War Department, had relayed an act of Congress that stated that chaplains must be "a regular ordained member of a Christian denomination." Twichell, of course, remained unordained.

A fragment of a letter Twichell wrote to his brother Edward, who was planning a visit to Twichell in Washington, follows:

When I returned the Reg. had moved about six miles from where it pitched last Saturday. We are now on Chapman's point, above Matthias Point and nearly opposite Acquia Creek, Ococquan [sic], Manassas Gap and Bull Run. What we are to do does not develop. We have Doubleday's Artillery with the division and yesterday it was thundering away at something, I know not what. It is some ten miles down the river. I have not yet visited any of the other camp for want of time. When you come, bring nothing but a valise or carpet bag. Leave your best coat at home. Bring no shirts, only woollen and under ones. A couple of pairs of drawers, some collars and handkerchiefs and stockings, will be all you will need. Put money in your purse, for until pay-day (shortly coming) I am not very wealthy. Immediately on your arrival repair to B street, almost within sight of the Depot, to the boarding house of Mrs. Smitson, which is near our Quarter Master's depot. . . . Tell Mrs. S. that you are my brother and that I sent you there to be called for. Stay there till I come, if it is a week, amusing yourself about town. . . .

> In a further letter to his brother, written from camp in Charles County, Maryland, on 2 November, Twichell speaks of heavy rains, high winds, and the accompanying results:

We have now on hand, or rather on foot, a most extensive and rich assortment of mud, from that kind of which you take up a ton every time you lift your boot, to that gayer and more sportive compound which spirts upon your knees, as you tiptoe through it. It is over-shoe everywhere. As we had just pitched our tents, and the boys had no time to build their rustic bedsteads, the rank and file have had a tough time. On visiting their quarters today I found many absolutely floating. Some sickness will probably result. . . . We appear to be settling down for a stay of some length on duty as river guard. Of this I have no assurance, beyond the *look* of things. . . .

> *In Camp—Chapman's Point, on the Potomac.*
> *Charles Co. Md—Nov. 3rd 1861.*

My very dear Sister,

If any man should at the present moment ask me why I have so long neglected to write to you, I should probably, for want of a better answer, kick him out of my tent, particularly if he dared to hint that it was from any lack of affection. It would be an impossible thing for me to give any satisfactory explanation of my silence, and if you will only believe that it hasn't been because I didn't love you, I will pass the matter by without any attempt to do so, or further observations. If you wish to know why I do it now, I can tell you. Night before last as our Surgeon and I were chatting before a cheerful camp fire, producing a letter from his pocket, he remarked, "Chaplain, I have this day received a thundering nice letter from a thundering nice young woman"! Or words to that effect. "Where is she?" said I. "At the Hudson R. Institute," he answered. "Why, mercy sakes alive!," said I, "I've got a sister there!," adding in my own mind, "If I don't send her a love-letter by our next mail I'll change my name for an uglier one"; so, here I am, Sis, with my pen in my fist, determined unless the rebels attack us before I can finish, to keep my self-made promise and retain our beautiful name.

Well, Sis, how are you, anyhow? It is so long since I have seen you, that I have only a faint idea of how you look at all. I remember the complexion and nose and a few such things, but the rest is fast fading from my remembrance. I hope that you are growing tall and stout and wise and white, indeed I suppose you are. Why, in the name of all the Twichells hav'nt you written to me? I suppose you have been too busy. Well, never mind! I forgive you. Yet, it would have been a very pleasant thing. Here I have been campaigning in this ill-begotten, secession region for more than three months, encountering cold and wet and niggers and salt-pork and pretty girls and other hardships, working like a horse and nearly breaking my heart over the moral condition of as rascally a set of vagabonds as ever united in wickedness—and all this time, never a word from my cherished sister to sweeten the coffee of my existence. Come to state the case, it sounds pretty bad, don't it? I don't know as I can forgive you so easily after all. The matter must have further consideration.

While I have been doing the apostolic here among civilized savages, I have always thought of you as pegging away at your education or prancing with the young women about you—little moved by the tragedy of the Union and hearing only a faint echo of the clangor of our national arms. According to your usual habit I suppose you are not very minutely posted on the status of the war. Perhaps you could give a brief synopsis of the campaign in Missouri, so far, and it may be you are watching with breathless attention the movements in Kentucky;° on the other hand perhaps not. Well, my dear girl, let it go. I don't know that you need vex yourself with such matters unduly. Give us your prayers and a few undershirts, as the rest of the ladies do, and I will let you off. Give yourself to reading and study and the general furniture of your head and heart, never forgetting that piety is God's best gift and that it peculiarly adorns the life of woman.

Since I attached myself to this regiment I have had some strange experiences. The pleasant and disagreeable, joy and savour, the dull and the thrilling have been strangely mingled. At one time a grievous sickness fell upon my flock, and I witnessed a great deal more suffering than I ever hope to again. . . . I tell you, Sis, I used to have the heart-ache then. Away in gloomy hospital wards, with home a thousand miles away, and no real friendly voice but mine to soothe them or none to hold their hand in the dread hour and speak a word of comfort, the most of my boys died. It was hard, hard enough. It made me homesick sometimes. We are now, thank God, in very good health, and one of these days anticipate a crossing of swords with those barking batteries just over the river. I don't know what sort of a job we shall make of it, but whatever the general result is, you may rely on hearing good news from the gallant 2nd. If they run, it will be backward. From our camp we can see the hills on which the Bull Run battle was fought, and the sight of it is aggravating extremely. I hope to see our colors in the middle of the fray, when that account is settled. The boys are not all fine gentlemen, or statesmen exactly, but they are spoiling for a brush with the rebels, and have some very sound, practical views on the proper mode of suppressing rebellion. They are hearty and rough and about two thirds of them think that getting drunk is rather commendable than otherwise, but all treat me very kindly and I have become much attached to the rascals. By the grace of God and through a Power not my own I have hope of showing some of them a better way than they have hitherto followed. I pity them from the bottom of my heart, for I can easily discern that very few, if any, ever had such a father as we have. The world has been rude and neglectful toward them and it would be strange if they were different. . . .

Together with the hardship of camp life, there manages to get mixed up now and then some real, royal, fun. Up in Prince George's Co. we used to hunt secessionists generally in the night, to be sure of finding the animal at home. The way we were in the habit of scouring through that region at a tearing gallop between the hours of 11 p.m. and 4 a.m. was a caution. Many a lank Marylander did we pluck from his downy pillow and lecture on his duty as a citizen of the United States, winding up the exercise by administering the oath of allegiance, while the victim stood quaking with fear and much more scantily clad than is usual at social parties. Whisky hunting is also put down in the catalogue of our sports. I have tonight returned late, and splashed with mud from head to foot, from this amusement. About seven miles from camp we (a Captain, Sergeant and myself) found a couple of barrels in a neat little cottage, which we spilled every drop, before the eyes of the owner. It is as a matter of necessity that this is done. Rum must be kept from the men. The depredations and cuttings up, of which people complain, are often a just punishment for giving soldiers liquor. I always enjoy the capture [of] this sort of enemies. . . .

I am just now very anxious to hear from home. . . . "The soldiers life is always gay" as the song goes. Very true, but sometimes it is less gay than at others, and at this particular moment, I should shed few tears if a blazing fire in a good, warm, room, with an easy chair, a pipe and a book, were at my immediate disposal—to say nothing about the folks to share it with. By the way, my dear girl, I wish to caution you against letting your young affections loose upon any of those chaps, fellows, opposites etc. who have the good luck of your acquaintance. You know I want you to come and live with me when I am settled down, as a sort of companion for Mrs. T. and to make jackets for the ragged boys of my parish. . . . Give my respects to all my friends at the

H.R.I., and if you know any pretty girls, give them my love. Now, Sis, I have written you a long letter. Let me assure you that it is brim-filled of love and no mistake. If I do not get a speedy, epistolary return for it as soon as mails can carry it, I shall eat myself to death or do some other dreadful thing. . . . We only get letters twice a week in this ungainly place, but we cherish them all the more—Your loving Brother. Joe.

the campaign in Missouri . . . the movements in Kentucky: General John Frémont was at this point pursuing Confederate general Sterling Price in Missouri. On 31 October, rebels had attacked a federal encampment in Morgantown, Kentucky.

On 8 November, Twichell reports to his father:

We are under fresh marching orders and shall leave here to-night or tomorrow morning early. It is understood that we are going to Budds Ferry about 5 or 20 miles distant.

He also speaks of Colonel Hall:

Col. Hall has not yet returned to the Regiment. We are all anxious about him, though it is generally supposed that he will be released without trial.

Washington, Nov. 15th 1861.

Dear Father,

I arrived in the city night before last at 12 o'clock after a ride of 50 miles over the most horrid roads I ever saw. . . . As was expected when I wrote last, the regiment left our camp near Indian Head last Saturday morning. The day opened with fair promise, but about noon a storm arose, that drenched us through and converted the road into a river of mud. Our fellows marched cheerfully on, however, and there was less leaving the ranks and disorder than ever before. . . .

Twichell describes the previous Saturday's events and the service he conducted the next morning, and then continues:

An hour's march brought us to our new camp and by night our city was built. We are about five miles below Budds Ferry and a mile from the river. Gen. Hooker's orders were that we go no nearer on account of the rebel batteries opposite. It is probably prudent to be out of sight, but we have a great desire to unfurl our colors full in the face of the foe. Standing on the river shore we can hear the drums of their parades and with a good glass they can be seen working the guns of the batteries as they blaze away at passing schooners, always without effect. One of these days we hope to go over and unearth those fellows. I really envy our boys the glory of the naval expedition.° They were lucky. I need not state my feelings at the look which our cause now wears. Yet, success can never cover the blood that has flowed and will, nor can it dry the bitter tears of cruel bereavement that drop on many a hearth-stone in the land. God give them better minds before the sorrow grows more great. Strange thoughts arise in one's mind, when standing in view of both armies. God moves in a mysterious way.

The region we now occupy is barren—as Wolcott.° We are reduced to first principles in the matter of rations. The wealth of the world could hardly buy a pound of butter. The health of the Reg. is as good as the health of any Reg. ever was. Not a man in camp may be said to be seriously ill. It is a great blessing. . . . I get little time to write nowadays, but love a great deal. Your aff. Son. Joseph.

I really envy . . . the naval expedition: On 7 November, Flag Officer Samuel F. Du Pont led a successful attack on Port Royal, South Carolina, that gave the Union a foothold on the coast between Savannah and Charleston.

barren—as Wolcott: As a boy, Twichell's father, Edward, moved to Southington, in the Quinnipiac River Valley, from Wolcott, a nearby hill town that like many in Connecticut saw a decline in agriculture in the antebellum period. Southington, by contrast, prospered by the development of industry.

In Camp—Sandy Point—Md.
Sunday night, Nov. 17th 1861.

My dear Father,

I really wish you were here tonight to sit down in my rather narrow but cozy quarters, to have a good talk and enjoy my comforts with me. I have nothing to say about the hardships of military life for, while the wind is blowing with genuine Yankee keenness outside, within here it is as warm as a good fire can make it. I have made an experiment of a little sheet iron camp stove and it is a complete success . . . and I sit down to-night with a feeling of luxury to write home in peace of body at least, not constrained in my movements as often hitherto by bonds of overcoat and blankets.

As usual on Sunday night, I am in a thankful mood to-night. My affairs to-day have prospered. Last night on my return from a laborious visit to Washington, I called on [Lt.] Col. Potter, as I often do, to talk over national and regimental matters. Just as I was leaving he offered me, all unsought, the use of his tent for service today. I did not finally use it, for a better place still developed, but I mention the fact to show how much I have to render my position a source of enjoyment and thanksgiving. Service was held in a large tent which had been put for Quartermasters stores, but not yet filled. It was well attended by men and officers, the Lt. Col. among the latter. The tent was crowded with as many as could stand in the space. . . . The men and officers who have stood by me thus far would endure anything in the way of discomfort, cold or wet, outdoor or in, which I should suggest for the sake of Sabbath day observance. Of this I have full assurance. A strong bond of sympathy has grown up between us, and as men will follow a captain into a galling fire, so would they come out in the absence of a better place under the open sky in a storm to help maintain the institution of Sunday religious exercises in camp, if I desired it. . . . To confirm each other in the faith by frequent words is an exercise of self-defence as well as a refreshment. Last Sunday as we were going out from our service in the barn, dear Capt. Rafferty remarked "Well, Chaplain, here is another green spot." We have many such, and I have no doubt God will give us many more. As soon as we are sure of being fixed for any considerable length of time, I am certain that the boys will build a chapel which may be warmed. . . . We have heard today that Col. Hall has been released from arrest by Gen. Hooker and that he will join his regiment immediately, probably tomorrow. The command is almost universal in its satisfaction at this result. [Lt.] Col. Potter is brave and a hard-worker. Wherever he is, *business* is first in hand—he is also a gentleman at heart and not addicted in a dangerous degree to any vices, but he lacks the experience, judgement, urbanity, in fact, the capacity of Col. Hall, who if he returns to us, and does as *well as he can*, will make his regiment as good as any in the brigade. I regard him as head and shoulders above any volunteer Colonel I have yet seen in ability to lead a body of men. That he may be warned by his arrest, and hereafter do himself perfect justice, is my sincere hope and fervent prayer to Heaven. If he comes to-morrow he will be just in time, for Col. Potter was this afternoon thrown from his horse—the horse falling on him—and received an injury in the chest which may prove serious, as the Doctor fears congestion. Since Col. Hall has been away, a few of the officers have seen fit to form themselves into an anti-Potter party, quite unnecessarily, which will yet I fear disturb our peace. Two of the Captains have already resigned and one or two others threaten it. Of these I can truly but confidentially say that the Reg. will sustain no loss by their absence. Selfish men cannot endure rough campaigning. It lays them bare. Deprived of the usual means of hiding a small character, their bad side is exposed inevitably. Col. Hall despised these fellows and sometime since meant to shake them off, but they got at him through his weaknesses and he dared not do what Col. Potter began at once when he took command, viz. advise them to resign.

Our position opposite the enemy and in sight is the occasion of some interesting incidents. Our boys do a great deal of impudent shouting across the river, which is responded to frequently with more force than elegance. Letters tied to boards, or the boards themselves inscribed, are occasionally sent across both ways according to the wind. Some that we have received were rare productions and showed that neither the schoolmaster nor the Preacher had been much abroad where the authors were reared. The rebels keep popping away at oyster schooners etc. passing down and up, never inflicting any injury however. This is a source of much amusement. A gun is fired. The ball strikes wide of its mark. A score or 20 of our boys looking on, raise a howl of derision, responded to immediately by a howl of defiance from the other side, and so we go for the present, exchanging nothing worse than ill wishes and windy words. Some day there may be less speech and more work. I have seen quite a collection of rebel shells picked up on this side. Some of them looked ugly. . . . I have had my photograph taken and will enclose a copy, also one of the General [Sickles] which I found at Brady's.° It does not flatter him at all. I dined with him last week and enjoyed it much. . . . Your aff. Son. Joseph.

one of the General [Sickles] which I found at Brady's: This was the studio of the photographer Mathew Brady in Washington.

In Camp. Nov. 30th 1861. Sunday night.

Dear Father,

Mr Bulkley has been over here this evening and protracted his visit so long, that I have little space between now and bed-time to occupy in writing. . . . We are led by some circumstances to think that our labors of simple preparation are nearly over and that the long looked for day which will reveal the stuff we are made of, is close upon us. Eddy and I passed a pleasant week in Washington although I had a great deal of business to do. We were joined . . . by Mr. Bulkley, whose errands were much like mine. . . . On Friday evening in the midst of a drenching rain, mounted on three good horses, we started for the brigade. The horse that Eddy rode was one which had just come into Mr. B.'s possession, and which fortunately needed a rider for the occasion. It was a bad night being very dark, but we rode fast. Eddy, having a good animal, took the lead and kept it most of the way in a most gallant manner. I was agreeably surprised at the spirit he manifested. Ten miles brought us to a tavern where we put up for the night, and starting early in the morning, six o'clock P.M.

brought us to my tent. The condition of the roads made travel very difficult. Everybody was glad to see us, and the close personal resemblance between the two brothers was generally remarked, at which the two brothers were both amused and surprised, not being of themselves able to detect the least ground for such opinion.

I found that the men had been suffering somewhat from derangement of the bowels, induced, the Doctor says, by the water. But it is probably nothing serious. One poor fellow is dying of typhoid fever, but none others are in danger. . . . Mr. Bulkley has kindly loaned me one of his horses for a while—a favor which will help Eddy's investigations considerably. The stores he brought from home were very acceptable. Grandma Higgins's gingerbread had the old taste° and the Deacon's big apple was a luxury. The last of the cake disappeared this evening, before an assault of several visitors, but the heavier groceries remain for longer enjoyment.

I am sorry to say that portents of coming troubles among ourselves are beginning to appear. I cannot make a detailed account of circumstances, nor do I wish to. It all arises from the arrest of Col. Hall and his return to the regiment. It appears that Col. Potter had been led to think that Col. Hall would be cashiered and that in consequence the command would devolve on him for some time, if not permanently. At the prospect of such a result, there was much grumbling among the officers, for Col. Potter was not very popular, while Col. Hall was exceedingly so. These grumblers were not much indulged by Col. Potter and they grew strong in their feelings against him. Some (who desired Col. Hall's return, as well) did not join the anti-Potter party for just and right reasons as it seems to me, and these were marked as not favorable to Col. Hall's cause. Upon his return he received representations from the Potter-haters which led him to treat the non-grumblers in a way which I deplore° and they resent. What will be the result I know not. Some resignations have already taken place, and others are impending. Col. Potter has gone home for thirty days to recover from his injuries. Hard words passed between him and Col. Hall, creating a breach which I fear will not be easily healed. I fear the Lt. Col.'s return. I pray God that we may have fighting enough outside, to leave no room for it within. After all, I am glad that Col. Hall is back again. He is a better manager of men than Col. Potter, although without the same energy. The regiment was wild with joy when he rode into camp. Excepting the matter I have spoken of, he has begun well, and there is much room to hope, that removed from the enticements of Washington and politicians he will do himself and the regiment justice. I cannot tell you how much I am grieved at what has taken place. Both sides have been often and amply represented to me, but I endeavour to avoid all expressions of judgment, and earnestly pray that we may be spared the blight of an unmanly, unworthy quarrel in our own house. It would seem that the great cause of our coming here and the apparent proximity of a day of battle would be a protection against it. I have some idea of asking an audience of all the officers of the regiment, and after careful preparation of thought and prayer, of calling upon them to sink the whole thing out of sight forever. Pray with me, Father, and counsel me in this business. Mr. B., Eddy and I celebrated Thanksgiving together at a restaurant in Washington. Had I been allowed quiet and leisure, I am sure it would have been a most solemn day with me. For six month I have been engaged in a novel and responsible work. There are many things to reproach myself for, in penitence before God, but nothing could more befit me than a psalm of glad thanksgiving. Bless the Lord, O, my soul! We thought of the folks at home that day and Eddy and I pledged our sire in a cup of temperate brewing. . . . Omit the *Rev.* in address-ing my letters, if you please. . . . I can hardly allow the honor, not yet attained. Love to all and a kiss. Your aff. Son. Joseph.

Grandma Higgins's gingerbread had the old taste: Twichell referred to Deacon Timothy Higgins and his wife Janette Carter Higgins as "Grandfather" and "Grandmother" all his life. They lived into the late nineteenth century.

led him to treat the non-grumblers in a way which I deplore: A letter from Potter to Sickles on 19 December describes the state of affairs under Hall as Potter heard it in New York, where he was recuperating from his fall from a horse. "Time is passing and the regiment is being ruined," wrote Potter. He enclosed an anonymous letter, signed "Excelsior," describing the pending resignations of various captains and lieutenants dissatisfied with Hall's command. The letter said Hall's supporters had put their perceived opponents—including "Chaplain"—under "a ban."

In Camp—Jan. 1862. Sunday Evening

Dear Father,

All that disagreeable weather, sleet, fog and rain, could do to disturb a man's equanimity has been the moist experience, for the last week, of all whose lot is cast on the Lower Potomac. I never saw the like. The porous, spongy soil of the country is completely dissolved to an indefinite depth. Our camp is a floating sea of mud. Walking is next to impossible and it is with the utmost difficulty that a horseman can flounder his way along. A land movement could no more be made by our Division now, than could the Egyptians move on through the Red Sea: indeed, I am inclined to the belief that a fair chance to swim would result in more actual progress than could be hoped for on these roads. We are, however, informed by the natives that the present is a mere joke compared to what will be in the spring. If that is the case we had better at once construct a regimental ark.

The past week has been to me in my official capacity one of surpassing interest, in that it has brought me the evidence that the Holy Spirit is at work in my congregation. . . . On Tuesday night two men called to see me at my tent. One of them I had before known as a Christian. He brought the other, to present him as a penitent backslider who wished to return to a blessedness he had lost by yielding to temptation. I talked and prayed with this man and urged them both to keep their armor bright by use, not only in quenching the fiery darts directed against themselves but also in testifying to their comrades the worth of religion. On Thursday night they came again bringing with them three others—young men who had been coarse, rough, profane fellows, but who had now been touched with conviction and desired to give their hearts to God. I was surprised to learn their case, so little was my faith, and at first labored under embarrassment in talking with them. After we had prayed and they were gone, I sat down to think and calmly consider what might be coming upon me. To be honest, my first mental exclamation was, "I am afraid we are going to have a revival!", and I almost trembled at the thought. "I can visit the sick and minister to them, and I can call to their mind the mercy of God in sparing them when they convalesce, or help them pray for salvation if they are appointed to death, but to have men asking of me direction concerning the divine life as it is to be lived on earth among men, with all the doubts and difficulties that may arise, I am unequal to the task." So I reflected and feared and shrank as the prospect opened on me, and so I continued troubled as long as I anticipated the responsibility as *mine* alone. But when the truer estimate of the case at length occurred to me—that it was *God's* revival, and *God's* work, that was coming, if any, and that He would direct and supervise, sustaining me by Grace and appointing both the means and results of my labor with which I had nothing to do save the present hour; the cloud grew less. I went to see Mr. Bulkley and counselled with him, deriving great courage and composure from his advice. He has been hungering for the time when *his* boys will come to the truth, and his joy under the circumstances was larger than mine, for he regarded it as a sign that the time had come. . . . And now, Father, . . . pray for us, that we may find a blessing. If it shall be my lot to witness the birth of souls here, how much wisdom, how much enlightenment, how much divinely granted power, how many gifts of grace I shall need in teaching the early steps. I wish that I knew more about it in myself, but God will provide for my poverty—I have taken up so much room with my affairs of office that other things will have to lie over. I hope you are all as well as I am. . . . Love to all.

Joseph.

Alexandria, Va. Feb 2nd 1862.

Dear Father,

I found that I could not dispatch my business satisfactorily and get back to camp Saturday, so I wrote to the Col. explaining my absence and deliberately resolved to stay away over the Sabbath. I have availed myself of the opportunity to do what I have long designed and desired, and am here with Harry Hopkins visiting him and inspecting the scene of his abundant, and I am persuaded, fruitful labors. I was for some reasons—rather selfish ones to be sure—willing to remain away from my congregation today, and should not, for the same reasons, be averse to a still longer absence. Had my own pleasure the right to rule me, I should not go near the 2nd Reg. Excelsior Brigade until its family quarrels were all over. I abhor and hate with perfect hatred such scandalous blots, such unworthy strifes—the results of selfishness—instigated by the devil—foreign alike to the spirit due to our cause and the attention due to our business. Yet there were many reasons conflicting with my repugnance which made me exceeding loath to spend the Sabbath anywhere but with my boys. I wanted to hear again the witness which a few of them are ready to give to a new found joy in forgiveness of sin, and to learn from their own lips the state of others who are feeling after God. . . .

But you wish to hear of my regiment. The coming of the Paymaster commenced a week of hard work with me, the engrossment of which debarred me from writing to you as I desired. I was deeply interested in events that were transpiring and desired to communicate my notes of them. The religious awakening, of which I gave you some account, has already led to some results over which I hope there is rejoicing in heaven and I expect greater things yet to come.

A prayer meeting was held last Wednesday night and another on Sunday night, conducted for the most part by the men. Two men expressed publicly their hope that they were born again and, almost as good, some Christian men who had before been silent gave the weight of their words to the impression of the occasion. I have rarely witnessed so hearty and deep feeling as seemed to pervade these meetings. . . . In the case of one man, who gives evidence of a renewed heart, I was intensely interested. He is a boy—19 years old—the son of a Methodist preacher now stationed at Norwalk—Rev Mr. Paynter. He came into my tent one stormy evening, evidently under strong excitement, and in an open, boyish way, with a candor that won me entirely, without preface or delay exclaimed, "Chaplain, I have been under conviction a whole year, and I can't stand it any longer." After a talk, I prayed with him and told him to come again. "May'nt I come to-morrow night," he asked eagerly. Next night he came, but still in trouble. Again we talked and prayed together. He was in a Company of which he is almost the only Protestant and lacked congenial companionship. I, therefore, introduced him to a Christian man of another company enjoining upon the latter to extend his sympathy and such spiritual aid as he might be able to furnish. I also urged Paynter to make confession of his state at the prayer-meeting Sunday night. He did so, asking prayers. All the while I was deeply concerned for him. . . . Wednesday night, he rose at the meeting, with his face all shining, and in the same open manner with which he first came to me, declared that he had found a hope in Christ. Join with me, Father, in thanksgiving for the great benefits wherewith God is pleased to crown my labors. I have talked with many in whom I thought I observed some sign, and the most have confessed that they were troubled about their souls. There was a fine fellow named [Charles or Thomas B.] Close whom I noticed lingering behind the rest after an evening meeting was dismissed. I knew him to be a straight-forward man who liked directness, so I walked straight up to him and put the square question, "Close, are you not interested in the subject of religion?" He was evidently stirred deeply. He looked at me for several seconds during which time the sweat started out upon his forehead— then answered, "Yes sir, I am, but I don't believe I could be a Christian in this camp." I had a long talk with him there and he promised to come and see me but had not done so when I left. If it please God, that camp will witness unspeakable glories. . . .

I see that I have little room left for the matter of our regimental troubles. [First] Lieut. [William H.] Ellwood of Co. I has prepared charges against Col. Hall, for which Lt. Col. Potter is regarded responsible and holds himself so. Consequently a most unlovely spirit is generated. Dr. McGowan is also under arrest, and to be tried on charges made by Col. Potter. Two of the Captains are also under arrest and charges have been preferred against one of them. It is all more or less a matter of feud, although I regard that in the issue some justice may accidentally be done. It is my effort and purpose to keep out of the rumpus altogether, but [I] shall not probably succeed as I am called as witness on two of the Courts Martial. If strict attention to my own business can help me any, I shall be helped. The mud is an appropriate physical embellishment to our unhappy camp. The incessant rain of the last two weeks has enlarged its dominion over man and beast. The Government must bow before it and own it King for the time. With much love to all I remain. Your aff. Son. Joseph.

In Camp—Lower Potomac. Feb. 9th 1862.

Dear Father,

I have seldom felt so strong a leaning toward home as I feel tonight. My spirits are depressed, I am heavy hearted, and the best thing I can do is to sit down and tell you all about it. Nothing can exceed the deplorable condition of our regiment—the glorious old 2nd in which I have felt so much pride and which I still love, or I should not sorrow for its troubles. The evil of discord, which has so long threatened us, now rages° in our midst with uncontrollable fury. It showed its head awhile during the latter part of your stay at Camp Selkirk,° and I shuddered to see it. What I could do to kill it, and it was little, I did zealously, and for a time hoped it was exorcised. But what Camp Selkirk began, the Lower Potomac has finished. Gradually the monster has been crawling from his den, until at length he stalks through our streets, unrebuked and free, hideous with claws and scales and foul pollution—a nuisance and a curse. It is a sorry spectacle to witness. The Colonel, Lieut. Col., and numerous captains and lieutenants are under arrest pending their trial on charges preferred the one against the other. Hate and envy rage implacably—generosity is a thing passed by and courtesy is bidding us adieu. Patriotism is not so much as named among us—even the flag droops as if conscious of dishonor. My own head, Father, is bowed like a bulrush in shame and grief. In a few days the Courts Martial will be convened and then other woes will come. God pity us. What the result will be no one can predict. Until the issue the regiment will rapidly demoralize in discipline, for the men must in great part be neglected. Hardly enough officers are left to fill the necessary commands and those who are on duty are constrained to do double work. Indeed, so hard are our circumstances, that I am detailed to act as Quartermaster for a few days, until the place vacated by our old Q.M. can be filled. I have little to do in the capacity, except to affix my official signature when it is needed, most of the business being transacted by the Quartermaster's and Commissary's Sergeants.

The only consolation in the premises is that of *hope*, that God will bring good out of evil, by causing a cleansing and refining, for which our present condition cries to heaven, to grow out of it. I am free to confess that a great change of feeling has taken place in me with regard to many officers with whom I am associated. I am thoroughly disappointed in their character and my emotions toward them have been reversed. I knew from the first that the pursuits and habits of some of them had been neither reputable nor decent, but you know how it was when the war arose. The great, all pervading idea of a holy cause, seemed to gild and elevate every one who called themselves by its name. Anybody, no matter what he had been, who would shoulder a musket or gird on a sword and march to the battle, was at once forgiven and went with a blessing. Under the flag, the high and low, noble and base, rich and poor, struck hands and on a common level took a common oath. It almost seemed as if loyalty to the Union were a recommendation to heaven. And so we met at first and so we lived at Camp Scott, every body admiring and harmonising with every body else. The times touched the same chord in every heart, and the general feeling had at least a likeness. The long, even days of Camp Selkirk, to which we followed our colors with one mind, permitted what was frothy and fictitious, the ebbulitive child of excitement, to die down. Men slid back from their temporary height into their old and real selves. The theatre was closed and the actors put on their own coats and talked their own words. Many began to feel that the charm was dissolving. Still, courtesy and external harmony staid with us. For my own part, engrossed entirely at the time with my own affairs, I only knew that I met general kindness, but having little leisure for inspection or gossip, I did not discover the change of atmosphere until overtaken by a perceptible chill. I then found that jealousies had begun. Little by little men showed their colors, and the process of uncloaking has gone on ever since until now we are torn with devils and I find myself compelled to withdraw my respect entirely, and my society in great part, from many whom I would fain have loved. . . . I should resign at once, were I not bound by ties not to be broken easily, to many a soul and many a heart in the regiment. If I am placed here by God, nothing short of an unmistakeable recall from the same source shall take me away. . . . I was probably led to a thought of resigning by the fact that Harry Hopkins extended to me a most cordial invitation to accept a station now vacant in the Alexandria hospitals which will probably be filled according to his recommendation. But after thinking it over I came to the firm conclusion that I could not leave my boys without a pastor and especially *now* of all other times. Eight months of mutual confidence and interest have woven a cord of obligation which must not be rudely broken. . . .

I now have an evening school of some half dozen pupils, varying in age from 25 to 45, all doing well in words of one and two syllables. I can foresee that this is to constitute quite an item in my system, for I find that the most illiterate so appreciate the arts of reading and writing, as to account them desirable elements of power, and I have the prospect of considerable work in this direction. The exercise would make you laugh sometimes. It does me—in my sleeve. What would my college fellows say?

I spoke of the fact that I am acting Q.M. [Quartermaster]. When the order was first served upon me I kicked against it. It was all very well as a token of confidence, but not very well encroaching on my other labors. With a feeling that it must not be, I mounted my horse and rode to Head Quarters through rain and mud indescribable, determined to do everything but refuse the duty— which I really might have done under an order of Gen. McClellan. The Gen. heard me out, acknowledged the cogency of my protest, but threw himself on my generosity, affirming that he could not avoid it, without calling an officer from another regiment, which is generally the very last resort in such a case. It was finally agreed between us that I should simply act as a show figure, so as to comply with the regulation requiring a commissioned officer to sign requisitions and returns. So I am Quartermaster pro. tem., probably for no more than ten days. Notwithstanding the fact that little is expected of me, I have an idea of doing some things for the regiment which it sorely needs and which have hitherto been neglected by the department. I do not know whether the real Quartermaster will ever come back. He has leave of absence for ten days to settle his acct's with the Gov't, which I fear were in rather a disordered state. That being accomplished he will either return or resign—the latter probably. In either case I shall be immediately relieved. If he resigns an appointment will be made at once.

I have had a prayer meeting this evening—a good one—conducted mostly by the men. Such things are refreshing and I must try to make them a greater part of my life. . . . I have forgotten to mention a tragedy that was enacted here last week. One night, under the influence of liquor and instigated by another, likewise half intoxicated, a soldier loaded his musket, walked to his tent door and deliberately shot a member of the same company for no cause whatsoever, inflicting a wound which proved fatal in sixteen hours. The murderer and the accomplice are in the guard house chained together. It is altogether probable that both will be sentenced to death. There are also some bad cases of desertions which I fear will call for the dread penalty. I have been to see the prisoners, but none of them appear to appreciate their situation. Even to tell them of it and urge the appropriate preparation seems to produce little effect. After their trial it may be different, but I am filled with horror at their present state. A dark page of our regimental history seems about to be written. How can I bear it? I try to think little as possible about it.

As if to furnish all our adversities a fit setting, the weather for several weeks has been the worst possible. Everything from fogs to hail storms has taken its turn upon us. Nearly the whole division has been out at work on the roads—to make it possible to transport subsistence—in fact, working for life. . . . Love to all the family friends. You see how long a letter I have written with mine own hand. It will be long before I write another such. Love to all. Joseph.

The evil of discord . . . now rages: On 1 March, a few weeks after this letter was written, the dispute between adherents of Potter and Hall erupted in a brawl for which Potter was court-martialed in April. According to his accusers, led by Colonel William Dwight Jr. of the First Regiment and Second Lieutenant Alexander M. McCune of the Second, Potter was guilty of conduct unbecoming an officer and a gentleman. They said that Potter, allegedly drunk but nevertheless affirming his ability to command the regiment, flourished a sword at subordinates, loosened Captain Thomas Glover's teeth with a blow, and called McCune "a little whorehouse pimp." Others in the regiment, including Twichell's friend Dr. McAllister, accused the accusers of drunkenness. Twichell himself testified: "Colonel Potter was not drunk and was fit to command. He is a temperate officer."

the latter part of your stay at Camp Selkirk: Twichell's father visited him during his stay at Camp Selkirk from mid-August to late October 1861.

Twichell updates his father on the regimental situation on 18 February:

The [Hall-Potter] imbroglio continues about as formerly and my relations to it have not changed. I have ceased to spend much time in thinking of it, indeed, we are already used to it. The recent victories have quickened the enthusiasm of our rank and file amazingly. The boys almost demand to be led to battle. Any ordinary discord, resulting solely from ennui or tedium would dissolve before the triumphs of our armies, but this is so deeply rooted in mean souls that it flourishes unabated. It is the opinion of Gen. Hooker (may be more than "opinion") that the Division is to depart hence very shortly, probably this week, where to go and what to do is not so certain. It is however affirmed that in conjunction with [Gen. Samuel B.] Heintzelman's Division we are to make a flank and rear movement on the batteries opposite, marching from some point below. Transports and barges have for some days been accumulating at Liverpool Point—an indication that the Lower Potomac is soon to be a memory.

In Camp—March 3rd 1862.

Dear Father,

I was in Washington last week three days, principally for the purpose of attending to the removal of some sick men from camp to the Government Hospital. While there I was rendered perpetually uneasy by rumours that were flying about to the effect that our Division was under orders to make an immediate movement—whither or with what intent was not clear. . . . I did not come back till Friday morning [and] found every thing quiet, with no signs of starting yet, indeed, the simple word of rumor had failed to reach the wilderness where we abide. It is however the impression that our quiet is not to be of very long duration. While we almost envy the troops to which such glorious work has been allotted in the West, we are sustained in our inactivity by the conviction that our flag will be borne into the great battle yet coming— the fiercest and hottest of the war by which Virginia is to be redeemed. . . . While in Washington on Thursday in company with Rev. Father O'Hagan of the 4th Regt. I paid a long anticipated visit to the Roman Catholic college at Georgetown and observed with much interest and some pleasure the habits of scholastic Jesuit priests who compose the faculty. I was received with great kindness and attention and found them rather jolly than otherwise. They appeared in view of the great physical mortification involved in celibacy, to regard all other fleshly indulgences as their purchased right. Such eaters, drinkers and smokers I never met. The long table at which we dined was punctuated by frequent bottles of wine, to say nothing of broad bellied decanters of "sterner stuff," from personal contact with which no one seemed to shrink in the least degree. I should have fallen from my chair drunk had I accepted a tithe of the proffered hospitality in that line. Dinner over we repaired to the commodious cell of the Holy Father Superior and it was not long before the picture of the Virgin on the wall faded from view in the clouds of tobacco smoke that rolled from priestly mouths. Father O'Hagan showed me everything about the institution, which appeared to be well ordered and complete in all respects. Not the least interesting was a visit to the Observatory where a fine glass subjected Fort Corcoran and its surroundings to our minute inspection. A tour through the nunnery hard by completed the day's work, leaving in my mind a vision of gowns and robes and round faces and crucifixes and white veils and Virgin Marys etc. Some impressions that I received were agreeable quite, but I bore away a more fixed and painful conviction of the conscience-lulling errors of Rome than I possessed before; still in the midst of all its dangers to the soul, I am persuaded that some who are called by its name live a life of real, fine faith. I have become much attached to Father O'Hagan and I have reason to think that the attachment is reciprocal. He is a generous, open-hearted and very intelligent young man with a superior education and a strong desire, so far as I can judge, of being useful. His labors, such as they are, abound. We have many friendly disputations on theological topics and never yet have exceeded the bounds of courteous earnestness. . . .

I have no particular news to communicate that would interest you much. Our regimental difficulties are unabated, indeed, the rancor seems to intensify daily. But, since it must needs be, I prefer that it should be as active as possible, in order that the issue may be hastened. Confidence and healthy patriotic feeling will be strangers to us until we know who is to lead us. The affairs of my office are much as they were . . . an object of great interest and solicitude to me. I now attend prayer meetings in the company quarters two nights in the week at least, and one on Sunday evening beside—and they are always a comfort and refreshment, especially the more general one on Sunday. I think that the interest is increasing rather than waning. It has not yet broken over the Protestant line, nor do I think it will, yet, after what I have seen, I do not feel like limiting the Lord. . . . Give my love to all the folks. I desire all to pray for me and mine. My school is flourishing. Capt. Rafferty and the Adjutant have been absent for a month on recruiting service. Love to all. Your aff. Son. Joseph.

Alexandria, Va., Sunday March 9th 1862.

Dear Father,

Again absent from my post—again with Harry Hopkins. Regret and enjoyment—uneasiness and pleasure—the bitter and sweet—compounded—a sort of neutralising mixture. This time I am absent by order and in consequence of one of the saddest events I ever knew. Last Tuesday night, Quartermaster's Sergeant [Michael C.] Cowell—a young man—24 years old—son of a most respectable Irish physician in New York—received a mortal wound by the accidental discharge of a sentinel's musket just as he was in the act of giving the countersign. He lingered in great agony for twenty six hours—during which he displayed amazing fortitude. His father was telegraphed to as soon as possible after the accident, but owing to delay occasioned by the removal on Thursday of the regular boat to our Division, did not reach the camp until Friday at 11 o'clock just as I was making ready to start for Washington with the body, where I was directed to have it embalmed and held subject to the order of his friends. The age and infirmity of the father as also the inexperience of a cousin of the dead youth who came with him, coupled with the overwhelming grief of both, rather increased than diminished the necessity of my going up to Washington with them, where by my experience of similar cases I could materially aid them in the matter of transportation. Compelled to wait at Mattawoman Creek for a government transport we did not reach the city till after 10 o'clock at night. Next day after attending to necessary business there was no time as well as no means for returning to camp. So here I am. Harry has gone out to attend his first service and I avail myself of the only hour I shall have to devote to the purpose, to write home. I find my friend oppressed and driven by the undivided spiritual care of nearly 800 sick men. It will afford me great pleasure under the circumstances to relieve him as I did before by assuming his Sunday duties this afternoon and evening.

The death of Mr Cowell as well as the manner of it threw an unusual gloom over the regiment. Although not connected in any way with our other troubles, save that it was the fruit of neglect in instruction, the sorrowful event seemed to take its place among our other misfortunes as if allied to and springing from them. He was with Col. Potter when the accident happened. They were going together to the 1st Regt. on some business connected with a court of investigation into our difficulties. So you see, that the association of facts is inevitable. This I deplore for it casts fresh bitterness into our already overflowing cup of unhappiness. I was at a prayer meeting in one of the company streets, and in the very act of prayer, when the report of the musket startled us. Word instantly went round, "Mr Cowell is shot." Going out of the meeting and repairing to the Hospital Steward's quarters, I found the poor fellow stretched out— a hideous wound in his abdomen—the dews of agony on his face. He was a Catholic, and the presence of Father O'Hagan was desirable. I went for him to the 11th Mass. Regt., he having told me the day before that he had been sent for to go there and remain a couple of days. It was five miles, in the dark and over a horrid road, and two hours at least elapsed before we returned. On my way, I was subject to strong conflicting emotions. I was going in behalf of a dying man—my friend—to procure ministrations enjoined upon him from youth up, but which I had good reason to fear would lull him into a false feeling of security just on the borders of eternity, separated but by fast vanishing veil of flesh from the dread realities. Yet, the dying man himself asked it, and I only did what would surely have been done by another, had I not volunteered to go. Moreover it has long been my conviction that to appear in some measure associated with the priest in such cases, paves the way for the kindly reception of my own efforts after the priest has gone and while the shadows of death are gathering. While riding slowly along I ventured in a friendly way to question Father O'H. concerning the nature of his exhortation to the dying, by what means he tried to lead to repentance and the acceptance of Christ etc. etc. His answers to all were ready and so far as I could see orthodox°—that extreme unction was predicated on evidence of hearty, godly repentance, that otherwise it aggravated the condition of the sinner etc. etc. I found that in this as in many other respects the theory was conformed to our own, but "by their fruits ye shall know them," and I cannot but regard the administration of priestly offices as involving always great danger to the soul by casting the priest, the church or the sacrament between it and God, when the struggle should be face to face. I urged Father O'Hagan with great fervor, permitted by our friendship and the fact that I was intimate with Mr Cowell, not to pronounce the word of absolution unless he felt persuaded that God did it first.

I left him alone with Mr C., and repaired to my tent to pray. In about an hour he came in, and apparently with much joy reported that he found him reconciled to the Divine Will and endeavouring by all means in his power to make his peace with God. Fath. O'Hagan then, wearied by his abundant labours, went to Capt. Murphy's quarters and retired for the night. I sought the bed of anguish and remained there till after midnight. Mr C. was writhing in pain yet free from complainings, and seemed to address himself to prayers for mercy with scarcely any intermission. I was relieved beyond measure when I perceived that he had received no spiritual narcotic from the rites of the church. "O Savior of Sinners! Have mercy upon me!" burst continually from his parched lips. I tried to guide his thoughts and pointed to the cross as well as I was able. I cannot begin to tell you all. He met all my efforts cordially and my heresy did not appear to stand between us in the least. When I went away he pressed my hand in a long grasp, asked me to see to it that his body was sent home, and remarked "Chaplain! I hope I shall meet you in heaven!" After that I saw him several times and never without a welcome. It was my design that a short religious exercise should attend the removal of the remains from our midst, but the Father who came at just that time, did not appear willing, so I let it go. Father O'H. gave his consent, although rather reluctantly. I knew Cowell well. His tent was next to mine and our intercourse was frequent and always agreeable. . . . Poor fellow! He was young and strong—6 ft and 2 in. high and so straight that they called him Ram-rod—full of plans as any man alive—expecting in time to become the Quartermaster and to go home from the wars in honor if not glory—and there he lies cold. . . . His father was an old man, evidently a gentleman and venerable in his appearance. His grief drew tears from many eyes. His mother is sick at home and not yet aware of her fresh bereavement. A son-in-law was killed at Bull Run.

The most agreeable event of recent date was the arrival of Mr Theo. Roosevelt of New York°—a government Commissioner appointed to visit the army and introduce the allotment system, designed to secure to the families of soldiers a just share of the pay received. He is a Christian young man and has long been active in Dr. [William] Adams' Mission Church and Sunday School.° He was handed over to me at once. . . . Mr Roosevelt promised the boys that he would request the special prayer of his praying-circle at home, in our behalf, and spoke many cheering words. In the morning I accompanied him as far as Gen. Hooker's Headquarters and we parted mutually edified, I think. If the allotment system can be made to work it will save me a great deal of labor as well as expense. It was a luxury to have a real Christian gentleman for a guest and I prized it the more by reason of its rarity. Our difficulties are I hope reaching their issue. Late events of which I have no time or desire to speak have hastened it. When I went down Friday morning to see about the transportation of poor Cowell's body, Gen. Hooker asked me a great many questions of which I answered some. He told me that he was about to take the matter in hand and would make short work of it. A new complication of trouble will arise from the failure of the Senate to confirm Genl. Sickles.° I am told that this is a fact and do not know what will arise from it. . . . The weather has now been good for three whole days and if I mistake not news will come of it. The occupation of Leesburg shows that our right wing has started. The left cannot long remain idle. I feel nervous away from the Reg. and shall join it immediately. Our boys are in much better trim than you would suppose. Gen. Hooker told me that he was amazed at their fine appearance at a brigade inspection a few days since and that he was resolved to do them justice. I regard it as the best regt. in the brigade, so far as material is concerned. . . . Pray for me, Father, that God will help me to a more entire consecration. . . . Love to all—Your aff. Son. Joseph.

His answers to all were . . . orthodox: Twichell is again wrestling with the anomalies of being a Protestant minister with a largely Catholic congregation. His questioning of O'Hagan about the last rites is characteristic of his attempt to find common ground with his friend while affirming his own Protestant beliefs. O'Hagan is able to reassure him that belief in Christ is a precondition for valid sacraments.

the arrival of Mr Theo. Roosevelt of New York: The father of Theodore Roosevelt Jr. (the future president, who was three years old in March 1862) was a wealthy businessman and philanthropist who had obtained legislation allowing part of soldiers' pay to be conveyed directly to their cash-strapped families. Soldiers were suspicious of this voluntary system, and Roosevelt made a personal tour of the camps to encourage participation. It was an issue in which Twichell, with his dangerous journeys carrying large amounts of cash to the Adams Express office, had a direct interest.

active in Dr. [William] Adams' Mission Church and Sunday School: Adams was a pastor of the fashionable Madison Square Presbyterian Church in New York City from 1853 to 1873. Twichell attended the church and taught a Sunday school class there during his time at Union Theological Seminary, 1859 to 1861. The Plan of Union in 1801 had formalized close ties between the Congregationalist and Presbyterian churches, and they were almost indistinguishable in doctrine.

the failure of the Senate to confirm Genl. Sickles: In fact, the Senate moved on 17 March to deny Sickles the brigadiership, forcing Sickles's friends Lincoln and Stanton, now secretary of war, to revoke it. Hooker put Colonel Nelson Taylor in command of the brigade, an order Sickles protested; as senior colonel of the brigade (his first rank had been colonel of the First Excelsior) he was entitled to its command, he argued. As the brigade prepared for the massive movement south that came the following month, he spent much time in Washington making his case.

On 16 March 1862, Twichell updates his father on news of the war:

When I left Alexandria Monday morning last, and went up to Washington, the city was in great commotion with the moving of troops.° All the forenoon they poured through the streets, over Long Bridge into Virginia—Infantry, Cavalry and Artillery. Everybody said, "It's coming! Its coming—at last!!" At about noon McClellan crossed with his staff and all their baggage. I heard that our Division was in the act of crossing, the rebel batteries having been already evacuated. My state of anxiety cannot be well imagined. It was a real affliction. I hurried through my necessary business at full gallop, sought in vain for some time for conveyance down the river, the regular boat having been withdrawn, succeeded however at last in getting on board a flotilla boat, and was set on shore in the small boat at Mattawoman Creek at 10 o'clock Tuesday night, only to learn that the Division had not stirred at all save to send over a few companies reconnoitering. I was delighted, but found everybody grumbling, and grumble has been the tune ever since. No one appears to know why we are kept here longer or of what use we can be. We shall see, however, in due time. Gen. Hooker says we'll get enough, yet.

The evacuation of the batteries was unaccountably precipitate. All the guns were left and a large quantity of valuable ammunition. At Manassas it seems to have been so. Lack of transportation does not seem to explain it, for they had a railroad. It looks queer. I intend to go over and see the rebel foot-prints as soon as I get time. The batteries I have a real affection for, for the amusement they have so long and harmlessly furnished. I really miss their cheerful music. It was an antidote for lonesomeness. It is rumored today that a skirmish has taken place just across, but I do not deem it worthy of entertainment as the enemy are supposed to be far beyond Manassas—the whole crowd of them.

great commotion with the moving of troops: Twichell is describing McClellan's 10 March advance on Manassas Junction, where since the Battle of Bull Run Confederate general Joseph E. Johnston had been building up a base and supply depot. Johnston decided the position was too vulnerable and abandoned it on 8 and 9 March, destroying supplies and rail yards. On the seventeenth, McClellan started moving men, horses, cannons, and supplies to the York and James rivers for the beginning of the Peninsula Campaign.

In Camp. March 23rd 1862. Sunday afternoon.

Dear Father,

Once more I am writing from the old place on the Lower Potomac, but I think it is the last time. Everything seems to betoken an early movement. For two days preparations have been active. All the sick and disabled were sent last night to a division hospital established in the comfortable quarters of the Mass. 1st—all to be left in competent charge. The Quartermasters are in a state of violent excitement and morose beyond description. The order is—only 4 wagons to a Regiment—barely sufficing for the ammunition and hospital stores. All else is to be left—tents, cooking utensils—everything. From this I gather that we are either to enter on a forced march to some point, or be taken to some fort where our property will soon follow us. For my part I shall be able to carry on my saddle enough to place me above want for some time.

I expect however that the boys may suffer considerably if it is a march and a long one. The state of the ground is most favorable—all frost having disappeared three weeks ago and the weather excellent for many days. Spring is close upon us. The birds have come and a tinge of green is gathering over the meadows. A lusty blade of grass springing up through a crack in the floor is my most fair and agreeable companion.

In going from this place we shall leave less regret than baggage. We have suffered here all manner of meteorological abominations in as pernicious variety as the plagues of Egypt—and almost without cessation. Hail, snow, pelting sleet, cold, bitter rains, suffocating, opaque fogs and stormy winds perverse as driven swine, have held dominion not only over the heavens, but more cruelly over the ground beneath. We have had enough of it. It does not seem as if there could be a real spring here and we are glad to go to where the elements will be kinder, shaking the mud off our feet as testimony against Lower Maryland. There is, however, an exception to this, thank God. To some, this untoward place, has been the very gate of heaven. Amid darkness and discomfort the Sun of Righteousness has arisen upon them. To all eternity this shall be their holy ground. . . .

The Independents I have received° have constituted a solid comfort and pleasure. It grows more wonderful yearly. I do not regard any other paper as approaching to it in real ability or character. I hope some day to have the pleasure of expressing to Mr. [Henry Ward] Beecher personally the grateful recognition I accord to his abundant labors. Your last letter was in answer to the one I wrote at Alexandria. Its opinions on the war correspond exactly with my own. Our private troubles have become fitted to us like a garment. Both parties have become pretty well blown with talking and a refreshing lull is upon us. Major Toler is in command—a gentleman and soldier—correct in habits and firm in action. Col. Potter has been undergoing Court Martial for a week. The issue is doubtful, but he will probably not be cashiered. Col. Hall's trial is still delayed,° for what reason I am not sure. I wish all were over. It may be that all will be temporarily returned to duty, if we are going to battle. . . .

The Adjutant returned Friday and Capt. Rafferty is daily expected. I shall rejoice to see his face. An able bodied contraband,° intelligent and well mannered, came to camp this morning and asked to go with us. The Adjutant and I assumed his protection and he is henceforth attached to our interest as Joe's 2nd Lieut. Joe is the prince of servants. Love to all. Your aff. Son. Joseph.

The Independents I have received: Helped by his mentor Henry Ward Beecher, the charismatic preacher of world reputation based at Plymouth Church in Brooklyn, journalist Theodore Tilton became editor of this Congregationalist weekly in the 1850s. Twichell refers here to Beecher's weekly contributions to the journal.

Col. Hall's trial is still delayed: As a result of the charges and countercharges that came out of the intrabrigade squabbles, Hall had also been arrested earlier in the month.

An able bodied contraband: By "contraband," Twichell means escaped slaves. In May 1861, slaves escaping to Union-held Fort Monroe on the Virginia coast had been designated "contraband of war" by General Benjamin F. Butler in an ironic comment on their status as Southerners' "property."

The following occurrence is not recorded in a letter but rather in notes entitled "Incidents, etc."

Lower Potomac. March 26th 1862.

Slave hunt°—For several days, owing I suppose to the prevailing rumor that we are on the point of departure, slaves have been coming to us from every quarter—some of them from quite a distance—and have asked to accompany the Regiment. Many of them—the most—are fine looking, well-mannered men, and a number of the officers have taken them into employ as cooks, grooms etc., nearly all of them having been accustomed to cooking and the care of horses. A gentlemanly negro, Benedict by name—about 40 years old—was taken by our mess. Of course so valuable property would not be allowed to escape the house of its bondage without an effort to retain it. This we had anticipated but not through open and avowed proceedings on the part of mourning patriarchs. It was not supposed that Gen. Hooker would give any countenance to a systematic search, being a Mass. man and not bound by army orders. Of Gen. Sickles there was some doubt,° yet, since there was a general Army Order forbidding active cooperation on the part of officers, in the matter, and since it was plainly Gen. Sickles' policy to construe the order liberally in behalf of the fugitives, the presence of slave hunters was not anticipated within our lines and in broad day-light. Therefore the runaways were instructed not to wander far from camp, and that otherwise they would be safe. This impression was deepened by the knowledge that in the First Brigade the work of seeking the lost within regimental lines had resulted in the ludicrous discomfort and defeat of the too presuming seekers.

This afternoon at about 3½ o'clock I was started by the sharp report of a pistol, evidently discharged at but a few rods distance from the rear of my tent. Thereupon followed a clamor and a rush of soldiers to that quarter. On going out, my eyes first encountered a company of some 15 horsemen—civilians—quite near the camp riding slowly along through the clearing made by our axes this last winter. Next, I saw a comely negro much excited, hatless, and nearly breathless, just reaching the crowd that had gathered, after an evidently hard run. He it was at whom the shot was fired by one of the mounted party. It appears that he was not identified but only assumed to be a runaway, for the man who shot first hailed him saying "Who do you belong to?" On witnessing this brutal act a Corporal called to the villain that to repeat it would be to commit suicide. It was afterward a matter of regret that a guard was not immediately sent to arrest the perpetrator. I was also informed that they ran another negro down, dashing him to the ground, by riding over him, but not securing him. Followed by the execrations of the boys the bloody men rode to the edge of the wood hard-by and paused for consultation. Soon after they rode en masse toward the camp. Nearly the whole regiment turned out to meet them. At the entry line they halted and called for the officer of the guard. He came (Lieut. [Benjamin] Franklin of Co. H.) and they presented a pass signed by Gen. Hooker admitting nine persons within the lines of all regiments and instructing commanders to allow them to look for strayed human cattle. Major [John] Toler (then in command) also went and inspected the pass. It was genuine and had the weight of authority. Lieut. Franklin was ordered to conduct them through the Regiment. In they came—the oppressors, haughtily sitting their splendid horses—looking for all the world as if bent on the noblest errand. In they came—the rich lords of the soil—gentlemen, Christians, I suppose—proud—honorable—white—while the animals whom they sought to find and lead away fled in dismay to the kindlier forest, or hid in boxes and secret corners, until the terror passed. How they did run. At one end of the camp the hunters came in, at the other the hunted escaped—leaping, straining, fleeing like frightened deer. Perhaps it was my hatred of the business in great part that warped the justice of my eyes, but these negro catchers appeared to me the most repulsive set of men I ever saw. They had not even the common courtesy to look mean, but lifted up their heads and gazed aloft as if looking into heaven. It seemed to me as I stood at my tent door and saw them pass, that I could lift up my voice and denounce them in God's name.

They rode down in front of the field and staff line until they reached the lower side of the camp, where they stopped as if at a loss how to proceed. By this time hundreds of the boys had gathered about them with lowering brows. Nothing was more evident than that the elements of resistance were stirring. I observed this with some curiosity and great satisfaction. I knew that the most—nearly all of our rank and file—and the officers almost without exception, hailed from that political party which in the last election had supported the traitor Breckenridge°—that by their votes they had declared their sympathy with slave holders, if not their lack of it with slaves. They are men who in words affirm the right of property in colored men and who have been accustomed to mob Abolitionists with hearty zeal—who maintained the inferiority of Africans in every point of view—that they were judiciously and properly cursed according to Scripture°—that, at least, they were better off as slaves than otherwise—men who loathe the "everlasting nigger" both socially and politically—caring little to discuss or investigate what might be his righteous dues. Of such material was the crowd composed which closed with scornful muttering around the hunters. Party vanished—politics sank into the ground or vanished in thin air, consistency was scorned—voting was out—acting was in—Conscience, divine and truthful—a heaven-granted Sense of Right—The man in the image and likeness of God shone out, scattering all vapors of ignorance and habit to the winds. It was grand, *glorious*, and I thanked God joyfully for the revelation of it. It was a proof, that low as man had fallen, he had yet the seeds of promise within him.

To go on with the narration—While the array halted as if to consult how to proceed, and things began to wear an aspect threatening disorder, the "deus ex machina" appeared in the person of Gen. Sickles and Staff, with Col. Hall (then under arrest) and others. He chanced to ride through our lines, when seeing the commotion he stopped and asked me, who happened to stand near, what was the occasion. "They are slave-hunters, Sir," said I. Just then Major Toler came up and exhibited Gen. Hooker's order, mentioning also the fact of their having fired at a man. Gen. Sickles without hesitation, and in a tone by no means trifling, exclaimed, "Order them out of the lines at once!"

Then followed a scene that for excitement and ludicrousness cannot be described properly. The lads heard what the Gen. said, and without waiting for the forms of law,—with one consent, groaning, shouting, cheering, started for the obnoxious party. Nor did ΣΠΣΑ ΠΤΣΡΣΟΝΤΑ suffice° to express their emotions. Whatever missiles were at hand were eagerly snatched and projected, in many cases with great precision, at the amazed equestrians. Clods of earth, sticks, and in some cases loaves of bread, leaped from strong hands on their errand of indignation. Like the javelin in a certain old-time battle, their multitude obscured the sun. In the hurling of the bread was displayed a heartiness and genuineness of emotion, capable of no stronger demonstration, for by it the hurlers mortified their own flesh not a little for the sake of proclaiming their principles. It was at the expense of a crying stomach that they did it and considering the objects on whom it was wasted, might be denominated, "Robbing Peter to pay—the d——l!"

The assailed did not long stand fire. Their horses began to plunge and rear—the crowd pressed closer with no joke in their faces, and in less than a minute these chivalrous gentlemen, the blooded nobility of the land, took to confused and ungraceful flight followed so long as the last horse tail was in sight by the vociferous execrations of an insulted throng—for not many but felt that the presence of such men on such business was a disgrace to the ground on which our tents are pitched. Had they stayed and nosed around (granting that the boys could have been restrained) their quest would have been in vain for the quarry was all safe. After dark they came back one by one, poor fellows, but with the look of the scare still on them. They tried to make light of it and laughed, but I fancied a look on many of their faces that told a different tale—a look that lay under their laughter as the sea lies under waves. Since they came to us they have been able to observe and make comparisons as never before. They have heard a great deal of sympathetic but incendiary talk among the poor whites of our rank and file. The difference between slave and free had been growing in their minds. Today, it has been portrayed to them in the strongest possible light. Why should *they* be forced to take refuge in a hospitable swamp more friendly than man, while the rest could stay and jeer in safety? Why should they be in terror at what others might deride? My Joe takes these things to heart. I can see that his spirit is heavy within him, for Joe prizes his liberty without regard to scriptures. How watchful an eye he kept for those he knew who were in danger!

Slave hunt: Twichell wrote a briefer version of this incident to his father on 30 March that noted the slave hunters were carrying ropes and handcuffs. Twichell also told his father that generals Sickles and Hooker were "at sword's points" over the incident. In 1880, Twichell published an article on the event called "A Jewel of Inconsistency"—that is, the inconsistency of the Irish-American Democrats' behavior when face to face with the real evil of slavery.

It was not supposed that Gen. Hooker . . . Of Gen. Sickles there was some doubt: The expectation was that Hooker, from Massachusetts, would take the antislavery side and Sickles, the New York Democrat, the proslavery side. In his order accompanying the slave hunters, however, Hooker named the slaveholders and required "that they be permitted to visit all the camps of this command in search of their property." On 13 March, Congress had approved an article of war forbidding officers and soldiers from "aiding in the capture and return of fugitive slaves from disloyal owners." Hooker may not have been aware of this recent action, or, more likely, the slaveowners may have been considered loyal.

the traitor Breckenridge: John C. Breckinridge (1821–75) was vice president under Democratic president James Buchanan from 1857 to 1861. When the Southern Democrats broke from the party in 1860, Breckenridge was their candidate. In September 1861 he tried to organize a Confederate provisional government for his native Kentucky, was expelled from the U.S. Senate, and became a Confederate brigadier general.

they were judiciously and properly cursed according to Scripture: This comment apparently refers to the tradition that Africans were descended from Ham, Noah's son whose offspring are cursed as "servant[s] of servants" in Genesis 9:25.

nor did ΣΠΣΑ ΠΤΣΡΣΟΝΤΑ suffice: The phrase *epea pteroenta* (Twichell has reversed the "Σ" and the "Ο") means literally "winged words." In the context of the *Iliad* (I, 211 in most translations) this metaphor describes Achilles' harsh words to Pallas Athena in a combat scene: "and his winged words went flying."

April–August 1862

General George B. McClellan, named general in chief after Scott's retirement in November 1861, conceived a plan to approach and capture the Confederate capital at Richmond via a long feint to the left, in an area called the Virginia Peninsula between the York and James rivers. To McClellan, well supplied with maps and intelligence showing easy terrain and only token opposition, it seemed a speedy route to victory.

But the general's idea that his route up the Peninsula would be relatively unimpeded was wrong. There was terrible, yellow, clinging mud that swallowed wagon wheels and the legs of men and horses. Unexpectedly, he found a line of fortifications at Yorktown.

He prepared laboriously to besiege this line, the scene of the battle by which the Americans and French had won the Revolutionary War eighty-one years before. A railroad engineer in civilian life, he could move large numbers of men and material skillfully. His weaknesses were a lack of aggression, a famous tendency to overestimate his enemy's strength, and a magnified idea of his own abilities.

Transported from the Maryland camp as part of this movement of one hundred thousand, Twichell shared the view that the fall of Richmond was drawing near.

On board Transport Rockland, Off Liverpool Point.
Tuesday Evening. April 8th 1862.

My dear Father,

After waiting—waiting—waiting—we at length have a prospect of seeing the actual front of war. I was telegraphed to last Thursday night at Washington, whither I went on Tuesday, to return at once as we were under marching orders. I rode the 50 miles intervening the Capital and camp as briskly as my good horse could carry me and found that the embarkation had commenced—although we did not leave our quarters till yesterday morning—even then 24 hours sooner than necessary, for the boys had to bivouac last night in the rain and suffered great discomfort, poor fellows, owing to both cold and rain. So far as I can judge the whole embarkation has been miserably managed. The transportation was quite inefficient and at least three days delay has been the consequence. This aggravates us, for tonight we hear that Yorktown has been taken,° and we were confident that some part of that job had been assigned to us. It may be a rumor, but if it is so, the boys will feel wronged at their forced absence. Notwithstanding the orders of Hooker, we have got our contraband all safely on board, Thank God. I fear that in some cases it was done at a sacrifice of truth, on the part both of officers and fugitives, yet who shall blame. We got our man on board, without being tempted to prevaricate—no questions being asked. His master was not ten rods from him when he walked up the plank. I will tell you all about it some time, Providence permitting. While I was absent in Washington, a bold reconnaisance, by details from each Regt. of the brigade, was made in the direction of Stafford, Va.°—full of excitement and interest. *The event* of it was a skirmish with rebel cavalry, in which our boys showed splendid spirit, charging at double quick after a most fatiguing march of more than twenty miles. One man had his leg broken by a musket shot, and several of the enemy are supposed to have carried off our lead. They fled in confusion. Mr. Bulkley was along, and I was sorely disappointed at losing the chance. You will probably learn the particulars from the papers. A sad sequel to the affair will mar the memory of it to our regiment. One of our men, Louis McFee of Co. H., on returning exhausted by 48 hours marching and loss of sleep, procured some vile whisky and drank it to excess. He was wild-drunk all Saturday afternoon—fell into a stupor at about 10 o'clock p.m., and was found dead in his tent the next morning at 9. Apoplexy of the brain, the doctors said—murder and suicide, every body else. It was awful, *horrible*. I could not let the occasion pass. A grave was dug near the camp and we buried him that afternoon (Sunday). At my request the whole regiment was paraded and, standing beside the coffin of the dead soldier, I spoke my mind freely and I hope in the fear of God. The occasion was one calculated to inspire the preacher and hold the audience. I had the advantage of breathless attention, and I have good reason to believe that by God's help, my words were not in vain. . . .

Gen. Sickles has been relieved from duty,° and, I understand, has gone to plead his case with the authorities. I hope sincerely that he will succeed, although the opposition is bitter and powerful. Col. [Nelson] Taylor of the 3rd Reg.—a most able officer—is in command of the Brigade. [Lt.] Col. Potter was sentenced to 15 days suspension from rank and the loss of a month's pay.° He received his sword this morning and commands the Regt. I am writing in a noisy, crowded, steaming cabin, yet send my love homeward as heartily as though it were from a palace. Your aff. Son. Joseph.

tonight we hear that Yorktown has been taken: In fact, Yorktown was not evacuated by the Confederates until 3 May.

a bold reconnaissance . . . in the direction of Stafford, Va.: On 2 April Sickles took a detachment of members of all five Excelsior regiments across the river. At Stafford Court House on 4 April this force traded shots with Confederate cavalry and, according to the brigade historian, ransacked the town and destroyed the courthouse itself.

Gen. Sickles has been relieved from duty: Sickles, who had been acting as commander of the brigade while his appeals to Hooker and Lincoln were pending, was finally removed on 6 April by Hooker.

[Lt.] Col. Potter was sentenced to . . . the loss of a month's pay: The sentence was reviewed by Hooker, who said, in effect, that serving in the contentious Second Excelsior was sufficient punishment "to an officer jealous of his reputation." But he upheld the sentence nonetheless.

> *Steamer Rockland—off Fort Monroe.*
> *Friday Morning, April 11th 1862.*

Dear Father,

The captain of the boat will take our letters ashore, whether we land at the Fort or not. As I am altogether uncertain where we are going or how long it may be before you will hear from me again, I embrace the opportunity to hail you again ere we pass from sight.

We have had a nasty voyage down the river. Wind, rain and heavy seas have combined to pen us in-doors and make us uncomfortable. Every source of amusement or occupation was used up 24 hours ago. The craft is a small one and we have but three companies of the Regt. aboard with their officers. I was at first located on the Massachusetts, a large boat and commodious, but came off and pitched in here, for the sake of Asst. Surg. [George] McAllister who was detailed to this position, and did not like the crowd. Joe is with me of course but my horse is on the Mass[achusetts]. Maybe we shall be in this region for some time. If so, you shall often hear from me. If the Pay Master comes soon, I shall be compelled to visit Washington, and then at least, I shall write to you.

Old Maryland, so far as we are concerned, is rid of us forever. We shed few tears at the separation. We met no hospitality from either nature or man. What has transpired in the country for the last week we know nothing of. . . . Love to all. Good Morning. Your aff. Son. Joseph.

Camp "Winfield Scott". On the peninsula between York and James rivers. 5 miles South East of Yorktown — Sunday evening. April 13th 1862.

Dear Father,

It is passing sweet to stop amid the large excitements of the hour and deliberately remember home. Until my blood is slower, I cannot give myself to systematic meditation on any subject while borne on the tide of such an army as ours. . . . Here we are at length. Monday we left our winter quarters — spent that night on the river shore — embarked Tuesday morning — lay in the stream till Wednesday morning — after twenty miles slow steaming against wind and tide, abetted by a sloop load of artillery horses in tow, lay to till Thursday morning — crept along another day as far as the Chesapeake Bay — forced by a heavy sea to halt till Friday morning — hailed Fortress Monroe about noon — caught a sight of the Merrimac and Monitor° — ordered to return to James river — entered a tributary of the same and anchored till Friday — disembarked in the forenoon — went into camp over night — started again at 7 o'clock this morning — marched nearly five miles to gain our assigned position, and here we are with upwards 120,000 others ready to commence the siege of Yorktown. Ten square miles covers both armies. Gen. McClellan's Head Quarters are about 2½ miles from our camp. For on every side is spread out our splendid army. The air is full of military noise, but the actual strike is yet delayed. So far as I can learn a long and severe artillery fight will precede the employment of other arms of the service. An intrenchment, fifteen feet in height, with a fosse ten feet wide and ten feet deep full of water, stretches across the peninsula from river to river 7 miles, which combined with an impossible morass in some parts, constitutes, as we hear, in the Commanding General's opinion, an obstruction equal if not superior to the defences of Sevastopol. A breach must be made in this work, before infantry or cavalry can be employed. For this purpose a large number of immense siege guns and mortars, each requiring 40 horses to drag it over the roads, are being placed. Meanwhile we shall sit here, till our turn comes. I do not know how soon the action will commence but when it does there will be a sound that will shake heaven and earth. I hope we shall be able to ride out and witness the operation, but we understand that strict orders will be issued to keep all officers within their lines. The situation is one full of interest and I shall watch the development of the plan as understandingly as possible. This it will not be easy to do, for one feels lost as in a wilderness. Rumors fly thicker than birds and we anxiously await the arrival of the papers from N.Y., to glean from them some slight knowledge of what is going on almost within ear-shot.

The Irish Brigade commanded by Thos. Francis Meagher° is about a mile from here, occupying the magnificent barracks of a rebel brigade which was driven out about two weeks since after a slight resistance, at least, so we are told. These barracks are built after a style of comfort and elegance wholly unknown to the Federal army. They must have cost a large amount of Confederate paper and negro labor. The houses in our neighbourhood are all deserted by men both black and white. Women of both colors remain, showing, I think, confidence on the part of the enemy in the character of our troops. I am now writing in the upper chamber of a neat little house within our lines. . . . The Lieut. Col. ordered Dr McAllister and myself to occupy it, to keep the other officers out. The husband is in the Confederate Army, and the wife, a quite pretty young woman with a child 12 or 14 months old, and an old negro woman with her grandchild, remain to take care of the things. Foraging is not allowed, and although our field and staff tents are pitched in the yard, and the Adjutant's office is in doors, where our mess also is established, none of the property is molested, and the landlady's geese hiss our regiment from reveille to tattoo unmolested. I even have been out with two other officers through the woods to find and drive into the barnyard a lean half-dozen cows lest they should meet violence. Still the woman laments without measure the loss of a few rails and the trampling of her land. If she were old and ugly I presume we should laugh at her and tell her she was in luck to fall into such good hands, but as she is young and interesting we give her our warmest sympathies and hold the baby by turns. Our boys are in excellent trim and seem ripe for anything that may turn up. We have only a few sick and if the good weather continues, shall have less. I have had no service called today for lack of opportunity. I much fear that our prayer-meetings must also be discontinued for lack of place. Save the field staff and line officer who have one small tent each, the regiment is quartered under the little shelter tents lately introduced, affording only room for three men to lie down in. All standing up has to be done out of doors. Still I hope when the evenings are warm to be able to gather the brethren about my own tent and revive our happy memories of the Lower Potomac. Mr. Bulkley called on me just after dark and took a cup of coffee. He was quite well and was in a high state of Anti-Slavery hopefulness. . . .

Col. Hall has not yet appeared at this camp although he is in the neighborhood somewhere. It is reported that Gen. Sickles will soon re-assume his command, but I hardly believe it. Col. Potter is conducting our regimental affairs satisfactorily and zealously. We, as you know, are in Heintzleman's Corps d'Armée,° and our division has the right of the Corps. I am told also that our Corps has the right of the army. If so we shall be likely to be in the advance. I hope so. If it seems to you that my vein is not very serious, you rightly apprehend my frame. To be near the event seems to take away the mood of general views. The catastrophe of the battle will I suppose recall deeper thoughts. It is a blessed thing that God does not forget men, when they forget him. May he cover us in the hour of peril, and by all our pains draw us up to His bosom in love and trust. I try each day to dedicate myself anew, so that if called, I may be an acceptable sacrifice. My love to the folks at home burns within me the warmer, as the leagues between us increase. In God's good time I shall see you all again. . . . Good night. Your aff. Son. Joseph.

caught a sight of the Merrimac and Monitor: The two ironclad ships had waged their famous battle in the stretch of water called Hampton Roads near Fort Monroe on 9 March. The Confederate *Virginia* (rebuilt from the Union *Merrimack*) had withdrawn up the Elizabeth River to safety but would emerge to threaten the *Monitor* and other Federal warships. Twichell saw the ships on 11 April as the *Virginia* made one of these forays.

Thos. Francis Meagher: The Union general was an Irish nationalist, transported by the British to Australia in 1849. He escaped to the United States, became an attorney, and was considered one of the foremost orators of his day. While a student at Yale, Twichell had heard him speak on Irish independence. Meagher became involved in New York politics and was part of Sickles's legal team during the murder trial. He had been confirmed a brigadier general by unanimous Senate vote in February and commanded what was to be known as the Irish Brigade.

We . . . are in Heintzleman's Corps d'Armée: The prewar organization of the army into divisions became too cumbersome as the numbers of soldiers increased and the move up the Peninsula was planned. After waiting for McClellan to designate corps and leaders, Lincoln himself named four corps commanders. The Excelsior Brigade was now the Second Brigade, Second Division, Third Corps—but Civil War commands invariably bore their traditional names or the names of their commanders in informal use. Twichell uses the full French term with its Napoleonic associations.

Before Yorktown. April 17th 1862.

Dear Father, . . .

I had it in my mind for some time after I entered the service to keep a full journal of events, but abandoned the idea at length for good reasons. It would often be likely to prove extremely inconvenient—it would before long become so voluminous as to add seriously to the slight baggage allowed on the field—it would be in danger of loss, and I should duplicate the most important part of it in my letters home, which after all would better subserve my purpose, both in the absence of the objections spoken of, and in affording the family the full benefit of my experience. By a little management, according to dates, I shall, if spared to return to you, be able to retrace my steps with sufficient accuracy from beginning to end. . . . I have today been to our outposts near the enemy's works. At about 9 o'clock the Major [Rafferty], two Surgeons, a Yale college Gamma Nu man named [Harvey H.] Bloom, formerly connected with the 5th Regt. and now on a visit to it and myself, mounted and rode out to see what could be seen. The fact that a portion of our Division has been moved quite to the front, where the rest will probably follow in a day or two, turned the order with reference to officers being confined within Division lines to our advantage. After a warm and dusty ride of about three miles over a road groaning under an almost unbroken line of army wagons, and lined on either side so far as was open to view by camps of every arm in the service, we began to meet signs of a present foe. Reserve pickets in battalions of about a hundred each were clustered about their stacked arms ready for a sudden emergency, while an occasional crack of rifles in the wood beyond showed that the sharp-shooters were doing hornet duty, trying to pester and sting the rebel picket into a display of their powers. A few steel rifled guns "all harnessed and saddled and ready for fight"° were stationed at intervals in the open fields near by, also in readiness for anything that might suddenly occur. But these were the exception. The great army lay quietly at ease on its back in the shade, writing home, or smoking a pipe, or reading a paper, else collected in groups in which the gossip and joke went round with laughing echo, as if it were a training day instead the verge of horrors. . . . An occasional boom of a gun, with the sounding flight of shot or shell, did not disturb them or us, for we are used to it. Proceeding a little further we passed the camps and met no soldiers except such as were on duty. . . . The rise of a little hill revealed to us the enemy's entrenchments to the extent of a mile—a huge dirt wall with an occasional dark spot, where the guns are mounted. We pause a minute, and then go on. Just before us, a general with his staff seems bent on the same errand with ourselves. They dismount in a sheltered place, at the edge of a ravine, and we do the same. Leaving our horses tied we cross the ravine, ascend a slope and enter a deserted house, from the upper windows of which a fine view of the earth-works is afforded. With a glass, we are able to discern the fact that large numbers of men are still at work on the wall and moat, also that they are negroes. It is a moving sight to see them throwing up their own prison, just as men serve Satan. The party before us proves to be Gen. Henry M. Naglee commanding the 3rd Brigade of our Division and with him is the gallant patriot [Governor William] Sprague of Rhode Island,° who looks but little older than I do. Gen. Naglee remarks that the fortifications are not as formidable as he supposed, but to me they look strong enough. At any rate, I trow the water of the fosse will be stained with Northern blood before they are crossed. We are in an interesting spot. To the rear, near where our horses are tied, are the remains of Washington's earthworks by which he kept Cornwallis in, and to the right is the field in which the Britons laid down their arms before the fathers, whose sons now stand within sight of the memorable spot, looking murder at each other over the cannons mouth. Will not that old blood lying under the grass refuse to mix with this new outpouring? We are ¾ of a mile from the enemy, and the barracks behind the works are plainly visible. In some places cotton-bales are piled up, à la New Orleans,° but they will not serve the rebels as well as they did Jackson. Modern artillery is quite a different affair from the old style. Quarter of a mile ahead of us, and nearer the works, are the ruins of a house of which the chimney alone is standing. A few days since, it was whole and used for observations like the one we are in, but the enemy, after sighting it for half a day, got the range and tore it down with cannon balls. While we stand looking, a white wreath of smoke belches from the wall—Whiz-z-z-z!! plump!—it buries itself in the ploughed field about 30 rods to our right, raising a great cloud of dust. "Not so near as the last one," says the sentinel stationed at the house. "That struck just over the fence there," pointing to a spot not three rods away. "They are going to try us again," smilingly observes an artillery officer with his eye to his glass. At this, I for one began to entertain the idea of evacuating our position. . . . While I regard these travels about the army as essential to an intelligent record of what is going on, nevertheless do not fear that I shall indulge in any reckless exposure. I am by no means insensible to danger. . . . (While I write—12 o'clock at night Apr.17th—some sort of affair is coming off up near where we went today. Both artillery and musket are hard at it. It may be a rally from the intrenchments.) We are led to suppose that the day of issue is yet a week distant at least. The defences of Yorktown were not known as they now are until our army landed in force and drove in the large outlying pickets, consisting in some cases of several regiments. We must wait till the means for a regular siege can be collected. This is going on as rapidly as possible. Seven companies of our regiment were yesterday detailed to go down to the landings and aid in unloading siege guns and mortars, many of them hundred pounders, which are being hauled into position with all the expedition possible. Good weather is rapidly improving the roads and nursing the health of our troops. . . . The Chaplain of the 5th Reg. resigned before we left Maryland and so far his place is not filled. The Regt. is largely Protestant and if I were not so attached to my own, I should be tempted to change. A good Christian brother came over to see me night before last, representing their destitute condition, and I promised to preach there on Sunday. . . . The effect of the impending battle is to sober the minds of all who have been religiously educated and, I doubt not, many about me are wrestling with God for preparation to die. . . . The Eternal Plan unfolds, and who shall question its process?

It is the faith of our army that Gen. McClellan will risk nothing in this matter. When he gets ready, he will strike and not till then. I think that this impression is productive of confidence, and will result in perfect trust and willing obedience when the time for action comes. "He knows just what he is about and will not send us on a fool's errand in the end," is the word among us. Men will fight when they feel that they are working on a matured plan, of which their particular part is a necessary link in a chain bound not to break. They may cut and slash out west° — cutting off the legs of the rebellion, but where the operation is near the heart there must be caution. God bring us through and have mercy on our souls. Love to all the family and neighbours. Your aff. Son. Joseph.

"all harnessed and saddled and ready for fight": The words are a variant of a children's rhyme: "Down in the dark dungeon / There sits a brave knight / All bridled, all saddled / All ready to fight!"

the gallant patriot [Governor William] Sprague of Rhode Island: Sprague, elected Rhode Island's governor in 1860 at age thirty, accompanied his state's troops to war and obtained a commission as brigadier general. To remain governor, however, he had to return to civilian life. He later served in the Senate and married Washington's most famous belle, Kate Chase — a marriage that ended in divorce and scandal in 1882.

cotton-bales are piled up, à la New Orleans: Twichell refers to a famous tale of the War of 1812. In the Battle of New Orleans on 8 January 1814, General Andrew Jackson's troops threw up bales of cotton to use as barricades against the British.

They may cut and slash out west: In general, the first months of 1862 saw a number of Union successes in what was then called the West, particularly in Tennessee, where in February General Ulysses S. Grant captured forts Henry and Donelson. In defending what is now generally acknowledged to be McClellan's slowness, Twichell may be referring to more recent news: the costly victory of Shiloh in Tennessee on 6–7 April.

Camp *"Winfield Scott." Before Yorktown. April 21st 1862.*

Dear Father,

Friday noon we were ordered to move to the front and join the rest of our division. After a march of upward three miles we halted and pitched in the midst of an open plain which was already covered thick with encampments, and lay down to sleep within two miles of the enemy and about half-a-mile from McClellan's Headquarters, a little in advance. Now and then a gun with the scream of a shell from the hostile works mixed with our drowsiness and made our dreams prophetic. Since skirmishes and sorties are of frequent occurrence we held ourselves in readiness to rise at any moment the alarm might be given. It was then our confident opinion that the next march would be a short one—without baggage—into battle, but at midnight a new order came detailing us to return to the landing on Cheesmans Creek to do fatigue duty. There was a good deal of growling but there was no help for it. At sunrise the regiment was in line and by 10 o'clock we had settled down in grassy field, about a mile south of the place from which I wrote my last letter. We are unloading ships, building roads, guarding public stores etc. etc. It is a business which the men do not like at all, but which is none the less necessary. A great part of the army is now employed on fatigue duty, connected with preparations for the "day of wrath" and I think that ours is as light and agreeable as any. The most are digging, which from the loose and quick nature of the soil is very disagreeable. We have the advantage of a clean pleasant camp, and a great saving of distance and labor in hauling forage and subsistence. We are learning the art of camp life. My tent is already a home of snug and cleanly comforts, owing to the genius and experience of Joseph the Incomparable. In coming here we relieved the 1st Conn. Artillery, Col. Tyler. It is a splendid regiment— an honor to our state. I have not seen in my whole travels through the army so fine looking, intelligent and well ordered a set of young men as compose it. Our rough fellows make a poor *show* beside it here. Whether we shall shine more dimly on the field of battle remains to be seen. I have grown to have a great opinion of genuine Yankees, though. Fighting is business, and the best businessmen do it best. . . . The more I look about, the more am I convinced that the siege of Yorktown is to be a great affair, not to be opened rashly or accomplished easily. Days will elapse, perhaps weeks, before the Federal hosts will take up their arms for the actual conflict. All of the skirmishing that you hear of is but a feeler put forth to ascertain the force and situation of the enemy. The particulars of such affairs we get as you do, through the papers. We hear the artillery and musketry at a distance of from three to five miles, note the length of its continuance, see, perhaps, the wounded in ambulances, next day, on their way to hospital at Annapolis, but know little of the real state of the case till the papers come three or four days later. Rumors are the commonest, most conflicting, and unsatisfactory in the army, of all places. A company of country beldames with their teapot could not shoot wider the truth in their gossip than these. . . . One of our heavy siege guns was discharged a few times yesterday afternoon, and made the solid earth tremble. . . .

I have seen one of the dark sides of war today. I spoke in a former letter of the capacious rebel winter quarters situated within the deserted batteries at Ship Point. Day before yesterday, two of our companies were sent down there—a mile in a straight line—to do guard and other duty. This morning a Lieutenant with a few files of men came up for rations, and reported that a sort of loose general hospital had been established in the barracks and that many of the sick, owing to deficient attendance, were suffering greatly. After a consultation with Dr. McAllister we decided to go down and see if any assistance could be rendered. After our own sick had been cared for we repaired to the landing near by, and stated our business to Lt. Col. Ingalls of the regular army, stationed there as Quartermaster. He kindly placed a small steamer at our disposal saying that he had heard of trouble at the hospital and desired us to investigate. We wormed our way through the forest of shipping which has suddenly grown up in Poquosin creek and were landed on the intrenchments. One of our Captains on duty there guided us first to the neat chapel in which the enemy have been praying for success all winter, and there lay 18 men all very low with the typhoid fever. Five of them were dying, some were insensible, others raving, only one seemed to have his mind, none of them had their clothes off.° All of these men, except one, with some 50 others, had the day before [been] placed in ambulances and driven two miles over corduroy roads to the landing near our camp (it is two miles by land) for transportation to Annapolis. Through some misunderstanding they lay in the ambulance for hours and were finally driven back to the hospital and unloaded. One man died during the operation and was taken out a corpse. A crime lies at someone's door for this thing. The body lay in a shanty close by, just as it was lifted out of the ambulance—the arms folded over the face—the knees drawn up—one boot on. In a box of rough boards lay another dead man. Our captain had caused this box to be made, as also another for the other body, and he assured me that it was with extreme difficulty that nails for the purpose could be procured. A corporals guard of our boys was marched to the shanty. With some difficulty the boot was wrenched from the stiffened foot which was stockingless. Tenderly the body was lifted into the box by men whose hands were coarser than their hearts—we drew his blanket over him (his overcoat had not been taken off)—four nails driven with a spade closed him in—the two were taken up and borne to their graves not six rods distant—just inside the earth-work, near the door of a bomb proof. Already the graves had two feet of water in them and their sides were sliding in. A rope was borrowed from a mule team at hand—they were let down—at first they floated but in a minute filled and sank—a little earth was thrown on—I conducted a short funeral service—a little more work with the spade, and they are left till the resurrection morning. . . . It seemed bitter hard, yet the dead wore calm faces as if their neighbors and not strangers were there. Both were young men, and that is about all I know about them. The spot will not be still until the army has gone. For weeks as today there will be clatter and rumbling of wheels and swearing of drivers and all the din of a sudden commerce about them, then the roar of battle, and soon they will be left to deepen the desolation of the peninsula.

We found the Surgeon in charge, who appeared to be a man of energy and ability. He told a sad story of much to do, with nothing to do it with and noone to help. . . . Who has time to look back from Yorktown and 150 regiments of warriors to care for a quarter regiment of sick men?

You remember that in my last letter I spoke of some firing that was at the time audible. It proved to be an attempt made by the rebels to capture a gun of ours that had been hindering them greatly in an effort to plant some heavy ordnance in a piece of woods a little ahead of their main works. The attempt was successfully repulsed, with a loss on our side of 35 killed and 100 wounded. . . . It was a desperate skirmish. . . . No word yet of Gen. Sickles. . . . Capt. Croker has left us. We mourn. He resigned. Capt. Rafferty is back. We rejoice. . . . My love to all and believe me to be ever your Affectionate Son. Joseph.

none of them had their clothes off: It was still early enough in the war that it was unusual to find hospital patients who were not wearing nightshirts or underwear.

In a letter of 23 April 1862, Twichell reports on a further visit to the sick at Ship Point. He also describes the poor state of the roads on a visit with Dr. McAllister to the Division Hospital:

I never saw the roads in such a condition as two days rain has effected. When we marched down here from the front last Saturday it was grievously dusty. Now our horses sank to their bellies in sloughs of mud, and the whole way was blocked with struggling teams.

On their return from the hospital, Twichell takes the doctor to "call on Mrs. White, in whose upper chamber we tarried for a season last week, before we marched up toward Yorktown."

There occurred quite a little event which is perhaps worth recording. The baby was not very well, yet in fair visiting mood, for I succeeded in drawing a smile from her diminutive ladyship by the exercise of arts known to baby-pleasers. We chatted awhile and went out into the yard to mount and return. After the horses were untied, but before we could get into the saddle, we were arrested by the most piercing, agonized cries I ever heard proceeding primarily from the house, secondarily from Mrs. White herself. The door was torn open from within with great violence. "Doctor! Doctor!! My child is dying! Oh! My child! My child!!," and much more of the same sort delivered most tragically. We tied our horses quickly and ran to her. "Take it! Take it!!," she shrieked, extending the baby toward us. The Doctor took it and at once perceived that it was in a fit. Its eyes were rolled up, and its white cheeks and dark blue lips were enough to startle any one, let alone a young mother. I hasted to get a pitcher of cold water which the Doctor directed me to pour on the child's crown. In a few minutes it revived somewhat and a second pitcher set it crying . . . naturally. . . . All this while poor Mrs. White was tearing about, utterly helpless and useless, uttering the most pitiful lamentations. With her beauty to set it off, on the stage, as a dramatic performance, it would have touched an audience of Armstrong guns. We told her to go into the next room and shut the door. After the fit had passed, the Doctor took the child in and laid it on the bed. This act, Mrs. White, full of the worst fears, unfortunately misinterpreted, for she raised a fresh, despairing cry—"She's dead! She's dead! Oh God, she's dead!" It was quite a while before we could get her attention to a better assurance. Then she caught the baby up and another scene of a different nature ensued. "I often have thought," said she, "that when John comes back, if he finds me and the child all safe, he will be satisfied to be spoiled of all things else." . . . As we rode away, at last, it occurred to me that war like chance—or *misfortune* is it?— "makes strange bed-fellows." Here was a Federal Surgeon, tenderly ministering to the child of a rebel soldier, while a Federal Chaplain soothed the mother, who politically desired our slaughter. If "John" could have witnessed the scene, it might have mollified his emotions toward the Yankees. At any rate it was a lucky chance that brought us there at the precise time. . . .

Camp "Winfield Scott." Sunday night. Apr. 26th 1862.
Dear Father, . . .

I have been down to Ship Point again this afternoon. Six corpses awaited burial. As I lifted the blankets from their faces I recognised some with whom I talked but two days since. We put the poor fellows in their boxes, and sadly covered them with the stranger soil—all but one who died this morning. Nails could not be found to make a box for him, so he was left till the next lot. The corner where we lay them is filling rapidly, and leagues away the monuments are set up in heavy hearts—here, there is not even a stick to show the grave. The resurrection morning will start a strange company out of that entrenchment— the dead Confederates sleep near by. They will not quarrel underground. . . .

I am glad to read that our boys are in Fort Pulaski.° Send them my love. We hear that Gen. Sickles has been re-nominated.° I for one rejoice thereat and hope his confirmation will follow speedily. The preparations still go on interestingly. The siege, as a work of military science, will, I think, be memorable. I like the style. Artillery is the arm of skill and fights dirt heaps. Infantry and cavalry kill men. The regiment is in good health and prospering. With much love to all, I remain. Your Aff. Son. Joseph.

our boys are in Fort Pulaski: The Seventh Regiment, Connecticut Volunteers, included thirty-two men from Southington. On 10–11 April the regiment took part in the successful attack on Fort Pulaski in the harbor of Savannah, Georgia. General David Hunter subsequently declared slaves in the area free.

Gen. Sickles has been re-nominated: On 25 April, on Stanton's recommendation, Lincoln renominated Sickles for a brigadier generalship.

Camp "Winfield Scott." May 2nd 1862.

Dear Father,

I snatch a little time from business to let you know that your letter has reached me and to say that I am glad to hear of the family welfare.

I do not know whether you have received all my letters as you say nothing of some articles I have sent along with them, viz, a long account of the slave hunt, a rebel paper and letter. . . . The news of David Beach's honorable wound° filled me with mingled emotions. I do not lament the fact, yet fear the result unless he receives the best of treatment. Gun-shot wounds are bad things at best. We are seeing more or less of it now everyday. Last night a 1st Regt. man had his leg so shattered by a piece of shell while at work in the trenches that amputation was necessary. Three others were more or less hurt. The rebels seem to have received accurate information of the position of our forces within a day or two, and begin to get troublesome. Today they threw a shell so near to Gen. Heintzleman's headquarters that a fragment went through his Adjutant's tent, and another came near summarily breaking up a court-martial convened at Gen. Hooker's headquarters, for the purpose of trying our Col. Hall. Another still exploded almost directly over Gen. McClellan's tent, and another fell in the midst of a camp of regulars. It seems strange that none of these took effect, but somebody will get hurt if it is continued. I have been to Ship

Point twice or three times since I wrote, and each time to come away heart sick. Tuesday I went down, and found the cot I had learned to love [that of a 19-year-old "fine looking young man . . . a remarkable person, religiously"] vacant. Going to the dead-house I found him lying cold. I turned down the blanket from the face—it was white and calm as sleep. . . . I gazed long, yea, tenderly, and there in the solemn presence, with a short but blessed retrospect sanctifying the moment, a look such as strangers do not give was bent upon thy dead brows, and a throb moved by no stranger's heart swelled full and true to thy sweet memory Oh! My Friend. . . . I feel a sob choking me as I write now, for I tell you, Father, this boy had a strange hold on me. The nurses—rough fellows—all said that it was queer how he took to me, and the last time I saw him, when he could not talk much, he looked unutterable things as I stood and stroked the brown hair off his forehead. . . . Next day I went down and buried him with six others. There was one sincere mourner for him. . . . I must write to his Mother, now, and I shrink from it, yet, if she is a Christian woman, I can tell her what will make her thankful, while she weeps. I hope she will never hear of the neglect he met in his sickness. . . .

For several days past we have had an addition to our number in the interesting shape of the sixteen rebel prisoners captured in front of their own works some nights since by a daring operation of which the glory belongs to Massachusetts. They are a quite respectable lot of men, or rather boys, for some of them ought never to have left their Ma's. They are intelligent and shown a disposition to cultivate acquaintance. Save a little hard staring, our boys have treated them with a consideration which surprises me. I have had little time to devote to them yet, but mean to canvass their peculiarities soon. With them in confinement is a deserter—an Irishman—to whom the others do not speak. He was impressed into the rebel service, and now desires to enter ours. A petition to this effect has been forwarded to head-quarters.

Several Yale boys have come to light since I wrote, and I have enjoyed a taste of the ancient days. . . . Love to all hands. Your Aff. Son. Joseph.

David Beach's honorable wound: The Beaches in Orange, New Jersey, were cousins of the Twichells. David Beach was probably a member of this family.

Camp "Winfield Scott." May 4th 1862.

Dear Father,

Last night there was a great deal of heavy firing. Gun after gun boomed and roared—while their echoes crashed and rioted through the woods. It took me [a] long time to conquer my ears and get asleep. So frequent were the discharges that between them I had not enough time to march my drowsy powers so far into the dreamy realms, but that the next screaming shell would flank and hustle them back without ceremony. This morning there was a great calm. Every body slept late, and woke up thinking, "Glad they've got decency enough to give a feller a little nap Sunday morning." At about nine o'clock the rumor crept around, "They've evacuated!"° As this was the twentieth time or so of a like whispering, no one paid much attention to it, but another hour made it certain. Sunday was, at once, put out like a candle. I had church call beaten, but no one came, save the Doctor and a Corporal. Truth to tell, I did not regret it or wonder at it, as I should have otherwise done. I was more in a mood for dancing than preaching, and no one would repress himself to listen to anything short of a Beecher, or some such. . . . It is probable that most of the troops moved this morning only went a short distance to occupy Yorktown and vicinity. I should have ridden out to see had it not been Sunday. A part of our boys are to be up all night loading back into the transports what they have worked so hard to unload. Tomorrow, in all probability, this part of the peninsula will be left bare as a desert and all the departments transferred to some point on the York river, which is much more navigable than Poquosin Bay. I can hardly imagine what will come next. After all I cannot repress a regret that the siege was not allowed to develop. Yesterday, Date Hannahs and I . . . went through the whole works,° up to the last parallel, and saw the machinery only waiting the word to move. The amount of labor bestowed is incredible, and the consummation would have been grand. I see not but that Yorktown must have fallen without much loss of life. The work at first thought seems to have been wasted, but the contrary is true. It is a victory in advance of an engagement. What the enemy expects to find better than the defences here, I cannot imagine. If he makes a stand on open ground his doom is sealed. The elation of our troops is worth 50,000 men. The deserters say that it will be hard work to get a discouraged army to fight. A great many were enlisted in the first place for ninety days, in view of this very battle at Yorktown, now declined, then the term was lengthened to three months, and finally, by act of the Confederate Congress, to the length of the war. They (the deserters) were pledged that they should be taken no further from home than Yorktown. Their families are near by and they appear very anxious about them. The wife of one came to see him just at evening, with her baby, and succeeded in getting up quite a little scene. This morning I carried to our other prisoners the materials for writing letters home, with the promise to use every endeavor to get them forwarded by flag of truce from Fort Monroe. I suppose it can be done; if not, they enjoyed the writing. Four or five of them are smart young men . . .

and will I think be worth something when Virginia is no longer a slave raising state. . . .

Since our boys have been working at the wharf, we have suffered considerably from rum. Although the most stringent orders are issued against its sale. Last night one of our Lieutenants captured a large quantity concealed on a sloop. The large number of crafts engaged in bringing stores, keeping the bay continually full, coupled with the cunning always displayed by rum-sellers, stimulated in this case by enormous profits, render its suppression a difficult matter. The war has made me a rabid teetotaller at least in avowed principle.

We begin to feel that the war is almost over. . . . I have written very hastily tonight for the reason that I am tired and want to go to bed. Love to all. Your aff. Son. Joseph.

the rumor crept around, "They've evacuated!": General John Magruder, the Confederate commander at Yorktown, had kept McClellan at bay for months in part through play-acting, marching his troops to various visible points in the fortifications and concealing the fact that he had only thirteen thousand troops to McClellan's more than one hundred thousand. McClellan estimated Magruder's strength at fifty thousand to one hundred thousand. Magruder withdrew when he knew that McClellan's siege guns were in place.

Date Hannahs and I . . . went through the whole works: Diodate "Date" Cushman Hannahs was another classmate of Twichell's in the Yale Class of 1859. He served in the Sixth New York Cavalry. In September 1862, after Twichell had left the Peninsula, Hannahs was murdered by a fellow soldier who was trying to steal his horse. Twichell's connection with Hannahs's family led him to meet and ultimately marry Hannahs's cousin, Julia Harmony Cushman.

Camp "Winfield Scott." May 6th 1862.

Dear Father,

Hearing that our Brigade was engaged yesterday with considerable loss, I hasten to allay any doubts you may conceive concerning my own safety.° Our regiment, and for some reasons I regret it, was not in the fight. We had to sit all day and listen to it without being able to carry in our own colors. Detached as we temporarily were, in the haste of the pursuit, there was no time to detail another regiment and restore us to our proper place. The boys look upon it as a bitter dispensation. It is rumored that our Division did a large part of the fighting and acquitted itself most honorably. We hear of many of our Brigade officers being killed, wounded and missing, yet are not reliably informed. . . . All day yesterday we held ourselves in complete readiness, expecting the order to shove on and mix in the fray every minute. From morning till dark the cannon roared in the distance almost without intermission. Of course we are devoured with anxiety to hear of our military family. It is the greatest pity in the world that Gen. Sickles could not have led his boys, especially as they behaved well from all accounts. The fortifications at Yorktown are splendid and have cost a vast deal of labor. I could not imagine better defences. All of our diggings look like the workings of a mole in comparison. Yet I think we could have made theirs untenable by superior artillery. We wandered all about this morning and saw much. Our troops were pouring in continually and by now the place is populous as last week before the evacuation.

Those torpedoes, Father, are a mystery to me. All through the streets they were buried, with sticks just peeping above ground to touch them off, or some article like a pocket knife tied to their combustibles. Woe to the curious soldier or civilian who should stoop to pick up the knife or whose foot should touch the stick. Several have been blown to pieces. I saw where a telegraph operator was killed. I am amazed at such barbarism. Are we fighting devils? Where is southern chivalry, or civilisation, or decency? Shall we deal gently with such? For more than a year they have been at work there and they must have been mad to have to lose it all. God hasten the end.

Love to all. Your aff. Son. Joseph.

any doubts . . . concerning my own safety: The army pursued the withdrawing Confederates up the Peninsula, and the rebels turned to face them near Williamsburg, the colonial capital of Virginia. Hooker's Division and the Excelsior regiments took the brunt of the fighting in the brigade's first real engagement, losing 772 killed, wounded, and missing. Both sides claimed victory in what historian Shelby Foote called "confusion from start to finish, with lunges and counterlunges and a great deal of slipping and sliding in the mud." Twichell's Second Regiment missed the battle, having been detached to reload transport boats with the equipment previously unloaded for McClellan's siege.

Camp near Williamsburg. May 9th 1862.

Dear Father,

I have a great deal to write—much more than time or energy places within my power. Wednesday morning I left our camp at Cheesmans landing with [Lt.] Col. Potter. He to seek our release from the authorities at Yorktown, I to push on to the late battle field with the design of rendering such assistance as I could, in the care of the wounded i.e. unless the regiment were ordered to join the Brigade at once, in which case I should return and join the march. A delay of two hours at Yorktown convinced me that I could not wait for red tape, and in company with Dr. McAllister who had come up meanwhile, I went on. A few miles over the worst of roads brought us to the neighbourhood. The signs began to appear full two miles from the scene of the conflict. Huge piles of knapsacks thrown off in the rush for the field—and guarded by sentinels left behind for the purpose—detachments of men collecting stores and property temporarily left etc. etc. At every turn of the road an intrenchment was thrown up commanding the approach, but these like other of the enemy's labours wrought them no benefit. I think they were not used at all. As we drew nearer, indications thickened. The road was trampled, as were the woods alongside. By-and-by we encountered a dead horse with a hideous wound in his side, then another, then four or five lying together, all mangled by shot or shell. This was in the road, in a place exposed to the guns of a fort in front, but beyond the actual battle field. . . . About a quarter of a mile from where the road emerges from the woods into the splendid plain of Wmsburg., were the spaces set apart for hospitals during the fight—strewed with clothing, rent and bloody. As we entered the open space, to the right was a field of newly cleared land with the stumps standing, to the left was an abattis consisting of large trees felled across each other in loose confusion. In that abattis many of our brave boys died.

We rode at first to the right. A rod or two further on, and our horses shied at a rebel corpse, lying stark and stiff, the hands clutched above the head, while the open bosom showed a ghastly wound—then another and another. It was horrible and my brain almost reeled.

Turning to the left we entered the abattis, tied our horses and went into the woods, and there I saw sights that can never fade from my memory. "Sin entered into the world and death through sin" kept ringing through my brain as I wandered among the slain unburied. They were all Confederate, the work of burying our own dead being nearly finished. They lay in heaps almost—a half dozen together. Wounds of every description were open to view, some horribly disfiguring, some scarcely perceptible leaving the slain with a look of sleep upon them. Many of them were boys. I saw one handsome fellow, with a beardless face and a hand small and delicate as a girl's. I took hold of it and even in death it felt smooth and soft. He was doubtless of gentle birth and rearing. I cannot now tell all I saw, but I shall remember it long.

When I had my fill of horrors there I went out, and repaired to that part of the plain on which our Brigade had pitched. The First Regt. was just on evening parade. As I glanced down its thinned column, my eyes ran over. One captain only stood on the line, a few lieutenants were left. Some companies had only non-commissioned officers. The loss of this regiment was heavier than that of any other, viz, killed 83 men, 9 officers—wounded 14 men, 10 officers—missing 115 men. The remaining officers appeared as in a dream—the men, less sensitive, were careless as usual. Our other regiments suffered more or less but none to such an extent as the First. It was as gallant fighting as the world ever saw. I can hardly realize that many of the men who have been my pleasant acquaintances and friends for a year now, are lying in bloody graves tonight within stones throw of where I am writing. . . .

The next day was passed in assisting to remove the wounded to the hospital boats on York river where they will receive every attention. All of our men are off now except those fatally or very slightly injured. The rebel wounded, about 300 in number, are still on our hands and received the best of care. I have been hard at work among them today. Their own surgeons who come under flag of truce to care for them seem to take less interest in them than ours. As a class they are very intelligent and many are gentlemen of education. I have been talking today with a young man just graduated at college with whom I was much pleased. His left leg was shot off. A poor boy belonging to a New Jersey regiment, dying of a shot through the lungs, asked me to pray with him, this evening. Suffering, suffering, on every hand. Wounds that are not serious, however painful, are made a subject of congratulation. The fact that it hurts is of no account.

As for the war we seem now to see the beginning of the end. I have prayed for peace since I have seen the bitter fruits of discord. I can't begin to tell you, Father, how I feel. If I had no faith in God, and did not feel that the plan, the *plan*, is unfolding in ways of His appointment, I should go crazy. I thought yesterday that I should not much care if I had done with earth, so full of violence. . . . Pray for me and may God bless you. Your aff. Son. Joseph.

> *In Camp near New Kent Court House° —*
> *25 miles from Richmond. May 16th 1862.*

Dear Father, . . .

I wrote last on Friday night from Wmsburg. Since then we have moved four times—all short marches except the first. As a historical fact this is our 23rd camp since the regiment was organised—a long way round to Richmond. The Division started Saturday morning with songs and merriment as though no dead were left behind—and this was their first battle to most of them. It is strange—this indifference of the soldier. He fights—a comrade who has shared his tent for months is shot down by his side—he himself escapes by a hair's breadth, yet he buries his friend with a sigh, perhaps a tear—sincere mourning but transient—and next day marches off whistling as he goes. If any seriousness remains, it is generally the brooding of revenge. The camp at night is noisy as ever. Death behind and before is out of mind.

At the request of Dr. [Thomas] Sim, Medical Director of the Division, I remained behind a few hours, to assist in transporting the last of our wounded to the floating hospitals on York river. . . . The study of wounds was interesting. Every freak that lead could play with human bodies, and not let their souls out on the spot, seemed to have been tried. I saw one man who received a ball in his cheek and, glancing over his jaw, it was taken out between his shoulders. Another, in our 5th Regt., was hit in the side, yet some how or other the ball found its way up to behind his ear. These are but two of numbers which I noticed. Narrow escapes were innumerable both among the slightly wounded and those not hurt. A great many were hit in the head with no more serious result than a momentary stun and a furrow through the scalp. Buttons, muskets, the little U.S. breast plate, articles in pockets, daguerreotypes etc. etc. saved many a life. Major [Thomas] Holt of the 1st had his coat almost shot off and his sword broken in his hand, yet was not even scratched. Col. [William] Dwight [of the 1st Excelsior] received three wounds and was taken, but on giving his parole till exchange, was left in Williamsburg. . . . I called twice on Col. Dwight, and found him in splendid spirits. McClellan called on him personally and praised him for heroic conduct. He wants nothing now but to regain his saddle, procure an exchange, and fish for new wounds with the accompanying glory.

What's that to those brave fellows we left in their graves? . . . The conduct of the enemy was in some respect characterized by that same barbaric treachery which planted torpedoes in Yorktown. The 2nd N. Hampshire was drawn up in line of battle, about to open fire, when a white flag of truce was observed approaching, borne by a committee of rebels. The fire of course was reserved, and a Captain of the Regt. with one of his Lieutenants and several privates advanced to meet the flag. They came so near to each other that salutations were exchanged, when our party was fired on, and every one except the Lieutenant killed. The Captain wounded and on the ground drew his revolver, and shot two of the devils, when a second ball finished him. This is a fact. Many of our wounded are said to have been bayoneted, but of this I am not so certain. Do you wonder that such things have the effect on a spirited army to rob the quality of mercy, or that revenge is talked about? A visit to the wounded of the enemy however tends to balance the matter. They suffer like our own, and in their doubly homeless state, no one can have the heart to treat them otherwise than kindly. They lay side by side with our own, and those slightly wounded fraternized immediately, one helping the other or talking together about the fight. In one instance two lying together recognised in each other a hand-to-hand foe the day before. "How are you, old fellow?" said one, "We had it hot for awhile yesterday, didn't we?"—"By gracious, is that *you?*" said the other looking at him, and raising his elbow to make sure. "That's so, and you're a darned tough fellow!" and more to the same effect. No difference was made in our Surgeon's care, except that our own were first put on board the floating hospitals. I spoke about a young Confederate who interested me. The more I saw of him the better I liked him. He was very intelligent, and being fresh from college we could understand each other well. I tried to do something for him, but that was very little. He confided to my care a letter to his father—[Robert C.] Grier D.D. of South Carolina, which I placed in proper hands to be forwarded. He bore his great loss of a leg with calm philosophy [and] the gentleman shone in every word he said. . . . Riding over to Williamsburg I stopped at several houses in the windows of which I saw ladies, and informed them that they would be allowed to contribute anything to the comfort of our prisoners which their sympathy might suggest, telling them at the same time where they were to be found. I did this having heard that they had bestowed much attention on those who were in the village itself, while my charge was a mile outside. Williamsburg is a beautiful place and reminded me somewhat of Farmington.° Many of the inhabitants were there as well as refugees from other places. I gathered from a citizen at whose house I staid two nights before the regiment came up, a multitude of facts concerning the internal workings of the rebellion. The high price of scarce articles seemed the most serious in his eyes so far, and he contemplated peace as the harbinger of cheap groceries. Salt had been sold for $60 to $70 pr. sack. Coffee for $1.50 pr. lb., as also butter. Some of our sutlers° would leave their regiments and open trade there, if any money could be started. They have oceans of scrip, but no cash. The man's wife was a Christian woman, and besought me with a trembling voice to be kind to her two soldier sons—Confederates—if they should chance to fall within my reach. I was sorry for her. . . .

What is before us between here and Richmond I can't even offer an opinion on. We are about eight miles from the rear guard of the enemy, and expect a battle daily, yet rumors are flying about of Richmond having fallen already by other hands than ours. We get no papers. . . . Immense enthusiasm was aroused yesterday by the news of Gen. Sickles confirmation.° We will give him a rousing welcome when he comes as we hear he will, notwithstanding the fact that Gen. [John J.] Abercrombie is now in command of the Brigade. Col. Hall is with us again by orders of Gen. Hooker. I am happy to think that our quarrel has worn itself out and that hereafter we shall work together happily.

It is currently reported among our Brigade officers that a serious rupture has occurred between Gen. Hooker and Gen. McClellan with reference to the conduct of the late battle and the subsequent face put on the affair. Hancock's brigade is sounded high° for a brilliant charge, when nothing of the kind took place. His troops took possession of a redoubt just as the last of the enemy was leaving it, while our Division toiled in a fearful struggle (unsupported till 3 o'clock, when Gen. Kearney came up) for thirteen hours, against overwhelming numbers of Confederates. Our 1st Regt. alone fought seven successive regiments without flinching, yet Gen. Hooker gets small room in the papers. Gen. Hancock is bruited a hero—whether he did a gallant thing or not, one thing is sure—he is the brother-in-law of McClellan. Hooker claims that he had to send his men to slaughter, because his numerous and urgent appeals for help were disregarded. Some one blundered, somewhere. There is no denying it. The dead of our brigade were not wholly victims of the enemy. I am sick when I think of it, and glad my boys were not there. Those who were there say, "We are willing to fight again but not after that fashion. We want some sort of a show for our pluck." Yet to a man they fought like heroes and redeemed Sickles' brigade from all reproach. At least, the mouths of prating meddlers are stopped. . . . Love to all the family, friends and neighbors—Joseph.

New Kent Court House: Following the Confederates, who were withdrawing to their lines around Richmond, the Army of the Potomac camped at this transit point between Williamsburg and the northeast approaches to the capital. Among those Confederates, unbeknownst to Twichell, was his college classmate and friend Robert Stiles, now in the ranks of an artillery unit called the Richmond Howitzers.

reminded me somewhat of Farmington: Like Williamsburg, Farmington, Connecticut had (and retains today) many substantial eighteenth-century homes.

Some of our sutlers: Sutlers were civilians licensed to sell drink and provisions to the troops.

the news of Gen. Sickles confirmation: After many months of lobbying, including a petition drive by *New York Tribune* editor Horace Greeley, Sickles was confirmed as brigadier general by the Senate on 13 May by a vote of nineteen to eighteen.

Hancock's brigade is sounded high: McClellan's report of the battle of Williamsburg credited General Winfield Scott Hancock's brigade as having won the battle with a bayonet charge. Hooker was furious at this, having spent the day holding the line against the Confederates without the support of idle nearby units. McClellan even used the phrase "Hancock the superb," starting that general on a successful career. "This blazoning about the bayonet charge of Hancock is all stuff," Hooker wrote a friend, and McClellan later revised his report to give credit to others as well. Despite Twichell's statement, McClellan and Hancock were not related.

In Camp. May 26th 1862.

Dear Father,

Your letter inclosing another from Sis, came to-day—a shower after a drouth. I was almost starved domestically, for my rations from home have of late been few and scanty. . . .

We crossed the Chickahominy yesterday at Bottom's bridge and instead of following the stage road to Richmond took the road, which you will find on the map leading almost due South toward James river, and advanced to a point about 14 miles from Richmond and seven or eight, I think, from the river. We compose the left wing of the army and are near the lines of the enemy—nearer I am informed than any other portion of our advance. . . . Orders of such a nature are out, consonant with arrangements vigorously making, as to induce the belief that we are to commence an attack from this quarter within the next three days. The pickets of the enemy retired along the road as we advanced and they are occasionally seen reconnoitering our position. All martial noises, such as unnecessary firing, drumming and music are forbidden, while no straying from camp is allowed. Everything betokens the event shortly to transpire. If we can succeed in flanking the right wing of the enemy—as is I suppose the intention—carrying the defences on or near the river, it will be a grand operation. I confidently expect to date my next letter in Richmond, yet it is not well to prophesy. We have a brave and desperate foe before us, and if God gives us the victory, to Him be all the glory. If He ordains otherwise, it is well.

The movement of McClellan's grand army up the Peninsula has been a great thing to witness. To feel oneself borne along on the surges of such a rolling tide, yet all the while conscious that the move was organised and in all its tremendous force subject to one mind, has been a sensation long to be remembered. Defective as some plans at times appear, inadequate as the management in some respect undoubtedly is, yet when the multitude of daily and hourly wants of such a mass of men is considered, it is wonderful that so few of them are unanswered. On the whole it has been a pleasant journey. The way has lain for the most part through a beautiful country, only needing free hands to make it a happy garden. As we approach Richmond all the houses, especially those of the better class, are deserted and the sight of a white native is rare. Our hospitals are established in these empty abodes, thus made in an essential point to contribute to our comfort. I think that the medical department of the Army is far behind all others in energy and capacity. There has been much unnecessary suffering among the sick. . . .

Gen. Sickles came back last week and we gave him a rousing welcome. . . .

Love to all. Your aff. Son. Joseph.

Much obliged for the stamps. We have not been able to have service for two weeks. Nearly every Sunday has been desecrated by marching and sometimes it has rained. Two weeks ago tonight (Monday 1st) I preached to the boys in the open air and had large attendance. To-morrow is my birthday.

Dear Father,

All Saturday afternoon, being on the extreme left of the left wing, we sat in camp and listened to hard fighting about five miles to our right° at about the centre of the wing. Toward night word came that the day had been a losing one to our side, the enemy having attacked in great force and fury, [Gen. Silas] Casey's Division [of the Fourth Corps] forcing it from its camps. Our impatience (for though it is hard work to fight, it is harder to be inactive but excited in the neighbourhood of a conflict) was relieved at about 5 o'clock p.m. by an order to march without baggage, not even blankets, at once. Cheerfully the boys fell into line and with shouts and singing started toward the firing. The six miles was soon traversed and we halted for the night half a mile from the enemy's line. Long before we got there, we met stragglers and wounded men all of whom told a hard story of the day's work. The night was warm, so that the boys slept well and rose in the morning at dawn, in the best possible condition. For once the sick were off our hands having all been left behind. It was the Sabbath and we were going to battle. At six o'clock I called my flock together, and we held solemn divine service so near the enemy that they could almost hear our hymns. The early morning, the work before us—all the circumstances made the occasion one to be remembered.

We waited under arms till 7 o'clock when the fight opened briskly right through the woods in front of us. An attack of the enemy was repulsed—a good opening. Our Brigade was speedily formed. Gen. Sickles was enthusiastically cheered as the regiments passed him. Down the road they marched, fresh and eager, our regiment to their first fight. The Surgeons, hospital attendants and Chaplains followed a short distance and halted under a grove of spreading trees. Ten minutes more and our boys were engaged. I stood and saw my regiment deliver its first fire. For a few minutes, they stood in line and fired by file after a volley° and then disappeared over a knoll, in a magnificent charge upon the enemy who filled the woods. Gen. Sickles gave the order and in two minutes the 2nd—so long in preparation—made itself a most honourable [sic]. A more gallant charge is not on record. A few minutes more and Lieut. [Theodore] Laurier of Co. K was brought back shot through the calf of the leg—a safe wound. Close behind Capt. [Patrick] Nolan [of Company A]—a soldier every inch—was borne to the rear shot through the fleshy part of the thigh—then seven or eight more of the men, none fatally wounded. One was shot through the eye, the ball passing behind the nose and out through the cheek—severe but probably not fatal. After the wounded were all in, I went

Twichell's Regiment, the Second Excelsior (which also had the designation Seventy-first New York State Volunteers) saw its first serious action during the Peninsula Campaign of March–August 1862. The regiment charged the Confederate line on the second day of the Battle of Fair Oaks, 1 June 1862. "They stood in line and fired by file after a volley and then disappeared over a knoll, in a magnificent charge upon the enemy who filled the woods," Twichell wrote (letter of 2 June 1862). Alfred R. Waud, artist for *Harper's Weekly*, sketched the Second Excelsior's successful charge, long remembered by veterans. (Library of Congress)

down and found three of the boys dead on the field. Another died in a few minutes. None of them, thank God, suffered much. After this short fight, in which the enemy were driven back over the ground they occupied for the night, the Brigade was halted, and our regiment, except in skirmishing, was not again engaged. Half a mile to the right there was brisk work. I rode around and spent most of the day remaining, in bearing a hand with the wounded there, both Federals and Confederates, chiefly the latter, who were left on the field necessarily by their retiring friends, and who outnumbered ours two to one. . . . The fighting ceased by 3 o'clock and at night I was used up. . . . The conduct of all our troops was admirable. The day before it seemed to be the old story— a surprise from neglect. Regiments were hewn to pieces in their tents. . . . I cannot stop to moralise or remark. Work is now the order of my day. I have risen with the dawn to write this, and the Division Surgeon has just called, to find out where his forces are, of whom I am one. I shall write as often as possible, yet you must not be alarmed if you do not hear. . . . All will be well, I hope. Love to all. Joseph.

hard fighting . . . to our right: On 31 May General Joseph E. Johnston, commanding the Southern forces, attacked the portion of the Union forces facing Richmond that had been separated from the main body to the north by the rain-swollen Chickahominy River. The Confederates managed to drive General Silas Casey's division back near Fair Oaks Station. The Excelsior Brigade was camped five miles to the south, near White Oak Swamp, when it was summoned to the field. The next day Twichell's regiment saw its first fire (the other Excelsior regiments had fought at Williamsburg) in a charge that veterans remembered and described for many years afterward. The significant outcome of the battle had taken place the day before, however: Johnston was wounded and replaced by General Robert E. Lee as commander.

and fired by file after a volley: In the line of battle, an infantry regiment formed into two lines of men, or ranks, one standing about a foot behind the other. Soldiers in the rear rank fired between the soldiers in the front rank. In a volley, all would fire at once; when they fired by file, each rank would shoot alternately to keep up a continuous fire.

Before Richmond, June 4th 1862.

Dear Father,

A little skirmishing is all that has taken place since the battle of Sunday. Until this morning, however, the Brigade has been in the advance, continually under arms and subject to the most fatiguing and harassing of military duty, viz. watching and scouting along an exposed line. Sunday night a fine fellow, Phillips of Co. B, was killed on picket by a ball through the head. The weather has been very hot indeed until last night when it began to rain and such pouring I never before witnessed. It slacked at about 11 o'clock today, but the sky is still overcast. All last night our boys lay out in the rain entirely unprotected and every man was as drenched as water could make him, yet their pluck is unabated. I was thankful and amazed this morning to witness their spirit. I tell you, Father, I did not imagine before now, how much men can endure. A merciful Providence seems to surround us all. I woke this morning after a sound sleep, to find myself partially submerged in water, and at this present moment I have not a dry thread on me, yet I never felt better in my life. I have not a particle of cold, or any ailment whatever. The Brigade has now retired about a quarter of a mile from the front and is trying to rest itself. It is gradually becoming revealed to me that our Division is one of the best, if not the best, in the army, and our Brigade is certainly the best in the Division. The men are full of fight as they can hold. The battle of Saturday was a disastrous one and undoubtedly owing to bad management. The enemy gained, at the expense of a fearful loss of life it is true, but they gained our entrenched and well fortified front, sleeping at night in the camps of Casey's Division. Two Brigades of our Division were ordered up and, Sunday morning, in less than an hour, undid all the mischief of the preceding day. Gen. McClellan was delighted. He left the important position thus regained in the hands of those who gained it till this morning. The charge made by our Regiment is the theme of universal remark and praise and it is this which helps keep up the ardor of our lads notwithstanding their hardships. Our Lieut. Col. [Potter] is winning himself a name by continued acts of daring which, in the end, will I fear cost him his life. Repeatedly he has ridden out alone till he could hear the roar of the streets in Richmond, and brought in prisoners from the enemy's pickets, in one instance a Captain. Our men who lay wounded on the field Sunday morning, till we regained the position, say that the enemy was in great force, drawn up in two huge lines of battle and in the most confident mood. Their vanguard of several Brigades advanced, through the woods, upon us, while the rest prepared to follow. It was designed beyond doubt to pierce our line at this point and flank the centre, thus taking possession of the rail-road and a vast quantity of stores, beside cutting off a large portion of our left wing and driving it into the Chickahominy. The plan was practicable and 40,000 men, at least, were sent to do it. But when their first onset was met with such instant repulse, and the vanguard came flying back, the whole array was withdrawn at double quick. This is authentic, for it was witnessed by our wounded, some of them officers. It is their opinion that if the retreat had been followed up, our Corps might have reached Richmond that day.

One hardship which our Brigade has encountered is almost too horrible to mention—viz. the stench arising over the dead bodies both of horses and men, lying on the field unburied. The enemy sent no flag of truce to ask permission to assist in this duty, and after our own were covered it seemed hard to ask the overworked men to complete the task. The field and roads for a mile were strewn thick. I counted in one space of not more than a square rod, thirteen of the enemy under the broiling sun, these corrupted so fast, that yesterday we were forced to cover them with earth, for they could not be moved. The air was so heavy with the smell that it was in some places hard to breathe at all. It turned the stomach even of the surgeons. The horses were most of them burned by making bonfires about them. The rain will do good, in purifying the air if nothing else. Several of the boys told me that their picket stations yesterday were in some places within a few feet of unburied corpses, and the graves are thick where we are camped this morning. Our loss in killed and wounded on Saturday was over 2200, that of the rebels not much less. On Sunday the loss was comparatively small on our side—the result of good fighting. It is the falling back and reforming before an enemy, in confusion and herding together, that is a fruitful source of loss. If the line of battle is preserved, and the men toe the mark unflinchingly, the loss is less, as you can readily understand. Our wounded all testify that while they were among the enemy, they experienced nothing but kindness, in return, as the rebels said, for the treatment of their wounded at Williamsburg. My hands have been full in caring for our sick and the Confederate wounded, most of which are still here, while but few of ours are left. . . .

Our sick suffer for lack of medicine, all of which was left behind and has not yet come back. I cannot judge how long this fight before Richmond is to continue, but fear that the four miles we have yet to go will be a bloody path. I pray continually that God in pitying mercy will end these dreadful times. I often am inclined to think that, after all, liberty [may] cost too much. If you could see what I have seen you would be thus tempted also. Give my love to all. Joseph.

Savage's Station. Before Richmond—June 7th 1862.

Dear Father,

Your letter dated June 2nd came last night. Our mails are necessarily irregular just now, and like yourself, I had been waiting hungrily. During the week I have written twice with pencil on leaves torn from a note book, the only means at my disposal. . . . [I]n the absence of envelopes I had to *pin* my pages together. . . .

The Brigade was night before last ordered again to the extreme front and lay in the rifle pits, or engaged in picket duty, till last night, when a New

Jersey Brigade relieved them. Of course the boys were tired out but a good, dry night's rest brought them out fresh this morning. The Division is kept close to the hostile lines, and our Brigade well in the front of the Division, as troops that can be relied on not to run at shadows. Gen. Sickles is among us all the time—at home among his own and his men feel confidence in him. Gen. Hooker is also not a sleeper and avows his determination not to meet his first defeat here. Wherever he has commanded he has always been victor and goes among his military acquaintance by the name of "Fighting Joe."

Lieut. Col. Potter is both vindicating and increasing his reputation as an intrepid soldier. Both Gens. Hooker and Sickles send him wherever daring is the key of success. He spends a great part of his time in sight of the rebel pickets. He told me last night that when our regiment was sent on a reconnaissance with him three days ago, that he took them much further than they or any one else had any idea of, and that he would stake his reputation that the 2nd Excelsior had been nearer Richmond than any other Regiment of the Army. He also gave me minute information concerning some of his captures. I will give you a specimen of his style. Take, for instance, a Confederate Major whom he nabbed in the course of the week. The Col. was riding out toward the rebel lines when he spied the Major cautiously approaching on horseback. Avoiding discovery the Col. rode slowly toward him and at length stationed himself behind a thicket to wait. When the unconscious Major approached within ten paces, Potter, his pistol in his hand, but hanging at his side, confronted him suddenly. "Good morning, Sir!" says Potter pleasantly. After a long, hard, stupefied stare the Major responds feebly, "Good Morning!" "Are you riding down this way?" says Potter pointing down the road." "I was!" says the Major. "Good!" responded Potter, "I am going in the same direction and will keep you company." That was all. The ready pistol admitted no fooling and the chopfallen Major had to accept the Col.'s polite invitation. He was so taken aback that he observed profound silence for some minutes. Finally he ejaculated, "Well! I suppose I must submit to the fortunes of war." "Oh! Yes!" said Potter, "take it easy and make the best of it." . . .

We are yet troubled considerably by the stench of the field on which both the battles of Saturday and Sunday were fought. We are encamped in the midst of it, for the position must be occupied. As our pickets advance they find the unburied dead still scattered through the woods. The loss of the rebels must have been tremendous. A flag of truce that came over yesterday expressed surprise that we had any of their dead to bury, to speak of, as they supposed they had done most of it, or rather, as they carried off large numbers Saturday night while they held the field. On this conviction it is probable their own estimate of the loss will be founded, but we know that we have buried hundreds beside. That battle field when I visited it Sunday after our fight was over, but before we occupied it except by skirmishers, was the most fearful scene these eyes ever beheld. I have written to you how the dead lay in windrows. Horses and men were mangled beyond all description, and every available cover—house, tent and tree—was occupied with wounded men. I went into one large hospital tent near the road and found it full of Confederate soldiers. Owing to the fact that the second day's fight was on the same ground as that of the previous day they had received little care, save a temporary dressing, some simple food and water. The tent was riddled with bullets and cannon balls, and they all said that they had barely escaped death that morning while lying helpless. I gave them some stimulants and water, from two canteens I carry with me all the while, and tried to tuck them up a little, promising to get them out as soon as ambulances could be brought to the place. One of them was dying of a shot through the lungs—a fine looking man—and asked me if I did not think he was sinking. As the fact was very apparent (part of every breath was drawn in and expelled through his wound) I told him he must die, and spoke a few words of religious advice holding up our Lord as a refuge to fly to. "I hope I have done so, Sir," he answered with calm manner. As I was leaving them, one asked me if I would be so kind as to remove two corpses which lay with them. I had hardly observed the fact, yet there they were, the dead among the living. One I drew out through the tent door, but, on account of the crowded floor and the painful wounds, I had to let up the side of the tent, and draw the other out in that way. He was a gigantic fellow, and I had hard work to drag him by the shoulders a space of three rods. About one-eighth of a mile beyond were other houses, full of wounded, but we did not go there as we could see the enemy drawn up in force near by, and concluded that the unfortunate fellows were not without care. The next morning however, the rear of the enemy retired and our regiment was sent on to observe their motions. Taking advantage of this, some of the Surgeons went up with some ambulances and we set at work to get them out. While we were in the midst of the business the alarm was raised, "Cavalry are coming"! The regiment, which was scattered about, fell back a few rods into line, and prepared to act. Four men who were at the moment lifting a Union soldier with a shattered leg into an ambulance, dropped him instantly and sprang to their arms, causing the poor fellow dreadful agony. The drivers were for running instantly and it took all the eloquence and threats of the Surgeons to keep them until we could finish the job. I own that my pulse started a little, to be left behind the regiment, and I kept an eye on the woods expecting every instant to see the cavalry emerge from them, but I was able to command myself, so far as to talk coolly and handle the wounded with caution till they were all loaded and started off. . . . It proved to be a false alarm. . . .

As late as yesterday wounded men were found in the woods uncared for, except in the matter of food and drink left them by the rebels. Where the battle is hot and neither side retires far from the field the wounded must suffer. It seems hard to accomplish any concert of action in the matter. Flags of truce do not perform so good a mark as they might. They have been too much perverted.

In an army constantly held in readiness for battle many accidents happen. Arms must be kept in order, and notwithstanding the care of officers that this be properly accomplished, it is the father of numerous casualties. We have had two men wounded in this way and one officer. Day before yesterday as I was sitting with the surgeon of the 1st Regt. we heard a shot and a shriek. In a few minutes, a young man, 25 years old, was brought in, although not of our Brigade. An examination showed that he was mortally hurt, and he died in five minutes on the Surgeon's table. His comrades took him away and buried him—the victim of carelessness. These dreadful scenes, you would naturally think, would have the effect to solemnize if not scare our soldiers. It does seem as if the sight of the slain and the continual stepping over graves would fill all with horror not unmixed with fear of a similar fate. Not so. For a day it may have some effect, but after a little the singing and swearing and laughing goes on as before. Men stand on their post in sight of a corpse, or pitch their tent hard by a fresh mound, with no emotion. On the other hand I think it dulls the fear of death and familiarizes the men with the idea of it. I make an exception in the case of Christian men, whom it brings near to God, while it does not harm their courage. It is a time and place for prayer and communion with Him who "maketh us to dwell in safety." Love to all family, kindred and friends. Your aff. Son. Joseph.

Before Richmond. June 12th 1862.

Dear Father,

I have [gone] back to the Division Hospital°—a distance of six miles—to visit the boys that are sick, to breathe untainted air, to take a bath and write a letter home. An occasional shell and some picket firing have been the only disturbers of our peace since I wrote last, and we have occupied the time in strengthening our position. . . . Our Brigade for a week has been taking its turn—twenty four hours at a time—with the two other Brigades of the Division, in the duty of occupying the picket line and trenches. The boys complain that the others always let the rebels advance their line, and entail upon us the work of driving them back. Two good nights rest out of three and abundance of food are fast recovering the Brigade from the fatigue at first undergone. As the defences multiply, confidence increases and everything betokens spirited action when the hour for it comes again. . . .

Jack Johnson [a Yale friend] has pitched with his corps of officers and men at Gen. Heitzleman's. I have been with him along our whole line this side [of] the Chicahominy and find every position to all appearances well chosen and fortified. One needs to make the rounds to gain any adequate idea of the magnitude of the business transacting. I found the signs of the battle as numerous two miles from where we fought as in our immediate neighbourhood. I was out this morning to take a look at our men on picket, and saw a grave wherein sixty four of the 4th North Carolina were buried—killed on Saturday. Their names and companies were written on boards stuck in the ground.

It seems to be the general impression that McClellan intends to work here as he did at Yorktown, by a system of gradual approaches, differing of course according to circumstances. I hope so, for I cannot rid myself [of] a great shrinking from the scenes and sorrows that would follow a series of desperate battles such as would otherwise ensue. Time and money—we have plenty of both—are not to be counted where life is in the calculation. My settled mood now is a vehement desire that this war be closed as soon as *honorable* peace makes it possible. It is not for myself that I am sick of it, but for the multitudes about me. God have mercy on them. . . .

I think of you at home a great deal now-a-days. Everything here calls it up by contrast. Never was it so inviting or dear, or sweet to remember. Yet, I know not what could induce me to leave here now. I wish to witness the "great day" which will blow the trumpet of Freedom for the oppressed, and proclaim to the world that the Republic is not a failure. I thirst for the hour, but am willing to wait for it, if only, when it comes, the rebellion, the reproach and the danger shall be joined together in one final fall. Give my love to all the family. . . . Your aff. Son. Joseph.

I have [gone] back to the Division Hospital: A huge field hospital had been established at Savage's Station on the Richmond and York River Railroad.

Before Richmond. Sunday afternoon. June 15th 1862.

Dear Father,

Again I am writing from the Division Hospital. The regiment is on duty in the front, hence divine service was impossible, so I rode over here under a broiling sun to see the boys and preach to the convalescents. . . . Aside from that I . . . visit with Dr McAllister who is my most congenial companion in the regiment, and whose temporary separation from it lessens my pleasures. Our sick are everywhere. Some are in hospitals at the North, others at Yorktown and others still at White House.° A few we have lost track of entirely having been left on the march to the care of strangers. Even here they are much scattered both through bad management and hard necessity. The army has been so depleted by sickness that all who have the prospect of soon being able to return to duty are not now permitted to go far to the rear. All those whose ailments are slight are kept in camp and compelled to take their place in the ranks when an attack is apprehended, although excused in other respects. At such a time you would be tempted to laugh at the sight of the maimed and halt, rheumatics and diarrhea cases hobbling to their posts with rueful visages, yet sharing the excitement of the moment and as able to load and fire as anybody. . . . Of course in our circumstances the main effort of all chief officers, beside the medical, is addressed to the work of keeping the *fighting* men in condition. In nine cases out of ten if you approach a Colonel or General in behalf of his sick men, you will meet a rebuff or be curtly referred to his M.D. in chief. . . . Just here is the evil. The Generals do their business better than the Doctors. With the latter there is a want of system and administration which it requires no great penetration to discern. On this subject I have spoken somewhat before, but the march up the peninsula and events since we sat down before Richmond, have deepened all my previous convictions. If wives and mothers knew some things that I have seen, they would start on foot at once or go crazy. The Sanitary Commission has done a great deal to mitigate the evil where they could get at it, yet there can hardly be said to be any cooperation in the matter, for the feeling displayed by Army Medical Officers toward this institution is anything but cordial. I think, indeed, that the Commission has been somewhat deflected from its original design and does not have an eye single to humane considerations. . . .

I am thankful to record that I regard our Division as an exception to this rule. Dr. Sim, its Medical Director, is a worker and although it is not possible to effect so grand a result as the *proper* care of the sick, yet we have little suffering from *neglect*. The soldiers themselves are not free from blame. . . . There is a vast deal of *playing* sick which, when detected, is apt to be visited in part upon the heads of unfortunate comrades.

The last few days have passed with little variation from the preceding ones, picket duty or digging in the trenches. Our position has been strengthened to such an extent that, if assailed in front, it is regarded very strong. There are rumours of an advance on our part tomorrow morning, but I doubt it. If so, we have all preparations for a splendid rally in case of repulse. On Wednesday [Lt.]

Col. Potter was ordered to take two of our companies and drive the enemy's pickets from a position too far advanced on our left. This he did most gallantly, fighting the boys against a superior number of at least five to one, yet so covering them, that he came off with only three wounded—not dangerously— but with any number of narrow escapes. Gen. Hooker commended the action with high terms of praise. He pronounces [Lt.] Col. Potter to be a remarkably intrepid soldier.

This morning the enemy shelled us briskly. I was sitting near my quarters quietly reading when it commenced. I took little notice of it till a projectile of infernal make came shrieking over my immediate neighborhood, when I changed my position to the shelter of a tree and felt safe. They got our range exactly, and succeeded in robbing a New Jersey Sergeant of Artillery of an arm, and hit two of our 5th Regt. The Sergeant is here tonight in good spirits and says that he means to apply for a position on Gen. [Philip] Kearney's staff (Gen. K is one-armed). . . .

Night before last a band of guerillas made an attack on a train conveying passengers and wounded to White House. The particulars you will learn from the papers. The re-wounding of some of the wounded was the worse feature of the affair. Col. Hall was on board, expecting to return next morning. He had not come back when I left today although assurances of his safety had been received but he had some adventure in the case of which we have, as yet, no account. This guerilla business must be suppressed at all cost, for the railroad is the main artery of the army.

As I hinted early in my letter, the weather is extremely hot. With the exception of drying up the marshy ground so productive of fevers, it is bad for the men. Heat produces thirst, and the water is so poor, that if drunk freely it produces diarrhea which in turn saps the foundations of spirit and energy.

I am not getting homesick, but I should very much like to come home awhile. This, I think, is a prevailing emotion in the army. We are tired. That is a fact. It is a weary, weary, thing to wait here in this swamp made so dreadful by its sufferings and awful scenes . . . and with the heavy weight of a great issue in suspense, continually weighing down the spirits. "Let us finish it and go," is the universal feeling so far as I can interpret it. Winter quarters were very well but this is wholly different.

I have formed my opinion of McClellan and have heard that of many others. It would require more space than I have left to unfold this. Suffice it to say that the New York Herald is by no means the echo of Army sentiment.° One thing is sure, everybody is heartily disgusted with the system of protecting rebel property which has been followed since we came to Virginia. No one knows how offensively this duty has often been required. It will come out yet. McClellan may not be responsible for it, but does not betray his repugnance to it. I will give one instance of this strange system. There are men in this hospital tonight recovering from fever, to whom milk punch is almost indispensable. A cow a few days since was caught straying near by and detained. Friday a Provost Guard came, conducted by a notorious secessionist, who has remained to care for his own property and that of his neighbors, and the cow was driven off to his barn yard and shut in with a dozen others. No argument of the Surgeons could retain the valuable service of the cow and the man will not sell a pint of milk. I call this an outrage on our soldiers. This is only one side of the McClellan subject. The points of capacity, courage etc. remain. . . . Peace dwell with you. May our united prayers bring us a blessing. Your aff. Son. Joseph.

others still at White House: McClellan had set up his main supply depot at White House Landing on the Pamunkey River, about fifteen miles behind the front and linked with it by the Richmond and York River Railroad. Twichell often visited there to see the seriously wounded off on transport boats to hospitals in Alexandria or Annapolis.

the New York Herald is by no means . . . Army sentiment: James Gordon Bennett's *New York Herald* favored reconciliation with the South before the war and was a strong backer of the Democrat McClellan as Radical Republicans in Congress became impatient with the general's delays. One point of contention, which Twichell refers to here, was McClellan's supposed overzealousness in protecting Southerners' property.

Before Richmond. June 19th 1862.

Dear Father,

I am here at the Hospital. . . . A New Jersey man died today and we held a solemn little funeral at the grave. The scene was so quiet, in the midst of these green fields, under a fair sky, and the whole effect was one not to be forgotten. One could hardly realize that a short ride away was a field sown thick with slaughtered corpses, yet an occasional reverberation of artillery revealed the neighborhood of the hostile lines. We rolled the dead in his blanket and lowered him to his silent abode, then the rough men who bare him paused while I conducted a simple ceremony to which they gave earnest heed. . . . "The ways of God with men" in their mercy and mystery rose before my inner view in changing emotions as I turned and left them to cover him.

I like to be at the Hospital, or rather I find it to be my place. Up at the front, where the enemy is in sight and an attack, at least a skirmish, is always imminent, men are excited—their blood is continually hot, and the gospel of love and peace and charity finds little soil to take root and grow in. Religion there seems to go back to the spirit and expression of the old Dispensation.

Men commit themselves to the care of God and try to live as his servants, as the pious Israelites did, and like them are largely occupied in a sort of savage zeal to smite the enemy. Killing and the Sermon on the Mount do not seem to go together, but where the sick or wounded are laid on beds in still places, the words of our Lord are more fitly spoken and heard.

I find that I have almost an infirmity in contracting attachments for individuals sick and wounded who excite my particular notice either by their looks, manner or condition. . . . While I endeavor to show no preference, or better, while I avoid neglect on account of individual interest, I confess at the same time to a great difference in the pleasure of ministering.

There is a boy here from our 4th Regt., only 17 years old, who was shot through the leg in a skirmish last Sunday afternoon. He is a handsome, black-eyed lad, full of fortitude. Today when they dressed his wound I held his head in my lap and helped him grin and bear it. After the Doctors had finished I remained and had a long talk with him. He told me his story. It is a hard one. As I said he was wounded Sunday on picket. The enemy drove back our pickets and he was left on the ground. The rebels moved him a short distance and put him in a deserted baggage wagon, took his gun, canteen and equipments generally, except his tin cup which they filled with water and departed, as their line after the skirmish was drawn back. This left him between the two lines of pickets where he remained helpless till Wednesday noon when some men of our regiment discovered and brought him out. All the long weary interval was passed in suffering and loneliness indescribable. His scanty stock of water was soon exhausted and the pangs of thirst were upon him. The outposts of both armies were occasionally in sight and he beckoned to them in vain. Once a party of Union scouts, seeing his signal, assumed it to be a trap and fired eight shots at him, all of which fortunately passed over. At length the agony of his thirst became so intense that he was forced to moisten his lips and throat with his own urine. For some time before he was driven to the resort he had to clear his throat with his finger or he would have suffocated. All this he told in a quiet, modest, uncomplaining way which touched my heart. It seems horrible, yet. I know that such things, nay worse, are not rare. In asking how he felt in his mind all this time, he answered, "I thought that God was punishing me for some of my sins." It is probable that the wounded leg will have to come off, and this alone troubles him. His only question of the Doctor is, "Do you think my leg is hurt?" and by that he means, broken. After the inflammation has subsided—in a day or two—the examination will be made. What is to be done with the multitude of armless and legless poor boys who will remain after the war?

The event of the week past was the death of Lieut. [Joseph L.] Palmer, Gen. Sickles' aid-de-camp [sic]. He was a splendid young fellow, just my age, handsome and bold. Sunday afternoon, during the skirmish spoken of above, Gen. Sickles sent him with a dozen cavalry to find out the strength and position of the attacking party. . . . It was raining at the time and I suppose he was not cautious in looking before him, however, having no idea of the point to which the enemy's pickets had advanced, he dashed into their midst before he knew it. Just as he turned a point of woods and hardly out of sight, the quick report of a dozen rifles was heard. Back came the cavalry pell-mell, led by poor Palmer's affrighted horse, but alas! without a rider. In a few minutes a party was sent out to learn his fate. Cautiously they advanced—the enemy had fallen back and there lay the brave young soldier—dead with a bullet through the brain. . . . Gen. Sickles mourned as for a son.

Yesterday the 16th Mass., just arrived from Fort Monroe and attached to our Division, was sent out to drive back pickets. Owing to their inexperience they fell into [a] bad position and lost 56 in killed, wounded and missing. It seems to me as if it was a blunder to send them. Outpost duty is a difficult thing, and requires skill, not to be gained without experience. [Lt.] Col. Potter could have accomplished the same thing with our regiment, with very little loss.

As I was riding into camp a few nights since I met Date Hannahs with his fine squadron pushing back in search of the guerillas. I turned and rode a mile with him. My thoughts would wander back to the peace and happiness of our golden life at Yale. The present seemed like a dream. "Can it be," I mentally exclaimed, "that these things are real? Here I am going to my tent pitched among the bloody graves of countrymen slain in civil war, and here is my old comrade, with whom when we were boys I lay warm summer afternoons like this stretched out under the cool elms, talking of life ahead and reading the book—a career just opening for each of which we could not imagine a page like this, now galloping with his hundred sabres to the rear on a perilous business?" "Which is the dream, this or that?"

I hope you are all well at home. Tell me how Eddy and Sis are doing. While I do not wish to have my private longings urge the General Commanding to any deed of rashness, if he knew how much I want to see you all, I am sure he would hurry up the siege. I shall be somewhat disappointed if I cannot reach the meeting of my class,° July 31st. God's will be done, not ours. Love to all— Your aff. Son. Joseph.

reach the meeting of my class: The Yale class of 1859 had scheduled its first reunion, the triennial, for 31 July.

In Camp before Richmond. June 25th 1862.

Dear Father,

It has been a day of hard fighting.° Scarcely an hour has passed since dawn when the sounds of it have entirely ceased. I have seen all the horrors and felt all the emotions, over again. This morning the first and second brigades of our Division were sent out to advance our lines of possession, all along the front of this position. Hitherto the hostile pickets have met about midway in a swampy wood affording cover to each alike and leaving to each the open ground beyond, both sides, to operate in as they pleased. If I understand it, it was regarded necessary to clear those woods of the enemy and establish our outposts in the further edge, thus giving us some jurisdiction over a wide plain beyond, in which they have, up to this time, been free to do as they liked. I had been so busy for two days . . . that my ear had failed to catch the gossip of the camp and so when the boys were marched out this morning, I supposed they were going to dig in the trenches and remained in my tent to write a letter. They had been gone less than half an hour when a scattering picket fire commenced, which being of ordinary occurrence did not particularly attract my notice. Soon however it grew warmer and began to extend along the line in a succession of volleys. I had my horse saddled immediately and rode out. At the intrenchments I found Gen's. Heintzleman and Hooker, beside a great many officers, awaiting orders, and everything bore the look of a day of action. The engagement was all the while hot through the woods, our boys holding their own and gaining. At first we outnumbered the enemy at the point of attack, but they were speedily and largely reinforced until they were much superior in force. The musketry was terrible. It crackled and roared along the line until the woods trembled. No artillery was used at this time as the contending forces were close together and in thick woods. Soon the wounded began to come in. Each regiment furnished its quota and it was not long before ambulances were in great demand. The first dressings were performed under the trees and in two houses just back of the intrenchments, then the patients were removed about half a mile to a hospital established near the rail road. As before, wounds of every description were to be found, from those that were mortal in an hour to those that were a slim apology for leaving the ranks. Dear Capt. Rafferty was shot through the leg—a bad flesh wound, but not dangerous. He accepted the fact, as you would suppose, without murmuring or complaint as became a Christian soldier.

About noon the musketry fell off and the artillery commenced, our men having gained possession of ground favorable for the purpose. I spent a good part of the afternoon at the general hospital above referred to, affording such aid as lay in my power and offering religious counsel to the dying, and in this latter I found great encouragement. At about 5 o'clock some cars were halted opposite and received a load of seventy men, or, at least, such part of them as was not cut off, and started for White House. Twelve of them were my boys. If the fight is not resumed tomorrow I intend to go down and see them once more, before they start for the north. Toward night the infantry became again engaged, and a great many were killed and wounded, but not from our regiment. At about noon Gen. McClellan and Staff came down to see us and were received with sufficient but not wild enthusiasm. He held a long council with our generals in the course of which [Lt.] Col. Potter, of ours, was sent for—as a man whose knowledge of the position was worth having. It was a first class honor for the [Lt.] Col. and we are proud for him. He is worth all the other officers of the brigade together for coolness, courage and the acquirement of valuable information. The result of the day's work seems to be the satisfactory accomplishment of the object aimed at—an advance of our outposts. It has cost many lives and much suffering, more, it almost seems, than the advantage is worth, yet it is not easy for one not versed in the art of war to judge. Our regimental loss is killed 3—wounded about 25–5 or 6 of whom will not recover. So small was the distance between the field and our camp that some of the wounded were brought direct to their quarters. Two poor fellows are wrestling with death here now. Capt. Rafferty is here and avows his intention of not going North, preferring the Division hospital. I think he is right about it. Several men of the 2nd New Hampshire have been buried within two rods of my tent today and this evening we buried one of ours, [George] Boughten of Co. A. His comrades dug his grave and brought his body tenderly, and laid it down. Wrapped in his blanket, they lowered him to his last resting place—it was an impressive scene. This morning he marched out full of manly strength, tonight he is forever still. Joe held a candle and by the flickering light I read the latter part of the XV Chap. of 1st Cor.,° spoke a few words and offered prayer. The men closed about me—they were all Catholics—and observed solemn silence with uncovered heads. I know that they did not feel the difference of creed there and, after I had done, they covered him sadly, speaking in low tones of the dead man's virtues and of a soldier's fortunes. It did not take long to raise the mound for the grave was shallow, and we left Boughten to his long sleep.

We shall feel the loss of Capt. Rafferty. He and Capt. Nolan were our best men. Gen. Sickles is brave as a lion and is much admired for his judgment. He has the making of a first class soldier in him which circumstances will not fail to develop. . . .

It is generally supposed that tomorrow will continue the fighting and perhaps bring on a general engagement and the issue. I am however led to think that McClellan does not intend to initiate the matter by the fact that the siege train used at Yorktown is now at White House making ready to come up here. If it is designed to effect this, we shall wait. If, however, the enemy shows his front, he will be met. So far as I can judge, the confidence of our army seems to increase with every trial of strength with the enemy. Some of their wounded were brought in today, among the rest a captain who lived but a few minutes. . . . Nothing can be so fearful, no event can be so clothed in horrors, but that the ludicrous will elbow itself in somewhere. I have often had men and officers tell how they were compelled to laugh at things that happened in battle when death was in the air, and they themselves expected to be hit every minute. Something of this nature occurred to me today. During the lull in the engagement—at noon—after our wounded had been all brought out and cared for, I rode into camp to have my horse fed and to take a look at those who had been carried to their quarters instead of to the hospital. After going around awhile, I went to my tent and sat down—tired. Just at hand the 2nd New Hampshire men I spoke of were being buried. Their comrades were digging the graves and the bloody corpses lay on the ground. Near my quarters on the other side, one of our men named Rednor of Co. D. was in his tent with a shot through the leg—a severe wound. I had been getting him water and tucking him up generally. As I said I sat in my tent, heavy hearted and weary, and fell thinking of where I was—death on one side—mutilation on the other. While I mused, I was started by the sound of a fiddle discoursing a lively air in my immediate neighborhood. It struck me harshly. "A funeral, a fiddle and a wounded man," thought I, "do not fit each other. I will stop the fiddle." I stepped to the tent door and looked around. One look sufficed to soften my indignation. It was Rednor himself, where he sat propped up, his bandaged leg on a blanket, drawing the bow as cheerily as if at a ball. The contrasts of war are one of its most notable features and often irresistibly funny.

I find that I am getting, not hardened, but accustomed. I always had a horror of blood. From a child I never could bear to see living flesh cut in any way. After I began to be among the wounded, I shrank from witnessing operations and more than once at first I was compelled to decline my aid, fearing that I should prove worse than useless when the knife appeared. At length however I have overcome all this and by a little care in observation, I have acquired a skill and handiness which enable me to act as an assistant in an amputation, satisfactorily to myself and others. Of this I am glad, for it earns me the right of being about the wounded at a time when every unnecessary person is in the way—even a clergyman, simply as such. It is a good thing too in enabling me to get a hold on the notice and confidence of the men operated on. If I can help take a man out of the ambulance, cut the trousers off a shattered limb, cheer the poor fellow while the painful preparatory examination is made, take a firm hold of his hand and help him grin and bear it, then administer the Chloroform myself and keep my finger on his pulse while his leg is being cut off, and be the first to speak to him when he wakes, and assure him that it is all over, I have the way prepared to say a word *for God* in behalf of his soul. He will at least give me his attention.

After all Father, it is an awful business. God alone sees the bright side of it. . . . Half the time I am like one in a dream, hardly believing that the things I see are real. I cannot *feel* what is going on—what a page of history is here filling. I cannot realise that I am before Richmond, unless I argue the case with myself. Do you wonder at it? If I can only hold on to God and feel that He and his mercy are real and that my eternal soul is real, and the souls about me, I can let the rest go shadowy. . . . Love to all. Joseph.

Pardon the slovenly chirography and composition. I am too tired to write carefully. . . .

It has been a day of hard fighting: In the first of what was to be known as the Seven Days' Battles, McClellan advanced a portion of his army toward a prominent group of trees called Oak Grove. The Excelsior Brigade was on the Union right. Twichell's regiment received an unexpected volley from a North Carolina brigade, panicked, and ran for the rear in what Sickles later called "disgraceful confusion." It was particularly galling that Hooker had witnessed their flight. By the end of the day, when Twichell wrote to his father, the Union forces had gained six hundred yards at the cost of sixty-eight dead.

the XV Chap. of 1st Cor: The biblical passage read over Boughton's remains contrasts the earthly and heavenly bodies, then contains the famous verses: "Behold, I show you a mystery; we shall not all sleep, but we shall all be changed, in a moment, in the twinkling of an eye, at the last trump; for the trumpet shall sound, and the dead shall be raised incorruptible, and we shall be changed. . . . O death, where is thy sting? O grave, where is thy victory?"

*In Camp. Near Harrison's Bar—
on James River. July 5th 1862*

My dear Father,

Until this morning I have been so surrounded by adverse circumstances that writing was impossible. . . . My experience for the last week is one which I have no fear of forgetting, indeed I doubt whether any week of the war will be so indelibly stamped on the memory of the whole army of the Potomac. The papers give you some idea of what has transpired, yet no adequate or wholly

"My Johnny has gone for a sojer!"

Much of Twichell's time was spent in hospitals, ministering to the spiritual needs of sick, wounded, and dying men but also serving as a nurse, litter bearer, and gravedigger. His friend, Surgeon Edward T. Perkins, sketched a number of scenes of military medicine, including this one—"My Johnny has gone for a sojer"—in which a surgeon binds up an amputated limb. (Courtesy Chase Twichell) truthful account, unless they depart from their usual custom. I cannot undertake to tell you the whole as it has fallen under my observation, but will give a summary to be filled in at some future time if we are spared to meet. We had a day of hard fighting on the left last week, Wednesday, of which I wrote you some account the same evening. Thursday afternoon the artillery on the right betrayed the fact that an engagement was opening in that quarter. This same night I went down in the cars to White House to take some articles to our wounded boys who were carried down the evening before. I found all along the road indications of some unusual movement or event close at hand. Stores were being packed on cars, others piled together in shape to be burnt if necessary, while rumors of the enemy were rife among the employees and soldiers we met. At White House the excitement was intense. It was said that guerrillas had been seen near etc. etc. To all this I paid little attention, the experience of a camp near the advance before Richmond having cured me of that excessive timidity which sutlers and civilians are subject to on the slightest provocation. I only concluded that something was to develop shortly; what I knew not. To my great disappointment I found the boat on board which my boys were bestowed gone. Hurrying up some business I had at the express office, I lay down on the floor of a barge till morning and started back by the first train in the grey of dawn. Arriving at Savages Station, I heard artillery on the right as on the previous evening, and was told that a battle successful on our part so far, was again opening.° As our part of the lines was quiet I bestowed little thought on the subject, but mounted my horse which was in waiting and rode over to the Division Hospital, which for several days I had been unable to visit. All day, while there, the roar of artillery and the fainter volleys of musketry were plainly audible, and the fact that it seemed changing in direction toward the right and rear aroused our apprehensions. I felt moved to return at once to the front, but the Doctor desired me to stay and assist the next morning in the amputation of that poor little fellow's leg, of whom I wrote to you. It was laid upon me to break to him the unwelcome news. He received it as I supposed he would like a brave boy, saying nothing of the operation itself, only shrinking from the loss of a limb. The job was accomplished skillfully and satisfactorily before seven o'clock, and after seeing Johnny comfortably reading a magazine I brought him, I started back with Dr. McAllister. Rumors that we had heard within a few hours led us to shape our course to Bottoms Bridge, where we found a sight that confirmed all previous whisperings. The bridge was destroyed, an earthwork was thrown up—artillery was in position with a force of infantry, and the cavalry pickets of the enemy were in sight. Then we realized that the right wing of our line had been turned and that strange times were at hand.

Delaying but a few minutes we pushed on for the lines. Arrived in sight of Savages Station, the plain was full of moving trains of wagons, and dark columns of troops appeared coming over the hill from the right. At a glance we read the story and our hearts sank down—down—down, until the very horses seemed to feel it. Further on we saw that all the reserve force of our left had been removed, leaving the second line of ranks empty both of men and guns. This change had been sedulously hidden from our boys in the front who still, poor fellows, stood on picket or lay in the outworks, gazing hopefully and bravely toward Richmond. We went among them. They were laughing over the absurd rumors of defeat on the right and consequent evacuation of our hard-earned position, which they had heard, and we prudently forbore to undeceive them. Gen. Sickles stood under a tree looking calm but anxious. Col. Hall was near and, riding up, Dr. McAllister told him in undertone what we had seen at Bottoms Bridge, and he in turn told it to the General, who seemed much incensed thereat, for he instantly, and not very mildly, ordered Dr McAllister to return to the hospital. He is so universally courteous that I attributed his manner at the time to his very great apprehension lest the men should find out what was going on and lose spirit. The fate of the Doctor warned me and I was very cautious what I afterward said. I staid with our regiment till it was relieved at 5 o'clock and went into camp with it. I cannot tell you how I yearn toward the boys since they began to face death and wounds, and now it appeared that they were to encounter the terrible dangers that always follow a rear guard. I felt then that nothing should compel me to leave them, but that whatever they were called upon to go through I would be with them. But my post turned out to be elsewhere, in a duty less agreeable, but probably less perilous. After the regiment had reached camp and the men, now always tired from overwork, had began to get quietly and unsuspiciously to their hard beds, I rode over to Division Headquarters to learn what was to be done with the sick. Dr. Sim showed me an order just received, to the effect that no transportation could be afforded to the thousands who were disabled—that all who could possibly work their way along with gun and ammunition were to start at once—the rest were to be left with surgeons, medicine and stores to become prisoners of war. The Dr. desired me to proceed at once to the hospital, announce the order and assist both in making ready, and subsequently in the march itself. Dr's Powell and McAllister were ordered to remain behind. I returned once more to camp, put my baggage on the horse and told Joe to get himself all ready, and go with the regiment. After informing the Colonel of my assignment, I turned and rode away out of the bloody field, past the graves of the dead, heroic multitude, over the ground drenched and drenched again in true blood, where we had hoped and feared and suffered for weary weeks, where valor had met valor and brave souls escaped through gaping wounds—I passed the point where my own lads first shook hands so gallantly with a soldier's perils—a little further on and Fair Oaks was left behind, maybe forever, to become the abode of death and stillness. I could not help a feeling of rebellion against the fate that forced the abandonment of ground that cost so much and was made so sacred, yet with a deep sigh and a fervent prayer for the boys who lay sleeping, thus far, in peace, I rode briskly away.

At the Hospital I found that the news had preceded me, and that every preparation was being made for a start at dawn. About 150 were to be left and the two good Doctors uttered no whisper of recoil from the duty laid upon them of encountering . . . imprisonment. We slept from 12 till 3, when the marshalling of the sick battalion was commenced. According to instructions they were divided into squads and placed in command of officers who had been inmates of the Hospital. Our Major Toler was in command, with one thigh well nigh immoveable through rheumatism. Such a crowd you never saw—the halt—the maimed—the disabled in every way. All had chosen to march and, under the impulse of fear, some were setting out who had before supposed themselves unable to save their lives by walking two rods. The sight was both sad and ludicrous. At length they were in motion slowly and painfully. The destination was James River, but what point of it was not known. The fervent hopes of every one made the distance short. Permitting the feeble cavalcade to proceed, I ran through the hospital to say good-bye and a cheering word to those I knew, and to add a last consolation to those I never expected to behold again in the flesh. I hated to leave those poor dying fellows, and offered my services to Dr. Sim to remain with them, in case he could send one of the Doctors on with the regiment; but he counselled otherwise. I gave the little hero Johnny whose leg came off the morning before, a kiss of true love, administered a hug to Dr McAllister, waved a farewell to the assembled assistants and nurses who were retained, and proceeded to overtake the Major and his command. It was not without fears that I contemplated the fate of those left behind. There were possibilities which I did not like to contemplate. If a formal surrender to the proper officer could be effected, all would be well. Both the Surgeons and the sick would be well treated and soon released, but a straggling squad might be their first entertainers, and something evil might happen. God be with them. To His mercy and protection let them be committed.

The pursuit of the Hospital column was not a long one. Slowly the convalescents crept along, with great pluck, it is true, but with small speed. Frequent halts were needful and the way wore wearily. Passing White Oak Swamp

The Union field hospital at Savage's Station, Virginia, after the battle of Gaines's Mill on 27 June 1862. Shortly after the battle, the field hospital was abandoned to the Confederates. Several officers and surgeons remained, including Twichell's friends Father Joseph B. O'Hagan and Surgeon George McAllister. Twichell was also ready to stay, but he was asked to lead a contingent of the walking wounded twenty miles to safety, just ahead of the retreating army (letter of 5 July 1862). (Library of Congress)

bridge, just where we were camped before our boys marched that Saturday night over to Fair Oaks, we dragged on till the sun began to relax the thin strained muscles, when we halted in a grove for the rest of the day, having accomplished six good miles. White Oak Swamp bridge is a point of interest now,° for it was there that a fierce battle lasting a whole day was fought when our rear had crossed. When we passed it, wagons were crossing at the rate of 100 to 120 an hour and so they continued for 36 hours. Nothing was allowed to stop the procession. The engineers were busy as bees and did their work nobly. The approaching battle was foreshadowed by the placing of batteries all over the adjoining eminences. The heat of the sun was not our only reason for so long a halt. Scouts sent ahead reported the enemy's pickets of cavalry on every road. Dr. Brown of our 1st Regt. who was along with us, and myself, rode ahead for information and ran right into a fight between some of the [Gen. Erasmus D.] Keyes artillery and a band of rebels. It was a short but very bloody affair resulting in the death [of] 9 of the enemy, and a number of wounded and prisoners. The poor fellows fell into a complete trap and our cannon, in two discharges, did all the mischief for them, but great service for us, as it made the enemy very cautious about approaching any portion of our advance. At about night we learned that the City Point road was open and that a long baggage train with a strong guard was to start upon it, and travel through the night. We resolved to avail ourselves of this protection, as, according to orders, we were most anxious to get the sick safely to the river as soon as possible. It was hard work for the weak legs to dodge among the wagons but we made about six miles more, and halted at 8½ o'clock in a piece of woods, where the exhausted men lay down on the ground and slept till 12 when the last of the train passed and we were compelled to rouse them up and push ahead, not knowing what might befall us if we tarried. As we proceeded we halted oftener and longed for the end. Thus far excitement kept our staggering line in motion, but this could not last much longer. Another hour's sleep between 3½ and 4½ o'clock by the roadside, another start, another weary pull of lagging miles and James River came in sight at 8½ o'clock a.m. We had been told that hospital boats would be in waiting, with comfort, rest, care and refreshment, and this goal we kept constantly in sight. Down to the river we crawled. A cavalry guard stopped us at the gate. The boats were not there. Too tired to indulge in emotion of any kind, half-dead with fatigue, the men crept down into a cool, grassy ravine by the river side, spread their blankets and sank into a stupor of sleep and exhaustion, having accomplished full 20 miles in 28 hours—a feat seldom equalled, I think, in the annals of war. Let us leave them here for awhile to rally their powers and travel back on the road, to look for the stragglers, who threw themselves down in despair, and see how the tide of battle goes. I felt great anxiety for the regiment. Ever since early morning the thunder of our protecting cannon had been sounding upon the air, and the frequency of the report showed that no boys' play was transacting. A careful count reported about 70 discharges to the minute and it was not far off. I started to see and learn the fate of my flock. After several hours of effort, I abandoned the design. The road was absolutely impossible. There was little real confusion, although to the uninitiated it might seem otherwise. Amid noise indescribable the army, with its stores contained in thousands of wagons, and all its munitions of war, was working rapidly and successfully toward its determined position on the river, but it was not in the power of man under ordinary inducements to stem the tide and make headway. I was quite near the gun boats when they opened their magnificent fire, and defeated a well-directed effort to pierce the centre of our vast column, by a movement down from Richmond and parallel to the river, at a distance of 1½ miles. Had this attempt not been timely frustrated, the Army of the Potomac were now only a historical fact. At dark I returned to the rendezvous of the sick. I have omitted to say that during the day I found some of our stragglers working their way along bravely and some that had secured a hard seat in the baggage wagons. As soon as I reached the river retreat I spoke of, one of our colored men came to me and said, "Please Sir! Johnny wants to see you." "Johnny!!" said I, "What do you mean?" "He came in an ambulance, Sir, and is close by here on the hill." Under the darkey's guidance I went and there was the noble little fellow placed on the ground on an ambulance bed, also a number of other severely wounded men from our Division Hospital. I was both amazed and delighted. It appeared that a few ambulances had been sent to the hospital after we left and filled with those best fitted for the journey in the Doctors' opinion. Johnny was in excellent spirits although tired, and his pale face lighted up with a smile of real pleasure when he saw me coming. I assisted a Surgeon in dressing his leg, and found it doing very well so far, although I have grave doubts as to the result. It was a strange sight, this dressing horrid wounds, out of doors, by the light of a candle, and the deep still river flowing by. Well! War has strange sights. Next morning, after endeavouring to secure something to eat to the men, who spite of all their hardship were more refreshed and in better spirits than you could expect, I again started back for the purpose of finding the regiment, and moreover of seeing and consulting with Dr. Sim, concerning the subsistence and disposal of the sick. This time I succeeded. I found the regiment in line of battle on a huge plateau called Malvern hill,° which hill was covered with artillery and troops. All the morning the fight had raged and the enemy were still held back. The infantry was stationed in support of batteries and there was little musketry from our side. The boys were thoroughly worn out with watching, marching and hunger, yet their courage was high. A vastly superior force crowding upon the position had been held at bay successfully and confidence was the result. Gen. Sickles looked pale but dauntless. [Lt.] Col. Potter (our pride) was lying under a tree reading, in sight of the enemy. A large brick building a little back, full of wounded with many more laid on the grass about it, showed what the fight had been. Most of the wounds were from fragments of shell and of the worst description. The fact that some of the Confederate wounded were brought in showed that they had been driven from points they tried to carry. I staid with the regiment for two hours to talk and learn the news. Two of our boys only had been killed, but several wounded. They left our old camp early Sunday morning and had been kept in various positions covering the rear, in support of artillery ever since—a duty most fatiguing and perilous. God was with them. "Some one must be praying for us, Chaplain!" said one of the boys to me. "I know of one!" was my reply. Several times by a hair's breadth, had the regiment escaped capture or slaughter, but so far there was every reason to be thankful, and I think we were. While I was there, at about 4 o'clock, the battle was re-newed with greater fury than before. You can gain by description no adequate idea of its fearful grandeur. The roar of artillery, the howling of shell and shot, the thick white clouds of smoke hiding the field, all remain in my memory, but stop at my pen. I could see the shells strike in the field and explode, hurling death on every side, yet fewer than you could believe were wounded by them. Soon the gunboats opened, throwing their ponderous projectiles entirely over our position into the ranks of the enemy where they produced fearful effect. The accuracy and efficiency of their fire, I gathered from a conversation with a rebel Captain of [Brig. Gen. J. E. B.] Stuart's Cavalry° who was captured in the course of the forenoon. In a few minutes the wounded began to be brought off from the field, when I repaired to the Hospital in the rear, and lent a hand till dark at the work of dismemberment and nursing. Dr. Sim was there. He told me that to keep the sick well in the rear (or rather, advance) was all that could be done just then, but gave me some cans of soup to take to them. After dark, finding that there was abundance of help at the hospital, I returned to my previous charge and found them pretty much as before. A boat had come and removed the wounded. I never expect to see Johnny again. In the morning we were awaked by the pouring rain. . . . [A] cavalry officer came riding around in hot haste. "Turn out! Turn out! Every one who does not wish to be taken prisoner must leave without a minute's delay! The army has gone on and the enemy are upon us!" For a moment I thought I would counsel all to remain and be taken. It seemed as though the men *could not* go. But they did not await my advice or any one else's. Hastily gathering up their guns and blankets, preternaturally strong through fear, they started. I never knew it rain so. The three hours already past of it had converted the soft rich soil into yielding mud from which it was not easy for a strong man to pluck his feet. But off they went, filing in long, forlorn procession across the fields, under the guidance of a dragoon, and parallel to the road which was full of troops and artillery. . . . The rear guard of the army had evacuated the position held the day before, after holding it, like heroes that they were, against tremendous odds until the rest were safe. It seems that we had been forgotten and here we were, compelled to hasten or be left behind. . . . Through thick woods, over ditches, and roads swimming in mud, thrust aside by the strong, cursed by the heartless, the heavy-hearted, helpless men struggled through six or seven miles to their final destination on the river. One large house and several barns were appropriated to the wounded, the sick were laid in the mud without a cover, and there they lay for two whole days, until the wounded [were] placed on board the boats of the [Sanitary] Commission. Hard bread was given them and occasionally soup and coffee, but their condition was almost irredeemably wretched.

Yesterday and today I suppose they are being attended to, and before long this hideous spot will not mar the face of our army. The memory of it will be more tenacious than the fact. . . .

In the last morning's march the Division was ahead of us, having passed during the night, with the exception of our own regiment which enjoyed the wearisome and miserable distinction of remaining drawn up before the enemy till the very last, when they had to come away on the double quick to escape capture. I joined it again in the afternoon and slept that night a sound refreshing sleep with nothing that could be nicknamed "dry" in the entire neighbourhood. The whole army was collected in an immense plain by the river side and there remained overnight in order for battle, but sunk in mud, until it was determined that the enemy was not in close pursuit, when the line was unfolded and positions taken. Thursday night the regiment moved out a mile. I did not follow till next day, having an eye to the sick. Last night (Saturday night. I am now writing on Sunday the 6th) we were ordered out just at dark, marched about 1½ miles, lay down till morning, remain still in the same place and know not what next, in fact, we little care. We are in a wide field at one end of which, the end away from the river, earth works are being thrown up. I have not even asked about them yet.

Such is my hasty and [in] many respects imperfect account of my travels since I wrote last. I have written in a hurry, fearing disturbance before I could finish and spurred by your anxiety as well as my own. Scenes, impressions, incidents which I intended to describe must be omitted. . . . But, as you might suppose, the period over which I have taken you will be most memorable to me, as a time when I saw men suffer. I thought I had seen misery before. It was comfort in the comparison. . . . All [that] weak, deserted, helpless, pain-pierced, despairing men can endure, I have seen borne and patiently confronted. . . . I have seen a man reeling mile after mile in half-delirium through weakness, and could do nothing for him. I have heard men call on God for mercy, when their comrades had no help for them. I have seen a man walk twenty miles, with a shot through both thighs. I have seen a man walking erect, with a face white as this paper, while a shattered arm swung on its fractures by his side, yet buoyed up by a will of iron. Time would fail me to tell of all I have seen, but long after this war is over, if I live, my dreams will bring it back. . . . We have no Surgeon at all now of our own. So many were sick in camp when we came away from before Richmond that Dr. McGowan also was ordered to remain. He is a very slight loss, although I wish him well.

The papers will discuss for you the general character and bearings of this late movement better than I can. I have, of course, my own opinions, but I am not sure of their foundation or justice. To be inside the wheel is a bad position from which to calculate the general principles of its movement. I think, however, that amid much evil there is some good. Undoubtedly the change was planned before it was necessitated by the battle of Friday. Undoubtedly we are in better position than before. Undoubtedly Richmond must fall, but when I think of how grand our army was last winter, of how much it has since cost in men and money, of how little it has been made to accomplish and of its present condition, reduced and far from elated, I am persuaded that something or somebody is all wrong. I hinted a while since that I might say something of our Commander.° I cannot now open the subject, but I have no doubt we agree in nearly all points concerning the conduct of affairs. We have not carried on this business in a way to claim the blessing of God, and we shall not have it until the free, Northern, *conscience* is a recognised element in the guidance of it. What is before us I know not. The prevailing opinion is that *this* position of the army, at least, must rest for some weeks, after its harassing toils. If this turns out to be the case I shall try to make my way homeward so as to meet my class. It is not at all sure and I am not very lively in my hope. Perhaps I shall come and stay but a day or so. . . . You wrote a Postscript regarding my remains in case I meet my death while away from you. Your wish in the matter, of course, has great weight with me and I shall take the steps you desire, in fact, I have done so already. For my own part, I have ceased to have any strong preference in this respect. I have seen so many noble fellows, the joy and hope of their homes, officers as well as privates, put under the sod of a battle field that it has dulled my care for my body after the soul has gone. . . . Many a mother's heart, for years to come, will yearn over some spot of earth, she knows not exactly where, which holds the ashes of her slain son. I should not for myself shrink from sleeping among my brave boys, God pity them. . . .

Joe is going to leave me. He is sick of the business and I do not wonder at it, yet I am displeased with him, at going when I want him most and after I have treated him with the utmost kindness. I shall get along however for there are swarms of contrabands about. Capt. Rafferty has gone home. He was in luck to get off as he did, for he would have had a hard time otherwise. . . .

I think of you a great deal now-a-days, and am pleased to hear that the family is at peace. God bless you all and bring us together in His good time. . . . That we may be wholly consecrated to Him and at last enter into his eternal joy is the prayer of

Your aff. Son. Joseph.

a battle successful . . . was again opening: In this letter Twichell writes about the remainder of the Seven Days' battles. Lee, the new commander of the Army of Northern Virginia, quickly took the offensive on the north side of the Chickahominy and convinced McClellan of his overwhelming superiority, although it was completely illusory. After Mechanicsville on 26 July and Gaines's Mill on 27 July, McClellan decided to "change his base" south to the James River, setting in motion the exodus from the lines in front of Richmond that Twichell describes so vividly.

White Oak Swamp bridge is a point of interest now: In a battle on 30 July, the day after Twichell and his invalids crossed the bridge, White Oak Swamp was the scene of a battle in which Lee's forces tried to keep McClellan from consolidating his forces.

a huge plateau called Malvern hill: Twichell originally wrote "Martins hill," but at some later date crossed it out and placed above it "Malvern Hill (?)." It probably was indeed Malvern Hill, at which Sickles's brigade played an important role. Union forces had been able to entrench themselves strongly on the hill and resisted a frontal attack, shielded in part by fire from gunboats on the nearby James River. Lee thus failed to prevent McClellan from concentrating his troops at the river, but the threat had been removed from Richmond. For the next month, camped at Harrison's Landing, Twichell and most of the rest of the army assumed the offensive would resume at some point.

a rebel Captain of [Brig. Gen. J. E. B.] Stuart's Cavalry: Stuart was a famous and dashing cavalry general. Starting on 12 June, while the two armies faced each other east of Richmond, Stuart rode his twelve hundred horsemen entirely around McClellan's army.

I hinted . . . of our Commander: Because Twichell speaks of national policy here, and the importance of making the "free, Northern, *conscience* . . . a recognised element in the guidance of it," it can be surmised he is speaking about Lincoln, because the president is designated commander in chief in the U.S. Constitution. The issue of conscience he refers to is probably the freeing of the slaves, something Lincoln had been reluctant to do early in the war, to the chagrin of New England abolitionists.

In Camp—Near Harrison's Landing. Va. July 9th 1862.

Dear Father,

A blue-pill last night, salts and senna this morning,° aided and abetted by the most ardent sun I ever saw, render the limits of my operations today exceedingly narrow. The grasshopper is a burden, and I shall adhere to a horizontal posture until the cool of evening, unless the Southern Confederacy makes some hostile demonstration sooner. Do not for a moment think that I am sick. I am only using precautions against it. A general sluggish feeling, with great disinclination to activity, told me that I was getting bilious, so without waiting for developments I instantly took the ancient, orthodox road out of the woods, which I have above indicated. . . .

My establishment is now by no means gorgeous. All our baggage, except such as we could carry on our horses, was ordered to be abandoned, consequently I am now existing on the simplest elements both of food and shelter. A piece of an old tent rudely supported on sticks is my sole habitation, while a tin cup, plate and pan comprehend my whole stock of kitchen and table furniture. The fact, however, is scarcely noticed or thought of in the midst of so many considerations of such a serious character that they crowd all ordinary cares into nothingness. We have not yet succeeded in folding our wings smoothly, after so long a flight. . . . While on the perilous way, with an exultant, multitudinous and blood-thirsty enemy surging angrily upon our rear, there was little time to think, but now that there is a pause and our new post is reached, the army does not cast itself at length along the ground, listless and empty-minded, but, yet panting with toil, asks the when and why and where. . . . Systematic deceits and false representations which have been imposed on the nation, and which have hitherto been denied exposure by censorship of the press, have had their day, at least I think so. Take for instance the correspondence and editorials of the New York Herald regarding this late movement. In many and important points they lie. Not only are facts garbled and dressed-up, but many things are affirmed which are fiction and falsehood. Blunders, palpable blunders and acknowledged at the time, before they get to public eyes and ears, are converted into the successful and anticipated developments of a determined plan. Humbug! Humbug! Humbug! It is beginning to leak out now and ere long it will be all uncovered. Think of what our army was when it rose from winter quarters in the spring. How magnificent and strong!

After the retreat to the James River, the Army of the Potomac waited at Harrison's Landing for the advance on Richmond to resume. *Harper's Weekly* artist Alfred R. Waud sketched members of the Excelsior Brigade in a log building where soldiers helped African American washerwomen fold sheets. Ultimately, President Lincoln ordered the army back to northern Virginia. (Library of Congress)

Three months have passed—months of battle and toil—months that drank our blood, consumed our treasure and filled our land with mourning, and where are we, what is left of us? What has been accomplished to offset the fearful cost? These are plain questions, and the men all answer them for themselves. Upon no one head does the blame all rest if blame there is. It is idle to charge it to the abolitionists, equally so to visit it upon the Government, or Gen. McClellan. One thing is certain, it has not been such a pull all together, as we shall be forced to yet. The course of Providence is often mysterious, but I think I can behold Divine Justice in this reverse, without drawing much on my faith for support. It has rebuked a pride which needed crushing as much as the rebellion. Suppose we had stormed Richmond a month since and all disloyal violence had ceased to show its face within our borders, I can scarcely imagine the disgraceful scene that would have followed in our own midst. How much pseudo-patriotism would have been unveiled, to betray its real ignominy of selfishness! What a clamorous rush for the spoils there would have been! What a canvassing of Claims! You are right, I firmly believe, in predicting that in the end, when it does come, the overcoming emotion will be disgust of war and an universal welcome of Peace. God grant that we may soon hear the rustling of her blessed wings, but not till we are worthy of her abode with us.

We are getting rested now and the face of things is brightening. Our line of defences has so far progressed that we have no fears of disaster here. The flanks rest on the river and supported by gunboats are supposed to be out of all danger. The pickets of the enemy are about a mile from here, but what their force is I have heard no reliable estimate. The sick and wounded who suffered indescribably during the movement and for three days after we reached here, are now either sent away or comfortably cared for. The Assistant Surgeon of our 1st Regt., Dr. [James] Ash, has been assigned to us for the present—a decided improvement on anything we ever had. I am anxious to hear some word of those we left behind, yet hope that all is well. The poverty of the rebels in medical stores and their immense need of them will probably put our boys on short allowance, while their distance from Richmond and the difficulty of transportation, even with a willing mind, suggests some apprehensions concerning their subsistence. It is presumed, however, that they were not permitted to remain just where we left them, on this very account.

I hardly dare to think of what may have been the fate of many poor boys left wounded along the track of the retreat. As our boys stood on picket Tuesday night at Malvern Hill where the fight had raged all day, they heard their pitiful groaning and cries for help, yet were not allowed to go to them. Federals and Confederates lay together, and the voice of their suffering as it rose on the still night air was a fearful sound. God alone knows the deep horrors of that time. Creeping away into the woods, many cried and moaned, and writhed and died, with no eye to pity save that of the Heavenly Father. That experience of a week made our army at least six months older as soldiers. That is one redeeming feature of all hardship. There is no doubt that 30,000 of our troops, as they now are, are more efficient than 40 or 50,000 as they were when they left winter quarters. Experience tells on a soldier peculiarly. . . . One great disadvantage hitherto has been that, while the rebels are not more courageous than our troops, they have been the best fighters, but this difference is fast vanishing. In another respect the generals of the enemy have surpassed ours, and that is in shrinking from no cost of life where a point can be carried. This is a quality born of desperation and with us there is yet no soil of circumstances out of which the same can grow. Many and many a time have the Confederate ranks been marched right up in the face of our grape and canister, when every discharge mowed a wide gap through their lines, yet without halting or breaking. In this way have positions supposed impregnable been carried, with dreadful loss to the enemy it is true and with little to us, but *carried*. This character of their fighting accounts for their enormous losses which I think are not generally over-estimated by our dispatches. It is not hard to explain. The ungodly ambition of which the rebellion is a hideous outgrowth, is recklessly lavish of what it cares little about—the deluded rank and file of the Confederate army. If every one of them perished it were of little account so that the leaders survived victorious. It is different with us. Every head that bows in battle is that of a citizen of the free Republic. Each man fights for what is dear to *him* personally and he in turn is dear to the nation as a son to whom his equal share of the universal inheritance is due. From all that I have seen and can gather, I conclude that the Confederate loss in killed and wounded since we arrived before Richmond is nearly thrice our own. On the retreat, when they were more than usually bold, there were times when from positions of comparative safety our artillerists slaughtered them by hundreds. God grant, that if the day is coming when our soldiers must be cast more thickly into the jaws of death, it may not be with any smaller view of the value of their lives or their dignity as citizens! . . .

I am happy to say that, so far as I can judge, the troops are in excellent humor—especially with *themselves*. Whatever opinions may prevail regarding the conduct of affairs at *Headquarters*, the army is satisfied with *itself* and justly. McClellan does well to be proud of his command, whether or no the pride is *reciprocal*. His proclamation, so full of laudation, was received with as much quiet complacency, as a man would pocket a debt duly paid. It was somewhat so yesterday when President Lincoln and Secretary [of War Edwin M.] Stanton paid us a visit.° As they rode along the lines the boys cheered stoutly like good, loyal soldiers, but there was the feeling—"We are the chaps to be admired! It is you, Abraham and Edwin, that ought to do the cheering!" The visit of our good President was a surprise. At about the middle of the afternoon a salute fired by the gunboats announced his coming, we were called out into line, and before night-fall he went the rounds. The first real information of his arrival I received was from colored Ben whom we "stole" out of Maryland. He was out foraging and came in, his black face all shining and cloven with a mighty grin, and with keen delight informed me, "Ise seen ole Uncle Linkum!" It is wonderful how these negro slaves contract their political views. Ben says that he never heard a *white* man in Maryland speak of Mr Lincoln in any terms except those of denunciation. He was described to the negroes as a monster, yet in those simple hearts the President attained the reverence due to a benefactor—and that without any abolition tracts or teachings. They hardly accounted him a real man, but rather as some half mythical, far-off omen of good, which some day would break the clouds above them. Simple minds apprehend *persons* rather than *principles*, and Ben says that when our Division came to the Lower Potomac the slaves did not regard it as the *Union Army* but as a visible sign of the coming of the long expected, benign reign of "ole Uncle Linkum." The story moistened my eyes.

I have seldom witnessed a more ludicrous sight than our worthy Chief Magistrate presented on horseback yesterday. While I lifted my cap with real respect for the man raised up by God to rule our troubled time, I lowered it speedily to cover a smile that overmastered me. McClellan was beside him, stout, short, and stiffly erect, sitting his horse like a dragoon, and the contrast was perfect. It did seem as though every moment the Presidential limbs would become entangled with those of the horse he rode and both come down together, while his arms were apparently subject to similar mishaps. That arm with which he drew the rein, in its angles and position, resembled the hind leg of a grasshopper—the hand before—the elbow away back over the horse's tail. The removal of his hat before each regiment was also a source of laughter in the style of its execution—the quick trot of the horse making it a feat of some difficulty, while, from the same cause, his hold on it, while off, seemed very precarious. I shall remember the picture a long time. But *the boys* liked him, in fact his popularity in the army is and has been universal. Many of our rulers and leaders fall into odium but all have faith in Lincoln. "When *he* finds it out," they say, "it will be stopped." I heard officers yesterday make the earnest remark, "With all their palaver and reviews, and Dukes and Princes, I don't believe they'll be able to pull the wool over old Lincoln's eyes." His benignant smile as he passed us by was a real reflection from his honest, kindly heart, but deeper, under the surface of that marked and not all uncomely face were the signs of care and anxiety. God bless the man, and give answer to the prayers for guidance I am sure he offers.

Joe has gone and I feel lonesome. He was with me a year lacking two weeks. . . . I say nothing about coming home for I have nothing to say more than what I last wrote. Love to all. Joseph.

A blue-pill last night, salts and senna this morning: Also known as blue mass, blue pill was a potent mixture of mercury and herbs. *The Medical and Surgical History of the War of the Rebellion* (Washington: Government Printing Office, 1879) says the use of purgatives such as blue pill, senna, and Epsom salts in cases of diarrhea was believed to "increase the diminished hepatic secretion . . . [and] modify favorably the condition of the intestinal mucous membrane."

President Lincoln and Secretary [of War Edwin M.] Stanton paid us a visit: Lincoln visited the camp to gauge the strategic situation and to consult with the army's generals. His and Stanton's observations helped them decide to order the withdrawal from the Peninsula soon afterward. McClellan took the opportunity to urge on Lincoln a conciliatory policy toward the South.

In Camp—Near Harrison's Landing, Va. July 19th 1862.

Dear Father, . . .

Important and exciting events with us succeed each other so rapidly that the experience of one day, by its engrossing excitement, throws a speedy veil of dimness over the day preceding and its record. . . .

We have settled down into unwonted quiet. Since I wrote the regiment has been relieved of picket duty and we have gone into camp on the brow of a smooth hill with here and there a huge pine tree to mitigate the sufferings of the burning noontide heat. We are just behind the breast-works, but the pickets are [a] mile beyond and report no enemy but an occasional cavalry squad, so we digest our food calmly and sleep in peace. It really calls to mind the palmy days of Camp Selkirk. Martial music is no longer forbidden and morn and eve sweet sounds from a hundred instruments are borne upon the languid air. Now and then a boom from the gunboats far or near keeps us from forgetting the business in hand, but the weary watching and incessant harassment of Fair Oaks no longer afflict us. The men are resting and, God knows, how much they need it. How long we are to enjoy the luxury, we cannot even guess. We are not anxious to have it continued much beyond the healing of our weari-ness, for a thousand homes unite us and delay is irksome. The feeling while we were immediately before Richmond was, "a few days, a great battle, a decisive victory, and it will be over. Lead us on! For it is toward home!" Now there is a prevailing disappointment, not so much that Richmond is not taken, but that the prospect of war lengthens before us. How many will live to cross their own threshold is yet to be revealed.

There is a great deal of talk now about the Brigade being sent away to some garrison or fort to recruit. Gen. Sickles has certainly been making effort to effect it, and is now absent in Washington on this business probably. I hardly entertain the idea that such an event is possible, yet the General has a way of getting what he wants. His difficulties with Gov. Morgan° and his strenuous maintenance of the position that we are independent of any state authority will operate to prevent the filling of our wasted ranks by means of the new state levy [of volunteers]. On the other hand we cannot remain as we are. Five separate regimental organizations cannot be continued with only 2000 effective men (we had 4500). Consolidation is not to be thought of for it would unjustly cast out brave and deserving officers. After all, the only apparent method of recovering our strength is to let us go to some convenient place, and fill up on our own hook. Should such a thing happen, it will probably enable me to pay you a visit of respectable length. . . .

Here are Dr. McAllister and Dr. Powell safe back again!° It is a happy event, and the regiment for the first time in many weeks is conscious of a joyous emo-tion. I have seldom in my life experienced a keener pleasure . . . than I did a few minutes ago when those two good friends walked into camp. . . . They were left [behind Confederate lines] . . . with very little constraint upon their move-ments until July 10th, when they were hurriedly removed to Richmond with their patients. From the time of their arrival in the city till they were sent aboard a boat yesterday morning, they were subjected [to] great discomforts and ill-treatment. Cramped in narrow quarters, they toiled like slaves from morning till night in stifling wards filled with our wounded—and in want of the most indispensable means of successful practice. Hundreds of our brave fellows who had lost limbs and been otherwise hurt, were lying so thick together that it was impossible to get at them properly, while the air foul from their festering sores was like the breath of a pestilence. Even stimulants in sufficient quantity were denied them, and many were dying for want of it. So great was this lack of nec-essaries that at length it was deemed advisable to stop operating, since in the absence of restoratives it only hastened the death of the poor fellows. This state of things the Doctors attribute partly to the multitudes of wounded collected in the city, but principally to the fact that Union soldiers are the objects of little care to the Confederate Authorities. How different from our conduct under like circumstances. A few days since, the enemy sent a flag of truce asking to be relieved of our wounded and a boat was sent up. This trip will be repeated till all or nearly all are removed. . . . The morning they came away, while the wounded were being conveyed on board the boat, a very interesting young lady approached Dr. McAllister and engaged him in conversation. She had some bandages and a few luxuries which she, with a few other females, was dispensing to the wounded. After a little general talk, the Doctor perceived that her political sympathies were with the objects of her charity. In answer to a question she stated her opinion that there were 10,000 Unionists in Richmond who dared not reveal themselves even to each other—so jealous is the Government of any look or sign not in sympathy with the rebellion. . . . The rations they were allowed were inferior in quality, and insufficient in quantity, but it was permitted to visit a neighboring market under guard, and purchase. The following are some of the prices° paid by Dr. McAllister.

Butter—	$1 pr.lb.	Eggs	1.00 doz.
Sugar 75.	[cts.] pr. lb.	Squash	1.00 doz.
Coffee	2.50 pr.lb.	Cucumbers	1.00 doz.
Beets	50. [cts.] bunch (5 or 6)	Carrots	30 cts. bunch (5 or 6)
Potatoes	50.c[ts]. quart	Asparagus	50 cts. bunch large as 4 fingers

A few days [of] such foraging as this would have emptied their pockets, and the prospect of subsequent existence was very slim. As luck would have it, though, they got off in the first boat and here they are contented and happy. They learned to their satisfaction that the enemy hates us, and have no doubt that the fighting will wax in bitterness till the end.

I have so far omitted to state that Dr. McGowan was released with the other Surgeons. . . . [S]uch was the regimental opinion of him that his reception was far from enthusiastic. I fear he is far from a noble man, although he is a skilful surgeon.

Col. Hall is in command of the Brigade during the absence of Gen. Sickles, consequently [Lt.] Col. Potter commands the Regt.—a very acceptable change to the most. I have had so much else to occupy my letters of late that I have said little about our regimental difficulties, nor have I regretted being able to avoid so disagreeable a topic. Internal peace has so long been a stranger here that we have ceased to miss its absence. . . . Give my love to all. May God bless and keep you. Your aff. Son. Joseph.

His difficulties with Gov. Morgan: Sickles had feuded with the New York governor ever since his independent appeal to Lincoln to designate the Excelsior Brigade as United States Volunteers at the beginning of the war.

Here are Dr. McAllister and Dr. Powell safe back again!: The two surgeons had been captured with the wounded at Savage's Station on 29 June and held in Richmond. Because neither side could deal with large numbers of prisoners early in the war, both sides used a system of parole and exchange: a prisoner swore not to take up arms again until formally exchanged for an enemy prisoner of equal rank.

The following are some of the prices: As in the letter of 16 May, Twichell is impressing Edward Twichell with inflated prices in the Confederacy. In New England at the time, one might expect to pay thirty-nine cents a pound for butter, twelve cents a pound for sugar, seven to twenty-five cents a pound for coffee, and thirty cents a dozen for eggs.

In Camp. Sunday night. July 20th 1862.

Dear Father,

The gods are propitious. My application for leave of absence has returned approved. Tomorrow, God willing, I shall start for Washington where my wardrobe is, and I trust to be able to make a descent on the Hudson River Institute by the evening of the 23rd or morning of the 24th. Will it be safe to appear unannounced? Will Sis survive the shock? . . . Probably I can remain at home till the 31st, but must imperatively start to return on the 1st of August. I never felt so much like a boy with delight as I do over this blissful turn of fortune's wheel. I need rest both of body and mind and shall hope to gain it before I come back. . . . In view of my seeing you face to face so soon, the pen seems unusually inadequate and I stop to bid you good night. God bless you all.

Your aff. Son. Joseph.

Twichell was granted a ten-day leave to deliver nearly five thousand dollars in pay to soldiers in hospitals in the North and to soldiers' families. But his clear personal reasons were to attend his sister Sarah Jane's graduation from the Hudson River Institute, to visit his family in Southington, and to attend the triennial reunion of the Yale class of 1859. He extended the visit into August by doing recruiting work in New York City, at one point sneaking onto the same platform as Sickles at the Seventh Regiment Armory, where the general made a speech of an hour and a half. He visited the wounded in hospitals in New York and New Jersey and visited soldiers' families before returning to Harrison's Landing by boat from Baltimore on 12 August. "I laid in a good store of messages, knicknacks, and children's kisses (not always cleanly) to be disbursed on my arrival at the regiment," he wrote.

In Camp. Wednesday night. August 13th 1862.

Dear Father,

I reached Harrisons Landing last night but so late that I did not go ashore till morning. At 9 o'clock I reported to [Lt.] Col. Potter and exchanged warm greetings with a goodly number of the regiment, both officers and men, the latter not less hearty or acceptable than the former. My sensations were extremely like those I felt on crossing the threshold at home, for after all the 2nd Excelsior is for the time the house in which I live and the abode of some of my quickest affections. . . .

> Twichell gives a lengthy account of his time since leaving the family, and before returning to the regiment. He concludes:

After passing Saturday and Sunday nights [in Washington] with my class mate Arthur Wood . . . I went up to Baltimore Monday afternoon, and took the night boat for Fort Monroe. Almost the first man I met aboard was Father O'Hagan likewise returning. Several other Chaplains were also at hand and the passage was a pleasant one. Some of my Protestant brethren were considerably amused that the Father and I occupied the same state room, seeming to think that some how or other Popery was of a gaseous or odorous nature calculated to hinder sound sleep. . . .

Again we are on the move. A large portion of the army has departed by transports and by land and the rest are soon to follow—tomorrow perhaps. Our goods are all packed and a few minutes notice is all we want. Whither? is the general inquiry, only to demonstrate the general ignorance. Col. [William R.] Brewster [of the 4th Excelsior] and some other officers came down from Richmond today.° They saw 30 of Pope's officers taken in the late battle,° who affirm that Pope was whipped. This is not regarded as conclusive evidence yet it sounds bad. We shall see. . . .

Col. Hall is in arrest again, on new charges. The fact has no novelty to give it interest. I am very tired indeed, and had I not feared a move to-morrow I should have put off writing. Having a thousand things to say, yet scant both in time, space and energy, I will close with a short-range grape and canister discharge of love to all hands. I remain. Your aff. Son. Joseph.

---

came down from Richmond today: Brewster and other officers had also been captured and paroled.

officers taken in the late battle: On 9 August Confederate generals Thomas J. "Stonewall" Jackson and A. P. Hill defeated an attack by General Nathaniel P. Banks at Cedar Mountain,

Virginia. The battle effectively shifted the eastern theater of war from the Peninsula to the line of the Rappahannock River, halfway between Washington and Richmond.

Near Yorktown. August 21st 1862.

Dear Father,

Here we are, retracing, retracing, retracing° steps that cost blood and glorious young life. It almost broke my heart to go by Williamsburg again. I seemed to hear the gallant fellows calling from the woods to hail us on our way. So you see the splendid "change of base" was all poppycock. I thought so at the time. I am told that we are bound for [Maj. Gen. Ambrose E.] Burnside who, when last heard from, was at Culpepper C[ourt] H[ouse]. All right! Burnside isn't afraid to fight. If I understand the move, McClellan's star is waning fast. After all, he may be worthy of better success, poor fellow. I have no right to say otherwise, although I can't think of the 30,000 corpses we leave behind without a bitter thought. The 30,000 corpses stand for a million sighs and tears which will not be stopped for a score of years.

We have been six days on the march, ever since last Friday morning. Taking it all in all it has been a great affair. For a whole day our division picketed the main road from Richmond just where it crosses the Chickahominy, expecting the enemy every moment, but he did not show himself. It would have been a bitter fight, for we had no place to retreat to. It has been in some respects a great march. Two days in succession we made about 20 miles through heat and dust indescribable. The boys couldn't have done it in the spring. We do not feel as if we were retreating, only, at last, going to work in earnest. I think that the fall campaign is to be an affair of strict business.

We shall probably embark today for the Potomac i.e. if our turn comes. The General is not yet with us but will probably appear before we find fighting. . . . Good-bye to the Peninsula! Its memories will abide while life does. The Conn. 5th appears to have seen a dreadful day at Cedar Mountain. . . . Love to all. Write often. In great haste. Your aff. Son. Joseph.

Here we are, retracing, retracing, retracing: At the end of July, Lincoln and Stanton had decided to withdraw McClellan's troops from the Peninsula—where the general had continued to delay and ask for reinforcements—to join with the army of General John Pope in northern Virginia.

August–December 1862

The battle of Cedar Mountain marked the beginning of the Second Bull Run Campaign. As Twichell surmised in his letter of 21 August 1862, McClellan's star had indeed waned. To reinforce General Pope as he opposed General Lee, the troops that had spent the long, hot summer at Harrison's Landing were ordered to the area near Manassas Junction, where the first Bull Run had been fought. After the long, disappointing march back down the Peninsula, the Second Excelsior boarded boats with the rest of the army and landed on the Virginia shore at Alexandria, just downriver from Washington.

About 4 miles below Manassas Junction, Va.
Aug. 28th 1862.

Dear Father,

We left Alexandria by R.R. Monday night and were set down at 2 o'clock in the morning in a field just beyond Warrenton Junction. It was a cold night ride, so much so that I had no emotion to spare for Manassas or Bull Run or patriotism generally, being wholly occupied in a protracted shiver on the top of a baggage car. Next day . . . orders were received that we should make ready to march at 6 o'clock with three days rations, leaving all baggage behind. Rumors were prevalent that the Rail Road over which we had just passed had been seized by the enemy in force at this point from which I now write. . . . Still we started at the time designated with our whole Division and a brigade of Kearney's, almost in the dark with reference to our destination and prospects. The day was hot and dusty and as mile after mile of retrograde was passed, the rations began to grow heavy, and as no enemy appeared, we began to feel victimized. . . . Another weary stretch brought us . . . in contact with the enemies videttes.° Our skirmishers soon brought a sharp rattling of musketry, the order of battle was . . . resumed, and in ten minutes we were in the hottest fight yet within our experience.° It has been a dreadful battle to us. For an hour and a quarter it raged incessantly and our Brigade was fearfully cut up. Artillery from three sides mowed through our lines, the woods all about poured deadly bullets in showers and, when unable to withstand the fierce onsets of our lads, the enemy fell back, the field was a sight which tempered our exaltation with the sorrow of affliction. Our regiment suffered severely especially in officers, [Lt.] Col. Potter, Lieut. [James W.] Powell, Lieut. [James J.] Webb, Lieut. [Benjamin] Franklin, Capt. [William H.] Greene, were wounded, Lieut. [John S.] Lowentrout was killed and Lieut. [Terance] Murphy wounded to death probably. Eleven privates were killed, a number more are dying, and some 40 hit. I am at this place with two surgeons attending the poor fellows. Some of our best men are among the disabled and I see not how we can recover from the shock. If filled up it will be another regiment. The conduct of the regiment and Brigade was all that their best lovers could desire. Under a most deadly fire they maneuvered with a coolness and precision that pertains alone to veterans. I went in with them and remained till the wounded claimed my attention. Again I have to record the mercy of God in delivering me from great peril. For a space of fifteen minutes I expected every minute to be hit. The sound of the bullets was like the humming of bees, while the roaring, crackling, shells plunged and burst on every side. I thank God, my dear Father, that I am alive to tell you this.

[Lt.] Col. Potter was splendid. He rose from a sick bed and *marched* to the field (8 miles), was wounded very painfully in the arm almost immediately, but continued at his post and fought like a demon till the end. Would that we had an army like him. The dressings of our wounded, where I could assist, were finished by 5 o'clock. I then went to the poor Confederates and worked as long as I could see. By nine o'clock I was perfectly used up, and laid amid the horrors of a hospital, and with agonised groans growing fainter in my ears, slept the deep sleep of exhaustion. Again and again during the day was my heart moved to its lowest deeps at the evidences I received that my boys love me, even while dying, and my gratitude was full when I saw that no religious differences were even hinted when I pointed to the Lamb of God. I am the only Chaplain with the Brigade, Mr. Bulkley not having returned and Father O'Hagan having attempted to make the journey by water and failed to reach us.

I must close. I have written now, when it is very inconvenient, for a specific purpose. Something is going on I know not what. All day baggage and troops have been pouring by toward Alexandria. . . . There is something brewing.

The baggage we left day before yesterday has been burned. If I mistake not there is a general falling back. I am here with the boys, and shall not leave them whatever happens. If the army passes and leaves us behind, I shall remain as a prisoner, so if you should not hear from me in a long time, do not be alarmed. . . . My love to all. I know you will pray for me that my strength do not fail and that my faith increase. Begging pardon for my haste. I remain. Your aff. Son. Joseph.

the enemies videttes: "Videttes" is a variant of "vedettes," or outlying sentries.

the hottest fight yet within our experience: A rapid advance by Jackson along the railroad toward Manassas Junction, which was at that point in Union hands and a major supply depot, resulted in the capture of Bristoe or Bristow's Station. In the bitter fighting, the Second Excelsior lost 114 killed, wounded, and missing.

Washington. Sept. 2nd 1862.

My dear Father,

I wrote you a letter on the 28th of Aug from the field hospital where were most [of] our men wounded in battle on the 27th. I hardly think it has reached you, for all mail communication with the army is much embarrassed. At the time of writing I fully expected that we would all fall into the hands of the enemy, as our forces were pressing on toward Manassas, and thus far no means for transporting the wounded had been furnished. . . . As it turned out we escaped the untoward adventures of captivity and I am here, much worn in body and sad of soul, but having much cause of gratitude to the God of all mercies. Perhaps it will be well to recapitulate in brief the events of which my last letter treated, so as to make later transactions more intelligible. We left Alexandria Monday afternoon last week—reached Warrenton Junction Tuesday morning at two o'clock—marched back next morning (our Division and a brigade of Kearney's) to Kettle Run—10 miles—and engaged the enemy at 11 o'clock. After a sharp, bloody, but splendidly fought battle of an hour and a quarter, the rebels fled leaving their wounded on the field. The conduct of the Brigade, but especially of the regiment, was gallant in the extreme. Our dead, with but few exceptions, fell in line with their feet to the foe and many of the wounded fought until loss of blood made it no longer possible. . . . Our loss was heavy. Only 250 or thereabouts went in; and of these between 80 and 100 were killed or wounded. . . . Artillery, we had none, while the enemy had three batteries well posted. It was an unequal combat and nothing but valor could have prevailed. I say "we," for under the circumstances it seemed best that I go with the boys, and I remained in the fearful storm of grape, canister and bullets, until I saw the wounded borne off. Ever since it has seemed to me a miracle that I escaped. It was a miracle. Thursday and Friday were passed in ministering to the souls and bodies of dying, stricken men, and in performing burial rites. . . . The men *all* died without murmuring. I was amazed at the lofty patriotism which some of them exhibited in their dying hour. It was something of which [I] had not supposed them capable. One man, a fine fellow—[John] Fitzpatrick of Co. A.—said to me, "Chaplain! I leave a wife and four children. My old woman and I always lived together happily and I love the young ones, but I could not die better and I leave them with the Lord," and added shortly, "They as raised this war have done a great wickedness, but if God forgives them, I have no right to give them . . . hard thoughts."

Saturday morning, the rail road was so repaired that all the wounded were placed on a train and taken down 1½ miles to Bristows Station, where they were transferred to ambulances and baggage wagons. Some were taken to Fairfax Station and there put again on board the cars, but the most were driven directly through to Washington. I secured an ambulance for Lieuts. Powell, Franklin and Webb and came on with them. It was a journey which I shall never forget. At Centreville all was confusion. All the cowards and stragglers of the army were congregated there, and everybody spoke of disaster. Working our way through, we drove out into the country. It was a sad procession. Every jolt of the wagons brought out piteous groans and shrieks of agony. No one who has not experienced or witnessed the same can imagine the suffering. I cannot describe the relief I felt when my charge was safely housed. . . . I should have returned immediately to look after the regiment, had I not myself been ill. I am much better today and shall probably go over to Alexandria tonight, and start for Centreville in the morning. It is supposed there will be a great battle today or tomorrow. I think it will be a decisive one, and have good hope for its issue. It has been *the* week of the war. Our blood is poured out like water. God grant that we may be near the end. . . . Love to all. Your aff. Son. Joseph.

Washington. Sept. 5th 1862.

Dear Father,

Perhaps you are surprised that I am still here. I did not anticipate so long a tarry when I wrote last, but was ruled by unforeseen circumstances. In the first place I have been quite unwell, so much so that the Doctor strongly counselled me not to return to the regiment immediately as I had intended. In the second place, I found that I could be very useful to the wounded officers whom I brought here as well as many of the men who are in hospital. The city is so full of the suffering victims of the late battles that, unless a man cares for his own, they are in danger of meeting, if not neglect, at least a small share of attention. . . . I also felt at liberty to remain from the fact that the regiment has not been engaged since I left, nor is it likely to be soon, unless a general engagement takes place in front of Washington. It now lies about two miles beyond Alexandria very near where it encamped before taking the cars for Warrenton Junction last week. . . .

My own health is not so bad as the mention of it might lead you to fear. . . . A diarrhea from which I have not been wholly free since I came home [in late July], aggravated by the vicissitudes of the journey from the peninsula and by the excessive fatigues of our never-to-be-forgotten *battle week* in Virginia, had quite taken the energy out of me by the time my groaning charge was safely housed last Sunday morning. I then felt that to return to the field before it was checked might expose me to the danger of its becoming chronic, and the Doctor concurred. I have since been taking medicine [and] dieting. . . . Already my strength and appetite have come to the surface, and I have every reason to expect that in a few days I shall be in fighting trim. . . .

I wrote to you that I had heard of the engagement of our regiment again on Friday,° but had no particulars. I have since seen several of the men who were taken prisoners and paroled at that time, also some officers of the Regt. Notwithstanding the great hardships already undergone and the terrible fight just over, the boys earned themselves fresh laurels and, as before, at the cost of life and wounds. Heroic actions were the order of the day. The color bearer, who on Wednesday received the sacred charge from a wounded predecessor, after conducting himself with a gallantry that will long be spoken of among us (waving the flag at its full height with cheery shouts etc.) received his mortal wound. He fell, but raising himself with a desperate, dying effort, hugging the tattered ensign to his bosom, he handed it formally to a comrade in the color-guard and sank to the earth a corpse. His name was John James. Few will know of this brave fellow, few will admire or mourn him, but some rough brother-campaigners will always thrill to think of his glorious death. . . .

On Saturday again the regiment was under a dreadful fire of artillery without being able to use their arms—the severest test of courage. On this occasion also the 2nd Excelsior was true to itself. . . . The fight of Friday I heard but could not see. All day the roar of cannon was in our ears as we tended our dying and suffering lads. On Saturday however, as we dragged painfully along the stony roads, the panorama of battle was spread out in the valley before us. Smoke enveloped everything so that we could not *see* the lines of battle, but I can never forget how my heart and my hopes went down into those sulphurous clouds, and how incessantly my prayer to heaven was ejaculated that God would pity the nation. Far into the night we could discern the livid flashes of artillery and it was not till Centreville was passed that we had darkness and silence.

Kearney is dead!° Let the nation mourn! To us it seems to *crown* all recent disasters. Phil Kearney and Joe Hooker were the men who, yoked, could move anything. They were the complements of each other. With much love to all I remain.

Joseph.

the engagement of our regiment again on Friday: In the Second Battle of Bull Run over the long weekend of August 29–30, Pope's forces were decisively defeated by Jackson's, who were aided by Confederate troops coming up from the Peninsula.

Kearney is dead!: The much-admired General Philip Kearney died in a battle at Chantilly, Virginia, in the aftermath of Second Bull Run.

In a 7 September letter, Twichell comments further to his father on the state of the regiment.

The Division was two days since ordered to cook three days' rations and be ready to march again, but Gen. Hooker caused the Surgeons to draw up a statement to the effect, that his command was unfit for more active field duty° at present and the order was countermanded. Only think of it! We left the Lower Potomac with 13,000 men, and two regiments were added on the Peninsula. Now rations are drawn for less than 4,000. Yet, the General [Hooker] has been as careful of his command as he could be. I perceive that he is now in high favour both with the Government and the public and it is just. His command is to be much enlarged,° in fact has already been, but I doubt if he will ever take his right eye off his old Division whose bayonets have wrought him so much renown. It was as it should be—a good General had a good Division. I regret exceedingly that Gen. Sickles was not with his Brigade in the late battles. I am sure had he anticipated so sharp work, so soon after our landing at Alexandria, he would have slipped all other business for the time to lead us. It is said that he has 1200 recruits and the prospect of enough to restore our numbers completely. I hope so. . . . I say nothing about my opinion of recent events, or those now pending, because I have no opinion. I am confused and confounded. If God designs our deliverance, it will in due time be accomplished, and no *man* will do it. I am content to wait. The best sign of the times seems to me the absence of all idea of giving up. . . .

his command was unfit for more active field duty: Exhausted and depleted by more than two-thirds of its men, the division sat out the next major campaign of the war—the Maryland Campaign, which culminated in the bloody Battle of Antietam on 17 September.

His command is to be much enlarged: In a reshuffling of military leadership, Hooker had been given command of the Third Corps of the Army of Virginia on 6 September. Shortly afterward the corps was redesignated the First Corps of the Army of the Potomac.

Washington—Sunday night. Sept. 14th 1862.

Dear Father,

I did not expect when I wrote last to date another letter from here. . . . My health is perfectly recovered. . . . Somehow or other I did not get through my pastoral visits till afternoon, then Capt. Murphy came to me with the request that I go with a flag of truce today after his brother's body. This detained me a little. Then it appeared not to be certain that the flag could go and I waited to find out; then it was decided that no truce could be negotiated at all owing to various blocks. That being settled, it was almost dark . . . so I concluded to stay, little pleased that it seemed best. I now purpose to start tomorrow morning, unless it pours. . . .

The wounded officers are doing well as could be expected. Col. Potter is not yet sure of his hand, nor Lieut. Webb of his arm, but both cases are hopeful. . . . Lieuts. Powell and Franklin are able to sit up a little. . . . I never look at these honourable wounds without thinking that, although war is a nation's curse, it is not wholly an evil thing that young men have been brought out from behind desks and counters and ploughs to walk through fearful perils and show that valor still resides in American bosoms. If God delivers us, at length, from utter ruin, the generations coming after will have sprung from the loins of heroes and bear the stamp thereof.

The whole aspect of the city is exactly the counterpart of what it was a year ago. I daily witness scenes which blot the last twelve months from my memory by reviving so freshly the sensations attending our coming. New regiments pour in night and day, looking just as I suppose we did. The heavy rumble of baggage wagons is unceasing and the old processes of preparation are evident on every hand. Yet it is not the same, after all. In many important respects I see these things differently. The spring and summer campaign have educated in me a military eye. These new levies come marching in with clean clothes and shining arms and each man feels the soldier, no doubt, and in time many of them will become such, but I have learned what a soldier should be, how he should look, and with all my hearty welcome to these fellows, I am often forced to smile at the sight of them. "Ah! Boys, your eyes are yet to be opened and your

After the Excelsior Brigade took part in the battles of Bristoe Station and Second Bull Run in August–September 1862, Sickles travelled to New York to recruit new members for his depleted regiments. He offered bounties for those who signed up. (Collection of the New-York Historical Society, PR-055-3-235, ac 03235)

views slightly altered on the subjects of bearing arms for your country." . . .
Sadder thoughts than this, of course, creep in, to quench any merriment which
may suggest itself. The man who has seen Williamsburg and Fairoaks, June 25th
[Oak Grove] and Malvern Hill, Bristows Bridge [sic] and Bull Run No 2, has
little laughter for men starting on a similar round of experience. "God bless
them! And have mercy upon them!" is the hourly language of my full heart as
they file by. . . . My love to all. . . . Joseph.

In Camp. Sunday night. Sept. 21st 1862.

My dear Father,

Once more I have passed a real happy Sabbath with my regiment—opening
with divine service and closing with a large and solemn prayer-meeting. . . .
I doubt whether a Protestant religious teacher ever had such a foothold in
the midst of a Catholic community. . . . Mr. Bulkley has resigned. I was both
surprised and sorry to hear it. Probably he has good reasons for so doing but
I cannot think that many who leave their regiments in the midst of a harsh
campaign are right in doing so. . . .

The loss of Gen. Hooker from the field is a serious matter.° We have no
good Generals to spare. . . . Our Brigade is beginning to look well again, but
still very small, although some recruits have arrived. Gen. Taylor (promoted
Col. of the 3rd Regt.) is in command and shows great administrative ability.
We begin to look for action again.

I could not for a moment think of leaving this regiment, unless it were to
take *the sword* elsewhere. . . . Love to all. May God bless you. Your aff. Son.
Joseph.

The loss of Gen. Hooker . . . a serious matter: At Antietam, Hooker was seriously wounded
in the foot.

In Camp—near Alexandria, Va.
Sunday afternoon. Sept. 28th 1862.

Dear Father,

The Regiment went on picket yesterday morning and returned at about
noon today. Service on that account was delayed till afternoon, and still further till evening by an order from Headquarters calling out the Brigade at 4
o'clock for inspection and parade. I have decided to dispense with preaching
and make the evening's exercise a prayer meeting, for the reason that I believe
it will do more good. . . . I regret this extra and unnecessary labor of show-

parading on the Sabbath. No General who feared God would ever order it. I doubt whether Gen. Sickles would, without a strong, special reason, but Gen. Taylor . . . seems to fix upon the day with profane and deliberate choice. When the Government and the Army are ruled more by what seems, after careful seeking, to be the Divine Will—when it is understood through all our ranks, in all our councils, and by all our citizens, that such is the *policy*, then . . . can our troubles begin to depart. . . . The President's Proclamation seems to me fraught with promise° on this very account. Not that it will benefit the present generation of slaves to a very great extent, or inflict much harm on the enemy through them, but that it seems the discharge of a *duty*, the results of which are where they should be—left with God.

As a military measure, I agree with those who think its chief effect will be a barring of foreign interference. The last week has been made painfully memorable to me and our little fraternity of Christians by the death of another godly man whose loss we shall keenly feel. Daniel Moran of Co. F died at Finley Hospital on the morning of Wednesday. He lost his right arm at the battle of Bristows station and for the first three days appeared to be doing well. The journey to Washington and the fact that a second operation was necessary to remove a bullet still remaining in his shoulder produced an exhaustion from which he did not rally. . . . He had a great domestic trouble in the shape of an unfaithful wife, and his heart was at times sorely troubled in behalf of his two children yet young. . . . I saw him several times after he was taken to the Hospital and shall long remember the manner in which in broken English (he was a German) he testified to the faithfulness of God toward his humble followers in time of adversity. Whenever he saw me coming he cried aloud, "Oh! My dear Shaplain! My dear Shaplain!" so that the whole ward could hear and his greetings were always those of a man whose thoughts were away from earth. . . . I went for the purpose of attending his funeral but the undertaker did not come, it began to rain and I could not wait, so with a last look at the cold body, I left him to other hands, but with a full heart and a humble hope that I should see Daniel Moran again some day. . . . Love to all the family old and young. . . . Your aff. Son. Joseph.

The President's Proclamation . . . with promise: Lincoln considered Antietam, which repulsed the attempt by Lee to invade Maryland, the victory he needed to present his Emancipation Proclamation from a position of strength. The proclamation, not signed until 1 January 1863, freed the slaves in the rebellious states only and not in border areas such as Maryland and Kentucky. But it lessened the danger that Great Britain and France would extend diplomatic recognition to the Confederate government.

Dear Father,

Since I rose this morning I have hardly seated myself till now. The regiment went on picket yesterday and did not return till 11 o'clock today, thereby delaying service at least till afternoon, but we had a funeral instead. . . . I did not get back to my tent till near noon and was just making arrangements to hold service at 3 o'clock when I received an order to report at 2 o'clock at the Headquarters of Division for the purpose of officiating at another funeral. I went at the hour designated and was sent to the 1st Virginia Battery of Artillery° attached to the Division, and encamped at least three miles from here. It was a battery of German officers and all the orders were . . . given in German. . . .

You ask about Col. Hall. I hardly know his whereabouts or prospects. He has been sick, but is now well and it is supposed that he will return to duty soon. I really regret it, for he is not a fit man to command a regiment. So far as his troubling me is concerned, I have no apprehension of it. He is afraid of Gen. Sickles and the Gen. is my friend, I think. Capt. [Walter A.] Donaldson of Co. F now commands the Regt.—a good and efficient officer. He has a notion of curtailing my liberty somewhat in respect to visiting Washington at discretion, but I have settled that matter by getting the General's verdict that the Chaplain's limits are extended to any place, not beyond speedy recall, where the sick and wounded of his regiment are to be visited. There are some officers, I suppose, who think that it is a nice thing to be a Chaplain and go when and where you please. This thought in my case is perhaps encouraged by the fact that when in W. I am the guest of Major McBlair, our Paymaster, who has two fair daughters. Of course, great power is attributed to the girls in drawing me away from the tedium of camp. I am sorry for this but can't help it. I cannot afford to hire a room and my board bill would be heavy. . . . I go with the desire to do good, and my *business* is to perform my proper offices. I shall continue as I have done, and let the envious misconstrue as they may. . . .

Gen. Sickles, as you hoped, will decline nomination for Congress°—at least I am so informed. He is getting fixed in his new place most successfully and will probably serve himself, as well as the country, better here than in the warfare of words. . . . The tattoo is sounding all through our glorious old Brigade, and I must go to bed. I cannot even surmise how long we are to remain here. The new regiments are pushed out beyond us and that looks as if we might be destined to inaction for some time. The Independent comes regularly. I do not like its *sarcasms* about McClellan. If it thinks a thing, let it be said right out. I am not sure, however, that its tone is unjust. The good weather is going. . . . Another month and the ground will give way under us. Then, a winter of *sus*pense and *ex*pense. Love to all. Your aff. Son. Joseph.

the 1st Virginia Battery of Artillery: Though most "Virginia" regiments during the Civil War were on the Southern side, the western portion of the state had remained loyal and supplied volunteers to the Union side.

Gen. Sickles . . . will decline nomination for Congress: Sickles was away from the brigade on a recruiting drive during the Second Bull Run and Antietam campaigns, and he made the decision to stay in the military despite pressure from backers to run for Congress again.

In Camp. Sunday afternoon. Oct. 26th 1862.

Dear Father,

It is the dreariest day imaginable. The rain is driving against the tent with dismal patterings and the whole "tabernacle" is rudely shaken by a pertinacious nor'wester. . . . These Virginia storms are great nuisances, yet such a choking dust as we have suffered for weeks renders them endurable if not welcome. It is not the wetting or the chill that make rain unpopular among us, for all that is triumphed over by a regular little cast-iron spitfire of a stove that fields a torrid heat at the least solicitation, but in this country rain is the father of mud, and mud is the father of all discomfort to a soldier in camp. A shower of twenty minutes seems to have power to dissolve the flintiest surface, such as has been subjected to the daily walk of a thousand pairs of feet, and convert it into an adhesive, slippery slime which even a duck would stay indoors to avoid. It is a costly way of getting rid of dust, but the only one that I know of. The cure is little preferable to the disease. . . . In one there is suffocation and blindness, in the other life is a burden in that no man can walk without danger of dislocating his hips. That will do for the weather. . . .

After morning service I took a large armful of religious papers, and a haver-sack filled with tracts, and went to every tent in the regiment. The "Chaplain's rations" were received with thanks in every instance, and I have no doubt were well digested by many. . . .

Last Tuesday I had a good time—a memorable time, in fact. I had heard that my classmate, [Hezekiah] Watkins, was Capt. in the 143 Regt. N.Y. Vols., and found that the regiment had come on and was encamped near Chain Bridge on the Virginia side. Watkins and I were fast friends (he was coxswain in our prize crew)° so I sallied out to see him. It was 10 good miles down to Chain Bridge, and I was not a little disappointed to discover that the 143rd had gone from there. However, after a long hunt and a sore journey to my brave horse, I found it at about 3 o'clock p.m., perched on Uptons Hill beyond Balls Cross

Roads. Riding up to Capt. Watkins' tent I hailed him in no gentle tones. Forth he issued and we embraced warmly; then turning he called out, "Ed!!," and to astonish my eyes out came Ned Carrington, my ancient comrade,° clad in the robes of a Lieutenant. You may depend upon it, the sentinel nearby stared somewhat at the vocal and other exercises that followed, and he was excusable for it. Ned in his letter had hinted at his entering the service in that Regt., but I had no thought of meeting him then. We had a good visit and promised each other a frequent repetition, if circumstances favoured. Both of them were full of warlike zeal, and I could not help thinking that a month of Chickahominy work might serve to modify their enthusiasm. . . . Love to all. Your aff. Son. Joseph.

P.S. I shall welcome you joyfully at any time you may choose to come. My only fear is about making you comfortable.

he was coxswain in our prize crew: On 26 July 1859, the Harvard rowing crew beat Yale and Brown in a regatta on Lake Quinsigamond near Worcester, Massachusetts. The next day, in a race for prizes offered by the city and with a crew in which Twichell rowed, Yale beat Harvard for the first time in the then-short history of intercollegiate athletics. The victory caused tremendous celebration among Yale fans and was long remembered.

Ned Carrington, my ancient comrade: Edward Carrington, Twichell's college friend and New York roommate, joined the army on the death of their classmate Diodate Hannahs in September. He was now second lieutenant in the 143rd New York Volunteer Infantry.

Centreville. Sunday afternoon. Nov. 2nd 1862

Dear Father,

It is 4 o'clock p.m. and we have halted, whether for the night or only to rest I do not know. We are tired enough for sleep at any rate. . . . We marched at 5½ last night but made only eight miles before we bivouacked—the whole Division on the sides of two contiguous hills. Today business has been pushed and we are here just behind that line of rebel works which frowned toward Washington during the winter of 1861–2. . . . I am sitting in a former Confederate hut—a very comfortable place considered as soldiers' quarters, with a large stone fireplace in which the boys have built a big blazing fire, for the air is chilly. At my elbow stands a steaming hot cup of coffee, just brought by my most attentive groom and servant, of which although milkless and sugarless I take an occasional luxurious sip as I write. So you see, considering that I am a traveler and only now arrived, I am not badly off. This place is a point of great interest, as every mile of the road hither is also. We passed through Fairfax Court House, and by the fatal wood of Chantilly where Kearny fell.

Almost within sight of here is the field of the battle of Bristow's where our boys are sleeping, and off to the right, facing south, is Bull Run—grown to be a name for disaster. What is to transpire here yet can hardly be even surmised. We were surprised at the order to march, and do not yet know our destination. The sights [and] sounds of the toilsome military journey bring vividly back the most thrilling days of our regimental history—Here we go again. The bugles blow and the drums beat. Fall in! Forward March! So good afternoon!

> *Manassas Junction. 9 o'clock Monday morning*
> *[3 November].*

A cool, stiff morning breeze is blowing across these beautiful but sadly tragic plains. . . . After I was called away yesterday we marched on about 4 miles and, crossing Bull Run at Blackburns Ford Bridge, bivouacked for the night very near the place where the regiment paused after the battle of Bristows Station. . . . It was night when I traveled this road before—a battle was progressing in the valley below—I was exhausted and moreover anxious for my charge of wounded—so that it is all new to me as if I had never been here. . . . The evidences of war appear on every hand all along the way. The rebel works and quarters occupy the frequent hills from beyond Centreville to here. Broken wagons, skeletons of horses, unexploded ammunition, remnants of burned houses, desolated farms, are continually in sight to remind the passer by that the curse is on the nation. The dark pine woods cast their sombre shade over the thousands of graves which hold their precious dust against the Judgement Day.

After we halted, I ate my dry supper and, spreading my blankets beside a log, lay down and . . . thought of God and home until my eyelids grew heavy and earth and moon went from me. . . . The next thing I knew it was early dawn clear and cold, the boys were up and about their fires cooking breakfast. At 5 o'clock we were on the march. How long we are to stay here is only a matter of conjecture but it is probable that we shall not advance much further unless it is for soldiers' work.

The fighting Division (it is *Sickles'* now)° is again in the field, and although containing but a small leaven of its original members, expects to sustain its reputation. I am told that the region is occupied by the three Corps of Heintzleman, [Maj. Gen. Franz] Sigel and Burnside, all under the command of Gen. Hooker, who is here, having traveled in our ambulance. The next two or three weeks may be decisive. . . . The wagons have come up and we are going to pitch tents. Perhaps I will write more when I can do it more comfortably. Love to all. Joseph.

The fighting Division (it is Sickles' *now):* With Hooker elevated to a corps commander, Sickles was placed in command of the Second Division of the Third Corps. He also received the rank of major general in November.

Washington. Nov 6th 1862.

Dear Father,

You will be somewhat surprised to know that I am here, since my last Sunday's letter was dated at a point so remote. It was not-at-all within my expectation while we were marching up to Manassas to return hither for several weeks at least, but a business arose which seemed to *send* me. The enclosed document will inform you what it was. I have accomplished what I came for. The poor creature is safely at home among the Sisters of Charity,° for which I render hearty thanks. It was, without any exception, the saddest case of sin and sorrow that I ever knew. She was a simple country girl, rather pleasing in her appearance, but crushed almost to death under the load of her dreadful misfortune. Shame-faced and silent, she betrayed none of that brazen hardihood which characterizes the professional harlot, while her utter helplessness appealed to every feeling of humanity. After the last battles of Virginia, the whole region was stripped of men. There was no surgeon or physician left in all the country and, threatened by a horrible death, she left her humble home to sue for help among strangers. From the moment I saw her, I forgot her loathsomeness in the fullness of my pity. Without delay, I made a report of the facts to Col. Hall, who asked me to go to the General. . . . There was talk of turning her over to the Provost Marshal, but as I thought it over, there appeared a vision of leering soldiers and impudent if not impure questionings, of joking officials and uncharitable alms-houses or jails, so at length I said "turn her over to me!" and so they did, giving me a pass for both of us on the Rail Road to Alexandria. I procured from Father O'Hagan a letter to the Sisters of Charity in charge of the home-like Providence hospital in Washington, but did not intend to make use of it if I could find a Protestant institution. The ride to Alexandria was an event which I shall long remember vividly. She was so bowed under her shame that it was long before she gave any response to my kindness, but what she did say and do swelled my pity until I overflowed. She was reared by Christian parents and had brothers and sisters. She said that she prayed sometimes and I tried to make her feel that although she had gone far astray, still the Lord loved her and desired her love. I cannot give all the particulars of my journey until she was off my hands. We could get no female attire for her, and I had to observe great caution lest her sex be discovered. Putting her in a carriage I drove to the Provost Marshal's at Alexandria, who is a friend of mine, and he introduced me to the Mayor, who after deliberation offered to send her to his Almshouse. An inquiry into the nature of the establishment settled my mind that it should be my last resort. . . . So we embarked for Washington. The ordeal of the ferry boat was safely passed. We had clothed her in a great army overcoat, for it was cold, but a long lock of black hair escaping from under the cap or a slender, small hand protruding from the coat sleeve were constant sources of apprehension. Not that I *feared* to have the facts revealed, but still it would have been rather awkward to have to explain if interrogated. It was dark when we got to Washington and I felt secure, but my wretched charge, in going aboard the boat while crossing and in coming off, clutched my sleeve as though I were a life-preserver and she drowning. She was bewildered and frightened, never according to her own statement having been so far from home before or in so large a town. I have omitted to say that in Alexandria I called on Harry Hopkins for his counsel, and learned that the Catholic Providence Hospital was the *only* suitable place to which she could be taken. A carriage soon brought us to the gate of its pleasant grounds. I entered, called for the Superior, presented my letter, made my own separate plea (rather excitedly I think for I was wrought up) and had not long to wait for the welcome words, "Bring her in." This is a meagre account of one of the notable events of my life so far. I have wondered not a little at the intense interest, nay almost affection, which took possession of me in behalf of so miserable, and under the circumstances so disgusting, an object, but I must confess that I guarded her all that day as jealously as if she had been a queen. . . . When I left her I gave her my blessing, said "Good bye! Elizabeth!" and asked her to write to me someday. The Sisters seemed to receive her with great kindness and I have no doubt she will meet nothing but charity at their hands, but I regretted that I was forced to place her under Roman Catholic influences, for I think she will be easily moulded. I shall endeavour to find out what becomes of her and help her still further if I can. Perhaps you did not care to hear all this, but I have told it out of my own emotion. . . . Tomorrow morning if nothing happens I shall start for camp. With much love to all. I remain. Your aff. Son. Joseph.

safely at home among the Sisters of Charity: This Roman Catholic order, founded by Elizabeth Ann Seton in 1812, aided wounded soldiers on both sides as well as sheltering fallen women in this home in Washington.

Manassas Junction. Monday. Nov. 10th 1862.

Dear Father,

Friday night, the Brigade, in the midst of a cold, driving sleet, was again on the march for Warrenton Junction. The Third Brigade under Gen. [Francis

Engle] Patterson had previously been sent but, on meeting a force of the enemy variously estimated at from one to three thousands with cavalry and artillery, retired. Gen. Sickles was very much enraged, placed Gen. P. in arrest, and sent our boys to do the job. They went, but the enemy had gone—beyond the Rappahannock as is supposed. The 3rd Regt. was left at Warrenton Junction, the 1st and 5th at Bristows station, while we, with the 4th and our new Regt. (the 120th N.Y.), returned to this place—thus giving about 15 miles of the Rail Road into our keeping. . . .

A glad day for the 2nd Regt. on Friday. Capt. Rafferty was appointed our Major and is now in command of the Regiment. You may imagine my joy. It was a matter of great importance for it is probable that the Major will command us through the whole winter campaign and who but Capt. R. was the man I desired? He is popular with the Regt.—as a gentleman and a brave soldier. I had taken the liberty some weeks since of speaking to Gen. Sickles in private about the matter, and only hope that my earnest recommendation had something to do with the result.

It is a good that Capt. R. is at the head° and will be our ruling spirit. He will see to it that justice and not flattery rule his administration. Hitherto the enthusiasm of the Regt. has had to suffer continual damp from a corrupt, palpably corrupt, conduct of its affairs. I have often wondered that our battle-days do not feel it more. You cannot imagine how much aside from fairness and common justice has been the award of merit in a multitude of cases. I have never dwelt much in writing to you on our dark side because you have a weakness for taking things at their very worst, and indeed, save an occasional shock at witnessing what hurt and disgusted me, I have generally kept *myself* looking on the bright side. The soul of New York city politics is our evil genius. Honor and truth are luxuries too rare to be commonly used. I hail then the elevation of good Capt. Rafferty as an omen of better times. He will do what he can.

Yesterday was the second Sabbath since we have been able to have divine service. If we are kept tramping up and down, my plans will be greatly interfered with in that respect. It is hard sometimes to keep in mind the great object of my presence here. I am often falling into the feeling that I am a member of the Regt., and not the bearer of a divine commission. God help me to keep in view the interests of Zion—to remember that my work is a *separate* one and to make adverse circumstances the source of greater watching and diligence. . . . Love to all. Your aff. Son. Joseph.

It is a good that Capt. R. is at the head: Captain Thomas Rafferty was a favorite of Twichell's, who saw his accession as bringing the long Hall-Potter imbroglio to an end. Technically, however, Hall remained colonel of the regiment until 1 May 1863, when he was succeeded by Potter, with Rafferty succeeding as lieutenant colonel. Twichell does not comment on a more significant change of command: on 5 November, Lincoln removed McClellan as head of the Army of the Potomac, replacing him with Burnside.

In Camp. Manassas Junction—
Va. Sunday, Nov. 16th 1862.

Dear Father,

The regiment went out on picket early this morning and, save in the matters of distributing some religious reading before it started and visiting the sick who are left behind, the day is one of perfect leisure to me. Both Major Rafferty and I regret the fact for this is the third Sunday that has passed without public service. Father O'Hagan was up bright and early and celebrated mass both in our regiment and his own but he has an advantage over me, in the item of authority. If he should choose to hold a service at midnight the Catholic Captains would rouse up their men, and almost *order* them to attend without a word of objection. . . . It is due to Father O'Hagan, however, to say that he is much beloved by the men as a kind hearted friend. I have never failed to be entertained, instructed and I think improved by his society. I went over this morning, after our boys left, to hear his sermon. It was made up of the commonest and plainest statements concerning sin and its consequences, the shortness of life etc., and the exhortations naturally derived therefrom. The *heart* of the service was the celebration of mass, all of which is in Latin and mumbled in a low tone by the priest. Meanwhile the audience kneeling awaits whatever virtue they may be supposed to derive from an exercise in which they can take little part. The attendance in his own Regt., which is of the "New York rowdy" religion, was very small—not more than 20—and I did not wonder at it for the morning was cold and blustering and even the strong inducements which the Church offers to a bare-headed prostration on the chilly ground, while a clergyman mutters and bows and crosses himself in the remote corner of a tent, could not rival the attractions of a blazing camp fire. It is not for Protestants to *boast* of a purer truth, but only to be thankful for greater light. . . .

Major Rafferty announced to us at the table to-day, since I began to write, that the Division was about to depart hence in the direction of Fredericksburg° and that he expected the order to march before many hours. It matters little where we go, and I have ceased to fix my affections on any spot having often been taught by bitter experience how vain it is, but this is an uncommonly nice place to abandon and I can't help a little disappointment [he and Dr. McAllister had fixed up a "really palatial abode, considering we are in the field" from an old rebel barracks].... Yet it may be a false alarm. Last week we were under arms for 24 hours owing to a rumor of another raid in the rear.

What you say about Thanksgiving makes me homesick. If it were fairly within the bounds of possibility and duty, I should be willing to suffer any penance for the luxury of a look around the family board that day, but I do not see how it can be.... I fear that few of the regiment will have even the qualified pleasure of regret that they are away from a scene of happiness and plenty where a welcome would greet their coming, for we have not been paid for nearly 5 months and I know that many, if not most of my poor fellows, are burdened with the hourly thought of want at home.... It is too bad! I can't tell you how I feel about it. Nothing so takes away the spirit of the men as the feeling that their family hearths are cold and cupboards empty.... With much love to all I remain. Your aff. Son. Joseph.

the Division . . . in the direction of Fredericksburg: Burnside was beginning to move toward Richmond via the more easily supplied route that passed through this Virginia city.

In a letter of 24 November, Twichell refers to an (unnamed) book he has recently read. The book obviously refers to slavery, for he writes:

So far as slavery is concerned, nothing could deepen my hatred of it. All that I have personally seen and heard has only confirmed what had before been told. My abhorrence of the system goes beyond my commiseration of its negro victims. I think sincerely that it were better that the present generation of *slaves* be exterminated than that the Curse of another generation of *Slavery* rest upon the shoulders of the nation. I do not see how this institution whose fibres clasp every interest of every community in the South can ever be dissected out by any skill of statesmanship and leave the separated parts still alive. Something must perish utterly, not in its relations but in itself.

In the same letter, Twichell also reports on a long-awaited change:

At length we are rid of our Surgeon [McGowan]. He has long been a dead weight and, while I am sorry for the man, I am glad for the Regiment. He was among my diseased crowd that I brought down here, so used up by his debauches as to be almost helpless. Capt. [Paul P.] Bradlee of Co. B., who after a year of immense, almost sublime, impudence of conceit, showed himself a whole coward at the first sight of the enemy, is also dropped from the army rolls in disgrace.

In Camp — near Falmouth, Va.
Sunday Night. Nov. 30th 1862.

Dear Father,

I succeeded yesterday in accomplishing a conjunction with the regiment after separation of ten days. . . . The boys are tired and not altogether cheerful as usual. The march from Manassas hither, lengthened by first going back to Fairfax, has proved an unusually severe one, aggravated in many cases by the want of shoes. Streams had to be forded, it was cold, rainy weather, and the large part of two nights was consumed in weary travel. I have no doubt it was a sorry journey, but those who call it our worst experience must have forgotten the retreat to James River last summer. Undoubtedly this march *dragged* unusually. It differed from all others before it in that it lacked those concomitants which contribute the help of excitement. Going up the Peninsula, Hope and Confidence put life in our heels. Returning via James River, the thunder of hostile cannon behind furnished a motive to push ahead. But now stimulus of either kind does not seem to exist. The army cannot be called disheartened, but dull. Its pulse beats, not feebly, but very moderately. This is my private judgement and may be very erroneous. The prospect at best is not charming. We are here with cold weather threatening yet having nothing for a defence against it. If we are kept active and meet with the grand success, our elation will be tempered by hardship. If we encounter defeat there will be tribulation. If we are held here in readiness, yet do not advance, we shall attain a condition which while it cannot be called discomfort, will yet be far from comfort—a kind of uneasy ease.

We are about a mile from the river, and about as far above Fredericksburg. I intend to ride down tomorrow and take a look. The hostile pickets are within easy talking range on either bank, and from this side I am told that we can almost look into the windows of the town. There is no firing at all, but the sentinels stack their arms, and keep an eye upon each other in silence—all communication being forbidden. The position here is to me an anomalous one, unless it be admitted that there is a disappointment on our part. This is, I think, the general opinion—that our plan is foiled through another miscalculation or mistake—so frequent hitherto that the enemy appear to depend upon it as a fixed element of advantage to them. I hope it is not so, and really *know* nothing to lead me to the conclusion. . . . My love to all the household. Your aff. Son. Joseph.

In Camp, near Falmouth, Va.
Sunday Evening. Dec. 7th 1862.

Dear Father,

Winter is upon us savagely. Snow lies on the ground and our water pail was frozen over this morning. We were ill prepared to meet it and our condition would not make a bad show compared with Valley Forge. The men are badly off for want of shoes and the little shelter tents not much better than nothing. We have no stoves and have to rely on camp-fires, which are only a mitigation. If we stay here, a few days will remedy these ills for the most part, but if called upon to move we shall have the chance to earn the name of "suffering patriots." Nothing is surely known about our programme but the general opinion favors an active one. Nevertheless the Doctor and I have risked a waste of labor, and entered upon the construction of a log house, which two days more will make habitable. That being furnished we shall be comfortable, but ever since day before yesterday we have shivered night and day. The snow did not much offend me, for it set me dreaming of home, and the look of the pine-covered hills loaded with snow—everything a spray of white—was as Northern as could be. I almost listened for sleigh-bells and shouting boys, but the prevailing spirit of the Army was neither delicious reverie nor boisterous fun. There arose a busy note of industry. The woods rang with the sound of axes. On every hand men were seen bearing logs on their shoulders. Spades were called into requisition and, by digging and walling, narrow dens were made which, though not fit for the abode of an American citizen, were a security against freezing to the Federal Soldier. It was work for dear life. "Move or no move," the men said, "we must live to-night." I think we are to see campaigning extraordinary this winter. Well! We can stand hardness if it only tells on the result. For my own part I was never so able to endure as now.

It was so cold this morning that I did not deem an early service feasible. After dinner, however, at the source of the "church call," a few faithful souls gathered in front of Major Rafferty's tent and we worshipped. The wind blew rudely and my audience looked chilly, but I think we enjoyed uncommon spiritual warmth, for all present were there in the love and fear of God. . . .

Tuesday we had a Brigade inspection—a tedious affair involving a standing still of some six hours—and Thursday the Division was reviewed by Gen. Hooker. The boys gave old Joe a most enthusiastic reception as he rode up and down the lines. We were honoured by the presence of some Confederate spectators, from the hills across the Rappahannock. Our proximity to the enemy is both novel and interesting. Standing on the river bank we are within pistol-shot of the Fredericksburg streets, and all the passers thereon, soldiers and civilians, can be inspected at leisure. There is a vast deal of mutual staring. . . .

Now to business. There is a strong probability that I shall be home soon, and my errand will be to seek ordination.° A new order has been issued reiterating the necessity of a regular induction into the ministry in the case of all Chaplains. While I do not feel guilty of dishonourable conduct, since my case is known and understood by my Colonel and General, and has been ever since I entered on my duties, I have concluded that it were better to place myself in such a position that the literal requirement of the law shall be satisfied. An enemy might charge me with equivocal conduct in the matter. I do not wish longer to run the risk of such an unpleasant though unjust an accusation. . . . Calling on the General I laid the subject open before him and he cordially approved my decision. I then formed the agreement with him that I should wait till the Paymaster comes, then taking the money committed to me, go to Washington and forward it; then go to the north and attend to my own solemn private business. . . . As soon as the long anticipated Money Man does appear, I shall notify you at once and there will be the necessary data on which to found arrangements. I do not see but that these will have to be committed to your care. I have a long cherished wish that dear Mr. [Elisha C.] Jones° preach my ordination sermon. . . . This is all I need to say now, we shall probably have time to communicate yet further on the subject.

I cannot tell you, my dear Father, with what feelings I contemplate this event. To me, [it] looms up gigantically. I feel weak and small and abashed before it. I know that I am unworthy, but I cannot turn back from it. In entering upon my present work I sought not only to do good to others, but to prove myself. While the trial has not delivered me from doubt, I find that, in seeking tests and the light that comes of experience, I have contracted obligations. I am bound to this place. I must remain with these poor fellows. Is not ordination indicated by Providence as a duty incumbent upon me? I cannot view it otherwise. An intermission of nearly two years in all my studies has rendered me less ready for it than I have been, in respect to theology, and spiritually, I fear, an equal unfitness. Yet, what am I to do? I am driven to the throne of Grace with a heavier burden—a sorer trial than has ever weighed upon me. Pray for me Father, that I may be helped from heaven, to give myself wholly away in perfect consecration—that God may be all in all to me—that I may find the clear light and a sure confidence, however humble. One thing is certain. I desire nothing so much as to be what I think constitutes a true minister of the Gospel. It is my constant prayer. . . . Am I about to make a dreadful mistake! . . . Pray for me, Father. Pray. Pray. Love to all. Your aff. Son. Joseph *my errand will be to seek ordination:* In September and October, the Adjutant General's Office had issued orders reiterating the provisions of the act of 17 July 1862 requiring that chaplains be ordained. Twichell decided to seek ordination "as an evangelist"—that is, without a settled congregation.

dear Mr. [Elisha C.] Jones: The Reverend Elisha C. Jones had been Twichell's boyhood minister at First Congregational Church, Southington, Connecticut. Although Jones differed with the Twichells and other abolitionists in his congregation on the slavery issue—Twichell's father nearly resigned his diaconate as a result—the family always regarded him with affection.

> *In Camp near Falmouth, Va.*
> *Tuesday Night. Dec. 9th 1862.*

Dear Father,

There seems to be little doubt of some movement of the Army within three days. Father O'Hagan was at Hooker's Headquarters this forenoon and saw the orders preparing. He was informed that we were to cross the Rappahannock at Port Royal, eight miles below here. An engagement is possible, perhaps probable. If this report (and it appears reliable) should prove true, it may be that the Paymaster, and hence my journey to Washington, will be indefinitely delayed. I assume that to cross the river now means action, and a giving way of everything else to the true business of the campaign. Still, I may be mistaken. . . . It would not be best to move, or make arrangements at all, in the matter of which I wrote Sunday night, unless it were to mention it to Mr Jones. . . . I should dislike having my ordination made an "event" of, or a source of, popular excitement, even in our own little community. The thought of so sacred, solemn, almost fearful an occasion furnishing a show or spectacle for the curious is revolting to me. To stare and gape at a man going to execution is a hideously barbaric amusement. That a transaction where God and angels are interested spectators, nay partakers, should be similarly observed, is worse: it is sacrilege. I wish I could be ordained as the apostles were, almost alone with the Lord.

Our gorgeous log-house is near completion, just in time to laugh at us with open door and wrinkled visage, for all our fruitless pains. A day more would have made it habitable and then we could have defied the North Pole. It is really a neat piece of work—about 15 ft. by 12 and high in proportion. The fireplace and chimney—the most difficult points—were ready for trial this evening and proved a complete success. To be able to say, "What a jolly place it would be!" is a poor consolation for having to leave it. . . . You would be surprised to see how much the boys have done during the last four cold days to better their quarters. Last night nearly every man slept in a warm apartment of some kind or other, often of very ingenious construction. I was myself amazed at the celerity with which this was accomplished. The coming march promises to be a grievous affair. . . . If we move, I shall write according to opportunity. Much love to all. Your aff. Son. Joseph.

In Camp near Falmouth, Va. Dec. 17th 1862.

My Dear Sister,°

When we left this camp last Thursday morning the thought of returning to it did not once occur.° Even the failure of an attempt to force back the enemy from the right bank of the Rappahannock did not by any means promise such a result to ourselves as the restoration of our lost log-house, and we said our farewells to the spot as for a final separation. . . . Notwithstanding those expressions, lo! here I am before the wide hearth of which I wrote before, seated to tell you what has happened to me and mine and all that I have seen during the five days of my absence therefrom.

Thursday morning (Dec. 11th) at 4 o'clock we were all aroused and ordered to prepare immediately for the march. . . . At six o'clock the regimental line was formed, and at half past six we emerged from the woods where our brigade lay, into the wide undulating plain that extends about a mile to the south west toward Fredericksburg. There we met the other regiments of our Brigade and Division, in fact, of the Corps and Grand Division,° with the Cavalry and Artillery thereto belonging. It was a magnificent morning, several degrees warmer than it had been for the week past, yet cool and bracing. The air was humid and the rising sun showed a face of blood, presaging, as it were, the terrible scenes about to be enacted. I have never witnessed so splendid a military display as that morning furnished. The long dark columns of infantry with fifty thousand gleaming bayonets and waving ensigns; the numerous trains of Artillery with guns of shining brass or black steel, heavily rumbling over the frozen ground; the quick moving bodies of cavalry with resounding hoofs and the jingling of sabres, combined with the music of the bands, the blare of bugles, the shouts of command, the galloping of aides and the tramp of multitudes; made up a spectacle not easily forgotten. Such was the nature of the ground that the eye and ear took it all in at once, and the knowledge that the display was but a prelude to a terrible tragedy in actual war, contributed a significance and intensity of observation which no mere show could have possibly evoked. I think that the influence of the hour was an inspiration of valor. The pervasive sentiment was that we were soldiers going to, and ready for, our soldiers' work. At about eight o'clock "old Joe" Hooker appeared, attended by his staff, but riding full three rods in advance. His coming, illustrious by his tall form and well-known white horse, was the spark that gave flame to an enthusiasm thus far expressed only in looks and words. The sky was full of shouting as he passed through the midst. It followed him in one vast wave, mounting from both sides till he disappeared in the front. Such a greeting must have been sweet music to the old fellow's ears and an earnest that he could rely upon his men to do his bidding. It was a voice saying, "Here we are, General, what shall we do?" As early as at 5 o'clock there had begun firing from over against Fredericksburg, and it had continued quite steadily yet not with great fury—until now, at 8½ o'clock, it burst upon the morning air all at once as if the thunders of heaven had broken their leash and were let loose upon the earth. A more terrific cannonade I never heard. It exceeded that of Malvern Hill. [Gens. William] Franklin and [Edwin V.] Sumner° had passed before us, the former to a point about 2 miles below the town, the latter to the hills directly opposite. Franklin was protecting his engineers while bridges of pontoons were constructing. Sumner, having been fired upon from the houses, was shelling the town itself. We were advanced over the plain a half mile further and there rested in reserve, two-thirds of a mile from the river, for the remainder of the day. Until dark the tempest of Artillery raged without ceasing, slackening at intervals only to break out again with increased energy. Its awful surges rose and swelled, multiplied by answering echoes boom on boom, crashing and roaring in one grand chorus of war. The hills about were crowned by clusters of spectators, and every high tree was laden with gazing men. In the course of the afternoon, accompanied by Ben Catlin [a Yale classmate, now a surgeon] and the two other Surgeons of his Regt., I went forward toward the town to see what could be seen. We found Sumner's men massed behind the hills nearest the river, ready to cross as soon as the way should be prepared. So dense was the smoke from the cannonade that one could see little. The enemy appeared to take little notice of our bombardment and, except when a column of infantry appeared, seldom fired. It grew dark while we stood looking and the troops were set in motion, as if the veil of night were to be enlisted as a cover to the ensuing movements. We hurried back to our place, lest some change might render it difficult for us to find our swarms in that vast hive. An aide riding by shouted to some comrade, "Two regiments are over already!," and we knew that more would soon follow. But we were destined to remain inactive for the night. Wearied from the day's excitement, we spread our blankets on the ground and, although in the morning my good overcoat, which I spread over me, was white with frost, I slept soundly and well. I must hasten my narrative of general events, of which you have been sufficiently informed by the papers, and make room for personal experiences.

Friday morning we advanced to the ground occupied the day before by Sumner and remained there till about 4 o'clock p.m. . . . Toward noon, with Father O'Hagan and a surgeon of the 4th, I rode down to the river (there was little firing) and, seeing that the bridges were open and the city occupied by our troops in large force, we crossed over. I cannot stop to describe minutely the sights afforded by a bombarded and sacked town. Every prank that shot and shell could play with houses of brick and wood was there manifest. The churches were riddled. . . . The streets were thronged with the soldiery. They passed in and out of the houses pillaging. Nearly every man bore some trophy of his search. Domestic utensils, articles of use or adornment, books etc. could be seen, suspended from the bayonet or carried under the arms of the licensed multitude. I saw one man, a coarse, rollicking chap bearing on his shoulder a board about 3 ft by 2 on which was fixed with arching back and tail erect a stuffed monkey, which was taken from some public or private museum.

The light of this universal appropriation . . . did not please me however lawful it may have been . . . It jostled my New England prejudices. After a general inspection of the town we started for the suburbs toward the . . . heights° for a view of the enemy's works which still remained to be dealt with. A narrow street attracted us by the absence of the usual crowd. We entered it, and riding a short distance, found it to be a "cul de sac" affording no exit. A number of soldiers were peeping through the fence which closed the end. Approaching them we hailed and asked what they were gazing at. Their reply startled us. "Back! Back or you'll be shot! The rebel pickets are but 300 yards beyond!" Suffice it to say we abandoned our plan of inspection with more precipitation than dignity. I did not feel exactly calm but we turned the corner of a brick house and again mixed with the throng. In a little while we started back. More troops had crossed and it was with some difficulty that we made our way. I have here to record a common operation of Father O'Hagans and mine which met a result at variance with its merits. Coming over we observed that boxes and packages of tobacco were in the possession of many who brought them across the bridge and sold at retail to the troops. An idea seized us. Our boys were famishing for want of the narcotic, the sutlers having failed to supply it, and here was a chance to remedy the evil and increase our capital of popularity. If any plunder seemed justifiable, it was that of bread and tobacco. We met a man with a 20 pound box on his shoulder. Being questioned he said that he bought it. After some "dicker" we owned it for $3.00 dividing the cost. I took it up before me in the saddle, and we proceeded with mutual congratulations. "How it would please the boys!" we thought and said. Alas! for our hopes! As we neared the bridge they vanished like the smoke of a pipe. The Corporal of the guard there stationed, halted us. "Gentlemen" said he respectfully, "I am very sorry, but an order has just been issued that no more tobacco be allowed to pass the bridge." And so, our property of the hour was confiscated. Father O'Hagan remonstrated in vain with an aid of Gen. [Darius N.] Couch's (the temporary Governor of Fredericksburg) who chanced to pass by, and we were forced to abandon our purchase and proceed empty. The sole yield of our investment was a pleasurable emotion of five minutes, alloyed on my part by the uncomfortable carriage of the box. We laughed dismally as we rode up the hill to our regiments, and tried to enjoy it as a joke. "Perhaps," said the worthy priest, "it is a divine revelation that the morality of the act was doubtful." Be that as it may, it was a slim business operation for a Yankee.

At about 4 o'clock the Division (Sickles) was ordered to return part way to our station the day before and bivouac for the night. We had just chosen our places in the woods and were preparing to cook supper when the order was countermanded and we were marched by a circuitous route of 5 miles to the neighborhood of the bridges over which Franklin had crossed. It was dark when we arrived and we bivouacked immediately in a wood by the road-side. Next day was Saturday, the day of battle.

Early in the morning we were moved a short distance and rested on a side hill facing the river, and ⅓ mile from the bridges, in full sight of Franklin's Division which was ranged in order of battle on the other side, along a plain reaching from the shore to a line of wooded hills, say ¾ of a mile. Occasional cannon all the morning kept us reminded of the impending conflict and as it were cleared their throats for the great vocal effort yet to come. It was not till near 8 o'clock that the muskets of the skirmishers were heard—the signal that infantry was in action. I ascended a high, bare hill near by where a battery of Parrott guns was stationed. From its elevation, it commanded a view of the entire scene of operations. To the right lay Fredericksburg and to the left our whole line was in plain sight to the very end of the wing, where a single gunboat at the head of navigation, from time to time hoarsely bellowed its martial rage. From this hill I saw the memorable battle of Fredericksburg. It lasted about five hours and five such hours work my eyes never before performed. I should think it was 9 o'clock when a whole line of battle marched out of the town and toward the fortified heights. The enemy's skirmishers retired before it. It was shortly followed by another line in support. I cannot describe my feelings as I saw these devoted battalions moving to carnage. Before them frowned in silence a hundred shotted cannon waiting but the touch of the lanyards. On, on they went and Death hovered near, smiling as he saw his cruel garner to be filled. Nearer and nearer they drew toward the Aceldama.° I seemed to feel their hearts beat, while my own stood still. All of a sudden from those black muzzles of the foe, there leaped the dreadful storm. It fell on the faces and drove through the bosoms of those brave men. Instantly the hostile ramparts swarmed with infantry and ten thousand small arms poured in their deadly fire. The valor that could for a moment withstand this torrent, was almost super-human. Some turned and fled toward the town. Many, alas, were stretched upon the field, but the most pressed on and gained the cover of a grove and a cluster of houses, whence they replied blow for blow. Then the rebel gunners left them to the infantry and turned their pieces upon the second line. Again I saw destruction rained down upon the sons of Northern men, and again they opposed an unyielding front. By this time the field was enveloped in smoke and it was impossible to trace the movements. A cloud gathered over the place, as if to hide from the pure heavens, so pitiful a sight of earthly wrath and suffering. From that sulphureous Pandemonium issued the din and clamor of martial strife. Hour after hour we waited for the issue but as the hostile cannon stayed not their riot, and finally as our fire slackened, we were forced to understand that the attempt to carry the heights had failed. It was evident that the slaughter had been immense, and that it should have been in vain, was sickening. Leaving the right with its piles of slain and thousands of wounded, and its troops dispirited by a bloody repulse, let us turn to the left.° All this time the battle has been raging there also, but not so easy of observation. Our own artillery filled the air with smoke early in the engagement. (On the right, our covering cannon were on the heights on the other side of the river and operated at long range, not able to command the rebel earthworks from the Fredericksburg side owing to their elevation above the level of the town.)

Notwithstanding the smoke, the eye assisted by the ear could in some degree trace the fortunes of the day. We could perceive that our batteries were gradually being advanced for the first three hours and the long gray fringe of light smoke that rises from the line of battle showed the infantry also gaining ground. The receding sound of the action also revealed our advance. If we could only manage to turn the enemy's right with our left the day would still be ours. All hearts went out in longing for this result; but, it was not ordained. At about 12 o'clock the fight waxed hotter and hotter. The roar of artillery was tremendous, and the rapid volleys of musketry showed that the conflict was close. Such work could not last long, especially as neither line was intrenched, except that the enemy held the naturally strong position of wooded hills. It turned against us. Our forces, it appears, had at one time gained an important if not decisive advantage, which the enemy perceiving, brought up a strong reserve, and we being not properly supported were compelled to fall back with heavy loss. This fact the spectator could perceive more by the hearing than the seeing. Just here, our Division [Sickles's, which was temporarily detached from its Grand Division to support Franklin] was ordered to "fall in." The general impression at the time was that we were now called upon to assist the waning fortunes of a disastrous day, and the bounding pulse of Thursday morning was sadly wanting. I descended from the hill where I had felt and seen so much, swallowed a cup of coffee that my servant had prepared, and followed the lads across the triple bridge of pontoons.

That hill I shall long remember. From it I looked down and felt all free America beating in my one heart, as I saw our standards plunged in the smoke of battle, rising and falling, advancing and borne backward with its mighty tide. From it too, I looked up and in the clear, peaceful, sky seemed to see God regarding this contending swarm of dust-worms with infinite Calmness and infinite Pity, Himself only seeing the end and the beginning of all things. . . .

After we crossed the bridge, there was no delay, but the division was immediately pushed out to the extreme front to relieve an over-wearied part of the line. The enemy had driven up from the woods that had once been carried, and under a considerable fire of artillery, we were formed in a wide field ¼ mile from the rebel front. The musketry had entirely ceased in this neighbourhood, some occasional exchanges between the pickets that were thrown out, and I may here state that, with the exception of the pickets, our Division came away Monday night without having been actually engaged at all. Our few wounded received their injuries while standing in this line inactive. I did not follow the Regiment to this position, but remained near the river shore and assisted in the organization of the Division Hospital, according to received instruction. . . . Although few of our own wounded had to be cared for, there was yet enough for every body to do, for the day's work had been a bloody one. By dark, our field surgeons were overwhelmed by the numbers that were brought to them, and at the General Hospital our operators had performed some 25 amputations— none of them from our own command. The usual scenes of agony and ghastly wounds and dying moans were repeated. I was surprised at my own calm witness of it. Two years ago I would have averted my face and stopped my ears, had I been compelled to be present at the cutting off of a finger.

During the afternoon I rode out to see the boys. They were standing in the field, waiting to be sent, with a coolness and quietude that became veterans. Several of the officers remarked to me, "Chaplain, if we have to go into the woods, you will never see many of us alive after it." Gen. Sickles sat on his horse, as unconcernedly as if riding before a plough, and directed the fire of our artillery. While I was there he ordered Capt. [Abner] Seelye (Battery K,

4th Regular Art.) to open on two rebel batteries that annoyed us. He did so and in a few minutes silenced both. The shell from the enemy came so fast that Major Rafferty told me to go away, which I did with reluctance and returned to the Hospital. Considering the probable consequences of an advance in the face of the enemy, I felt that the end of the 2nd Excelsior might be at hand, and I hated to be away. . . .

After dark again, at the request of Dr Sim, the Division Medical Director, I accompanied him out to the field hospitals and to the line of battle. . . . On going to the Division we found it lying at its post in utter darkness. No fire of any kind was allowed and beyond our previous knowledge of the fact, there was nothing to indicate the presence of 10,000 men. It was with profound emotion that I thought, "Underneath that silence and darkness lies an armed host which a single word of command would arouse and develop in terrible strength." It was the most striking impression of hidden power that I ever experienced. Gen. Sickles and staff had withdrawn over a little knoll and were sitting about a fire chatting, rather seriously, I thought, for the morrow was uncertain. We staid and talked a while, then returned and slept in the ground at the hospital.° Sunday morning, in view I suppose of our return across the river, it was directed that a Hospital be established on this side and the wounded transported thither. . . . Five of my charge suffered amputation on Monday, and all got through it well.

One mortally wounded man was the object of my chief solicitude. He was shot through the back and lungs, and paralyzed above and below. His mind also was affected, and though I tried often to direct his thoughts toward his eternal interests, I fear he did not rightly understand his condition. He died last night (Wednesday).° Another poor fellow shot through the lungs was dying when brought in, and fully aware of his situation. I talked with him and asked if he had any word to leave. He gave me his wife's name and address, saying, "tell her to bring up my child right." A comrade coming in at the moment, he exclaimed, "Oh, Jim! I'm going to die." Within two hours I buried him. At this hospital I worked hard both as nurse and minister, and had the satisfaction of feeling that it was to some purpose. . . .

Monday night our troops commenced recrossing the river. Our Division was relieved at 1 o'clock that day, having remained in the same line of battle 48 hours. I was called up at 12 o'clock to attend a . . . burial and saw the withdrawing column returning the way it came. It was a windy night and the sky was black with clouds. I was filled with gloomy thoughts. The midnight funeral— the darkened heavens—the repulsed army, were all in accord. The wind lifted the blanket from the face of the dead and I saw that he was a beardless boy of

Twichell's friend, Surgeon Edward T. Perkins, drew this mordant commentary on the Union disaster at Fredericksburg in December 1862. "It was evident that the slaughter had been immense, and that it should have been in vain, was sickening," Twichell wrote after witnessing the battle from a nearby hillside (letter of 17 December 1862). (Courtesy Chase Twichell)

delicate features and fair complexion. So far as I could judge by a dim lantern he was not more than 17 years old. I thought of his home and mother, and of his seemingly vain sacrifice. (The question would arise, "Why is it? Does God know?" The grieving winds could not sigh too mournful a dirge for such a burial).

Toward morning, there was a heavy shower which lasted till about 7 o'clock, by which great physical discomfort was added to the other trials of our dispirited soldiers. The roads were converted into an almost impossible condition of muddiness, and all movements were effected with extreme difficulty. The Division was ordered back to its old camps and by night had become settled in them.

The wounded, (about 100 in number) of which we had been taking care, were brought in ambulances to the Fitzhugh house ¾ of a mile from here, where they were comfortably bestowed in warm rooms, and have been carefully attended. It was a trying ride to most of them, especially the cases of amputation. Every jolt or side motion of the ambulance shot a pang of acutest pain through the lacerated body and forced out groans, cries, and often shrieks of agony. After seeing my "ward" unloaded I rode to camp and found the log house all safe. . . . Yesterday I went down to the Fitzhugh house and today I have been again. . . . My amputated boys are all doing well now, but it is hardly possible that all of them finally recover. One in three is the usual percentage of men who survive an amputated thigh.

I have omitted hitherto to state that during the comparative suspension of hostilities on Sunday, by an arrangement conducted under flag of truce, our wounded who had fallen into the enemies hands were brought to their outposts and there delivered to us. Some of our stretcher-bearers were even permitted to enter their lines, and all day a sort of free friendly intercourse was kept up between our pickets and theirs. The enemy made the first move toward the transfer of the wounded, more, I suppose, to be rid of the burden than from motives of humanity, although I would not deny them the latter altogether.

Such then is my record of the battle of Fredericksburg as it came under my observation. I may not be altogether correct in some general statements, as I have to depend on the evidence of my bodily senses, which cannot be relied on to convey a just impression of events where the line of battle is so extended. . . . This much is certain. It was a great effort accompanied by great loss to us, and ending in a failure.

The general estimate of our loss in killed, wounded, and missing is 20,000. That of the enemy, judging from the nature of their positions, could not have been more than one third as great. I saw about 500 prisoners, yet even in that respect I think our loss exceeded theirs.° It is impossible for me to depict adequately my inner private record of those momentous days. On my own memory it is indelible. I can discourse of it but, in thought and emotion, I receive and ponder it as a Divine visitation.

What is to be done next is uncertain. There is much talk, and seemingly not without foundation, that the Division is to be restored to Heintzleman's command, from which it is temporarily detached to follow this standard of Hooker. This change, if it takes place, will take us to the neighborhood of Washington, a consummation devoutly to be wished. . . . The Paymaster has not yet appeared and there will probably be abundance of time to consider the matter of my ordination. . . .

My Dear Sister: Twichell's original salutation was "Dear Father"; this was crossed out and replaced.

When we left this camp . . . it did not once occur: Burnside moved his 102,000 men quickly to the Rappahannock River, where he planned to cross, occupy the city of Fredericksburg, and drive on toward Richmond. Delays in crossing, however, allowed Lee to entrench 75,000 troops in the hills behind Fredericksburg. The frontal assault on 13 December was a disaster for the Union side.

the Corps and Grand Division: Burnside had reorganized the army into three "Grand Divisions," each comprising two corps. Hooker commanded the Center Grand Division, which included the Third Corps.

[Gens. William] Franklin and [Edwin V.] Sumner: These two generals commanded the Left and Right Grand Divisions, respectively.

we started for the suburbs toward the . . . heights: The Confederates had taken up a strong position on Marye's Heights to the west of the town.

toward the Aceldama: In Matthew 27:7–8 this is the field purchased with the money Judas received to betray Christ; in Acts 1:19 Judas himself buys the land and dies on it. Twichell may have been using its literal meaning, "field of blood."

let us turn to the left: With the horrendous carnage on Marye's Heights, many, like Twichell, put hope in Franklin's Grand Division on the left. The failure of this effort resulted in censure for Franklin in one of the wrangles among generals and politicians that typically followed military disasters.

We staid . . . and slept in the ground at the hospital: In years of speeches at Memorial Day observances and reunions after the war, Twichell told a story of this bitterly cold night, 13–14 December, as a parable of the reconciliation of Protestants and Catholics. He and Father O'Hagan combined their blankets and overcoats for warmth, but shortly the Jesuit began laughing quietly. Twichell asked him why he was laughing, and O'Hagan answered: "The scene of you and me—me, a Jesuit priest, and you, a Puritan minister of the worst kind, spooned together under the same blankets." Both chaplains agreed that if the angels were to look down, they would approve the sight.

He died last night (Wednesday): Either the letter is misdated, or Twichell has resumed writing this letter on Thursday, 18 December.

I think our loss exceeded theirs: The estimated Union losses at the battle of Fredericksburg were 12,600 killed, wounded, and captured. The Confederates reported 5,300 lost.

On 21 December, Twichell wrote to his father with a brief update on conditions in camp.

It is bitter cold today but our men have made themselves quite comfortable—an art which I perceive is not yet acquired by the new regiments. It is enough to make one's teeth chatter to see their little shelter tents simply pitched on the frozen ground. The thermometer was 10° above zero this morning. There are rumors of coming movements, and indeed some things, such as the keeping on hand of six days rations, seem to indicate it. If it takes place there will be great suffering.

In Camp. Near Falmouth, Va. Dec. 28th 1862.

Dear Father,

I am still waiting for the Paymaster. The Government is tardy beyond all reason and humanity in a matter which seriously effects the welfare of thousands [of] poor people. Gen. Sickles went to Washington yesterday and it is supposed he will effect our speedy relief. If the Government has not money sufficient for its current expenses, let it either get more, or reduce its expenses. It is miserable policy to run up a long account with the Army. Men will lose confidence in an Administration which does not keep its promises to women and children. Today is as balmy as spring. We held divine service out of doors at 11 o'clock without the least discomfort. This afternoon we have buried Richard M. Fuller of Co. I. He died last night after a long sickness. . . . I think if the poor fellow could have gone home three months ago he would, humanly speaking, have recovered. His disease was chronic dysentery, cured less by medicine than by diet and nursing, two things at best indifferently attained in a field hospital. Many soldiers die who might be saved by timely furloughs. These are very difficult to procure now, the privilege having been grossly abused during the early part of the war. The innocent here, as elsewhere, have to suffer for the guilty. . . .

The Thanksgiving, which I supposed safely digested a month since by one of my boys in Washington, reached here very unexpectedly today. By some hocus-pocus the box itself had disappeared. Only the chicken pie, covered in its pan by a mince pie, was left of the original package. How far it had travelled thus naked I do not know. But it was not in danger of being coveted, for it had, by age, assumed the appearance of a mass of blue mould. I opened the top of the chicken pie and found the contents fast returning to dust. The Doctor, more anxious than I, for I had a raging tooth-ache and didn't feel hungry, dived deeper and near the bottom of the dish discovered some fragments of fowl, not wholly decomposed and committed to the cook the task of separating such edible part as yet remains. It is a pity that so kind intentions should be so poorly accomplished. I thank you all the same. If the cook succeeds in rescuing any portion of your gift from utter waste, I may yet be able to pronounce my opinion of mother's culinary effort—of course, with a charity due to the circumstances. Last Wednesday, the wounded from our Division Hospital were started on their way to Washington. It was two miles to the cars and, being over a rough road, the initial journey was a sore thing to the lacerated bodies, especially the cases of amputation. . . .

Gen. [Joseph W.] Revere (formerly Col. of 7th N.J. vols.) has been assigned to this brigade. He took command yesterday relieving Col. Hall who had been acting ever since we left Alexandria. The Col. started immediately for Washington and New York on leave of absence, for the purpose, it is supposed, of entering the list for a Brigadiership. I sincerely trust he will not succeed for he is not worthy of promotion, if indeed he is fit to retain his present place. I am sorry to say this but it is true. . . .

It is currently reported that we are to move for a short distance during this week, for the purpose of securing better located camps and a more systematic arrangement of the Division. This will turn us out of our grand log-house, which is and has for three weeks been our glory. If, however, we pitch again within reasonable distance, we can in a day or two cart these same logs to the new place and put them up in much less time than it would take to cut the timber afresh. . . .

Other news I have none, save that I have a most persistent and peace-ruining tooth-ache—the first of my life. It occupies most of my attention. Please ascribe to it the lack of care, perhaps intelligibility, characterizing this letter. . . . Tomorrow morning, if the offending grinder does not suspend hostilities, I shall give it no mercy. Give my love to all who ask for me. . . . Your aff. Son. Joseph.

January–April 1863

After the disaster of Fredericksburg the army returned to its camps across the river in Falmouth, Virginia. As the winter wore on, Twichell concerned himself with political matters. In a letter to his father on 15 March, he makes clear his advocacy of a military takeover if need be to deal with perceived traitors in the Northern states. "The strong Life of the Nation is under canvas tents to-night," he writes. With spring came changes in army leadership, a visit from his father to camp, and an unexpected personal tragedy.

In Camp. Near Falmouth, Va. New Years Day 1863.

Dear Sis,

I am very tired tonight having been in the saddle a great part of the day, but I cannot think of going to bed without hailing the folks at home . . . and saluting you all, as I have saluted hundreds whom I love less, with a wish for your Happy New Year. . . . This morning everybody was astir early. . . . The air was full of cheery cries. "Happy New Year" rang out on every hand. My poor fellows seemed absolutely happy and it was a delight to see their lit up faces: yet they had nothing to enjoy whereby this day differed from all other days. . . . I think, however, that a loaf of soft bread sent to us from Washington, and a ration of whiskey, were dealt out in the course of the day.

At 12 o'clock Major Rafferty called his officers together and we went in a body to pay our respects to . . . General [Revere] but found him absent from his quarters. Then, Drs. [James] Ash and [John] Younglove, with my-self, mounted our horses and rode some three miles to call on old Joe Hooker. We found him amiable as the weather, which I have forgotten to state was of the finest. We staid at Gen. Hooker's half an hour with great satisfaction. He is one of the most courteous, affable men I ever met, and never puts on airs except to the enemy. He expressed himself freely with reference to the late battle and the conduct of the war generally. He said, "there seems to have been a special study how *not* to do it." Also, concerning the Banks expedition° —"It is the only movement of which the Government kept its destination a secret. The common sense of the nation scouted the rumour of a southern mission as a concealment and a blind, saying, 'It must be going to James River for it is wanted there,' and lo, it sails away from us, out of sight, and contrary to the advice of a People." I was told that he remarked a few days since of the same expedition, "It has gone President-making." I hope that the result will prove Gen. H. to be wrong in his verdict. . . .

At 3 o'clock the officers of the brigade met at the camp of the 1st Regt., and from thence, headed by Gen. Revere, proceeded to Headquarters of Division to visit Gen. Sickles. We found everything in real gala-day order. The wide street lying between the staff tents, which face each other, was spanned by arches of evergreens, adorned with appropriate devices, and all the place was gaily attired. At a short distance stands a small house. This was used as the eating and drinking rendezvous. On its piazza, a band of two violins, two flutes, an accordion, and a man who chirruped like a bird, discoursed sweet music and drowned the noise of mastication. Swarms of bright uniformed officers filled the grounds, galloping in from near and far. The programme was to first salute the General, then salute his victuals and drink, but Father O'Hagan and I, who stuck together, observed that rum was flowing freely and so, having made obeisance to the Gen., we omitted the refreshments and retired to his (Father O'H's) quarters where we devoured a quiet dinner and consumed some tobacco in peace. The day has gone quite happily throughout the army. Games, horse races etc. have abounded, and with the exception of a far too free use of liquor, it has been a source of innocent pleasure. . . . May 1863 continue the happiness and prosperity of our house. . . . Your Aff. Bro. Joseph.

concerning the Banks expedition: In the western theater of war, General Nathaniel P. Banks had been given command of the Federal Department of the Gulf, replacing General Benjamin F. Butler in an expedition to New Orleans whose aims were initially concealed. Both Butler and Banks had been active in Massachusetts politics before the war—Banks had been governor—and it was natural for Hooker, also from that state, to impute political ambition to Banks.

Dear Father,

With but an hour's special warning the Regiment was moved yesterday noon about a mile eastward. The movement was simultaneous with the 1st and 2nd Brigades—the 3rd retaining its place. The advantages sought by this change are, I suppose, an improved order of location and better facilities in the way of wood and water. It seems to indicate that our stay in this region may not be as transient as some have anticipated, yet is no surety thereof. . . .

After months of absence, Rev. Mr. [John W.] Alvord appeared again Friday. I was delighted beyond measure to see him. He is a good man and a very Paul for fearless energy. Most winning in his address, understanding all sorts of men, fertile in resources for making his way and establishing confidence, he has accomplished a vast amount of good in the army. I never saw his equal in cheering and encouraging a Chaplain who feels depressed. Last summer, after the seven days battles, moved by the prevalence of unalleviated suffering among the sick and wounded, he stirred up some godly people in Boston to send him stores. The result was that in a few weeks he distributed, mostly with his own hands, 100,000 lbs of varied comfort, and all this outside of his main business as agent of the Tract Society. His wagon is a widely and well-known institution. There are many Generals' quarters at which he is always a welcome guest. Friday night he staid with me. . . . We called on the other chaplains of the Brigade, including Father O'Hagan and Mr. A brightened the face of every one. This reminds me that the new Chaplain of the 1st Regt. has arrived—Rev. G[eorge] W. Horton. He is a young man and I like his looks. The only deficit observable is that he is not robust. I was not a little amused to hear him remark on the inadequacy of a tent to shelter the human frame. His opinion of tents will improve after he has bivouacked on frozen ground a few times. Mr [Robert] Sittler of the 5th goes in strong. He is a man of uncommon simplicity, in fact, so much so, that I fear he will get some of his men to laugh at him—a most undesirable thing—although not altogether incompatible with respect. *Utter* simplicity will not do in fishing for such wily gudgeons—regular sharpers—as abound in the Excelsior Brigade. While keeping in view a strict rectitude of conduct, one has to use somewhat of this world's wisdom if he purposes to acquire influence among them. Let me illustrate. Mr Sittler, in meeting his parishioners individually, addresses them, I judge, after this fashion— "My dear friend," with strong emphasis on the "dear," or if the proper name is used, it is in a tone soft as that of a sighing lover. He will find in a short time that his *"dear* friend" and gentle appellatives will become engrafted in the common vernacular of his men. He had better study the prevailing style of salutation and, where it is not unbecoming, use it. His full heart and yearning desire should not be always dancing off the tip of his tongue, else, on special occasions he will find himself lacking special expression. Sacred things must be mentioned or unfolded to rude men, at a time, if possible, when their rudeness is not in the ascendant.

Gen. Sickles told me yesterday that the Paymaster would be here in a very few days. I drafted a certificate such as you advised, setting forth the circumstances of my connection with the Regiment without ordination, and submitted it to him. He altered it slightly and ordered it to be copied for his signature. . . . Love to all. Your aff. Son Joseph.

> *In Camp, near Falmouth, Va.*
> *Sunday night. Jan. 11th 1863.*

Dear Father,

Again no public service. It rained hard yesterday and nearly all night, leaving the ground soft and the air heavy with chill mist. . . . The Major did not think it best to assemble the men out of doors, neither did I, though I was loth to give it up. Whatever may be the cause of omitting the Sunday service, however imperative it is, I never feel quite reconciled to it. . . . I visited the regimental hospital and talked a little with the dozen patients, but that I do everyday. I also went about among the boys and gave them a few tracts that I had, but that is not a work limited to the Sabbath. . . . At times I am overtaken by the thought that my situation is lacking in the stimulus of external circumstances. Neglect of the most sacred duty on my part, or a partial attention to it, would pass unnoticed save by a very few, and probably without rebuke from any. So long as I remained benevolent and helpful, I should be called and esteemed a good Chaplain, even though I forbore almost entirely to preach Christ Crucified. In this mood I desire a change to some post where public opinion, and a general appreciation of what is due from a Christian minister, would arouse and quicken me. . . .

The Regiment was on picket, eight miles from camp, from Monday till Thursday. . . . No certain signs yet of the Paymaster, although I should not be surprised if he appeared tomorrow morning. I shall be disappointed if the week passes without his coming. He must come, or the men will grow into a serious hostility and bitterness toward the Government. For my own part, I have anticipated coming home until I am actually homesick. It seems as if I never sighed so longingly for the air of Plantsville as I do now. The great cause of my journey thither is continually before me. The more I think of it, the calmer I grow, I hope it is not indifference. . . .

Col. Hall, having returned from Washington without the Brigadier's star, assumed command of the regiment this afternoon. Lt. Col. Potter is daily expected, although not wholly recovered from his wound. I presume the old quarrel will begin anew, and disgrace the service as of old. . . . Love to all. Your aff. Son. Joseph.

> Twichell wrote his father from Washington on 20 January. In the letter he refers to his coming ordination, and, briefly, to army movements.

I left camp this morning and reached here at 3 o'clock p.m., bringing the men's money, upwards $10,000. I have already telegraphed that I shall probably reach home by the middle of next week. . . . I trust that the arrangements for my ordination will bring it about with as little delay as is consistent with convenience, for I shall be anxious to be back with my boys, especially if there is to be fighting. . . .

We had been three times ordered to march when I left. The order each time was countermanded for 24 hours. This morning the extreme right . . . was in motion, but I do not know whether it was general. It was bitter cold. . . .

> Twichell was on his way home to Plantsville and was ordained by the Reverend Elisha C. Jones, his family pastor, on 30 January. On his way back to his regiment he stopped in Washington, staying with the McBlairs.

Washington. Sunday Evening. Feb. 15th 1863.

Dear Father,

It really seems pleasant to sit down and again commence the regular Sunday epistle. Long indulgence has so confirmed me in the habit that I fear it will prove ineradicable. I can hardly imagine myself living without it. Whether I have anything to communicate or not it makes no difference; I must write. It enters into my inevitable and needful functions, without which there would be a sense of disorder or incompletion. . . .

I review my visit home with great satisfaction. It was a season long to be remembered with profound emotion and devout gratitude. How the events it incloses will tell on my future, God alone knows. I hope, yet have hours of troubled reflection. "I am an ordained minister," is continually in my mind. Sometimes I am strong, again I am pitiably weak. Sometimes the thought is grand, and sometimes awful. But I have put my hand to the plough. I am cursed, surely, if I look back. "I will look unto the hills from whence cometh my help." More than ever now shall I need the faithful prayers of those who have prayed for me. . . . With my best love to the folks at home. I remain. Your affectionate Son. Joseph.

In Camp, near Falmouth. Va. Feb. 22nd 1863.

My dear Father,

It is a day of elemental wrath. Last night, after a fair, sunny day, the sky put on sackcloth. This morning the snow lay nearly a foot deep and the storm was not abated. There is a high wind and the air is thick with flakes. It is a real northern affair and an hour since as I waded a drift, leaning against the blast, all the old snowstorm sensations of boyhood rose vividly within me until I fancied that I was again struggling my way over the hill toward Lewis Academy.° . . . The old-time exhilaration revived and, forgetting that I was a man and a minister, I was invaded by the juvenile instinct of snow bathing. The dive, the somersault, the labors of mine-digging, were only prevented by my awaking to present realities — to the fact that my free mittened and tippeted period is left behind and that my way now and henceforth lies through a sober land. My early life was so exceeding happy that my visions of memory are always sweet, and I sigh when they vanish. Occasionally I get back so far that I happen upon Innocence, and then a pang of regret closes the retrospect. . . .

The storm was sufficient of itself to make the camp, with its narrow quarters, a place of gloom and discomfort, but even the tolerable mitigations were denied the Excelsior Brigade. Late last night the order came to make ready for three days picket duty. It was a bitter thing to march this morning but they did it — the poor fellows — with more cheerfulness than you would suppose. I went out to them after they were drawn up on the color line behind their stacked arms. All were stamping their feet and rubbing their hands to keep up circulation, but jokes were flying thick as the flakes and, while there was a deal of grumbling, there was little anger. I could easily pardon merriment, nay even admire it, under such circumstances, if it did chance to be on Sunday. Three days picket in such weather involves formidable hardship. A long line of outposts is to be maintained and no fires are permitted, except in the rear where the "relief" is stationed. I did not go, for the double reason, that I could be of no use, and also because tomorrow I must be busy establishing my quarters, which have vanished during my absence. The log house was dismantled when the army marched on Burnside's last movement, and has since been turned into a hospital cookhouse. . . . I had my choice between turning in with our new Dr. Younglove, and setting up a private establishment. I chose the latter unanimously, for I have often experienced great inconvenience from not being alone, especially in the matter of holding religious conversation with the men who call on me. I find that it is distasteful to the Surgeons to have privates familiarly received in their quarters. I do not blame them for it, yet it is my duty and pleasure to receive them cordially and render it agreeable for them to call on me, hence I need a place of my own. In pursuance of this idea, as soon as I returned I procured a tent from the quartermaster, and my man Martin° has since been employed in making it habitable—no slight task, since it involved digging, laying up log walls, the construction of a fire place and chimney, and various furnishing. I reached here Thursday afternoon and was welcomed most flatteringly by all, excepting perhaps the Col. [Hall], who made no outward manifestation, but who secretly I think loves me little. The good Major gave me a joyful salutation, and importuned me to share his tent till mine was made ready. He wanted to know all about my visit and the ordination and I was a good while occupied in giving the details thereof. . . .

At 12 o'clock today there arose a sudden fire of artillery to the southward, almost simultaneously a dull booming came from the North, and again the heavy air brought a similar sound from the East. "Good Gracious! What can it mean!," thought I, and for a few minutes the suspense was considerable, until some one solved the mystery by saying, "Why, of course, its Washington's birthday." I did not hear any salutes from the other side of the Rappahannock. *Their* Washington is not yet known. . . .

My visit home abides with me as a theme of thought. Many things connected with it I shall never forget, especially the evidence I received that our family is bound together in sincere love. I did not say much about it, Father, but I felt more deeply than words can tell that, in my Father's affection, I posses a wealth that may not be measured or lightly held. I do not merit it. Your eyes are shut to many things, but I was born to the inheritance and I thank God for it. My love to all our folks and friends. Your affectionate Son. Joseph.

over the hill toward Lewis Academy: Twichell attended Lewis Academy in Southington from 1850 to 1855. The "tippet" referred to in this snowy reminiscence was a scarflike garment.

my man Martin: In his 1864 journal of the Wilderness Campaign, Twichell identifies his servant as "Martin Furniss, private in Co. H."

In Camp. Near Falmouth, Va. Sunday, March 1st 1863.

My dear Father,

If the old saying concerning this month—"In like a lion, out like a lamb"— is true we have some very delightful weather due in four weeks. It rained last night and there has been more of it this morning with a high wind, although the sun is out for a few minutes just now. The camp is a perfect sop and a sucking sound betrays the feet that plod past my tent. But notwithstanding the above facts, the service was well attended and, as far as I could judge, well enjoyed by all. . . .

The week has passed without excitement or incident of general interest. The Regiment returned from picket Wednesday afternoon fully persuaded that, after all, camp was a luxurious place. Tuesday morning, taking the mail, I set out to pay the boys a visit. . . . The roads were awful. Several times my horse floundered in mire of such depth that I contemplated his chances of extrication as exceedingly slim. Howbeit, after six hours of toil, [I] returned to camp, having abandoned the search as fruitless.

I am now snugly settled in new quarters and am better satisfied with my arrangements than at any time since last winter on the Lower Potomac. My tent is of linen, very light, yet sufficiently warm by the aid of a most cheerful fireplace. The bed is a perfect success, and Mart has made me a chair which, though ungainly to look at, is comfortable to sit on. . . . The advantages I anticipated from being alone have already begun to appear. Private conversations have taken place which seemed only to have been waiting till they *could* be private. Before, a few words now and then of warning and exhortation were all that convenience allowed, whereas a good long talk is what men want and need and here it is invited. . . . [A] German Sergeant [Henry] Funck dropped in to visit. I knew him well and had often seen him at service. He . . . confess[ed] that he regarded his soul's salvation as his first interest and that [he] was always uneasy in view of his sinful state. I may here observe that the Germans, although generally stolid and phlegmatic in habit, appear in their *religious* emotions to be eminently tender and demonstrative. I have seldom talked with a Christian German without his weeping. . . .

There is tonight, at Gen. Sickles' quarters at the Fitzhugh House, a grand supper. Genl.'s Hooker and [Franz] Sigel are guests, together with a large number of Generals beside, none of a grade below the Brigadiership, being summoned—with two exceptions, Father O'Hagan and myself. The Father called on me this afternoon to inform me of my invitation as he received it from Gen. Sickles. We consulted and unanimously concluded not to go, on Christian, professional, and politic grounds. 1st. It is Sunday, though the Father said he would not decline for that alone, since it is at so late an hour (8 o'clock). 2nd. There will be free drinking and we should be annoyed by solicitations to join in it. 3rd. It will be such a gathering of stars that we should feel ill at ease. 4th. We did not consider ourselves of sufficient age and calibre to appropriately sustain the dignity of the cloth in such a presence. Therefore, heartily thanking the General for so distinguished a mark of his regard, we concluded to stay at home and read good books, leaving the warriors to their own society. I confess that curiosity, if nothing else, urged me to go and, had the Father agreed, I would have risked it for an hour. It would have been a memorable occasion but I am now glad that we refrained.

Two Captains of the Regt., both young men, have called on me today to witness their agreement to abstain from the use of liquor as a beverage while they are on duty as officers of the Government. I received their pledge gladly, for they were in great danger through the practice of tippling, and I hope this beginning will introduce a general reform in that respect among our young officers. It gave me pleasure also, as it often has before when the correction of conduct has been undertaken, that *I* was deemed essential to the completeness of the transaction. May it always be the case in my parish, that "swearing off to the Chaplain" is regarded as adding significance to a promise or validity to a bond.

After supper this evening, I paid a pastoral visit to Major Rafferty, and, as usual, to my enjoyment and edification. He is in low spirits about the national prospects and rendered uncomfortable by some circumstances of the regiment, but in matters pertaining to Zion full of brightness. He is one of those men who are pre-eminently Christians. . . . Would that all Chaplains had such a Major. . . .

Your counsel, Father, I thank you for, knowing as I do the appreciative solicitude that prompts it. I have scarcely yet myself realized my ordination. When I do confront the fact and think what I am, I almost wish it undone. But that can never be. My vows are irrevocable. I see no promise of peace but in leaving all that is behind and pressing forward and upward. I have many hours of deep depression, almost horror, yet I know that my only deliverance from such is to work, watch and pray. If I am wrong, I cannot right myself. God must do it, and will do it. . . . With much love to you all, I remain. Your aff. Son. Joseph.

In Camp. Near Falmouth, Va.
Sunday night. March 8th 1863.

Dear Father,

The week has passed flying. It hardly seems possible that my "letter night" has come again. . . . I long for the end of this war, the solution of this darkness, the lightening of this suspense. Let the time flee as fast as ever it may—let the weeks chase each other scarcely distinct—like the fence posts beside a railroad to one who is whirled by them—the greater the speed the better, for it promises the End and with the end, if God will to bring me to it, comes a fresh beginning. This is a *feeling*, I know, and a false reckoning in view of daily duty, yet I am invaded by it. It afflicts me also in another way and leads up a temptation. Every day, in contemplating the future and placing an estimate on it in comparison with the present, I find myself prone to regard the time I am passing in the army as *lost* time, for which I must make amends when I return to the old order. It assumes the character of a gap or recess—a break in my life which it will require great diligence to repair—a putting off (necessary and excusable) of my business, until I may resume it. Now, while in an inferior sense, there is some ground for this feeling; in the wider view—taking into the account my Life Work and the interests of Zion to which I am nominally devoted, it is groundless and I fear dangerous. I do not know that I shall ever again be placed where I can preach the Gospel with such an advantage as here and certainly I shall never be placed where it is more needed. I ought to feel that I have come to that for which I have been preparing, *now*, and set at work as having found the object of my search and desire. Here I can honor Christ if ever. My circumstances relieve me of no duty, a return to civil life will develop no new one. I have always the same thing to do—to preach the Gospel. If the Union is saved, that will devolve upon me. If it is dismembered, I shall still be a minister of the Truth of God in Christ. . . . The obligation is upon me now, it can never be stronger. These are my deep convictions yet I have often the feeling of which I have spoken. The temptation it brings is to mingle my estimate of the time, my desire of its hastening, with the duties that exist in it. In urging on the days, there is danger that I slur over their solemn significance as days of probation to immortal souls. . . .

Friday, my turn having come, I visited the Division Hospital and spent a large part of the afternoon. I was received by all the patients with courtesy and by most with evident gratitude. . . . To some, after a short inquiry into the nature and length of their illness, their regiment etc., I plainly stated my errand. "I wish, if you please, to talk with you on the subject of religion." I did this because I am convinced that, too frequently, the system of smuggling in the subject, or sugaring it over at the start, is pursued with the best intention . . . but sometimes to the annoyance of the listener, who, if he is ordinarily keen, can see what is coming and would prefer to have it spoken out candidly. . . . Two men with whom I talked were moved to tears, the only tears that it is pleasant to see dropping from mortal eyes. . . .

Friday night I was destined to a great surprise. After returning from the hospital, as I sat before my fire musing and peacefully burning tobacco in my pipe, I heard the Adjutant's voice outside, saying, "This, gentleman, is the Chaplain's tent," and on going to the door, lo! Messrs Hotchkiss, Smith and Pratt.° I was astonished . . . and, of course, delighted. . . . After supper at which the knees of my guests served them for tables, I gave myself to the enjoyment of their visit, and with great success. We canvassed thoroughly the local interests of our native town and collated our war opinions till near 10 o'clock, when . . . they retired to their severally appointed beds. . . . I was up betimes in the morning making ready to give them a view of Fredericksburg for which they had professed a wish. Without difficulty I procured a horse for each and after breakfast we mounted, rode to the Lacy House, inspected rebeldom, and returned to Falmouth Station in time for the 10½ a.m. train. I hope they were satisfied for I did all that lay in my power to secure them the objects of their visit. I am truly thankful to them for the honor they bestowed by calling on me and shall remember it with pleasure.

Since they departed I have been thinking that if . . . those gentlemen can come here and survive it, you can also. That I should be delighted to see you, you well know. My invitation is cordial, and would be urgent, if there were not something to be left to your own judgement. If you had been here, enjoyed the visit, and were safely back without damage, I should recur to it as glorious event. If you will try it, nothing that I can do to make you comfortable shall be left undone. . . . My love to you all.

Your aff. Son. Joseph.

Messrs Hotchkiss, Smith and Pratt: Charles A. Hotchkiss, various Smiths, and Horace P. Pratt, all of Southington, served in Connecticut regiments. Edward Twichell's business partner in the carriage hardware business was Henry D. Smith.

In Camp. Near Falmouth, Va.
Sunday Evening. March 15th 1863.

Dear Father,

Your unusually long letter of Mar. 8th came only day before yesterday. . . . I fully concur with your opinions of public affairs, especially in your assignment of Military Success to the dignity of the Nation's Hope. If an Army was *to be* raised, we might, in view of a divided sentiment, a faltering loyalty, a feeble confidence in our Chiefs of Administration, and straitened finances, be faint at heart, with reason. But the Army *is* raised; it is in the field confronting the enemy. For the time the army *is* the nation. It is regarded such the world over. According to the rise or fall of its banners, not according to the fluctuating tide of wordy but unarmed politics in the background, we are to frame our opinions regarding the status of the country. Not that collateral circumstances are to be left out of the account entirely, not that the voice of the unenlisted public is to be banished in the estimate of hopes and fears, but that the already mustered bayonets of the Republic constitute the great central Repository of issues.

Let our principal strength of emotion, our confidence, our prayers, follow the coming campaign, leaving the broils engendered by demagogues comparatively unheeded. While we may regret and in a measure fear the perversion of our *voting* forces, let us remember that it is to the men who throw bullets, and not votes, that we are to look for deliverance. Until the peacemongers grow so strong as to *recall the army*, their power to do harm is exceedingly limited. Moreover, I am persuaded that the army is thoroughly loyal, and never more willing for the test of battle than now. It will be a matter of more difficulty than peace democrats may think to spike our cannon. Washington will have to be *chained* first, and even then, have we not muskets in our hands that can be turned two ways? I tell you, Father, the Army is boss of this job. If home enemies succeed in turning things upside down, the Army can give things *one more* turn and make the *Connecticut Resolutions* try standing on their heads.° Two negatives make a positive. A double confusion may develop order. Violated obligations are the parents of Anarchy. We have not come to that yet, but perhaps we need such fires for our purification, for we do not seem to become sufficiently molten to release our dross by present calamities. If anarchy *does* befall us, those who carry the cartridges are the masters of the situation. Let them look well to the matter who would stop us this side [of] our legitimate goal. The day that hears the order, "Cease firing!," dictated to the Army by a peace democracy triumphant at the ballot box, will be a day long to be remembered in the annals of gunpowder. Look to the Army, Father. Hang your faith on it as, under God, the grand Security of a troubled people. How *can* they recall us? Will they refuse supplies? Will they stop the pay? Will they resist conscription? But, I tell you again, we possess 700,000 muskets that can be pointed in *any* direction, and all, I firmly believe, unalterably sworn to wage active warfare against all enemies of the *United States of America*, whenever, wherever or however they shall *openly* assert themselves. I think that we do wrong in regarding the Army as depending on the people. True, there is a certain reciprocity of dependence, but the people stand *behind* the army in which *Force*, humanly speaking the arbiter of our destinies, principally resides. We have so long been an unmilitary nation that it is not easy for us to comprehend or admit the real significance of our armed soldierings. The vicissitudes of the times have *exalted* something that we had abased as a tool of despotisms. "What do our rulers *say?*," was once our most eager inquiry. It has given place to another, for the time, viz. "How will our soldiers shoot?" Once our arms

were locked up in forts or kept out of sight away on the frontier. Our difficulties with all except the Indians were settled on paper. *Now*, the case is well
nigh reversed—not wholly, but well nigh. Our documents are sent away to
the garrets to mould with our compromises etc. Great orations are only a cent
apiece—prices of statesmanship are down—the grand power—the strong Life
of the Nation is under canvas tents tonight. If it is not now fully realised, the
circumstances are possible that will develop it in unmistakeable light. History
at least will be compelled to confess it.

As usual, I have followed my own nose too far. It was my intention to write
you only the news of the week and make my letter respectably brief. . . . Service
was held this morning at 10 o'clock—before Inspection. . . . My service was
more numerously attended than before this winter; indeed the congregation
has increased every Sunday since I returned. . . . After the last singing I repeated an invitation, which I have often given but not lately, to all who wished
to talk with me on the subject of religion, to come to my quarters without
reserve and at any time. I told them that they need never fear interrupting me
or delaying me in any engagement, for to receive such visits was not only my
first pleasure but my first business also. I have reason to thank God that He
put it into my heart to give that invitation. A man was waiting for it. He has
been in since I began this letter, told his feelings, declared his deep anxiety. I
have counselled him as well as I was able, prayed with him and dismissed him.
What the result will be God knows. I can only wait for it. . . . I hope that he
is the first of many—the first who has confessed voluntarily what others are
keeping hid. Pray for us that the Outpouring may hasten. . . .

Friday night, Gen. Sickles gave a ball in honor of his accession to the Major
Generalship.° At 8½ o'clock in the evening a mounted orderly left the enclosed
invitation at my door, and inquired the way to Father O'Hagan's. I dressed
speedily, called for my horse and rode over to the 4th, in time to join the Father, who had dispatched a messenger meanwhile to ask it as a favor. We set
out. The night was dark and before we were 20 rods from the camp of the
4th, the Fathers horse stepped into a hole, fell and threw the unlucky priest
in great confusion upon a pile of rubbish near by. The suspense was short.
No harm was done barring a general soiling and disarrangement of toilet, and
we proceeded on our way. Arrived at the Fitzhugh House a scene of festivity,
quite foreign to our habits here, burst upon us. Large tents were erected so as
to eke out the narrow accommodations of the house, and the whole was gaily
decked with flags and green festoons, while the light of a thousand candles
and lively music wrought up the effect to the point of bewilderment. Hundreds of bright uniformed officers were assembled and a wedding party (the

wedding took place Thursday in the 7th N. Jersey Regt. One of its Captains was the bridegroom—a novel and interesting affair) embracing nine bridesmaids beside the bride, borrowed second-hand for this occasion, completed the brilliancy of the entertainment. The guests were made up of Generals with their Staffs and Commanders of Regiments exclusively, excepting, of course, the two humble black clothed individuals who felt a little out of place. When we reached the scene the dancing had begun and all was going "merry as a marriage bell." As soon as possible we pushed our way to the General, saluted and congratulated him. He welcomed us with warmth and immediately drew us aside into an inner room where (I must confess it) we took a sip of wine with him, and engaged in conversation for nearly half an hour of the most familiar and agreeable tone. Then when the supper was announced he called us to partake with the "quality" present (numbering about 25) of the first installment thereof. Afterward, the rabble—Colonels etc.—had a chance to fill their maws. At the supper we had an opportunity to speak with Gen. Hooker and were introduced to Gen. [Hiram] Berry, now commanding our Division. Shortly after 11 o'clock we retired in good order, leaving the gay party, to which clerical abstemiousness were no object, to wear the night away in light-footed pleasure. You may imagine that we were highly gratified with the treatment we experienced. I will not omit to mention that the Gen. apologised to us for asking us to supper Sunday night a week ago. "It was not my deliberate purpose to have it on Sunday," he explained. "I asked Gen. Hooker to name the day, and he said March 1st, so I ordered it for March 1st and neither of us knew the day of the week." . . . Tuesday is St. Patrick's day. I intend to visit the Irish Brigade. With much love to all. . . . I remain as ever. Joseph.

P.S. Col. Hall is again in arrest, and under charges. Col. Potter has returned. Major Rafferty goes to morrow on 10 days leave. . . .

the Army can . . . make the Connecticut Resolutions try standing on their heads: Connecticut's statewide elections for governor, state senators, and state representatives were scheduled for 6 April. In February, the Democrats had held a convention in Hartford and issued resolutions that denounced secession but said "all true lovers of the Constitution are ready to abandon the 'monstrous fallacy' that the Union can be restored by an armed hand."

Gen. Sickles . . . his accession to the Major Generalship: In January, Lincoln removed Burnside as commander of the Army of the Potomac and replaced him with Hooker. Hooker scrapped Burnside's system of "grand divisions" of the army and restored the corps system. Sickles, who had befriended Hooker in the year since their disputes over returned slaves and issues of command, was placed in command of the Third Corps. The Senate again delayed, but not as long, confirming Sickles's promotion to major general on 9 March.

My dear Ned,°

Father had written that, as soon as he can spare a week from his boxes, he will pay me a visit. Will you be so kind as to transact for me a little business in the meantime, to wit—Go to Brooks Brothers, Tailors, on Broadway where I have left my measure with the cutter . . . and order for me a pair of dark (black if possible) *corduroy* pants, double seated for the saddle. Pay for them and have them sent to your office so that you can forward them by Father when he comes down. Inform me of the amount of the bill and I will remit immediately. Will it be too great an inconvenience? If so, don't hesitate to say it. . . .

The Brigade has seen some service since you inspected it last, and in numbers is not what it was then. . . . Under Gen. Hooker's efficient regime we are polishing up our tools for another campaign which we hope will result in breaking the backbone etc. I am persuaded that the Army of the Potomac never had more fight in it than now. The general health is remarkably good and a spirit of confidence prevails. This, at least, is certain; however the Copperhead virus may poison the loyalty of the Northern voters,° the Northern soldiers are untainted by it. The old Jacksonian creed is what we are sworn to° and by it we will abide. Before many weeks the sound of loyal cannon will offset the hand-organ din of disloyal croakers. If any man says that the North is divided, let faithful patriots point proudly to the *Arms* of the Republic— remaining unalterably fixed in the purpose to which they were originally sent. Within our lines the stars all stick by the flag, or rather, the flag holds on to all its stars.

We are not all Republicans or antislavery men. Some there are who hate colored folk with all the intensity of depraved ignorance—who feel above *dying* on the same day with a negro. Some there are who think the present Administration a dead failure and Abe Lincoln an imbecile (though Hooker doesn't let them say much about the matter). There are a few who think we are bound to be beaten—many who would rejoice to see Horace Greel[e]y hanged—many who would be pleased to load [Henry Ward] Beecher into a cannon and fire him off—many who consider Wendell Phillips worse than Jeff Davis—many who wish Massachusetts sunk in the Dead Sea, but we have not one who [does] not deeply feel that the Copperhead Peace-Democratic party is a mighty mean set of fellows. They are a stench in all our nostrils. Had they sufficient courage to come down here with their blatant noises, that same hour would witness the universal cry, "Turn 'em out!!" Nor would we degrade good honest Union *bayonets* to the drudgery of accelerating their departure. Our *toes* itch for the job. Abolitionist, Republican, Democrat, negro-hater, whatever we may be—despondent, despairing, hopeful, confident, brave, timid—however we may feel, all agree in loathing the persons and principles of those political reptiles who smear the loyal North with the slime of a sneaking secessionism. We *love* the rebels in comparison, and I think they *love us* in comparison. If we should be compelled to give up the contest and ask terms of peace because we were utterly routed, I am sure both sides would immediately join in ducking the whole Copperhead Peace party in the filthiest pool that could be found on the continent, as an expression of our mutual regard.

"Them's my sentiments." I have a good mind to copy just what I have said and send it to my friend [Cyrus] Northrop, editor of the New Haven Palladium.° I partly promised him a letter, and it would give me great pleasure to ventilate in the Connecticut press my opinion of those dastardly Hartford Resolution makers.

I left you, my dear Ned, with the most agreeable impressions of your condition and prospects. Especially was I gratified with my short visit to Brooklyn. I gathered from it the firm conviction that you had set out to make your life something beside a period devoted to making money or enjoying yourself. I do not think you are called to serve your country as a soldier, but I do think that you are called to serve it as a Christian. . . . Wishing you, my good Brother, all the blessings of a well-ordered, successful life. I remain. Yours affectionately. Joseph.

My dear Ned: Twichell's brother Edward was then living in Brooklyn.

the Copperhead virus may poison the loyalty of the Northern voters: The antiwar or "Copperhead" faction of the Democratic Party opposed turning the war into a total war against slavery, favoring instead a settlement that would restore the union "as it was." After two years of war, with a draft imminent, the group was gathering strength. To Republicans like Twichell, Copperheadism could be equated with treason.

The old Jacksonian creed is what we are sworn to: At a banquet in 1830, President Andrew Jackson gave a famous toast: "Our Federal Union—it must and shall be preserved."

my friend [Cyrus] Northrop, editor of the New Haven Palladium: While at Yale Twichell had made the acquaintance of Northrop, the young editor of New Haven's Republican newspaper. Northrop later taught at Yale and served as second president of the University of Minnesota.

Camp of 2nd Regt. Ex. Brig. March 23rd 1863.

Dear Ned,

Father appeared last night totally unannounced. I have hardly recovered from the shock yet. As an introduction I have today taken him a ride of 15 miles and he complains of a slight stiffness in the thighs. Tomorrow morning it will probably have all passed away. Don't you think so? He has now retired and while tucking him in I felt that the tables are at last turned. For once in my life he is under my care and a guest in my house.

You have before this received a letter from me requesting you to order me a pair of pants and hold them in readiness for Father's coming. I now write to tell you to order them notwithstanding and hold them subject to my order. . . . Yours affectionately. Joseph.

> *Camp of 2nd Regt. Ex. Brig. Near Falmouth. Va.*
> *March 29th 1863.*

Dear Father,

You have not been long enough gone for much news to accumulate, nor yet have I much of other matter to communicate since we canvassed the whole round of mutually interesting topics so thoroughly during your visit. The echo of the train that carried you off has hardly died away and the impressions of your bodily presence are still fresh. It was a sore affliction to have you leave in such a hurry. I am not wholly reconciled to it now. Two days more would have made me a comfortable meal; as it was, my appetite was keen when the dishes were removed. Returning from the Station I found the review just in process. The Division was larger than ever I had in mind as the measure of it and, ranged in three lines, made a grand show. I was more than sorry that you were gone. Especially the next day at the races on the same ground, where under a genial sun were assembled the "beauty and chivalry" of Hooker's army and the very air was full of enthusiasm and pleasing excitement. I was moved almost to indignation at the thought of your absence. The remark was often made to me during the day, "Your Father ought to have staid." Everybody was in festive mood and the influence of the occasion on the tone of the army was undoubtedly good. It relieved the hum-drum monotony of winter quarters, which is one great cause of discontent and homesickness. The greased pole, sack races, wheel of fortune and "buckfight," beside the horse races, contributed a rare feast of amusement and fun. You remember that we saw a party at work with spades as we passed on our way to the cars. They were digging the ditches to be leaped in the races. Several horsemen were thrown during the day but none permanently injured. Among them, and the most seriously hurt, was Prince Salm Salm of Prussia,° Col. of the 8th N.Y. Vols. His horse fell at one of the ditches. Dr. Ash was called to attend him. After the programme was finished and the general public allowed to try the track there was fine sport. . . . Father O'Hagan returned from Washington in time to participate, and entered into the spirit of the day with true Irish zeal. He was disappointed to hear that you were gone, bade me send you his best regards, and assurances that the invitation to visit Plantsville should be well heeded. . . . I am deeply grateful to you for coming to see me . . . and shall long remember the event, as conspicuous for satisfaction and, I think, profit. If you are content, I ought to be also. It is a most agreeable thought that you went away with an improved opinion of our army, and I hope it will brighten your mood hereafter when pondering on national affairs.

Preparations are daily making for future movements. We are ready to go at any day. Do not be surprised to hear of it. Next Sunday, I surmise, will be our last in this camp, but maybe not.

I have just received your note from Washington. Before this you are doubtless safe home again rejoicing the family at the house and wrestling with boxes at the shop. My love to all of the folks. . . . Your aff. Son. Joseph.

the most seriously hurt, was Prince Salm Salm of Prussia: Prince Felix Salm Salm, after a career in the Prussian and Austrian armies, came to the United States in 1861 to escape his creditors. He received a commission as a colonel and commanded the Eighth New York Volunteers.

Camp of 2nd Regt. Ex. Brig. Near Falmouth, Va.
April 5th 1863.

Dear Father,

It is quite late. I have passed the evening reading the last Independent (today arrived) and . . . now finish the day with a short look homeward. . . . Your March 30th letter came yesterday announcing your safe arrival home and your experience by the way. The two notes from Washington are also received. For Mr. Upson's benefit I may state that the pay of a Chaplain *is* $118 pr. month, including allowances. It *was* about $145.° I am anxiously waiting to hear what Connecticut will do tomorrow.° How can we endure the success of the worse than lukewarm loyalty that gives character to the peace-men. Can you not manage to spue [sic] out that Laodicean patriotism? I hope that ballots will be taken the same day in all the Conn. Regts. in order that, if the civilians go wrong, the corrective Army vote may be tacked on to show the reason why, and help our state repute a little before the public. I regretted to know of the baby's illness.° . . .

The weather is going from bad to worse. Yesterday the wind blew a tornado all day. I found it impossible to keep a fire in my tent without the danger of being burned out. . . . Soon after sunset there was a partial lull and snow commenced, continuing all night. This morning it was four or five inches thick and drifted in places after the fashion of January. The sun struggled out at 9 o'clock and it has thawed all day, yet the air has been disagreeably raw. . . . Of course this conduct of the elements will still further retard our movements. Yesterday we received notice that either today or tomorrow the Corps would be reviewed, and it seemed to be the prevailing opinion that the President was to pay us a visit. I do not believe that Mr. Lincoln would review troops on the Sabbath. If he did so, it would cause great grief to Christians in the Army and all over the country. . . .

This morning owing to the untoward weather the attendance on service was smaller than usual. . . . In the afternoon I held a short service in the hospital and enjoyed it exceedingly. One poor Irishman named Jimmy Smith, a bad case of rheumatism, sat up in his bed and listened with all his senses. Being unused to Protestant ways he hardly knew how to conduct himself, and responded to my remarks, which were delivered in rather a conversational style, with frequent bowings of his head and such confirmatory ejaculations as, "Oh, yis Sir" . . . yet with such evident sincerity that it did not disturb the general gravity. After I had finished, I reaped more than one hearty, "God bless you!," and went out comforted. The Doctors have received instructions to discharge all disabled men, and have selected thirteen as worthy of release—three of them men whose old wounds unfit them for duty.

The religious interest of which I have written appears to abide, but with less outward demonstration than last winter. The Christians seem to be in earnest and are doing good. My sermon today was designed to quicken and instruct such in their duties. In two tents of the Regiment, at least, prayers are formally observed after tattoo at night and comrades are invited. The boys call them "*Family* prayers." . . . All of last week was passed in waiting for the Paymaster who was daily expected. It is almost certain that he will be here by the middle of this, when I suppose I shall go to Washington again. . . . I have not been exactly well for four or five days and yesterday had recourse to blue-pill and castor oil, by which bodily penance and mortification I expect absolution from my ailment. . . . I wish you were here tonight. I have been inclined to lonesomeness since you went away. With much love to all, I remain. Your aff. Son. Joseph.

For Mr. Upson's benefit . . . the pay of a Chaplain is $118 pr. month. . . . It was about $145: The paymaster general of the United States, Colonel Benjamin Franklin Larned, sought to have the army chaplaincy disbanded. Instead, the pay was cut from $145.50 a month plus three daily rations and forage for a horse to $100 a month plus two daily rations and forage for one horse "while on duty." Twichell's classmate Henry Upson was by this time chaplain of the Thirteenth Connecticut Volunteers.

I am anxiously waiting to hear what Connecticut will do tomorrow: That is, he was anxiously awaiting the results of the 6 April statewide election.

I regretted to know of the baby's illness: Anna Walkley Twichell was born 8 October 1862 to the fifty-two-year-old Edward Twichell and his second wife, Jane Walkley Twichell.

> *Camp of 2nd Regt. Excelsior Brigade.*
> *Near Falmouth, Va. April 12th 1863.*

Dear Father,

We had real spring sunshine this morning and the boys were all out of doors enjoying it. At the church-call a full audience assembled. We had a most agreeable service. I have never seen worshippers gathered together bearing more evidences of a devout and earnest spiritual frame, than those whom I speak to every Sunday morning. There is a reason for it. None are compelled to come. Neither law nor public opinion nor curiosity moves them. They come because they deliberately choose to. The ordinary motives to frivolity and inattention are almost wholly lacking, hence our solemn worship has always been marked by seriousness and a strict regard for the proprieties and objects of the exercise. In this is an advantage to the Chaplain, for which I am thankful. . . . This evening we initiated evening prayers and hope to continue it whenever possible. A hymn and a short prayer, ending with the Lords Prayer in which all joined, is the exercise. I think it will be a comfort and refreshment to all our religious men, as well as a pleasant manner of closing the day. . . .

Tuesday the officers of the 3rd Corps were invited to meet at Gen. Sickles Headquarters for the purpose of welcoming Mr. Lincoln. 3 o'clock was the time appointed but it was 5 before the distinguished visitor appeared. The day was raw and gusty and it was cold business waiting, but plenty of food and drink kept the crowd patient and good natured, so that a hearty reception was accorded to our good President when at length he did come. We all shook hands with him and I took occasion to thank him for the "Day of Fasting and Prayer" lately appointed by him.° He looked pale and careworn yet not dispirited.

It is said that he was greatly pleased with the appearance of the Army. Monday he reviewed the Cavalry (12,000). I never saw a finer display of horsemen. There was a general Chaplains meeting that morning at Mr. Alvord's quarters. About 25 were present and, on breaking up, at least a dozen of us went over to the review in company—presenting such an array of black cloth as is seldom seen. The meeting was a most interesting one. Many gave their experience and some had hard stories of difficulty and hard usage to tell. A Methodist made the speech of the meeting. He was one of the "swearing" kind, and used some very strong language. Among other things he told how his Colonel challenged him to fight, and how he accepted the challenge, but the Colonel backed out. Wednesday there was a grand review of Four Corps. . . .

Your letter of April 7th has arrived. I had eagerly watched the returns of the Conn. election and rejoiced at the success of Liberty—thankfully. Your personal defeat, I regretted much more than you did,° I suppose, for I do not judge you to be devoured by political ambition. I trust this victory will be vigorously followed up, by measures calculated to confirm the State loyalty by instructing every citizen, through the press, pulpit and platform, in the *true logic* of the war—enabling men to give a *reason* for faith that is in them. Has there not been a lack in this respect? . . . With much love to all, I remain. Your aff. Son. Joseph.

the *"Day of Fasting and Prayer" lately appointed by him:* Lincoln was visiting the army under Hooker, its new commander, at Falmouth, Virginia. The president declared days of fasting and prayer nine times during the war. This one was to be observed on 30 April to "humble ourselves before the offended Power, to confess our national sins, and to pray for clemency and forgiveness."

I had eagerly watched the returns of the Conn. election. . . . Your personal defeat, I regretted: The "success of Liberty" was the reelection of the Republican war governor William A. Buckingham. Edward Twichell apparently had stood for a local position. The Hartford *Daily Courant* reported that two Southington Democrats had been elected as local representatives to the state legislature, which indicates the way the vote went in the town.

> *Camp of 2nd Regt. Excelsior Brigade.*
> *Near Falmouth, Va. April 14th 1863.*

Dear Father,

I write as has been my habit on similar occasions, to warn you that a longer time than usual may elapse before my next letter. We are again under marching orders. Some affair is brewing of which we know nothing except by surmise and inference. Monday a large cavalry expedition was dispatched, with a support, we are told, of 10,000 infantry ([Gen. Henry W.] Slocum's Division, rumor says). We are now ready to go with five days rations, and three more to be drawn and cooked when the final orders are issued, and these we expect in the course of the night unless the plan is changed. No wagons at all are to be taken. The eight days rations are to be carried on the backs of horses, mules and men. Everything not absolutely necessary is to be left, even the blankets. Eight days rations—that indicates that we are going off the direct lines of communication.

No wagons—that indicates speed—the prospect of circumstances in which a baggage train will be an unusual incumbrance—perhaps a route impossible to wheels. It seems to be a general movement, for I found the 1st Corps, six miles from here, making the same preparations this noon. It is reported, I know not how truly, that Heintzleman is at Dumfries with a large force, either to join us, or take our place. The sick are all removed to the neighbourhood of the Rail Road.

We all trust that the Army of the Potomac is about to furnish the nation the refreshment of Good News. Vicksburg drags°—Charleston is below par—North Carolina looks more than dubious—Kentucky is skirmishing—let Virginia improve the record, redeem the past and brighten the future. If the Lord wills. I think there is more of that feeling all through the country now than ever before, likewise in the Army. Yet when the horrible wickedness of our armed host comes up for review, there will come with it a sinking heart. I do not mean by this that we are worse or as bad than civilized armies in general. I am persuaded otherwise, but no one passing through our camps would conclude our cause to be a *holy* one. When I think of man, I am hopeful. When I think of God I am fearful. If we prosper it will be not that we deserve blessing, but that the enemy deserve cursing. There is our best security with Heaven. . . .

Tonight there were, by Dr Younglove's count, 39 at sunset prayers. I expect that our evening hymn will gather about it sweet, sacred associations and influences which our hearts will feel for many a year. . . .

I cannot help thinking that tonight may end my enjoyment of these snug, little quarters. It is one of the places which my memory will hold dear. I leave it regretfully. Within these few square feet, I have enjoyed much. Many prayers have gone up hence—both mine and others. Anxious, troubled souls have here confessed their burden—here Christians have rejoiced—here I have read books, written and received letters, entertained my friends—my Father has been here—here my sleep has been sweet, my waking pleasant. Altogether it has won my affection. Many a time, if I live, I shall look back and think how [I] sat cosily before this glowing fire (it may never be kindled again and I forgive it for smoking sometimes) and felt at home in the midst of a strange country. Love to all. Peace abide with the dearest household of the world. Do not expect to hear soon again. Your aff. Son. Joseph.

Vicksburg drags: Since the previous October, General Ulysses S. Grant had been trying to capture the significant and well-defended Mississippi River port of Vicksburg in an elaborate series of land approaches and canal-building. In fact, two days after Twichell wrote, Union gunboats ran the batteries of the city to rendezvous with troops for a roundabout approach from the south that ultimately succeeded.

Two telegrams from Twichell's brother Edward are included in the correspondence, both sent from Plantsville on 16 April 1863. The first is addressed to Major General Hooker:

Please inform Chaplain Twichell second regiment excelsior Brigade that his father is dead. Have him telegraph when he will be here.
E. W. Twichell

The second telegram is to Harry Hopkins in Alexandria:

Please send Jos. His father is dead. Telegraph when he will be here—E. W. Twichell.

Washington. April 25th '63.

Dear Ned,

I reached here this morning, have procured my pass and intend to go down tomorrow. Your telegram overtook me at New York. I inferred from it that my leave was extended five days. If so please forward me the document immediately, for I shall be reported by the Provost Marshall here as five days beyond my time and hence shall have to show my authority. Your telegram is not legal evidence. I was thankful to know that the baby was better, yet expect to hear that the respite was brief. . . .

Give my love to Mother, and Sis. I think of you all continually and our common sorrow. I feel utterly lonesome, almost discouraged. . . . Love and blessings to all. I will write again when I get to camp. Your aff. Bro. Joseph.

Camp of 2nd Regt. Excelsior Brigade.
Near Falmouth, Va. April 26th 1863.

Dear Mother,°

I take up my pen in great heaviness of spirit. I write the superscription— that is familiar, I write the "Dear"—that is familiar too, but there I pause to lean my head on my hand and think. Can it be so? Back through seven years my memory travels and recalls how often and in how varied circumstances I have thus begun my letters. Sweet recollections flood that happy period and I wander over it like a child in a garden, till arousing myself, I come face to face with the hard, bitter Fact—our common, unspeakable sorrow—my first great grief in life. Then I put my pen to the paper again, and with the heaped up mound of Father's grave before me, write on, "Mother." Not that I do not love you, Mother dear, but, O, my Father! My Father, where art thou? Is it I, or is it he that is lost? I'm very lonesome here tonight—the night of the week when I have always felt that he was more than half with me—and, not many night ago, he was here in the body. There is my bed—it is hardly a month since he lay on it—three blessed nights—thank God for them. Then I tucked him in and drew the blankets up over his shoulders and he nestled down and said—"That's it, Joe! First rate!" Now with unutterable yearning I grope round the shadowed world after him, and find nothing but the fresh grave. Mother; it's trouble, trouble, trouble—empty dreariness. Oh! For another touch of his hand!—an hour of his company—the sound of his voice! Would that I could hear him call me "Joe" again. Nobody ever did, or ever can speak it as he did. Of late he never uttered it that I did not feel like falling on his neck. I only wish he had known how much I loved him. I hoped to show it someday, but now, Oh God! Blankness gathers about the future. It is not as he would wish it, I know, nor is it thus that I feel when I sit down to reason and plan, but I am writing as I feel tonight. I am afraid, when I think that perhaps the happy dead visit us who yet for a little remain, for then Father must know that I am not what he thought me, but, this at least he sees clearly, that I loved him and love him still. I shall never write "Dear Father" again—never. I do it now in fond sadness, as I would set up his tombstone. My pen lingers about them, its favourite words—"Dear Father"—sacred and sweet forever shall they be to my soul. How many times, when I was inly [sic] disturbed, has the mere writing of them called me to peace and a better mind.

But I am talking too much about myself. Away and alone, sitting here in silence with my grief, I am selfish. Nobody here knew Father. I cannot unburden myself to human ear. They saw him and liked him, but I am the only one that knew him. I wish I were at home among those who love to talk about him. I have thought of you nearly all the while since I left. Eddy, Sis, and the widow with her girls have been continually before me. God bless you all, and deal gently with you. Your loneliness is somewhat different from mine—more bodily and sensible. You miss him from morning till night and in every place, yet, I would like to stand where his feet have trod. More than a week now, he has walked the "golden streets," seeing "face to face" and knowing "as we are known."—He has seen the Lord, he has heard the "Alleluia"—a week, I say, and I mean one of *our* weeks. We cannot tell what the weeks of heaven are. "One day is with the Lord as a thousand years." Perhaps he already looks away back upon his earthly life as a thing long past—a vapor almost forgotten since the Light of the Throne dispelled it. We must try to rise toward him and all, by Faith and Patience, journey that way, until such time as he shall meet us at the Gate. We are not to get him back. He is to lead us up.

It gave me great joy and relief that Eddy was able to telegraph that Annie was better. Poor little thing, her baby face with its wan cheeks and bleeding lip haunts me. I am anxious to hear of her, yet am prepared to hear that she has been called. . . .

I am very tired tonight. Coming down in the cars Friday night I did not sleep much and this morning I had to rise early in order to catch the boat. Mart was waiting for me at the cars and I reached camp at about 1 o'clock. The boys gave me a welcome and all offered me kind sympathy, as also did all my friends in New York and Washington. The whole Division was ordered out in the afternoon to be reviewed by the Governor of New Jersey—a flagrant crime against the Sabbath. At Sunset I called my congregation together for service. The evening was beautiful and our worship seemed unusually delightful. The lads spoke to me softly or went quietly away after the benediction in deference to my affliction. Poor fellows. They have lost something in common with me— Father's prayers. I have often thought that our blessing was to come from the closet at Plantsville rather than from my ministry—so unworthy and weak. . . .

Some of you will write to me, I know. It will seem strange not to get the familiar envelope. My love to all of you, dear folks—dearer than ever now. I commend you to God and His promises. Your aff. Son. Joseph.

Dear Mother: Twichell's letters are now addressed to his stepmother, Jane Walkley Twichell; his brother, Edward Williams Twichell ("Ned" or "Eddy"); and his sister, Sarah Jane Twichell ("Sis").

May–July 1863

In January 1863, Hooker was named commander of the Army of the Potomac, replacing Burnside. During long preparations for action, Lincoln advised Hooker to direct his efforts at Lee's army rather than attempt yet another overland campaign to capture Richmond. Hooker moved across the Rappahannock in late April and engaged Lee at Chancellorsville. On 2 May, in the course of this battle, Confederate forces under Jackson made a surprise flanking movement that caused a rout. Union losses continued, and on 4 May Hooker withdrew his forces back across the river. Once again, Twichell found himself working among the wounded.

House near United States Ford. Stafford Co., Va.
May 9th 1863.

Dear Ned,

My present situation is probably in many respects more singular and interesting than any in which I have been placed since I entered the army. I am here with only one attendant (a private of the 12th New Hampshire) in charge of thirteen wounded Confederate prisoners. During the night of Tuesday our forces recrossed the Rappahannock. The wounded were all brought over the afternoon before and disposed in the various houses available on this side [of] the river. I had been employed in their care and transportation till at dark I established myself at this place, set up my tent and waited for the returning troops. It was a cold rainy night. Hundreds of poor, helpless fellows were huddled together both out and indoors. Many, it was utterly impossible to put under any sort of shelter. We passed nearly the whole night in arranging them on their stretchers in circles about such fires as we could make in the storm. The ground was perfectly fluid and some lay in the mud. Such suffering I never witnessed. The lacerated bodies, drained of their blood, were keenly sensitive to the cold and wet, and I saw more than one armless, legless man shaking and shuddering with a violence heartrending to behold. All their clothes were soaked, a dry blanket was not to be found; warm drinks and fires were all the means we had for combating the evils of the situation. Fast as ambulances could be procured they were loaded and sent on, only to suffer yet more from jolting over horrid roads. At daylight the troops began to pass. The drenched, weary columns marched by in appearance anything but gay soldiers. By noon so many of the wounded were removed that we were able to place what remained under some sort of cover, tent, barn or out-house—though very inadequate for purposes of comfort. Our regiment passed in the course of the forenoon. I went out and told the Colonel that I should remain with the wounded, even if captured. Three surgeons beside myself were assigned by Dr. Sim (Medical Director of 3rd Corps) to stay. That same night they all left, on various pretences. The last one accompanied a train of ambulances which removed all but fifty of the patients, and I was left alone in charge with three attendants. The desertion of these Surgeons was an outrage. Cowardice and laziness were the chief causes of it. They were afraid of being taken and wanted to shirk duty. Thursday noon more ambulances returned and took away all but the present fourteen Confederates. Two of my attendants also left at that time. Since the Surgeons left, two of my charge have died, both Federals. The first was a mere boy, shot in the side. He had been apparently doing well, having been able to get up and walk about a little. Suddenly he grew weak, lay down and called for me. He wanted to be raised up. I lifted him, he sat a minute, then fell over and died immediately. None of us knew his name or regiment. I searched his pockets for some clue in vain, and we had to bury him, nameless. The second was a New Jersey Sergeant—a noble fellow—shot through the lungs. The night before he died I sat with him till 3 o'clock in the morning when he grew easier and slept. He wanted more to see his mother than anything else. At 11 o'clock he asked me to read from the Testament to him. At 20 minutes of 12 he said he felt better—at 12 he was dead—filled up with blood and strangled. The Chaplain and two grave-diggers were all that attended his funeral. We buried him in the garden. These Confederates are under the jurisdiction of the Provost Marshal. I have sent him (Gen. [M. R.] Patrick) word three times that they were here, but thus far he has not sent for them. A cavalry scout passed by yesterday, the Captain of which promised to cause the matter to be promptly brought to Gen. Patrick's notice. I therefore expect the ambulances every minute. Day before yesterday I sent Mart along with the most of my baggage, on a mule which we picked up, but kept my horse, whose forage I have picked up as best I might. With regard to provision we have fared tolerably. The Sanitary Commission, flying with the rest, were unable to carry off all their stores, and left with me a supply of beef-tea, jellies and dried fruit which has lasted till now. A Quartermaster also, being compelled to abandon part of his stores, kindly allowed us to take what pork, coffee, crackers and sugar we wanted. The great lack has been medical attendance. Simple wounds I can take care of sufficiently well, but we have three cases which demand surgical knowledge. The house is warm and the blankets have become dried, and the poor fellows are as comfortable as wounded men usually are, with the exception of clean beds and underclothing. Some of the wounds are suppurating, all the garments are bloody, and the stench is anything but pleasant.

A small bottle of morphine is all I have had to work with in the way of medicine, but that has been a good angel—blessed be its memory! Many a restless pillow has been smoothed by it, many a tired body has drawn sleep out of it. They are a very nice set of fellows, these confederates, and I have rather enjoyed myself with them. One little fellow 17 years old, I have contracted a real affection for. We have talked some politics, but without bitterness. Every night I have prayed with them, to their evident pleasure. A few of them are religious men. We are fearfully lonesome. The army has all gone back to its old camps. Once in a while a few cavalry appear to relieve the picket at the Ford. There are five poor women in the house, who have been nearly frightened to death, and mourn to have their house so despoiled. Their chickens are in the garret, their mule in the bedroom, and the hog in the closet—for safe keeping. I hope we shall be able to leave them to themselves today, to repair as best they can the damage they have suffered.

I am totally without news. My supposition is that the army has met a reverse, but what the real state of the case is, I am ignorant. . . . The excitements, labors and distractions of the past week have stood between me and the sorrow at home, so that at times I have suddenly remembered it as a thing almost forgotten. Yet I think of you with love and prayers. . . .

I presume, by this time, you know all about the great battle. It was a terrible engagement—the fiercest I ever witnessed and the losses on both sides must have been enormous. All the grandeur and misery of war, in a high degree, characterized it. The quality of the fighting, with the exception of the 11th Corps, was better than ever before.° Some of our troops stood six hours under fire without flinching. Several of my army friends were killed—fine young fellows whom I mourn. I understand that the Army will shortly move again, when I suppose these scenes will be repeated, and so on till the end. Give my love to Sis and Mother and all the children. The neighbors—I never can forget the sympathy they showed us in our dark time. God bless them. Write to me occasionally. Your aff. Bro. Joseph.

P.S. Sunday Morning—in the old Camp. All right—ambulances came at 2½ o'clock yesterday.

The quality of the fighting, with the exception of the 11th Corps, was better than ever before: Jackson had struck the Eleventh Corps in his flanking move at Chancellorsville. Many of the men had been resting or preparing dinner, and the corps was driven back two miles in disorderly flight.

In Camp, near Falmouth, Va. May 31st 1863.

Dear Mother,

The week past I have been very much occupied in visiting the hospital. . . . Wednesday (27th) was my birthday also. I am twenty-five years old—a thing well nigh incredible. I miss Father's good letter on the occasion. That day, for the purpose of honoring it a little, after I had finished my rounds at the hospital, I set out on a tour of visitation, calling on three college friends in different parts of the Army with whom I enjoyed much pleasant talk of old and present times. In the early part of the week I went down to the First Corps to see Ned Carrington who is aide to Gen. [James S.] Wadsworth, commanding a Division, but to my great disappointment, he was absent on ten days furlough. Last night, however, he came to me and spent the entire evening till 11 o'clock, when I mounted and rode a couple of miles with him on his way back. He had much to tell all about his visit to the North, and I enjoyed it hugely.

I have moved my quarters twice since I wrote. A Medical Inspection of camp resulted in an order that the Hospital be moved to an adjoining hill for finer air. The Doctor had to go with it, and asked me to accompany him. Without much reflection I did so, but soon found that I was too far removed from my parish, and so took up my tent and pitched again in the old camp. The Doctor (Younglove) has been quite sick for a week and will probably go home for a few days.

The Quartermaster has very kindly caused a kind of summer chapel to be erected for my accommodation. It consists of a large canvas cover, and walls of green boughs, and will hold about 100 easily. This morning we held service in it for the first time, but the strong wind blew the dust through our rather open walls in such quantities that it was anything but a luxury, either to preach or hear. In calm weather it will answer every purpose, and I feel truly thankful for it.

Dear Mother, I am very grateful to you for writing to me so often concerning the affairs of our house. I think of poor little Annie in her suffering, and am only consoled in the persuasion that better days are not far off—health in heaven or an abatement of her disease. . . . Precious is the letter from Plantsville! It comes, always, freighted with sweet memories—blessed associations cluster about *it*—before I open it, I almost seem to have taken the hand of the man we loved. I am glad that you are able to look upon the consolations that God provides for your affliction. It is fitting that whoever mourns for Father should do so without *unhappiness*. . . .

The Photograph of Father I was disappointed in. It is not as good as I expected, yet I am glad to have it. That of my mother is a slight improvement on the old, but I am sure we can never have a good likeness of her. . . . There are no signs of motion here yet, and if we are doomed to summer quarters I shall try to get home in July. My love to all of you. . . . Your aff. Son. Joseph.

> On 7 June, Twichell wrote to his sister, returning to his father's death and its relation to military events since. Speaking of her care of their sick infant stepsister, he continues:

I wish I could divide with you the care of nursing her, or any other of your cares, Sis, if it were possible. Father used to assume most burdens for us, or at least, share them in his true heart, but who can we call on to enter into our trouble and lighten our grief at his loss. No human being surely. . . . Even here, I carry a continual sense of something gone or greatly changed. The rush of events, since that sad Sunday when we buried him, has had the effect to lengthen my retrospect. The 19th of last April seems a weary distance back. The battle of Chancellorsville is now an old event and Fathers death, having preceded it, shares the effect of this most strange experience and mode of life to a still greater extent. The old measures of time fail when applied to the present—I mean, with respect to the sensations of memory. I *feel* about Father's death about as if it had taken place six months ago. . . . I am glad that Mr. [Elisha C.] Jones' sermon is to be printed. I shall want half a dozen copies, at least. Has any proper obituary notice been published in the religious papers? I have seen none. . . . Thursday morning . . . I visited the great Convalescent Camp where our paroled prisoners, many of them, are kept. I found nearly twenty of my boys who were abundantly glad to see me and tell what a time they had in going to Richmond. . . .

Movements are in progress, but exactly what, or for what purpose, I haven't the remotest idea, nor indeed do I take much pains to find out. I shall know soon enough, especially if it is to be fighting. . . . Your aff. Brother Joseph.

Camp near Falmouth, Va. 3 o'clock p.m. June 11th 1863.

Dear Ned,

Again we are on the wing.° Our tents are struck, the baggage with three days rations is packed, we are only waiting for the men who went on picket this morning to return; then we shall start—where for or what for no one known. There has been fighting for two days at the Fords above here, and the report is that we are to march as far as Hartwood Church (i.e. 10 miles) tonight in the direction of United States Ford where we crossed before; but there is no reliable information. Some are disposed to think that the enemy has advanced on us; no one supposes that we are to enter upon offensive operations. The former opinion finds some warrant in the comparative smallness of our army. The two-years men have gone home,° and we have never been so few. In that sense, it is an opportunity for Gen. Lee; but I assure you, Ned, he will find it no sport to drive what are left of us. However, time will tell. Maybe I shall be able to write as usual Sunday night but, if not, this will furnish you the reason. The Colonel just now . . . gives his judgement that the enemy is either falling back, and we are going in pursuit, or, as I have said before, that he is advancing and we going to meet him.

I am sorry to leave these quarters—the most delightful I ever had. Although the regiment has three times marched out and returned hither again, it is hardly possible that it so happen for the fourth time. While I was in Washington last week, Mart raised my tent on posts, and arranged curtains, or rather a "valance," around the sides, easy to be hooked up [on] warm days; also he brought abundance of cedar boughs and planted them round about and put a thick arbor over the door, so that I lived in a cool, green bower. My bed was delightful and my chair a luxury. I am enjoying the table for the last time. The place is precious for the reason, above all, that Father has been here. I found an old letter of his today in my valise. The familiar look of it recalled one of the finest pleasures of my life as well as its deepest grief. I laid it aside with a moist eye.

My chapel, too, with its evergreen walls, and seats and platform, is well worth the regret I feel in leaving it. . . . Sunday night we had a good prayer meeting in it, and another Tuesday night. I am thankful that I can declare my opinion, that a good work is being wrought in many hearts of the regiment. More than one has announced his having begun the "new life" and others are solemnly inquiring the way. The deep fervor and excellent spirit that pervades our meetings are full of promise. . . .

I expect every time a letter comes from home to hear that the baby has gone. Her little life has been shadowed. . . .

Of course, you are waiting almost breathless, with the rest of us, for the issue of events at Vicksburg. If that point is gained, much is accomplished. We who are in the field, sick of exile from civilized homes and anxious beyond expression for the end of the war, are growing thin with the intensity of our wishes in behalf of Grant's gallant army. It would be foolish to crow a single note before we actually enter into possession of the place, for we have a foe to contend with both brave and skilful. But, Edward, failure at Vicksburg will give us no right to whine or drop our hands. The greater our reverses, the more tenacious should we be of the grand principle with which we started. While we have men for an army, and bread for their mouths, we should not abate one jot or tittle of our original claim for an undivided Union. Much blood has been shed and not in vain. All that is behind urges us forward, and what is before beckons us on. Hurra, for the Star Spangled banner!! Give my love to all our friends. . . . Write to me according to your opportunities. Your aff. Brother. Joseph.

Again we are on the wing: In early June, Lee invaded the North, moving his army from the Fredericksburg area through Maryland into Pennsylvania. The move would not only carry the war to the enemy's country, Lee reasoned, but also provide needed supplies, encourage the Peace Democrats' movement, and perhaps even reopen the question of foreign recognition of the Confederacy. Hooker was slow to determine Lee's plans and oppose them. On 27 June, Lincoln replaced Hooker with General George Meade.

The two-years men have gone home: Some of those who enlisted early in the war had only agreed to serve for two years. Inducements and bonuses for staying were offered to them, as they were to "three-years men" like Twichell the following year, but many left nonetheless.

> *In Camp. Near Rappahannock Station, Va.*
> *Sunday. June 14th 1863.*

Dear Mother,

We reached here last night after a hot, dusty march of two days. When we halted the boys were utterly wearied, but today they appear to have thoroughly recovered. We march again at sundown for Catletts Station, says the Colonel, and 20 miles at least. So you see we are returning to the old ground. August 27th last year, we fought at Bristows Station, only six miles toward Washington from Catletts. It begins to look as though the old battles might be repeated and maybe a third Bull Run placed on record—though, I trust, not as a third Federal defeat there. The enemy is just across the river and entrenched. By climbing the little knoll in front of our camp their principal earthwork is distinctly visible. I rode over yesterday afternoon so near that I could see their cavalry grazing their horses in a field. It is immediately opposite here—across

Beverly Ford—that the fiercest of last week's cavalry fight took place. Our presence here in force is supposed to be unknown to the enemy, and we are not permitted to show ourselves much. It is to keep our movement secret that we are to march in the dark tonight I suppose. Our Division seems to be the main force at this point. Whether the whole of it is going, or only our Brigade, I do not know. . . .

The march hither I shall never forget. It will be memorable to the end of my life as the scene of an event which for importance and terrible interest surpasses nearly all of my experience hitherto. On Friday afternoon at a little after two I was called to a professional duty from which in anticipation I had always shrunk in horror, hoping that it might never befall me—which indeed I doubted my ability to perform. It was to attend and minister unto a poor wretch who was shot for desertion. His name was [John P.] Woods, a private of the 19th Indiana Vols.—1st Division—1st Corps. My being summoned to administer to his last moments was a matter of chance, or rather unusual Providence. It was as follows. Our Brigade, the last of our Corps, having been delayed in the start by the absence of a portion of it on picket, became mixed with the advance of the 1st Corps. While we halted for breakfast I asked and received permission to ride on, purposing to find and visit Ned Carrington who is on the Staff of the 1st Div., 1st Corps. I succeeded and, soon after meeting him, he informed me of the execution about to take place. My only emotion was one of commiseration and horror, for I had not the least thought of seeing the unfortunate man, much less of witnessing his death. Soon, however, as Ned's General—Wadsworth—with his Staff were resting by the roadside, the ambulance containing the condemned drove up surrounded by a heavy guard and stopped close by. As the thousands marched carelessly along, or only thought of their bodily fatigue, this man, in their midst, knew that he would be in his grave before the setting of the sun. The order for execution read "between the hours of 2 and 4 o'clock." It was now two and the Division was halted. I had by this time perceived to my amazement that no clergyman was with the man. On mentioning it to Ned, he said that for several days they had been with him constantly and till a late hour the night previous, and he presumed they thought that they could do no more for him. Yet to me it seemed hard that the poor fellow was left to pass through the fearful trial alone—that some *friend* should not have been with him to sorrow and sympathize with him, at least, during his last earthly day, and help him meet his fate like a man. Still I had no thought of visiting him myself, because he was not of my own part of the army, and I felt my blood chill at the bare idea—

Good night. Must get ready to start. Will resume (D.V.) [*Deo volente*, or "God willing."]

Heigho! How tired we are. Leaving Camp Sunday night we marched till eight o'clock next morning (yesterday), then halted under a broiling sun till half past one o'clock, when the order to "Fall in!" awoke us from noon-tide slumbers and started us on the way hither where we arrived at midnight, thoroughly used up. All that heat, dust and forced marching could do to exhaust men we have endured, yet this morning but nine of our men are absent. I never witnessed such suffering from marching. The poor fellows lay stretched all along the road choaked [sic] and panting, and many a one was sun-struck. So many were enduring the unusual hardships and manfully bearing up against unwonted fatigues, that I felt it right to use my horse but part of the time. Most of the way I yielded him to some one of my parishioners feebler than myself. The loss of sleep is as hard as anything to endure. We are evidently under some strong pressure of necessity, but we have no news. Rumors, the most startling, are in circulation, yet nothing is known. Last night, just about sunset, I rode aside to visit the graves of our boys who fell June 27th [sic; it was 27 August 1862] at Bristow. They were as I left them and the sight thereof inclined my heart to sadness and meditation. I suppose we shall march again this afternoon.

But to go on with the story I commenced Sunday. As I was going on to say, in the absence of any other Chaplain, I was asked by the Provost Marshall, who had the prisoner in charge, to go to him and afford him whatever counsel I might be able. Trembling I went, not daring to decline. I took hold of the manacled hands, looked in the face, declared myself a friend, and immediately began to seek out his spiritual condition and wants. He was a young man—about 25 years old, I should think—an American, and as far as I could judge a man of medium intelligence and of the middle class society. He was perfectly calm and fully able to give himself to the work of preparation for death.

At first he seemed to regard me as actuated in part, at least, by curiosity and did not immediately give me his confidence. But I soon persuaded him otherwise and kneeling on the ground we had a season of prayer together. He said that he had tried, earnestly tried, to commit his soul to Christ . . . but had not the Assurance of hope that he longed for. After a while I left him to himself, until the Marshall came again and, saying that the execution would take place in half an hour, asked me to accompany the doomed man. For this I was unprepared yet, as before, dared not decline. Giving my horse to an officer, I got into the ambulance with the prisoner, and the sad procession started. I never can adequately tell all that passed in the ambulance—the agony of soul—the intensity of prayer—the anxious inquiry—and the black shadow of the event just at hand always present. As I never prayed before I prayed for divine guidance in what I should say to my companion, and I think I received it. He seemed better and better (as we rode along) to appreciate the office of Christ and its immediate availability. He drank in all that I said about our blessed Lord—prayed as they only pray whose death is at hand, and often ejaculated, "I *wish* I could see and feel Jesus!" He was, as I have said, perfectly self-controlled, and by his own composure assisted mine. Had he been strongly possessed with fear, I could hardly have remained in his presence. As it was, although as I have said, the shadow was on us continually, yet he and I were both enabled to refrain from dwelling on the approaching tragedy, and gave ourselves entirely to spiritual exercises. I did not see the throng about, nor perceive the route we took. That a man, whose eternal judgment at the bar of God was to be pronounced in a few minutes, was looking to me for guidance and sympathy, was enough to shut out all things else from my senses.

At length the ambulance stopped. I had a dim impression that a large body of troops was drawn up in order and that the executioners were there. The day was warm and sunny. It was in a wide green field, and immediately on alighting we both kneeled down on the grass beside the coffin which had been brought in a second ambulance; and passed a half hour in such wrestling with God, for mercy, for help, for light, for peace, for Christ, as I think brought calm upon his troubled spirits. His last prayer was different from those that preceded it. He seemed in it to have a stronger sense of God's personal presence, and to ask for just such things as he needed—oh! how earnestly, then! The Marshall touched me on the shoulder while we were still praying. I gave the man my benediction. We rose to our feet. "Now," said I "meet it like a man!" and so he did. "Lord Jesus receive my spirit!" was the last I heard him say. I withdrew a few paces. They seated him on his coffin, tied his elbows behind him, bound a handkerchief over his eyes and opened his shirtfront so that his bosom was bared. Still it did not seem possible that he was to die. He was young. I had just touched him and heard his voice. It was a fair day and in a green field; one could not believe it to be really an execution. He sat quietly where they put him. I could not see that he was even pale. He had asked me once to speak to the Provost Marshal and request that he be permitted to stand up, but it was ordered otherwise and he willingly acquiesced. At a signal six muskets were raised, cocked and aimed—the distance was about 10 paces. Another signal and the dread suspense was broken. He swayed a little forwards, then with a single convulsive straitening of his body, fell back over the coffin. Then a Sergeant and one man stepped up and discharged their pieces through his head, although five bullets had already pierced his breast. This is a custom—

dictated by humanity—in all military executions. They lifted the body into the coffin—a plain fine box. It was over. He had seen the bar of God and the Christ toward whom he was praying in such agony a few minutes before. No longer seeing in part, but face to face. I hope, nay, from what I afterward heard, I believe, that his soul was saved. The scene on the field now changed from one of utter stillness to one of noise and motion. Orders were shouted along the lines of troops, and the march was resumed as if nothing had happened. Ned rode up and bade me good-bye, and went away with his Division, while I remained to afford the remains a Christian burial. While the grave was being dug, the mystery of life and death broke over me in such waves of emotion as I have seldom been caused to experience. A few minutes since, my hand was on his living head in blessing, I heard him speak, I felt his flesh; he was as well as I, yet how we differed then! I was looking forward into life, he was taking his last look at the sun. Now he was gone. The body whose hands I had held, whose eyes I had looked into, which had walked and knelt beside me, was a mangled corpse. The soul, which had been gazing with unutterable straining of vision out through its dim fleshly windows was away—where? Set free from the flesh, at least.

We buried him and I rode away from the memorable spot to rejoin my regiment. The experience was strange and providential. I hope it did me good. Next morning while riding along with Father O'Hagan, the Marshal of the day before hailed me from the roadside. He had something to tell me. While he was tying the poor fellow's arms and covering his eyes, the latter had said calmly, "You need not do this. I am ready to meet my savior." Also, "Tell that Chaplain that I thank him. I believe that he has showed me the way to eternal Life, by leading me to Christ." Of course he magnified my office, ascribing to me the work of an illuminating Holy Ghost, but my soul was greatly comforted when I heard this. Truly I had reason to praise the Lord.

We rather expect to march again tonight—for somewhere. I shall write as opportunity offers. . . . I hope that you are in peace at home, Mother, full of all heavenly consolations. . . . My hearts love to Ned, Sis, and the rest. Kiss poor little Annie for me if she is still alive. Your affectionate Son. Joseph.

Washington—Sunday. June 21st 1863.

My dear Sis,

Friday morning one of our men broke his leg and I was dispatched to see him safely housed in some Alexandria Hospital. . . . I sent a letter to Mother Wednesday while on the march from Manassas to Centreville, which I hope she has received. We rested at Centreville two nights, and never was rest more grateful. The last day of the march especially was fraught with sore hardship. The roads over which so many troops had preceded us, through days of unbroken drought, were thoroughly pulverized to the depth of two or three inches. The foot sank in dust as it were ashes. The moving columns were shrouded by its suffocating clouds, while the scorching fires of an ardent sun fell with withering power on the panting soldier's head. Numbers sank on the arid fields utterly exhausted. Giving my horse most of the way to those who were weakened by the heat and burden of the four preceding days, I found myself no more than equal to the labor of maintaining the journey wholly unencumbered, and could but wonder at the endurance on the part of those who toiled on beneath knapsack, musket and ammunition, unconquered. I have regarded myself as no weakling, yet it would take a long apprenticeship to enable me to march beside many of my brave comrades. Nothing is so trying to a soldier's spirit as a long midsummer march. A battle does not compare with it, and the remark was frequent that to stop and fight would be a refreshment joyfully welcomed.

I noticed with no small surprise that two women (wives of soldiers) kept pace with us all the way, one of them actually carrying a sizeable knapsack on her shoulders. What do you think of that, Sis? What grand times a lady might have trudging along some 60 miles beside her lord, enjoying his company, and shouldering the contents of a trunk the while! Perhaps the Capt. would give you a chance to try it° if you expressed the wish. . . .

Capt. Smith (Mrs. McBlair's new son-in-law) has just come in to say that the sound of firing indicates a battle progressing on or near the old field of Bull Run. I shall go to Alexandria tonight and be ready to start by daybreak. If it is really the case that the same ground is being contested for the third time, it is time for us to win it, but the battle will be a sanguinary affair. I am thankful that the army has had 48 hours of rest. The more vexed our national affairs become, the more public mourning we are called to hear, the darker grows the record of slaughter, the more do I feel reconciled to Father's removal from earth. His true heart was destined to many a pang, had he remained. . . . Now my darling, good afternoon. . . . Pray for me and believe that I am. Your very aff. Bro. Joseph.

Perhaps the Capt. would give you a chance to try it: Twichell may be referring to Captain Charles H. Weygant of the 124th New York Volunteers. It appears Sarah Jane Twichell had a romantic interest in Weygant.

In Bivouac—Point of Rocks—Md. June 26th 1863.

My dear Ned,

I seize upon a little time which my heavy eyelids claim for another purpose to tell you where and how I am, fearing that I shall not soon have another chance to do so. . . . Monday morning I crossed to Alexandria . . . and set out for the Regiment which had moved to Gum Spring since I left it on Friday. My journey—a ride of 30 miles—prospered as far as Fairfax, and was providentially so ordered from that point that I escaped by a half hour an encounter with Moseby's guerrillas.° They attacked a wagon train and burned three, killing and capturing several horses. I met the wagon-master at a short distance from the scene flying in terror. I did not join him but proceeded cautiously and secured the protection of a squadron of cavalry which had been sent in pursuit of the rebels. Altogether it was an interesting adventure but I cannot stop to detail it now. It will make a good thing to tell, if I get home again. Just where the wagons were burning, I met Col. Potter with 100 men of our Regt.,° who had been dispatched to support the cavalry—on the double quick for two miles. Our camp at Gum Spring was on a pleasant green field—the whole brigade lying together. Every evening while there we had a religious meeting of some sort. . . . There is a lively religious interest in our midst which has promise of good things. Yesterday morning we were again ordered to march—and a memorable day's march it was. The day was delightfully cool and the boys moved easily, but toward dark it began to rain and then our miseries commenced. The route lay from Gum Spring to Edwards Ferry, where we crossed the Potomac on pontoon bridges, thence up the towpath of the Chesapeake and Ohio Canal to the Monocacy where we halted at a little after midnight, having marched fourteen hours without a halt of sufficient length for making coffee. The towpath was clayey and slippery, so much so that walking was extremely difficult, and the men suffered greatly. Most of them fell out by the way—less than 50 remaining with the colors till the final halt. I marched a large part of the way, giving my horse to the fagged-out little drummer boys, who perched on his back by twos. I stuck them up as you would fasten clothes pins on a line. One of them brought me some cherries tonight as a thank offering and another stole a sheaf of wheat for my horse. Speaking of stealing, I must, with shame, record that the conduct of our troops at Gum Spring was in that respect utterly unworthy [of] our cause. Foraging parties ranged through the country and drove in flocks of sheep and cattle or anything eatable that came in their way. To be sure we had not many luxuries and were in enemies country but to me the whole business seemed an outrage. To conquer the Confederates we must fight them, not despoil their families of food.

This morning we set out again after an insufficient sleep on the soaked ground, under soaked blankets. . . . Many of the boys who fell out last night joined us before we started—all looking blue and cold, and some overtook us in the course of the day, so that on halting tonight, a little before sunset, we looked like ourselves again. It has rained almost continuously till mid-afternoon and we have tasted all the unpleasantness that soldiers are exposed to. The roads are fluid—everything is dirty. Tomorrow I suppose we shall proceed to Harpers Ferry. What next you will learn in due time. Why we are here and what is before us is only the subject of surmise, but all agree that it means fight. God prosper us this time—at last—at last. . . . Since we have halted I have changed all my underclothes, am warmed and filled—as is also my pipe—so that I feel serene. From where I now sit—or rather lie—writing— the bivouac fires of the Division gleam on all the hills around—a scene of rare beauty and romance. I wish it could be photographed. Passing the bivouac of the 1st Div. just before we halted, I turned aside to find Capt. Weygant, and succeeded. He was well. . . . He said something in a very vague manner about his not having been able for the last month to write or send any letters to his friends—hoping that they would not misconstrue his silence. I could not comprehend his drift. Perhaps Sis can make something out of it. I think of you at home a great deal, my good brother, and with deep affection. . . . Keep a stout heart, Ned, for yourself, for the family and for the country. All will be well. . . . Love to all the folks. Your aff. Bro. Joseph.

an encounter with Moseby's guerrillas: Major John Singleton Mosby, the leader of a band of about eight hundred irregular Confederate guerrillas, had won fame by catching a Union general in his bed ten miles from Washington in March. Southerners admired and embroidered Mosby's dashing exploits. He raided supply wagons and Union outposts and brought home prisoners, funds, and horses.

I met Col. Potter with 100 men of our Regt: Potter had become full colonel of the Second Excelsior on 1 May.

Bivouac near Taneytown, Md. Tuesday June 30th 1863.
Dear Mother. . . .

I wrote to Eddy from Point of Rocks last week. From there we have wearily journeyed on day after day, mile after mile, passing on the route the towns of Jefferson, Middleton, Frederick, Walkersville, Woodborough, Middleburg— until last night we halted here. We are all tired out and had been allowed insufficient rest, never halting till dark and being aroused before sunrise almost every night. The weather has been mercifully cool and favorable to marching. I have walked a large part of the way, unable to endure the sight of men dropping with fatigue or treading with pain on account of blistered feet while I sat in a saddle. Many such a one has my good Garryowen borne on his able back since we left Falmouth. One circumstance has operated greatly to mitigate our discomfort and revive our drooping spirits, and that is our meeting friends and receiving friendly greetings. The set Virginia sneer and frown are left behind. Here another mood prevails. The farmers as we passed had pails or tubs of fresh, clear water at their gates and the loyal kitchens of their wives yielded abundance of good bread—but better still are the smiles, and waving flags and cheers with which they meet us. At one place a bevy of country girls sang Union songs as we passed—Bless their dear hearts! It was better than their mothers' biscuits. Through the towns we have marched in column by company with bands playing and colors flying—altogether we are refreshed in the inner man. We are not to stay in this place long, orders having already been issues to make ready to start. . . .

Last night as we entered the town we passed a tanyard°—the first I had seen for years. The very sight of it with all its familiar surroundings struck a very deep sacred chord in my memory. A substantial house was near and a group of solid, honest-looking people, male and female, stood at the gate. I made up my mind that if we halted within a mile or two, I would return to inspect the premises more minutely . . . and so I did. It was too dark to go into the shop, but I looked at the outside and then spoke with the proprietor at the door of his house. His wife came out and other persons old and young, among the rest a very fair young lady. I told them why I came back and we had a pleasant talk about tanners and tanning. It wound up with my being invited to walk in and take tea, also to return in the morning and take breakfast. . . . I . . . reported myself there duly at 8 o'clock again to see the hostess and young lady of the previous evening and partake their hospitality (sausage, preserves, pickles etc. etc., all good). This time, after breakfast, I sauntered down to the shop and asked an aged employee, who was sharpening his shaving knife on a stone outside, to open the doors. It was the same old place and I became a boy at once. There was the barkmill at which I toiled for many a day. I was tempted to "h'ist the gate," but alas, this one moved by horse power. There were the tables and shaving beams and vats and hanging sides, and piles of horns and hair, the scrapers, the steels—everything to translate me to other, happy days, when our home was glad and I not yet a man. My guide through the establishment was a tanner indeed. His shirt was yellow with oak stain and his back bent with working over the beam. And the smells—the same as of yore. It was my nose that called up the most faithful memories. For a long time I walked about the old building (like ours it was adorned with every possible patch and temporary, rude repair, in which, as material, leather was supreme) and mused. I was at home and Father was alive. At every turn, I seemed to see him. All the place was redolent of his memory and my mind was thronged with recollections. . . . Sweet and sad was my visit to the old tannery and I shall not soon forget it.

Gen. Sickles came back to us yesterday and received a most complimentary welcome. Great cheers swelled along the lines as he rode by and all hands feel relieved at his return. Poor Gen. Hooker, it seems, has finished his reign. I'm sorry for it, for I had faith in him. Gen. Meade has an excellent name among soldiers. God guide him.

I grieve for you about poor Annie. It is hardly possible that she is yet alive, and I think of you as sitting together in a house again made lonely. . . .

Since I began this we have struck tents and marched five miles further to Bridgeport, encamping in a field for the night. My love to all. Your aff. Son. Joseph.

Last night . . . we passed a tanyard: Twichell's visit to the tanyard, so similar to that of Timothy Higgins where Edward Twichell was a partner, is particularly poignant in light of the elder Twichell's recent death. Tanning leather in early-nineteenth-century America was a messy, smelly, and slow business of soaking hides in lime, scraping them, "bating" them (extracting lime with a solution of chicken or pigeon dung and salt), and tanning them in a hemlock or oak bark solution, the bark having been ground in the kind of mill Twichell describes.

3rd Corps Hospital—Near the battlefield. July 5th 1863.
My darling Sis,

I need not tell you that I am safe. I am glad to inform you that *he* is also.° I saw him this morning, a little the worse for wear but unharmed by the enemy. It was a merciful deliverance, for he is left as senior officer in command of the shattered regiment, all above him having been killed or wounded. It has been a terrible battle—one of the hardest fought, if not the hardest, of the war. Once more the fearful tragedy is enacted. Another libation of blood has been poured out to Liberty. Thousands of souls have been called to sudden judgement—thousands of homes are desolated.

I cannot give you more than an outline journal of the last few days. I wrote to Mother last from Taneytown. Thence we marched to Emmetsburg—thence, with the sound of cannon in our ears, to the position from which we advanced to battle. July 1st, the 1st and 11th Corps were engaged about and beyond Gettysburg,° and after a bloody fight withdrew to the line from which the next day's battle proceeded. The morning of July 2nd arose sunny and warm. Nothing save the proximity of the hostile forces portended the storm about to burst.

I occupied the forenoon in visiting the 1st and 12th Corps—the former to learn the fate of Ned Carrington, about whom I felt great anxiety—the latter, to visit our boys from home.

I found Ned safe. His horse was shot but he escaped unscathed. Capt. [Samuel S.] Woodruff's company was in excellent order° and I spent a few hours with them most delightfully. After calling on a few other friends I started back to my own regiment. Ned had shown me [the] formation of our lines, and I had an opportunity of watching the operations of our sharpshooters, also of seeing a regiment of rebel cavalry dispersed by one of our batteries. I had not reached our Corps before it became evident that the action was about to commence, and on returning to the place where I left the regiment I learned that it had been advanced.° Following, I overtook it, formed in line of battle with the rest of the Brigade, preparing to go forward. After a look and a little talk, the bugles sounded and with a firm step with colors flying, the bravest men in the Army marched into the open field. It was a splendid sight. Far to the right and left the dark lines of infantry moved on, with the artillery disposed at intervals, while the stillness was unbroken save by the scattered fire of skirmishers in front. My eyes and heart followed the flag which I love best and I stood unsuspicious of danger, but full of anxiety. Of a sudden, from the left, a point not apprehended as concealing the enemy, a battery opened upon us the most terrific fire I ever witnessed. The first shell struck not more than two rods behind where I, with several other non-combatants, were standing, expecting to see it begin from the front. We all retired rather precipitately to the partial shelter of a brick barn hard by,° and there remained until our artillery silenced the guns that had opened. It was awful. For half an hour it raged incessantly. Grape, canister, solid shot and shell whizzed and shrieked and tore past us. The trees near by were torn and dismembered. My packhorse was tied to one of them. Twice the poor animal was within a foot of being killed, but I did not dare let Mart go to bring her behind the barn. A fragment of shell killed two chickens within a rod of where I sat. Every moment I expected to be struck, but at length perceiving that our soldiers had advanced further up the field, the fire was diverted from that point and we were released. I never experienced a deeper sense of deliverance. We retired a little and then the wounded began to come in. One of our boys was brought to us with both legs gone. Poor fellow, he lived but a few minutes, having given me his wife's address and commended his soul to the mercy of heaven. Before he expired, a battery from the front again rendered our position unfit for a hospital. The doctors went still further back and as soon as poor [Private Timothy] K[e]arns died I followed them. All the afternoon the battle continued with great violence.

The rear was one vast hospital. The wounded were everywhere, and scenes of sickening horror were presented on every side. The fortunes of the day were of varied aspect. At times we were forced back, but generally the appearance was hopeful. Both sides fought with the utmost desperation. At nightfall it was plain that our arms had gained an essential victory. The plan of the enemy—to turn our left flank—was foiled, although he held portions of the field—the more deplorable because we could not get at our wounded. The ground on which our Brigade fought, including the brick barn, was in their possession. At a little before sunset the sad intelligence spread that Gen. Sickles was wounded. He had been the master-spirit of the day and by his courage, coolness and skill had averted a threatened defeat. All felt that his loss was a calamity. I met the ambulance in which he had been placed, accompanied it, helped lift him out, and administered the chloroform at the amputation. His right leg was torn to shreds, just below the knee—so low that it was impossible to save the knee. His bearing and words were of the noblest character. "If I die," said he, "let me die on the field," "God bless our noble cause," "In a war like this, one man isn't much," "My trust is in God," were some of the things he said. I loved him then, as I never did before. He has been removed, but we are informed that he is doing well.° That night I was so exhausted that I had to sleep. The next day the enemy made another desperate attempt to turn our left but failed.° Again and again they hurled their masses against our batteries, only to be slaughtered and recoil. Since the first I have, of course, been among the wounded.

90 of our regiment are gone—killed, wounded and missing—of the latter very few. Six have suffered the amputation of a leg. One died last night—another cannot probably live. The fortitude with which they bear their terrible sufferings moves me almost to tears. . . . I leave nothing undone that I can think of to assuage their pains. My own conscience and their gratitude furnish sufficient incentives. Yesterday (4th) I got away awhile to bury our dead on the field and look up the wounded that had been left to the enemy. The Confederate line had been withdrawn a little so that this was possible. In a pouring rain we performed the last sad offices for the fallen and left them in soldiers' graves. We found five of our wounded. They had lain two nights on the ground—three of them with broken legs—suffering God alone knows how much.

It was the most terrible battle field I ever beheld. The stench was almost unendurable and the dead lay everywhere. In one place more than 30 were gathered together and the look of their bloated, blackened corpses was a thing to murder sleep. I saw where two Confederate officers had tried to screen themselves behind a stump, but a shell passing through had taken off both their heads. I grieve for our poor boys. We had none to spare and now can hardly

During the crucial second day of the Battle of Gettysburg, Twichell took refuge during a cannonade in a barn owned by farmer Abraham Trostle. "For half an hour it raged incessantly. Grape, canister, solid shot and shell whizzed and shrieked and tore past us. . . . A fragment of shell killed two chickens within a rod of where I sat" (letter of 5 July 1863). (Library of Congress)

be called a regiment. We sent but 13 line officers into the field—of them 6 were wounded and one killed. The Adjutant also was wounded. . . . The Army of the Union has fought as if appreciating its Cause. The accidents of war are dreadful, but the fruits of such a war as this amply pay the cost. As Gen. Sickles said "a man isn't much," weighed against Faith. We have undoubtedly gained a victory. God be praised! The Army will probably be set in motion again to-morrow, for the enemy has gone. May the day be hastened when war shall cease. All this I have written without saying a word about you at home. I have thought of you much, but this is the first time I have found to devote to you. I have little idea that the baby is alive° and think of mother with great sympathy. Give her my love.

You must forgive my ill-looking letter. I have to write in such a constrained position that anything like neatness is out of the question, but I love you, Girl, notwithstanding. Your aff. Bro. Joseph.

I am glad to inform you that he *is also:* Twichell is speaking of the Battle of Gettysburg and is probably reassuring his sister about Weygant. Weygant's regiment, the 124th New York, was on the extreme left of the Third Corps line in a rocky area known as Devil's Den, which saw some of the fiercest fighting.

July 1st, the 1st and 11th Corps were engaged . . . Gettysburg: Union forces clashed with Confederate troops commanded by generals James Longstreet, Richard Ewell, and A. P. Hill on the first day of the battle. The Union forces were driven through the town and took up position on the ridges and hills to the south. The Confederates' failure to press their advantage allowed the Northern troops to reinforce and dig in for the next day's battle. The Third Corps arrived during the night.

Capt. [Samuel S.] Woodruff's company was in excellent order: Woodruff had raised the first company of volunteers in Southington before the war and was now an officer in the Twentieth Connecticut Volunteer Infantry.

on returning . . . I learned that it had been advanced: On the afternoon of 2 July, Sickles advanced the Third Corps—without authorization from the army commander, General George Meade—from its assigned line to slightly higher ground closer to the enemy. Sickles's move ignited a controversy that continues among Civil War scholars today. Sickles maintained that if the Confederates had occupied this ground, they would have dominated and destroyed the Union line, and that Meade's inattention to this part of the battlefield justified the preemptive move. Most historians believe Sickles endangered the left of the army by the maneuver, which was almost immediately followed by a Confederate attack that shattered the Third Corps. Meade rushed other parts of the army to the area, finally reoccupying the original line. Sickles spent the rest of his long life defending his action. Twichell was one of his foremost advocates at veterans' gatherings and Memorial Day speeches.

We all retired . . . to . . . a brick barn hard by: The Trostle barn, still standing on the battlefield, still has shells embedded in its brick walls.

He has been removed, but . . . he is doing well: Sickles survived, carrying on an extensive

The Trostle barn still has some of the shot fired from the Confederate lines embedded in its brickwork. Near this barn Sickles, by now a corps commander, was hit in the leg by a cannonball. The shattered limb was amputated while Twichell administered chloroform (letter of 5 July 1863). The general was out of the war and may thus have avoided a court martial—earlier in the day he had advanced his corps without orders, a move still debated in Civil War circles. (Steve Courtney)

diplomatic and political career. He attended (with Twichell) the fiftieth anniversary of the battle in 1913, when he was ninety-four. Sickles died the following year.

The next day the enemy . . . attempt to turn our left but failed: This refers to the action of 3 July, actually against the center of the line—the so-called Pickett's Charge.

I have little idea that the baby is alive: Eight-month-old Anna Twichell had died on 27 June.

After the battle, Twichell stayed on to aid with the wounded in one of the vast array of hospitals in and around Gettysburg. In a letter to his brother, he describes a short and recuperative visit with friends of Father O'Hagan, some ten miles from Gettysburg.

At the pleasant house of Miss Lilly.
Conewago, Pa. July 15th 1863.

Dear Ned. . . .

We are to start back soon and I embrace the opportunity of the morning hour in a quiet chamber to send my love to the folks at home. I would have written oftener but for the absolute want of time. Owing to the scarcity of Surgeons—as few as possible having been left behind—much more than usual has devolved on Chaplains. . . . Within three days the condition of our hospital has much improved. Nearly all of the slightly wounded have been sent away, making more room for the bad cases, and assistance has reached us in the shape of stores, nurses and surgeons sent by the authorities and benevolent persons of various cities. I intend to start for the regiment in two or three days. If another battle takes place soon, as is probable, I wish to be with my regiment. I have not heard from it since it went away from Gettysburg. I shall never forget this hospital. It has been a scene of great sufferings, also a place in which the love of God and the preciousness of Redemption have been strikingly manifested. . . . All the country round about is a graveyard—not an acre for miles but has some mark of death left upon it, yet if it only brings the blessing, we will rejoice.

I have been considerably among the Confederate wounded. Thousands of them were left in our hands and they fared miserably. Many were not taken from the field till the fourth day. The Confed. surgeons left with them were too few to care for a twentieth of the number—we had more of our own than we could attend to, and the poor creatures had to suffer and die for want of care. Nearby us is a barn, within and around which were 150 of the wretches, mangled in every way, left for days without hardly a look. Some of us would snatch an hour to go over, and fetch them water—bind up simple wounds etc. etc.—but their misery was almost unmitigated. It was a heart-rending sight to see them. Their appeals for help would have moved a heart of stone. Food they had, and a few men were sent to keep them from dying of hunger, thirst or cold, but, as wounded men, they were in great tribulation. Now, those that are left are well nursed, but many a one did not live to be helped. . . . Many of the Confederates are gentlemen, evidently of good birth and education, and there are not a few pious men among them. There was one, a sweet handsome boy with beautiful deep eyes, with whom I fell in love. He was mortally wounded and for days bore his sufferings with most admirable fortitude. I procured a bed and a pillow for him and went to see him often as possible. He possessed a most cheerful Christian spirit and was really a lovely character. One night I went to him, and was so touched by his nobleness that I stooped down and kissed him. The poor little fellow burst out crying. I buried him yesterday before I came away, and mourned for him sincerely.

How are you at home? I have not heard since the battle. . . . To all of you my love. . . . Your aff. Bro. Joseph.

Hospital of 2nd Div., 3rd Corps. Near Gettysburg, Pa.
July 20th 1863.

Dear Mother,

I am a little unwell today and so have time to write, though little really to say. The programme here is uniform—a round of watchings—comfortings— prayers, closing of dead eyes, and funerals. It seems almost impossible that I have become so accustomed to the miseries of life and the solemn mysteries of death. I can sleep the night through when the air is full of anguished cries, or witness the most rending agony, not unmoved but with composure. Once I could hardly bear the sight of a surgeon's knife. Now I can keep my finger calmly on a man's pulse while the keen blade is plunged into his quivering flesh. The horrible scenes of the late battlefield would have driven me crazy a year ago, and a thousand things I could never have dreamed before I went to the war are almost familiar. At the same time I am not aware that my sympathy with human suffering is any the less, and I certainly know better how to minister to it. If I live, my experience here will prove of great value to me as a clergyman.

Our hospital has been thinning out daily as patients become able to be removed, until now the most dangerous cases only remain and they in turn will be taken to Gettysburg as soon as will be safe. My work here is about finished and I would return to the regiment if I knew its whereabouts. We have not heard a word from it since it started with the rest after the retiring enemy. . . .

Yesterday was Sunday, and it is marked by an event which made a deep impression on me. There was a boy in the ward where I have been most busy who did not belong to our Corps. By chance he was brought here and cared for, of course, like the rest. His name was William Morgan of the 126th N.Y., 2nd Corps. At the very first I was attracted by his fine appearance and the fortitude with which he endured the pain of his wound (amputation of right arm at the shoulder joint). . . . The more I saw of him the better I liked him. He had his ups and down like the rest and had a fair chance until yesterday, when the whole prospect changed. . . . Early in the morning . . . Morgan suddenly called a nurse to him. The blanket was lifted. There was fresh blood. In an instant three Surgeons were there and the hemorrhage arrested as soon as possible, but in vain. Such cases are almost surely fatal. His chance of life was gone and he knew it but did not murmur. I prayed with him and sat by his bed until it was over. For an hour and a half he suffered agony, then grew forever still. Poor boy! I closed his eyes and composed his body for the grave, and I am not ashamed to confess that I wept while doing it, for I loved him. I trust he was transferred from earthly to heavenly worship. . . . The Confederates are dying very fast, but are cared for now as well as our own. . . .

My desire to see you increases daily, and I shall make a great effort to come home soon. The events of the last few months have been so momentous that I am almost confused by them, but morning, noon and night, above all other things the sad words, "Father is dead," rise to my lips. My love to Sis and Ned and your little girls.° Your aff. Son. Joseph.

My love to Sis and Ned and your little girls: Twichell's surviving stepsisters were Mary Delight Twichell, eleven; Olive Newell Twichell, eight; and Julia Emeline Twichell, three.

August–December 1863

General Meade, credited with a great victory at Gettysburg (though not by Sickles), did not pursue and destroy Lee afterward, as Lincoln had wanted him to. In the Bristoe and Mine Run campaigns late in 1863, very little changed in the comparative position of the two armies. Twichell was granted a leave that he used to visit his family in Plantsville and to travel to New Haven, probably for the Yale commencement. In an 1896 speech at Yale (see the afterword), he recalled meeting the college president, Theodore Dwight Woolsey, on his way to the chapel. Woolsey plied Twichell about the Battle of Gettysburg "and the Yale men that had borne part in it."

> *Camp of 2nd Regt. Excelsior Brigade.*
> *Near Beverly Ford, Va. August 10th 1863.*

Dear Mother,

I enjoyed a delightful time at New Haven. Very few of my own class were there, but I found friends in abundance, and all apparently glad to see me. . . .

Reaching New York Friday noon, I went first to see Gen. Sickles. I found his house—a charming place on the Bloomingdale Road—but he had gone out to ride. After chatting an hour with Mrs. Sickles and her Mother° I returned to the hotel promising to call next morning. I then found my General, sitting up on a sofa, writing letters on a table before him. He received me graciously and I talked with him for an hour. He was pale and languid, and seemed yet to be suffering, but wonderfully well under the circumstances. He had ridden out [in a carriage] several times and expected to try the saddle in a few days. I have since learned that he has made the experiment successfully. A movement is on foot in the Corps to present him a carriage and horses, for his use on marches, etc.

He made my call very agreeable, especially by discoursing most eloquently and profoundly on a subject that was incidentally brought up, viz. the best method of studying Rhetoric—a subject which he thoroughly understands. . . .

I had designed leaving for Washington in the evening, but Gen. Sickles' surgeon, Dr. Sim, desired me to remain over till Monday morning, for the purpose of assisting him in buying stores for our wounded men. It appears that the Stock Exchange had given the Gen. $800 for his boys. With this we were to buy such things in New York as would serve the purpose, and proceed to Philadelphia and Baltimore and distribute them through the hospitals. I consented to the arrangement, rather reluctantly. During the afternoon I called on Mons Smith.° "Just in the nick of time," was his almost first observation—and proceeding to explain, he told me that Billy Boies and Frank Houston of our class were to meet him at night in Brooklyn, where he is boarding for a few weeks. It was really a happy thing to contemplate. We passed the evening deliciously rambling in our talk over past, present and future, and went to bed to dream of Yale. The next day was the celebrated hot Sunday. The rest staid under the roof while I sought Mr. Bulkley's church,° and, after a most perspiring journey, found it just as he commenced his sermon. After the benediction, I presented myself before him greatly to his surprise. He walked with me a distance to hear and impart news, then I returned to Mons' abode. . . . Monday morning I bade them good-bye and was at the place appointed by Dr. Sim quite early. After waiting till 11 o'clock and seeing no sign of him, my patience became exhausted and I proceeded down town to take the first train for Washington. By the aid of a sleeping car the night passed profitably, and early morning revealed the dome of the Capitol again. First I found Father O'Hagan and learned that my horse and servant were at Georgetown College. The Father had ridden down from Gettysburg through the country, in a sweltering sun, and was well nigh consumed. Next day I met him at the College, inspected Mart and the horse, and once more partook of Jesuit hospitality. . . . On Thursday . . . I . . . was detained to meet Gen. Hooker° who had promised the holy Father a visit the same afternoon.

He came looking handsomer than ever and in the most buoyant spirits. He is certainly a remarkably attractive man. Toward Father O'Hagan and myself he was cordial in the extreme. It was my design to start for camp that same day, but the heat was excessive and I backed out. . . . Finding, Saturday morning, that my horse could not be taken on the cars till the next day, I left Mart to bring him on, and myself set out—reached Bealton Station at sunset—bivouacked on the cold ground—and found my parish early Sabbath morn. Talked all day about our wounded men and answered all manner of eager inquiries. . . .

I enjoyed my short visit exceedingly, yet long for another soon. Father O'Hagan has gone North. He told me that perhaps he would call on you. If he does, I know you will like him. . . . He is one of my best friends, and I want him to think well of my home. . . .

I have learned the particulars of the skirmish at Manassas Gap, July 23rd.° All agree that it was the neatest, most perfect operation ever performed by the Brigade. But two of our regiment were killed and 13 wounded. The 1st and 5th suffered most. Two hills were cleared of the enemy as you would sweep dust with a broom. For the present we are quiet—picketing the river—but are ready for action whenever it is ordered. I hope that you are well and send you my love. Your aff. Son. Joseph.

After chatting an hour with Mrs. Sickles and her Mother: Twichell's attitude toward Teresa Sickles had changed considerably since the early days of the war, when he chose not to share a carriage with the scandal-tainted lady and her mother, Maria Bagioli (see 12 May 1861). Teresa Sickles, her mother, and her daughter, Laura, lived in relative seclusion in a mansion in Bloomingdale, in Manhattan's northern suburbs.

I called on Mons Smith: Twichell's classmate Eugene "Mons" Smith had graduated from Albany Law School in 1861 and opened a law practice in New York City.

I sought Mr. Bulkley's church: That is, Charles H. Bulkley, the former chaplain of the First Excelsior.

I . . . was detained to meet Gen. Hooker: Hooker was in Washington awaiting reassignment. Meade wanted no part of the outspoken general in the Army of the Potomac. As a result, in September General Hooker was given a corps command in the Army of the Cumberland, which was then active in Tennessee.

skirmish at Manassas Gap, July 23rd: The Excelsior Brigade's success at Manassas Gap, Virginia, was not reflected in the strategic outcome of this skirmish. The delay caused by the fighting kept Meade from his goal of dividing Lee's army.

In a letter to his sister on 16 August, Twichell reverts to the subject of Father O'Hagan and his impending visit to Plantsville.

I hardly suppose that Father O'Hagan has yet appeared in Plantsville, though he partly promised to visit you. If he does come, beam on him, Sis. Thaw out his Jesuit heart if you can. You need not be afraid to speak, laugh or trot in his presence, for he is an Irishman and likes hilarity. There is a possibility that, if I come North [to perform his first wedding ceremony for his college friend Arthur Hollister], Harry Hopkins will come with me. I know you will like him. He is a true gentleman. . . .

We are under marching orders. It is more than probable that I shall not find the regiment here when I return. The general opinion is that we are to fall back toward Washington, not having sufficient force here either to attack or resist an attack of the rebel army in front of us. I have not seen Capt. Weygant since I returned. His Division is at Sulphur Spring, seven miles away.

Twichell was able to travel to New Haven to perform the ceremony for his friend Hollister, and, as usual, he combined this duty with a visit to his family in Plantsville.

Washington. Sunday Evening. Sept. 13th 1863.

Dear Ned,

I had so good a time at home, so satisfactory a visit face to face, that it is with a sigh that I sit down to commence writing again. I hoped to have been with my regiment today but various allurements so delayed my progress through New York that I failed of it. Arthur [Hollister] and his wife reached Hartford Tuesday night . . . The newly married folks conducted themselves with uncommon sense, refraining from harrowing up the feelings of their less fortunate friends with any needless display of bliss. I was really quite delighted with my professional handiwork. The ride to New York seemed amazingly short through the sweet charm of Miss May Warner's company.° She is a perfect audience for a talkative man. . . .

Thursday morning Mr. Warner gave me a delicious drive through Central Park, after which I went down town. Mons Smith saluted me rapturously and we lunched together. Calling on John Hannahs° I encountered another day's hindrance. "Hurra!" said he "Just the fellow—dinner tonight! One seat vacant!—pretty girls! Just the fellow!" I protested in vain but at length compromised the matter by extorting a promise to be let off at 10½ o'clock, that I might take the 11½ o'clock train, which of course I missed by just a few minutes. The dinner was gorgeous—much more so than anything of the kind I ever before saw, but the company was not such as I relished. I wasn't posted in the town-gossip, so consequently "let my victuals stop my mouth." Friday . . . I passed most delightfully with my dear Dr. McAllister. He has not entirely recovered his health,° and has so little hope of doing it speedily, that he has tendered his resignation, at which I grieve, for he is a good friend to me. . . . Arrived in Washington, I hurried through a budget of business and reported myself at my Washington home—the McBlairs, where I met my usual warm welcome and good cheer. . . .

To-morrow morning (D.V.) I start for the regiment with Major McBlair, who is going down to pay the Brigade. I shall be glad to see my parish again but love home better than ever. What a grand time I had! . . . Your affectionate Brother. Joe.

the sweet charm of Miss May Warner's company: Sarah Jane Twichell was now a student at the Hartford Female Academy, where May Warner of New York was a fellow student. Twichell was clearly enamored of his sister's classmate. They apparently traveled by train together to New York City after the Hollisters' wedding, Warner to return home and Twichell on the first leg of his return trip to his regiment. The outcome of Twichell's interest is unknown.

Calling on John Hannahs: Probably the brother of his classmate Diodate Cushman Hannahs, killed the previous year.

He has not entirely recovered his health: McAllister had been recuperating ever since January, when he had suffered what Twichell called "an abscess so malignant in its nature that an operation has been necessary."

In Camp. Near Culpepper Court House, Va.
Sunday afternoon. Sept. 20th 1863.

My dear Girl [Sarah Jane Twichell],

I reached the regiment last Monday just in time, for we marched Tuesday evening at sunset. Father O'Hagan was one of the first to welcome me—and a regular, warm Irish greeting it was too—the warmer in prospect of our permanent separation at hand, for he had resigned and was all ready to turn his back on the Excelsior Brigade next morning forever. I prevailed on him to stay one day more and we devoted it to a last ride together—over to Warrenton Sulphur Springs, eight miles and back. We were both merry and sad, for our two years of acquaintanceship furnished many a pleasing reminiscence, while the thought of parting "for good" tinged our converse with a real regret. He is gone now and I can't help feeling solitary—not a little bereaved indeed, though in general Presbyterian ministers shouldn't mourn much° over the absence of Jesuit priests. I shall always remember him with tender emotion, as a gentleman, a charming companion and an honest-hearted friend. It would fill me with gratitude to feel that he is a true Christian. Today a letter came from him beginning "My own dear boy." I have a fancy that, since he saw my sister and other friends at and around home, his regard for me has magnified. He certainly seemed to have conceived a most flattering—beg your pardon, I mean, *just* —opinion of your individual and collective virtues, for he spoke of you all, especially you, with the utmost enthusiasm while we rode to Warrenton, but it is hard to sift the wheat out of the chaff of Irish blarney. However I am sure he thought you very nice respectable people. He appeared to suffer somewhat from the idea that he made rather a poor show on his own account, through previous over-work and weariness, but promised, sometime when he had "the O'Hagan on," to come up and correct the matter. I hope he will. . . .

We (i.e. 3rd Corps) marched Tuesday night . . . and with a vengeance. It was a march, and nothing else. Our first destination was Fox's Ford on the Rappahannock. This being neared, our course was changed, by order, toward Freemans Ford. Then commenced our tribulations. Through forests and morasses, through highways, byways, through hedges and ditches, we groped, huddled and floundered. Vain the splendor of the night, with crisp air and stars and thousand voices and blazing camps, consigned to abandonment and flames—vain indeed, the songs and quips and laughter of the merry rank and file. Mart was sick and I insisted on his occupying my saddle while I plodded, unrecognized in the darkness by men that jostled and swore and mules that brayed—sore of foot and stubbed of toe, remembering what I had just left; home and you and—May Warner, perhaps, which things, however comfortable to pore upon, stretched at length in one's tent, burning the meditative pipe, then only served to exasperate by taunting suggestions of what might be but was not. Well, we marched and countermarched, and filed right and filed right, until the "noon of night" was past when, after half an hour in the thick woods so dense and dark that candles were necessary to light the column on its way, we emerged, not at the river crossing which was our quest, but upon the very field from which we set out, and lay down with mingled cursing and laughter to sleep in the old camps. There was blundering somewhere. Next morning the General of our Division was placed in arrest° to account before a Court Martial for our nocturnal vagaries, and we started afresh—crossed the Rappahannock and at night bivouacked within a mile of Culpepper, having marched more than twenty miles. Thursday morning we were moved around to the west side of the town where we are at this present, pitched on the side of a hill near the road. The enemy withdrew his pickets from the region about us last Sunday and we perceive no hostile signs but an occasional cannon from the Rapidan five or six miles away. What the programme is I have not heard, but whatever it is, the Excelsior Brigade will burn its powder in good style. . . .

But today is Sunday, and I must tell you about it for it has been a day of rare delights. I found on coming back to my parish, while the boys gave me their welcomes—honest, hearty, soldiers' welcomes—that during my absence a religious interest which began at Falmouth had grown and spread until it was quite general. The Christian Commission had established a large chapel tent° in the midst of the Brigade, which was crowded every night with eager audiences, and not a few had been led to the Cross. . . . As I was walking up and down before my tent—arranging my sermon [for morning service]—an Irishman of the regiment and a Catholic drew near and saluting me said, "Chaplain, I want to ask a favour of you." "Say on!" I answered. "Well Sir!" said he, "If I am wounded in the next battle, and like to die, I want you to come to me!" Not exactly understanding his meaning I questioned him further and found to my mingled surprise and astonishment that he desired beforehand to enlist my services as a clergyman. "Father O'Hagan is gone," he said "and you are next to him in my love and confidence." Deeply touched . . . I promised to observe his request if circumstances should require. . . . He promised before we parted to come to me some evening for further sympathy and that we might pray together alone. With the glow of this strange—it seemed to me—wonderful incident still upon me, I entered upon the regular public service of the day. A goodly congregation assembled . . . and an unusual solemnity pervaded the whole worship. I felt how grand a thing it is to preach the Gospel, and how divine a gift—with its frequent terrors of responsibility—is the great ministry I have received. . . . This evening again, at our Hospital tent, we held a prayer meeting—a gracious one, where all hearts were bowed and full of gladness. We sang "Rock of Ages" and some poor fellows prayed, in bad English it may be, but in language that Heaven joys to hear. So you see, my darling Sis, there is an occasional rose in our wilderness, and I am not without my consolations. . . . Your loving Bro. Joe.

P.S. The Surgeon of the 1st has called to ask me to go over and try to make his negro servant confess the theft of some money. Truly the work of a Chaplain is varied and interesting.

Presbyterian ministers shouldn't mourn much: Twichell is referring to himself as a believer in the presbyterian form of church government instead of the episcopal form of the Roman Catholic and Anglican churches—not as a member of the Presbyterian Church.

the General of our Division was placed in arrest: General Henry Prince was apparently not court-martialed for marching the Second Division in a circle, but he was soon reassigned to noncombatant duty.

The Christian Commission had established a large chapel tent: Like the Sanitary Commission, the Christian Commission, formed in November 1861, aided the wounded and sick of the army but with a heavy emphasis on evangelism and the distribution of Bibles and tracts.

In Camp near Culpepper. C. H., Va.
Sunday afternoon. Sept. 28th 1863.

Dear Mother,

A lovelier day than this cannot be well imagined, from the early morning when the sun shed a most grateful warmth upon my chilly bed through the tent side, to now. . . . Autumn nights do very well when one can kindle a fire at sunset and roll up in numberless sheets, quilts and blankets on a good bed in a snug chamber to sleep, but here they are a serious matter. The evening passes tolerably with a pipe and a gossip with fellow officers around a glowing camp fire, which at the expense of a little smoke keeps off the first damps, but the subsequent seeking for rest covered by only a summer's allowance of blankets is a process devoid of romance. Toward morning it grows decidedly unpoetical. However, I have luxuries, compared with my poor parishioners. Before we left Falmouth for Gettysburg, it was ordered that each man turn in either his blanket or overcoat for the sake of lightening the journey, and these have not yet been recovered. Consequently the 2nd Excelsior for the present sleeps poorly enough. . . .

Last evening our hospital tent was crowded with a most solemn congregation, and such a prayer meeting as it was is seldom enjoyed. Numbers unable to get in gathered around the entrance and stood through the whole hour. . . . Thursday night I was asked to go and preach to the Artillery of our Division. It lies about half a mile off through the woods and I was near losing my way, but heard a hymn and, following the sound, found about a hundred men collected around a clump of bushes. It was a right pleasant thing to speak to them and I continued the service till the bugles called them away. So general an interest in religion never prevailed in our midst before. It ought to rouse me completely and lead to all the devotion of heart and life of which I am capable, but I find myself lagging behind the occasion, led rather than leading. . . . What I pray for, for others, I need myself in large measure. Often and often I long for Father, to write to me and stir me up. His words always used to be so fit and inspiring that I waited for them to confirm my purposes. . . .

Wednesday a poor wretch of the 3rd was drummed down the Brigade to the Rogues' March, with his head shaved, for striking his officer. I pitied the rascal although he looked funny with his brown face and white skull. My love to all. . . . Yours most affectionately. Joseph.

In Camp near Culpepper, Va. Sunday afternoon.
Oct. 4th 1863.

Dear Boy [Edward W. Twichell],

I have been thinking today how I would like to be home a few hours, just to take a peep. I really believe that if I hadn't been able to be there at all since I entered the service I should not desire a taste of you half as acutely as I do now, having lately returned from a respectably long visit. The fact is it hardly seems as if I had been there. When I think the affair over—the day at Compounce,°

the climb up mountain, the talks with which we wound up the days in your room, Arthur's wedding, the ride to Hartford with Sis and May Warner, and all the other delights of my sojourn, there is a veil of unreality over them. I seem to have dreamed it for one night. I suppose the track behind us always grows dim in that way, and that is one reason why life seems so short. It is also an exhortation to fill the day we have on hand full of usefulness, since it is out of sight so soon and we can't get hold of it again. Father told me once that he never felt right in the evening unless he was conscious that the day had borne fruit through his exertion. It was an old saying but, coming from him, was clothed in new force. It was the secret of his extraordinary industry and great success in everything that best deserves the name of success. . . .

According to Mother's letter, Sis is probably away by this time. . . . God bless her wherever she goes and in all that she does. I received a short call from Major Weygant a few days since. He wears his promotion modestly and if he escapes casualty will doubtless rise further. He is a good, honest fellow of sterling worth every way, and sufficiently smart to do well at almost anything. At any rate I had rather trust Sis to him than to nine out of ten twice as brilliant. Not that I think a hum-drum man safe, even if Weygant were such, which he is not by any means, but I believe in manliness more than I do in cleverness. That a man possesses first class abilities does not by any means prove that he is or will be a first class man.

Now for my journal—Monday I went to the Artillery Reserve to see my classmate, Charley Fitzhugh. . . . [He] told me that another classmate, Frank Hamilton, who like him left Yale for West Point was in a horse battery (i.e. a battery of which every man is mounted) attached to [Brig. Gen. Hugh J.] Kilpatrick's Division of Cavalry. Anxious to see him, for we had been quite intimate, I set forth Tuesday morning to seek him out. . . . I rode for four miles over a beautiful road through the woods, almost without meeting a man, . . . until I reached the Cavalry and found Kilpatrick's Headquarters, where I paused to inquire for the battery. Kilpatrick I knew somewhat through a classmate that came from the same town, and his Adjutant Major Edwin F. Cook I knew still better. He came to see me in camp once in the fall of '61 with Gen. K's wife. I had met him riding with the General a few days before in Culpepper and exchanged a few courtesies, but was not quite prepared for the boisterous "bowld dragoon," "Hillo, Joe Twichell!" with which he (Cook) hailed me. He told me where the battery was, but utterly refused to let me go further till after dinner. So I staid and dined with the "young Cavalry lion" and his staff. I listened to their yarns and swallowed all their recited exploits with courteous credulity, Oh-ing, Ah-ing and Indeed-ing with as large wonder as they could desire. These cavalry chaps are big talkers and Gen. K. is by no means dumb. I will do him the justice to say that modesty will never be his drawback. After dinner, thoroughly posted in cavalry and urged to call again, I once more bestrode Garryowen and continued my quest of the battery. I found it and my friend. . . . Altogether it was fun. I staid till after dark, when he mounted his horse and, having procured a pass which the lateness of the hour made necessary, rode with me as far as the infantry picket where we parted, mutually pleased with our visit, I think. At least, I was.

It was very dark and but for Garryowen's most admirable sagacity—retracing exactly the path by which we came through fields and woods and camps, a thing I could not possibly have done—I should have had a weary job in getting home. While passing through a perfectly dark forest road, I heard a shuffle and quick steps following me. Depend upon it "the roots of my hair were stirred," but an open space with moonlight revealed that my pursuer was a dog—a very handsome one, who for some unexplained reason had adopted my society. I said nothing and he kept on. When I dismounted to show my pass to a guard, he came to me and submitted to my caress with evident ecstasy. I resolved to receive him into my family, flattered a little perhaps by his unsought attachment, and at once named him Calvin Culpepper. He was a youthful pointer, fair to look upon. Arrived at my tent I took him in and he abode for the night. Next day "the Chaplain's dog" was the popular theme of camp. I fed him, as dog never before was fed, and his gratitude was intense. While I wrote he would sit with his head on my knee, keeping an affectionate eye on my movements. He also affectionately turned over my inkstand and exhibited many similar proofs of the fact that he considered himself as one of the family. I began to paint his future—how nice it would be to take him home after the war and tell the rather touching story of how he came to me, how he had been with me ever since, on marches, in battles etc. etc. That night we had a prayer meeting and, fearing to invite him lest he should disturb our devotions by his displays of affection for me, I left him behind tied to the tent pole with a rope. That was the last I ever saw of Calvin Culpepper. Dexterously slipping the noose over his head, he departed to seek other victims of misplaced confidence. . . .

We had a good meeting that night and another little one in the woods Thursday night, and yet another Saturday night. Today has been a pleasant one in every sense—a real Sabbath. The morning service was solemn and well attended although not as fully as usual owing to a general excitement and discussion concerning an offer made by the Government with reference to the re-enlistment of veteran troops for three years more. . . . The religious awakening continues to occupy much of our attention and is still on the increase.

I ought to have said more about it, and meant to, but my letter was too long before I knew it. Love to all. Your aff. Bro. Joseph.

the day at Compounce: Lake Compounce, on the town line of Southington and Bristol, Connecticut, was then and still is a recreation area.

Union Mills (near Centreville), Va. Oct. 15th 1863.

Dear Mother,

I have not written as usual, simply because I could not, and now I may be interrupted before I can finish a page by an order to march. For more than a week we have been in an unsettled state, and endured considerable hardship. Last week, Thursday morning at 3 o'clock, our Division left the camps it had occupied three weeks near Culpepper C.H. [Court House] and marched through the outpost lines toward James City, for the purpose of observing, in conjunction with Kilpatrick's Cavalry, the movements of the enemy. It seemed comparatively lonesome to have only 10 or 12 thousand men about, but I enjoyed the seclusion. For a whole day (Friday) we remained under arms waiting for the troopers in front to find out what was going on. Being close under the Blue Ridge I had leisure to witness the morning and evening glories of that beautiful range. In the evening the brethren gathered together in a place aside and we held a prayer meeting. Next morning, at daybreak, word was brought that the enemy was crossing at a neighboring ford. The Division was immediately put in order of battle° and the general pulse beat quick. Soon the flying artillery opened and we knew that the cavalry was engaged. A regiment of our brigade (the 120th N.Y.) had been sent six miles to the front on picket, when we first reached the position, and for the fate of it no little apprehension was felt. It proved to be well founded. At about 9 o'clock all that was left of it came in, reporting that they had been attacked by three brigades of rebel cavalry, but aided by thick woods had been able to keep them at bay while retreating, leaving in their hands, however, all the wounded and a number of prisoners, amounting to near a hundred. There was some misunderstanding about the cavalry that was to support them, that left them so badly exposed. This event, although deeply regretted by the rest of the brigade, only quickened the desire, already strong, to try our hand with Stuart's cavalry, but it appeared that a very large force of infantry was also in front of us—much larger than we could cope with, and the order was given to face about and return to the army lines. This we did while Kilpatrick held the enemy in check. They pushed on hard and it was once thought that we would have to halt, form line, and give them battle, but the flying batteries worked busily and we escaped. At midnight we bivouacked within a short distance of the camp we left Thursday, tired enough and chilled through, for it was cold. Next morning (Sabbath) we received eight days rations and marched early. During our absence the whole Army had been set in motion. Our reconnaissance revealed a vast column of the enemy moving to the right. Once more the army of the Potomac was compelled to fall back and cover Washington. 11 o'clock Sunday night saw us bivouacked across the Rappahannock. Since then we have hurried along, guided in our course by the enemy's, till tonight (Thursday) we are here. The incidents of the march have not been very diverting or exciting. It has been real, hard work and the boys are wearied. The enemy has pressed us continually. Yesterday the rear guard (2nd Corps) was hotly engaged, but with great success, repulsing the enemy in fine style, taking both guns and prisoners. I was so tired from having had but one hour's sleep the night before that, although the cannon and musketry roared and crashed, I lay down on my cloak and slept soundly through the whole of it. This happened while we were covering the crossing at Bull Run. Today our 3rd Brigade has been engaged just in front of where we are now bivouacked and, although suffering loss, has maintained itself bravely. Sunday night, before we crossed the Rappahannock, while marching through the dark woods, an alarm arose, and for a few minutes the panic was fearful. In the midst of it, my horse broke away from Mart and stampeded through the forest, throwing off his forage and tearing away the saddle-bags, which held my books and all my treasures, against the trees. Some of them were gathered up but the most were left to the enemy. The horse I gave up for lost, but he made his way back to the column and was caught by a soldier of the 1st Regt. I received him right thankfully, and almost felt as if I had had a horse given me. The rascal felt no remorse for his evil deeds, but looked perfectly lamb-like when I reproached him. . . .

To-morrow may bring battle. The enemy is before us. Whether he will attack, fall back, or pass around our flank into Maryland is uncertain. I dread an engagement. So often have I beheld courage and blood, that I would I might never again. I forgot to mention as an incident of the march that night before last, the head of our Corps Column was suddenly and fiercely attached by rebel artillery and cavalry. [Maj.] Gen. [William H.] French escaped as by a miracle.° His bodyguard was badly cut up. A brigade was wheeled into a line and soon drove the assailants away, but it detained us for two hours. . . . If we have a great battle I shall write as soon as I can. I pray God to cover my poor boys if they are brought to the field of slaughter, and you must pray for us too. Give my love to all the folks—I begin to feel as if I had not seen them in a long long time. Your aff. Son. Joseph.

The Division was immediately put in order of battle: During the autumn of 1863, Meade and Lee crossed and recrossed the Rapidan and Rappahannock rivers, facing each other in skirmishes rather than major conflict. In the so-called Bristoe Campaign of 9–20 October, Lee tried to turn the right flank of the Army of the Potomac.

[Maj.] Gen. [William H.] French escaped as by a miracle: French was now in command of the Third Corps.

In Camp. Union Mills, Va. October 18th 1863.

Dear Boy,

War has no Sabbath days and we are all yet in order to start again, after two days rest, and continue our travels—whither I do not know, nor indeed, do I much care. My manner of life for two years and more has bred an indifference concerning destination and prospect, to which in my first campaign I was an utter stranger. Then I fretted and wondered and worried, anxious to find out what was brewing—time, place, why and wherefore, as if, forsooth, it was at all necessary or expedient that I should be in the counsels of our chiefs. But now, having concluded that my responsibility in the premises is exceedingly limited, that I shall not be glorified by success or changeable with failure, I have drawn in the nervous feelers of my curiosity and reside contentedly within my own shell and parish, wherever they are located. When the column is formed for march, I mount my horse serenely, take my place and, wrapped in meditations, or talking with some comrade, or peering into some book, or observing the immediate surroundings, follow along unquestioning and in peace. Often, indeed, after a day's travel, not even having observed the points of compass . . . I have lain down under my blanket and slept without knowing or asking the geographical locality of the bivouac. I have confidence that all is going as well as may be under the circumstances, have no doubt that we are in the way of saving the Union, feel certain that Providence guides the whole affair, and that is enough to keep me from small perplexities. . . .

When we first reached here (last Thursday) I . . . learned that my friend and classmate Charley Hatch (Capt., 13th N.Y. Cavalry) was at Fairfax C.H. [Court House] convalescing from a typhoid fever. Next morning I set forth to find him. . . . The poor fellow had been very sick and lonesome and was delighted to see me. Saturday morning I returned, via Centreville, and met Gen. Sickles in a carriage riding in state with his staff behind him. At my salute, he did me the honor to stop the whole establishment, shake hands and inquire of my condition. He was looking magnificently and showed no signs, save the missing leg, of his misfortune. We had been expecting him for two days, and the boys were all primed to give him a rousing welcome. Upon his saying that he was then on his way to the Corps via Fairfax Station, I hasted on . . . and arrived in camp just as the Division was being marched out to greet him. I knew it would be a splendid spectacle, and outside of my personal desire to welcome back my general . . . would not have missed the occasion, as a sight worth seeing. Two Divisions (2nd and 3rd—the 1st was at Fairfax Station) were formed along the road, massed a regiment deep. After some delay the General appeared, mounted on a horse which he sat like an emperor, and followed by a great cortege of officers. The moment he hove in sight, the uproar commenced. It was thunderous. Enthusiasm begot excitement, and excitement, wildness. Officers waved their swords and soldiers their caps, while cheer on cheer, huzzas, shouts and "tigers"° swelled down the line, one after the other rolling the length, like sea waves. It was soul-stirring and not a little affecting. I know some officers that wept. The object of all this clamor rode slowly along, bowing with uncovered head and looking proudly, as well he might. Some say that they saw a tear running down his cheek. The old Brigade strained its individual and collected lungs to the utmost and the results were immense. I am today quite hoarse, which ought not to be on Sunday.

We were downright glad to see the General and he to see us. The last time he looked on our ranks was in the midst of the terrible, bloody fight at Gettysburg and everybody was thinking of it as he passed before us. He did not come to stay—only for a visit. When he will resume command I do not know,° but the Corps will never be contented with another Commander.

I am ashamed to write such miserable letters, but they are as good as the times afford. I have to sit on the ground and it makes my back ache so that I hurry to get through. On no account let one of these "literary gallops" go out of the house. I enclose a melainotype of Ned Carrington and myself° which we had taken at Culpepper. Love to all. Your aff. Bro. Joseph.

huzzas, shouts and "tigers": This was a student cheer that consisted of shrieking the word "ti-i-i-ger" with a prolonged yell at the end.

When he will resume command I do not know: Sickles's attempt to regain his command by meeting with Meade on this visit to Virginia was unsuccessful. It was generally believed that Meade would have court-martialed Sickles for his actions at Gettysburg had the corps commander not lost his leg. Theirs was clearly not a good relationship: Sickles had already regaled Lincoln with his side of the controversy, in which he declared Meade to be an incompetent leader bent on withdrawal from Gettysburg. Sickles remained unoccupied until late 1864, when Lincoln sent him to Colombia as a diplomat.

I enclose a melainotype of Ned Carrington and myself: A melainotype was a photographic image on metal, also known as a tintype.

In Camp. Near Cattells Station, Va.
Sunday night. Oct. 25th 1863.

Dear Mother,

We have been here four days. I have a good bed of boards, hard but level, and a fireplace that behaves beautifully. Today I have been congratulating my-self on my comforts and indulging in anticipations of pleasant pipes with a new book before my glowing hearth for many days to come. An hour since, however, an order came to pack up and be ready to start early in the morning. I don't mind it much though, for I am used to such rude proceedings. Maybe this unsettled style of living is a timely experience, preparing me for that rov-ing, changing, career that many ministers are doomed to. I shall learn the art of moving to perfection. . . .

We left Union Mills last Monday morning at dawn in the midst of a driving, cold, storm. It was awfully wretched business to begin with, but Providence was kind, and the sky cleared by 9 o'clock. Halting at about noon near Bristow's Station, our regiment was detached from the Brigade and sent off a mile on a by-road to hold a picket line. At a house nearby, the Major and I found some poor but well mannered people who sold us some butter and furnished din-ner at a moderate price. The man of the place was a cobbler and I submitted to this artistic skill one of my boots that had given way, with the most satisfactory results. Just before dark we were relieved from the picket and returned to our place in the Brigade. Next morning while the column was preparing to march I galloped over to the house again to get another vent in my boot sewed up, which had escaped my notice the day before. While the man was at work and I reading, the woman (one of the lean, dragged out, Virginia sort, but rather pleasant withal) came to me and quietly asked what religious denomination I belonged to. On my replying, she added that she was a Methodist, but had been a long time almost entirely without the privileges of the church and min-istry and that her four youngest children were yet unbaptized. She wanted me to christen them. "Certainly," I said, "Bring them in!" So she brought them in—two boys and two girls, one a baby—from 8 years to 8 months old—and with a short introductory and concluding prayer, I baptized them out of an earthen mug of water, and added to the good mother's satisfaction by kissing the baby, though it was far from clean. It seemed to do the poor woman a great deal of good. She hugged the baby and said, "Now you little deary, you've got a name!" and, turning to the rest, remarked, "You'll have to be mighty good after this!" It was really quite affecting and I was glad it happened for their sakes and mine. My boot was finished (I performed the ceremony in one stockinged foot) and I mounted and rode away with very pleasing emotions. I do not know what the family name was, but I shall long remember the event.

That day a letter was brought me on the march which may have a great influence on the next few years of my life. It was from Harry Hopkins, telling how a friend of his and mine, Major [Samuel C.] Armstrong of the 125th N.Y.S. Vols., was setting out to raise a negro regiment° and that he had written to Harry saying, "Nothing would be so delightful to me, nothing would so certainly ensure the success of the enterprise, as to have Joe Twichell Lt. Colonel and yourself Major, of that proposed Regiment." You cannot imagine my astonishment. It was a long time before I could fairly take in the idea and for the rest of the day, indeed ever since, it has been uppermost in my mind. Harry wanted to know what I could answer to Major Armstrong's proposition. . . . I did as well as I could under the circumstances—looked on all sides—tried to view it conscientiously, and at night wrote to Harry that I would go if he did. . . . To tell the truth I think he will decide against going. It is a problem that I hardly feel able to solve alone. Oh! How I wished I could counsel with Father about it! The subject has two sides, and it is not easy to tell which is stronger. I would glory in bearing a part in the grand movement that is putting the colored man right before the world. The very thought sets me on fire with zeal, but my ministry is not to be laid aside, even for a year, without the clearest indication of duty. The position offered is one that I am not now fitted for, but I could attain a fitness by hard study. Major Armstrong's estimate of my worthiness is gratifying to me, and I shall try to verify it, if I once set out to. . . . I do not think of going without Harry, indeed, I shall feel very sure that to abide by his conclusions will be to do what is best. It isn't very pleasant to anticipate continuing a soldier for an indefinite period, but whatever God and the country set before me, woe is me if I do it not. . . .

The religious interest continues but not with such results as I could desire. Many are convicted, but few converted. . . . Wherever we go, I think much of you at home and look forward to seeing you with impatience. Love to all. Your aff. Son. Joseph.

Major [Samuel C.] Armstrong . . . was setting out to raise a negro regiment: The militia act of 17 July 1862 had allowed the enlistment of African Americans in "any military or naval service for which they may be found competent." Twichell wrote in 1893 that Armstrong gave up his plan temporarily, so he and Hopkins never had to decide whether to take part. Armstrong later organized the Eighth and Ninth United States Volunteers (Colored). After the war he founded Hampton Normal and Agricultural Institute, which taught both African American and Native American students.

Dear Ned,

We have shifted our location about one third of a mile since I wrote and now lie in a smooth open field near the rail-road, but on the other side of both it and Kettle Run than before. The change was made, I suppose, in view of an anticipated attack by the enemy. In case of repulse a stream is an awkward thing to retreat over; again, it is an advantage to have it in one's front for defensive purposes. But no attempt has been made to disturb us, though hardly a day passes without a cannonade from some part of the lines, and we have settled down quite comfortably again. . . . How long we shall stay is an uncertainty, but I suppose until the rail-road is finished—a week or so. The enemy did the job thoroughly this time. Every bridge was demolished, every culvert blown up, and some cuts filled. The ties were used to heat and bend the rails, some of which were actually wound around the trunks of trees. But Uncle Sam is a wealthy and patient individual and not easily discouraged. The work of re-ducing this chaos to order goes bravely on, having already reached Warrenton Junction—a mile beyond here.

Monday, our regiment was ordered out to escort a supply train (i.e. of wag-ons) to and from Bristow Station. I went along. . . . On the way down I rode aside to visit for the second time since that dreadful day, the battlefield of Aug 27th 1862. I found the graves of my boys that fell there trampled by a drove of grazing horses belonging to a battery encamped near. It grieved me to see them so despoiled yet there was no fault to be ascribed. I straightened up the headboards and wrote the names over again, where they were growing dim. Poor fellows! They lie there humbly enough, but oh! how honorably! It was hard to think that all I was permitted to do in respect to their memory was to take out my pencil, and keep their resting-place from being nameless a little while longer. I felt, while doing it, with profound emotion that if one's name is "written in Heaven" he can afford to have his dust lie lowly, and prayed that I and those I love might possess that "better part."

The battle between our 2nd Corps and [Gen. A. P.] Hill's Confederates°
week before last took place in part on the same ground. Twice baptized in blood for Liberty's sake, it will be a place to which in after times pilgrimages will be made by those who reverence the glorious, through suffering, past.

We returned to camp without seeing any sign of guerrillas, to the disap-pointment of some bold hearts, which panted for brush with the thieves.

Ned Carrington, to whom I unfolded the negro regiment scheme of which I spoke last week, gave me his views against it decidedly, and at length, having been led to consider the matter before. I listened to his exposition of the subject and was persuaded of its justice, yet feel no less that it is a grand business in which I would like to have a hand, as I already have a heart. I have not heard from Harry Hopkins yet in reply to my letter but have little doubt that he will think it not best to enter upon the undertaking.

Thursday night we were well settled and the weather was so mild that I appointed a prayer meeting in the hospital tent. It was filled. Evangelist John Vassar of the New York Tract Society° was with us—the most wonderful Christian I ever saw. . . . He, by fervent prayers and exhortations, stirred us mightily. Since then we have had a meeting every evening and goodly seasons they have proved. I begin to feel that a great work of Grace is coming—is now being wrought. The brethren (some of them converted since they entered the Army) are awake. I wish you could hear them pray. My own coldness is rebuked daily. A number who never came to preaching or prayer-meeting before now find their way into our midst often, and some of them confess freely that they want to be Christians. I was amazed last night to see a man whom I had esteemed the wickedest in our regiment—a blasphemer—a scoffer—walk into the tent and sit down. "Nothing is impossible with God," thought I, but I could hardly conceive that man with a regenerate heart. After the benediction I went up to him, almost trembling. I saw in his eyes that he was softened. "Jim," said I, "don't you wish you were a Christian?" "Yes, Chaplain, I do!" was his instant and hearty reply. I could have fallen on his neck and kissed him. We talked a while and parted, he promising to come and see me today, I to reproach myself with little faith. . . .

There are others . . . who are under conviction. . . . Never, never, since the country had a name was there a time when a great Awakening from one end of the land to the other—from the President to the humblest citizen—from the General-in-chief to the poorest private—was so to be longed and prayed for. Oh! That a Pentecost would sweep through the nation! When we call upon God, He will hear us and give us what we want—and that is neither dominion, nor gold, but Holiness. It affects me unpleasantly—it makes me afraid—to hear of Prosperity at the North. It is not a sign of promise in my eyes. I think, "Surely God cannot give us peace, while our store houses and purses are full, and our hearts otherwise engaged than in contrition and humility." . . . Christian citizens and soldiers ought not to expect or desire the Republic to be let off on any less terms than such as will leave us a people after God's own heart. . . . I long to see the country shaken by the Holy Ghost, and our countrymen giving in their allegiance to the Lord, till He whose right it is actually reigns in the national heart—then—Peace, blessed Peace, will come to abide forever.

Col. Potter came back Thursday, looking very thin and pale but apparently mending from a worse condition. He has now got through the first few days in camp without any drawback and has a fair prospect of strength again. . . . Love to all at home. Your aff. Brother. Joe

The battle between our 2nd Corps and [Gen. A. P.] Hill's Confederates: On 14 October, Hill's corps attacked the Army of the Potomac's Second Corps at Bristoe Station. The subsequent Confederate defeat was ascribed to the impetuous Hill's advancing without reconnaissance.

Evangelist John Vassar of the New York Tract Society: "Uncle John" Vassar was a lay preacher and member of the Poughkeepsie, New York, brewing family that founded Vassar College. He travelled extensively during the war evangelizing among the troops. "Just before the battle of Gettysburg he was captured by General James E. B. Stuart's cavalry, who were glad to let him go to escape his importunate exhortations and prayers," says *Appleton's Cyclopedia.*

Near Rappahannock Station, Va.
10½ o'clock a.m. Sunday. Nov. 8th 1863.

Dear Mother,

We have halted and stacked arms to wait while the order of advance is forming. . . . Mart has built a cheery fire by which one side of me, at least, is kept comfortable enough for a soldier's utmost desire. The Major is at my elbow reading the paper, a pot of potatoes boils temptingly before my toes— altogether the situation is not one to complain of. I am far from being merry, however. On the contrary, there is an oppression on my spirits and not with- out cause. We are probably marching to battle—today perhaps, tomorrow probably—but certainly, as the appearance now is, before long. I cannot look at the column as it moves on toward the tragedy, especially at my own regiment— my beloved parish—without gloomy forebodings. As I think of what is coming and anticipate the scenes to which we haste—the death groans—the hideous mutilations—the burials—the graves, a dread comes over me more profound and disturbing than any personal apprehensions could possibly inspire. The great Reaper seems to lead us on with exultation at the food soon to be fur- nished for his ready scythe. Once it was hard for me to realise, as we gaily advanced, that it was to such fearful places, but now I seem to see them all portrayed before they are reached. . . .

But to give my journal of events. We marched from Cattell's day before yesterday and joined the rest of the corps at Warrenton Junction. Early yes- terday morning the whole army started for the Rappahannock°—the 2nd and 3rd Corps being ordered to cross at Kelly's Ford, the others at fords above. We reached the hills commanding the ford at 3 o'clock. Our 1st Division was before us and had succeeded in effecting a crossing with the loss of about 25 in killed and wounded. Our batteries of artillery from an advantageous position rendered it a comparatively easy job. The enemy was evidently taken entirely by surprise—a rare thing, and what [might] have been a difficult task was accomplished with a rush. A few rifle pits that commanded the ford on their side were suddenly flanked and yielded about 400 prisoners who, poor fellows, I regarded as lucky beyond measure. Until dark the cannonade was kept up and we had a fine opportunity for observing the movements of the infantry that had crossed. No line of battle became engaged, but the skirmishers maintained a rattling fire. A similar operation was as successfully performed by the Corps that crossed at the next ford above—resulting, as we hear this morning, in the capture of quite a body of the enemy with some artillery. I can only hope that these preliminary successes are but a foreshadowing of what will result from the greater attempts about to be made.

At nightfall we crossed and took our position in line on the left of the Corps and threw out pickets. Our bivouac was in a cornfield of which the sheaves were standing—large material for good beds and forage. The Colonel [Potter], Major [Rafferty] and myself combined our resources in the way of blankets and in one another's embrace slept both warm, long and soundly. At sunrise the bugles sounded. A hasty breakfast and we pushed on. The enemy had disappeared from our front and as we advanced evacuated several entrenched hills to fall back, and probably will take a position somewhere between here and Culpepper. Some of their dead were left unburied, and I felt no joy at seeing them stretched on the plain. We have now joined again the right wing and are prepared to show a full Army front. The general mood is hopeful and the fighting will be good.

If Lee has suffered much diminution of his forces through the necessities of Chattanooga and South Western Virginia, we may outnumber him. That he was surprised, leads us to think that he supposed us to be already in winter quarters and himself at liberty to part with a portion of his army. The prisoners taken belong to Ewell's Corps. They affirm that they had supposed themselves settled for the winter and in no danger of attack. We passed a large number of their shanties this morning—very strongly and comfortably constructed. An unqualified victory just now on Virginian soil is an event devoutly to be wished. I pray for mild weather in behalf of those who will lie wounded on the field. Sufferings from cold are both harder to endure and mitigate, and aggravate injuries.

Your last letter with Father's photograph has reached me. I think the likeness better than the former one, but yet far from good. One of the eyes is somehow distorted and mars the whole effect. I do not think we ever will have a satisfactory picture of his face. His memory will be green without it.

Eddy's urgent invitation to come home to Thanksgiving made me wish, but did not make me hope. It will probably be impossible, but how I should like to be there. . . .

I wish you might see the maneuvering of thousands now going on in the field before me. War is grand in some of its aspects, but God give peace as soon as Honor can accompany it. Love to all. Joseph.

Early yesterday morning the whole army started for the Rappahannock: Meade crossed the Rappahannock again, contending with the Confederates at Kelly's Ford and inflicting a surprising number of casualties. Lee withdrew behind the Rapidan, the next river to the south, restoring the status quo of the previous month.

> 2nd Regt. Excelsior Brigade. Near Brandy Station, Va.
> Nov. 15th 1863.

Dear Ned, . . .

There has been a brisk cannonade this morning on the left of our lines. I have not heard what occasioned it, but we have been ordered to be in readiness to march at a minute's notice, and though I am of the opinion that it is simply a precaution, I nevertheless wish to make sure of my weekly document, for I am so conceited as to think that you will be disappointed by its delay.

The battle which I prophesied with such confidence did not take place, contrary to universal expectations. Even while I was writing the troops were being formed for action and skirmishers were feeling the way all along our front. Everyone was surprised that the enemy retired before us and we moved on, the whole army compactly arranged, toward Brandy Station where it was thought he certainly would make a stand—the country being open and well calculated for defence on the Richmond side. I have seldom witnessed a more splendid array than the Federal arms presented that day. From some points of the march the whole army could be taken in at one view—the hosts of the Union advancing in combined grandeur. The 2nd, 3rd, 5th and 6th Corps stretched out across the plain—shoulder to shoulder—pressing on with equal step—and the 1st Corps bringing up the rear. It was a magnificent spectacle. One's pulses leaped with enthusiasm, pride and hope at the sight. From the cavalry away on either flank no firing was heard and our vanguard met no opposition. It began to be whispered that the Confederates had declined the proffered challenge and such was found to be the case when Brandy Station had been reached. They had left at 12 o'clock—the last of them—and fled beyond the Rapidan, leaving for our use their winter quarters just finished. There we halted and went into camp, for already our railroad communication was far behind, the track having been completed but little distance further than War-renton Junction. It is now in working order nearly to the Rappahannock, and the bridge is being reconstructed. In three or four days it will reach us here and we shall be ready to advance again. Meanwhile we are comfortably housed in the cabins reared at great expense of labor by the enemy, who must gnash his teeth at the very idea. I declare it seems almost cruel to have turned them out into the cold so unceremoniously, and ourselves profit by the industry. It is something like slavery in that respect. Our regiment is making itself at home under roofs intended for the 23rd North Carolina Vols. I have a shanty all to myself—very commodious and well made. I would ask no better fortune than to winter in it, although it needs a little Yankee contrivance to make it perfect.

Our recent activity has, of course, interrupted entirely the order of public religious observance in the regiment, and just at a time when it seemed least desirable. . . . Friday night the hospital tent was up, the weather was mild, and we got together to begin anew. It proved a more than common blessing. . . . The brethren were rejoiced greatly to see [one] of their comrades rise for the first time and hear him tell with much emotion how once he had thought he was a Christian and felt peace in his soul, but had gone astray sadly, and now wanted to come back to his Lord and start afresh to love Him. . . . Next we were made happy by Asst. Surgeon Younglove rising, also for the first time, and speaking such things as became a Christian man. I tell you, my dear Brother, I have full faith that a great work of Grace is coming to our army. Everybody appears to be stirred by sacred influence. . . . May the day hasten that shall reveal the Holy Ghost with power. . . .

My old and well-esteemed friend, Mr. Alvord of the Boston Tract Soc., came to see me on the march and propose that I accompany him on a tour through the States for the purpose of making public addresses, and moving the people to deal liberally with the army in affording it religious privileges. It was a tempting offer and a most complimentary one, but I said, No! at once, yet I would dearly like to do it and I think I could succeed. After my regiment is mustered out of service, I will go with him if he wants me.

There is some talk of our Brigade's being ordered to New York to recruit as mounted infantry but I have little expectation it will result in anything. If it should come to pass, why, then I shall be almost the same as at home. Dear me, how glorious even to imagine. . . . Write and tell me how you prosper. God bless you, my dear boy.

Your aff. Bro. Joe

Dear Mother,

Yours of the 15th inst. came duly, and had no cause for jealousy in the attention I gave it, for it has been almost my only comfort from the mail for the past week. This is very unusual and in some respects a relief, for I receive a great many letters from wounded men in hospital wanting this or that done for them, and the families both of the living and dead asking information, and lawyers seeking certificates and other documents on which to found claims against the government for pensions etc. — to comply with whose requests and answer them is a great chore and consumes of both time and stationery. The lawyers I treat very coolly, sometimes giving no attention to their applications, for many of them are shysters and sharks, leading poor people to expense by false representations, and themselves pocketing a large share of what they succeed in extracting from the national treasury, if indeed they succeed at all. Beside that, many of the discharged men in whose behalf the pension is to be applied for, as having become disabled in the service, I know to be entirely unworthy of it, and am unwilling to do anything in aid of swindling the government, in a respect in which it has already been too much victimized. . . . But all this miscellany of letters of which I speak only makes me glad to get the occasional love-letters, from home and elsewhere, that shine out from the mass like diamonds in rubbish. If they fail to appear, I feel as though I had received nothing, and I wait for them with daily longing. . . . I find, dear Mother, that you after all are my chief reliance. All the rest are fitful and irregular. One meagre morsel is all that Sis has vouchsafed since I left home. She is treasuring up wrath. Eddy, I make no charges against, but I shall soon grow so unfamiliar with his signature as to be in danger from forgery should any one try to get money from me by its means. You see, these remembrances from the north are my social provender. Here are only husks. . . . I crave better. A pleasant note from Arthur has assured me of Sis' continued convalescence,° and the more definite news of yours leads me to hope that she is quite herself again. . . . Your comfort in the little girls, so gratefully mentioned, is often in my mind, a source of thanksgiving. Your widowhood, bitter as it is from the constant memory of a great, irreparable loss, is peculiarly relieved by such consolations and blessings as few widows have. Aside from the sweet, sacred, priceless recollections of a past companionship with the best man we ever knew. . . . A multitude of homes may well envy ours. Hearts are breaking all over the land at the thought of mangled bodies and nameless, unknown graves. . . . How differently was it

with your dead! And there is little Annie. I had almost forgotten to mention her, yet I know you buried part of a mother's heart with her tiny, wasted frame, and the pang is not so soon dull. Well! The Lord has carried her in his arms now near half a year, and she has seen His face all that while. "No more pain". . . .
. . . Your aff. Son. Joseph.

Arthur has assured me of Sis' continued convalescence: After returning to the Hartford Female Academy in the fall, Sarah Jane Twichell suffered from a fever and convalesced at the home of the newly married Hollisters. By mid-December she had recovered.

> *2nd Regt. Excelsior Brigade. Brandy Station, Va.*
> *Dec. 3rd 1863.*

Dear Ned,

I am back in the cabin I left a week ago this morning feeling as old and worn and generally used up as ever before in my life. When I reached here last night I was in a condition to do nothing but roll up in my blankets, although I did make a cup of tea for the Major who was, if anything, worse off than I, . . . but a good long sleep, a wash, a shave and breakfast have so revived me that I undertake to give you an account of our campaign across the Rapidan° — a campaign that the Army of the Potomac will always remember as attended with peculiar hardships and sufferings, and resulting in failure, or at least, a want of success.

Thursday morning, Nov 26th, Thanksgiving day, we were early aroused and at sunrise the column set out. Our Corps was ordered to make the crossing at Jacob's Ford which we reached after a march of 7 or 8 miles. A few shots dispersed the enemy's cavalry picket stationed there, the pontoons were laid, and our division was over before dark. We proceeded directly on by a wood path for two miles or so till we ran into a hostile picket which retired skirmishing. The incident is noteworthy from the fact that a dog belonging to one of our advance guard was wounded by the first fire and made the woods resound with his piteous yelpings. It was just there discovered that by somebody's blunder we had taken a wrong road. The column was faced about and marched back a short distance when we bivouacked. It was a very cold night and every mother's son of us was chilled to the heart, yet no fires were allowed but small ones sufficient to make coffee by. The Colonel, Major and myself combined our blankets and snugged in together for warmth's sake. So passed and ended my Thanksgiving day. From the midst of my own discomfort I sent many a thought homeward. . . . But to resume my journal—Friday morning we (i.e. 3rd Corps) changed our course and at about 9 o'clock again encountered the enemy's pickets. For two hours then we felt the way cautiously with skirmishers—the hostile pickets falling back, until at a little after noon we came upon Ewell's Corps drawn up in a thick wood with dense undergrowth, making it very difficult to form our line of battle. Soon, however, the 1st Brigade of our Division was engaged hotly° and our Brigade was ordered in to its support. I rode in to see where the boys would be posted, not intending to expose myself, but just as our line was forming in a little open space and I was sitting on my horse just behind Co. E., taking a view of the situation—whiz-z-z-*thud*! and down tumbled Sergt. [James J.] Brady, almost catching my rein as he fell. He was immediately placed on a stretcher and I accompanied him off the field, thanking Heaven for my narrow escape. It proved not a bad wound—the ball having pierced the fleshy part of his thigh. I took good care of the Sergt. that day, as I felt under peculiar obligation to him for stopping a bullet that might have broken my ankle without going much out of its way.

I cannot give you all the details of the battle. Suffice it to say that it continued till dark, neither side gaining much ground. Our whole Corps and one Brigade of the 6th (which had come up, having crossed after we did) was engaged. The musketry was terrific. Very little artillery was employed, and that mostly by the enemy. We had no place to post it in, but the little open space I mentioned, approached by a narrow road which would almost certainly have ensured its capture in case of repulse, while they had open ground beyond the woods.

Our regimental loss was slight, more so than one would have deemed possible listening to the fire. Only one man was killed—Sergt. Richard Easterby of Co. B. Poor Dick! He was an old soldier and a good one. Years ago he had been an orderly of the present rebel general [Charles F.] Henningsen, when he was with Walker . . . in Nicaragua.° His life had been checkered and eventful, but Nov. 27th 1863, in that dark wood, put an end to his roving forever. In his pocket was his wife's daguerreotype and two of her letters, one of which I enclose, that you may know how sad a duty I have to perform in writing to her of his death. About a dozen only were wounded.

The loss of the Corps was about 500 in killed and wounded. Late in the afternoon the Surgeon in Chief of our Division became apprehensive that our hospital would come under fire (it was located to the rear of the left wing), [and] ordered the wounded to be removed to a more secure place. Our left being at the moment forced to retire a little before a charge of the enemy, the order was executed with more speed than system. There were no ambulances nor stretchers at hand and the poor fellows were hurried away in every species of litter that could be devised or framed. I took Sergt. Brady on my horse, and though it hurt him cruelly, he stuck to it, I leading, for a mile or more till we became benighted, when we came upon the 3rd Division Hospital and there I left him. Returning to the vicinity of the field, I found Mart with my pack-horse and inviting Chaplain [William R.] Eastman who was with me to share my blankets,° bivouacked for the night after a vain search for the rest of our wounded. Saturday morning it rained! Daylight revealed the fact that the enemy was gone, leaving all his wounded behind (we had brought in a number from the field the day before). On going to my regiment I found it ordered to march, and even then the column was moving. Riding out over the battlefield I found a party engaged in burying the dead. . . . The march that day was a hard one. Rain and mud were against us and until we struck a turnpike the progress was slow. You have no idea of the difficulties that have to be overcome by a column under such circumstances. The artillery is bestowed along it at certain intervals, as also the wagons containing ammunition. Under such heavy weights the ground yields, so that after a few batteries have passed the wheels sink to the hubs and frequently a gun or caisson will be stuck fast. Then the whole column has to halt till it can be hauled or pried out. This walking and standing tires men more than straightforward work. A mile often has all the weariness of ten at a common pace.

After we reached the pike, signs of a fight of the 2nd Corps, whose cannon we had heard the day before, began to appear. Hasty rifle pits made of rails and dirt—little protections thrown up by sharp-shooters etc.—and at least one rebel corpse, marked a contested route. We (the 3rd and 6th Corps) had crossed at the right of the whole army, the rest having made use of the three fords next below. Indeed, at one time, during our battle, Col. Potter remarked that our regiment held the extreme right of the old Potomac Army, and that his boys well sustained the honorable position, making three as gallant charges as are on record. We were on this day marching to rejoin the other Corps, and the position subsequently assigned us was almost on the extreme left. Toward night, to continue, we left the pike and once more were bemired. A tannery that we passed held 128 rebel wounded. It was late before we bivouacked, but the clouds had broken and we had starlight to march by. During the evening we passed the 1st Corps, and their fires looked cheerful enough. An incident of this day's march is worthy of remark. Capt. [Henry J.] McDonough of our 3rd Regt. had been killed the day before, and some of his boys, anxious to have him sent home for burial, undertook to bring his body with them. It was a touching sight to see the noble fellows struggle along bearing the remains of their dead Captain on a stretcher. He had led them long and now they carried him. Sweet labor of affection! It started my tears to witness it. It accomplished all it desired. The cold weather aided their loving purpose, and today the body has been sent to Washington for embalmment [sic].

Sunday morning our Division was detached from the Corps and ordered to report to Gen. [Gouverneur K.] Warren commanding the 2nd Corps. This involved passing through several miles of forest and an entire separation from the rest of the army. It was a very cold day and a slow job. One Brigade (the Jersey Brigade) skirmished ahead, and the other two followed, it seemed an inch at a time. It appeared to be a perilous business to be feeling our way though those thick woods, not knowing what might be there. However, by dark, we had worked through so far that communication was opened with Warren and we bivouacked in a beautiful pine grove. . . .

Monday morning we started again at 4 o'clock, marched to the plank road (from Fredericksburg to Orange C[ourt] H[ouse]) and before daylight were in our position in the line, massed by brigades in a low damp field. Soon after, our 3rd Division, also detached from the Corps, came up and formed on our right. The 2nd Corps was on our left. It was a terribly cold morning—one of the coldest I ever saw. The ground was frozen hard as flint and the morning star had a chilly glitter such as made one's teeth chatter to behold. But we had something else to think of than the cold, for it was rumoured that an assault on the enemy's ranks was to be made at sunrise, and it was a serious subject overtopping all others. "Silence" and "no fires" were the orders, and no sound was heard but the clatter of feet and commands almost whispered. These facts and the sight of the dark masses as they moved back and forth made it a scene long to be remembered. To me it was dreadful, for I had had forebodings heavy in my bosom of the tragedy that was to follow. The thought of what those wounded that bitter cold morning would suffer oppressed me like a weight of lead, and I looked at my boys with the feeling of one who takes a last look. Every few minutes some one would bring me his money to keep and tell me where to send it if—, and my throat would swell to think of that brave fellow lying stark. Indeed I could not bear to stay there, and left for the ostensible purpose of looking up the hospital arrangements. Sunrise came, but no assault. Eight o'clock came. There was a little cannonade to the right (that was to be the signal) but no advance on the left. I had seen Gen. Warren with his staff ride down to the line and wondered what the matter was, and kept on wondering as hour after hour passed and no assault. By the middle of the afternoon I was told that the hostile works appeared so formidable that Gen. Warren had concluded not to attack them without further orders, and that Gen. Meade had been over to see him and inspect the situation, moreover that the plan of storming was given up.° . . . We moved off with an unutterable feeling of relief, for the men had all day been creeping to the top of a little hill in front and looking at the works they had to take, and all now felt that they had experienced a great deliverance. . . .

All day Tuesday we lay quiet. . . . "To the old camps" was the order [on Wednesday]. The Col. sent me ahead to keep our shanties from being pillaged by the stragglers of other Corps and, with the Adjutant of the 1st Regt. who was sent on a similar errand, I plunged into a strange country—got lost—found myself again—met no guerrillas and dismounted at this door at 3 o'clock in the afternoon, stiff from the long ride, hungry as a graven image and completely beat out. At dark the head of the Column appeared and what few had managed to keep up crept into their old beds and slept as men only can sleep who have marched with knapsack, gun and ammunition 35 miles in 24 hours. Tonight they are all arrived. The Campaign across the Rapidan is over, and such is my story of it, jagged and hasty it is true, but in the main correct, I think. Hurra for Grant and Chattanooga!° That is glorious anyhow! Poor old Potomac Army! How it is knocked about! I have not yet received a mail. I expect a feast when it comes. Your affectionate Bro. Joseph.

our campaign across the Rapidan: Meade crossed the Rapidan with his eighty thousand men on 26 November in the Mine Run campaign, but the movement had been delayed by heavy rains and spotted by Confederate scouts. Lee, with his fifty thousand men, parried the move and ultimately built the extensive earthworks, which Twichell, as part of French's Third Corps, called "formidable."

the 1st Brigade of our Division was engaged hotly: The battle of 27 November, during which Twichell was nearly struck by the bullet that felled Sergeant Brady, was called the battle of Payne's Farm, or Orange Grove.

he had been an orderly of the present rebel general [Charles F.] Henningsen . . . in Nicaragua: Henningsen, an Englishman who had fought in the Carlist army in Spain in the 1830s, joined the unlikely adventure of American William Walker in Nicaragua in 1856. Walker and his fifty-seven followers joined a civil war, and he briefly took over as the country's leader.

inviting Chaplain [William R.] Eastman . . . to share my blankets: William R. Eastman had been a classmate of Twichell's at Union. When an opening for a chaplain came up in the Third Excelsior in late 1862, Twichell suggested him to fill it.

the plan of storming was given up: Meade had planned an assault on the Confederate works on 30 November but was informed by Warren that the move would fail. On 1 December Meade withdrew across the Rapidan.

Hurra for Grant and Chattanooga!: During these indecisive movements of Meade and Lee, General Ulysses S. Grant, having captured Vicksburg in July, was advancing through Tennessee toward Georgia. Grant won a major victory at Chattanooga, Tennessee, on 23–25 November.

2nd Regt. Excelsior Brigade. Near Brandy Station, Va.
Sunday, Dec. 6th 1863.

Dear Mother. . . .

From [Mary] Delight's letter and Eddy's galopade on the back of it I glean but meagre accounts of your Thanksgiving day. The young man was evidently suffering from young woman "on the brain." As soon as he cools off I trust he will give me a coherent report of that day's history as well as the events immediately preceding and following it. He whips by and is gone, seeming to say, "Halloo Joe! How d'ye do! All right! I'll tell you as soon as I get back!" It is almost as good as being there myself to know that he enjoyed it so. It was a pleasant time. That much I gather and shall suck the fact contentedly till the details arrive. . . .

I am perfectly recovered from our trans-Rapidan excursion and ready for another if it is the royal decree, although I feel a decided leaning toward winter quarters. I do not think we are to stay here long. It is the general opinion that our permanent establishment will be the other side of the Rappahannock.

Twice since we got back (once in the night) we have been packed up "all sad-dled, all harnessed, all ready for fight"—or flight—in consequence of hostile demonstrations, but each time the enemy proved to be only reconnoitering, and we subsided into calm again. I see by the papers that the Confederates regard our 3rd Corps battle of Nov. 27th at "Orange Grove" as an important affair. It appears that we came near doing them great damage, wounding two generals, imperilling their train etc., but though we called it a sharp action and ourselves lost nearly, if not quite, 500 men in it, the idea of a great general engagement just ahead led us to undervalue it as a preliminary operation—an introduction only to the grand tragedy. The boys are perfectly content to fight no more till spring. They have not been really quiet since we struck tents last April to go to Chancellorsville. We have been a hard-worked Army if Rich-mond does remain untaken.

When I shall make my way home is so uncertain that I can hardly give a probability. It will not be Christmas, though I should dearly like to see the tree and pluck my share of its crop. . . . I am now so near the end of my term of service° that I begin to sniff the air of freedom already. It will seem passing strange to be my own director, but I can never cease to love the 2nd Excelsior and revert to my campaigns with it with a glowing heart. . . .

Service today was usually attended and to me very interesting. Tonight there will be another meeting, but it is so cold that I shall make it short. As soon as we strike winter quarters I mean to have a Chapel built, with a large fire place, and then, if God wills, His work will proceed. . . . Love to all. Your aff. Son. Joseph.

I am now so near the end of my term of service: Twichell was due to be mustered out, along with others in the brigade who did not reenlist, in July 1864, three years after having been mustered in on Staten Island.

Brandy Station, Va. Sunday. Dec. 20th 1863.

Dear Ned,

Your full four page commemoration of Thanksgiving and other events of interest were a great treat. I was entirely satisfied with the accounts you gave and could without straining my credulity believe that you had been enjoying yourself rarely. . . . If I envied you a little while reading the story of your felicity you will forgive me, for I do assure you it was not that sort of envy that wishes its object's loss, but the rather a species of natural grumbling that only concerns the grumbler himself. My observation leads me to conclude that it is an insepa-rable characteristic of camp bound soldiers. . . . That a member of the Potomac Army should always be cheerful and serene of mind is more than can justly be required of mortal man. Everything from wormy crackers to congressional en-actments affords ample scope for this harmless exercise (i.e. grumbling), and the indulgence operates as a sort of sauce or relish for the tedious daily routine. None but he who has tasted it knows what a luxury it is to find a little fault with everything that happens and everything that everybody does. It is only acquired by patient practice. . . .

The week has been remarkable for its disagreeable and diverse weather. The first half of it we were compelled to an amphibious mode of existence. It seemed as if the deluge had come again. Then it turned cold as it had been wet, and froze all nature stiff, converting the sea of mud in which we had been well-nigh wrecked into a horrible, stony surface . . . over which one has to walk his horse slowly for fear of dislocating the beast's ankles. By the token Garryowen has the "scratches"° and I fear if the frost gets in that he will be afflicted all winter. It is a torture to me to have anything out of the way with him, and he has never been exactly in a condition to satisfy me since I became his owner. Indeed he is not so fine an animal as his colt-ship seemed to promise. There appears to be an admixture of Canadian blood that crops out in shaggy hair and thick legs, but he is endowed with great strength, and will make you a good cart-horse if nothing more.

Monday morning I rode over to the 1st Corps near Kelly's Ford and staid till the next day with Ned Carrington, to our mutual delectation. . . . Saturday there was a Chaplains' meeting at the Christian Commission tent in the 1st Div. It is proposed to make it a regular institution and I am appointed permanent secretary. If properly sustained it will prove edifying. After the meeting I called on Major Weygant and was received with the extremest courtesy, in fact so far beyond anything my own dignities or merits invoked that I was not a little amused. He was in command of the regiment, and I verily believe would have ordered out the whole force for my inspection if I had desired it. Anyhow he is a fine fellow and a true soldier. If it is fated, I shall be quite ready to accept him as a brother-in-law. The girl might do worse. Indeed, I hardly think she could do better.

The Colonel went away Tuesday, to be gone, on recruiting service, probably the rest of the winter, and I have moved into his quarters—very neat and comfortable they are. I hope to entertain you in them before spring. I have been most cordially invited to spend Christmas at the McBlairs in Washington, but have no expectation of going.

My anticipated journey home next month is in my mind continually. It will be a short visit but yet a relief after four months imprisonment. . . . Love to all. Your aff. Bro. Joe.

Garryowen has the "scratches": The scratches, or greasy heel, is an infection of the hoof and hock of a horse. It results in swollen, scabby cracked areas and is often found in animals that have been exposed to wet and muddy conditions for an extended time.

2nd Regt. Excelsior Brigade. Dec. 29th 1863.

Dear Mother,

Your short note announcing Eddy's illness came yesterday. Though you described his condition as not alarming, I shall be in suspense and trouble till he is well again. . . .

I returned yesterday from four days "Christmas" in Washington and Alexandria. Mrs. McBlair had sent me a most cordial and urgent invitation which I felt bound to accept if possible. I applied for only forty-eight hours leave but by the surprising kindness of Corps Headquarters received double. I passed two nights with Harry Hopkins, who without doubt stands first on my list of friends. How we enjoyed it I know, but cannot tell. At the McB's they entertained me with accustomed hospitality and added to the great burden of obligation I was already under to them. I spent one evening at the house of Senator [John C.] Ten Eyck of New Jersey, with whose family I became acquainted at Mrs. McB's. . . . They are very fine people—of sound principle and with tastes much more congenial to mine than most persons whom I meet in Washington.

The Senator is an unpretending man and so modest that one feels at ease in his presence, but his talk is marked by such wisdom and evident thoughtful discretion as to inspire the feeling that he is worthy of his high position. His wife is one of the loveliest of characters and my esteem for her has increased with every interview. . . .

At present we are suffering from a visitation of extraordinary mud. It is almost impossible to go anywhere. A large number from the Brigade have re-enlisted for three years and will in a few days receive 30 day furloughs.

We intend to begin our Chapel in a few days and make it a grand affair, but so far the Hospital tents have answered very well. I intend to call a meeting tonight. Sunday night I preached for Harry, but did not myself enjoy the exercise as I do before my own boys. . . . I think of nothing so much as my journey to Connecticut next month, if the Lord will. My love to all of you. Your aff. Son. Joseph.

2nd Regt. Excelsior Brigade. Dec. 31st 1863.

[To his sister:]

It is the last night of the year, girl, and in this region as dreary a night for dying as ever brooded over the earth. Poor old 1863 is going out in a tempest fitful as his own expiring pulse. Grieved sobs and sighs fill the dark air and mingle with rainy drops of weeping: at intervals the dole increases to shrieks and moaning wails—louder voices of lamentation. I pity thee, Old Year! Hard as thy yoke has been and heavy thy burdens laid on me and mine, I wish thee no ill, and had rather peaceful starlight and the gentle moon should cheer thy exit than this rude storm add to its bitterness.

I undertook to give the evening to pipes and appropriate meditation, but I found it too ghostly for comfort. Between goblins without and mournful thoughts that thronged within, a weird, unearthly feeling began to creep over me, as if there was a corpse in the tent, and I craved company—yours, Sis, upon reflection, hence I have chosen it. . . . I don't know where you are to-night, my darling; whether in New York with that dear little pattern of silence, May Warner (to whom I send New Year's greetings and a kiss) or at home, warned thither by our good Ned's untoward illness, which caused me two days acute anxiety till the news of its abatement changed me to thanksgiving. In either place I hope my prayer for your happiness is answered, even now while I am writing. Not so much the happiness that finds utterance in merry words and songs and laughter . . . but chiefly that blessed inner calm—that peace of God which is our divinest earthly joy. . . .

The farther back I range over bygones—and tonight memory wanders to its limit—more and more beautiful grows the image of our beloved [Father]. All the retrospect gathers about him. I find the same central figure everywhere. From the most indistinct impressions—the faint glimmerings of childhood that remain with me—down to the last good-bye and blessing at Falmouth, Father is never out of sight. Nothing is sweeter than his approbation, nothing so sad as to have grieved him. Whatsoever thing I do, whatsoever thing I purpose, he is in the reckoning thereof. Strong, generous, gentle, just, it is easy to yield him my confidence, and where I have done wrong it is misery not to do so. I did not know all this before he died as I know it now. . . .

The year that has almost reached its verge will never to us be common with other passed and passing time. We cannot linger behind, but it will follow our journey. Whatever life shall bring us, whether joy or sorrow, whatever great memorial days are to rise out of the future, never, Sis, never can we forget the year 1863.

I have little space left for news etc., but if there were more I couldn't use it. Your letter of the 16th inst. pleased me well in its matter and besides possessed all the charm of novelty. I have a feeble hope of receiving another sometime. . . . You were cruel to mention squash pie. It led me to the sin of envy. Don't say any more about it, though the subject is fascinating. . . . Write soon [deleted and replaced by "waste of ink"]. Your loving brother. Joseph.

January–July 1864

Unlike other Civil War battlefields, Cold Harbor, Virginia, is a grim place, with few monuments. It is not a place the veterans wanted to remember. By the time the new general in chief of the army, Ulysses S. Grant, reached that desolate and oddly named place, men were dying in slaughterhouse numbers as he relentlessly pressed Lee's army. Grant did not get what he wanted in the Overland Campaign and in early summer settled in to long-term trench warfare in front of Petersburg, Virginia. Lee won battles, but knew that Union forces were driving deeper into the Confederacy both east and west, that the South's men and resources were destroyed and depleted, and that there was no longer any chance of foreign intervention. Chaplain Twichell counted the days until July, when the Excelsior Brigade's term of service was up.

2nd Regt. Excelsior Brigade. Jan. 3rd 1864.

Dear Ned,

I feel it a real privilege to sit down tonight and address you. . . . I do not remember in a long time to have received such grateful tidings as the news of your illness abating. . . .

1864 has shown us a savage front. Day before yesterday was, I think, without exception the coldest day I ever saw in Virginia. I found it impossible to keep comfortable, especially at night. On the 1st, though the mud was bottomless and the more formidable because it was just stiffening, I managed to flounder to Brigade Division and Corps Headquarters with a party of fellow officers, and pay the due respects to authority, but it was as cheerless an act of courtesy as I ever performed. When I had completed the business my coat was fairly "nubby" with clots of mud that were thrown up by horses' feet and froze in place. I celebrated the evening by writing to Sis. I had many mournful meditations that day for I could not forget that 1863 had brought great and sad changes with it to our house.

The army has been deeply exercised for the last fortnight on the subject of re-enlistment. The plan has proved a great success. It is my impression that not less than 30,000 of this army alone have accepted the offer—and they are 30,000 worth thrice their number of recruits. Nearly half of our Brigade is mustered in anew—and about 80 of this regiment. It was a touching and glorious sight to see the war-worn remnant—so large a part of it—that has survived the slaughter, lift the right hand and, with uncovered head, swear to fight for three years more. It seemed to me the strongest insurance of success that had yet become manifest. The boys ask me every day if I will stay too, and I don't know what to answer.

I perceive that the Independent of the 31st has given a casual production of mine a much more prominent place° [than] it merited or aspired to. I sent it, partly to keep a promise I made Father once, and though Mr. [Theodore] Tilton acknowledged it in a very complimentary note, I thought to find it in some out of the way corner. In my private letter (of which an extract was also published in the two preceding numbers) I was as modest as a violet and hardly hinted that I expected it to be printed. Please send the paper to Sis. . . .

> *the Independent of the 31st has given . . . a much more prominent place:* Twichell had written a letter to this religious newspaper, edited by Theodore Tilton, praising its companionship through his 2½ years in the army: "My marching library has always been my Bible, Shakespeare . . . and the last Independent."

2nd Regt. Excelsior Brigade. Sunday Evening.
Jan. 10th 1864.

Dear Mother

The service is over, I have dined, and now until the evening meeting I am at leisure to write home. The great event of the week past has been the beginning and partial building of our brigade Chapel. At the prayer meeting Tuesday night we gave notice that all who desired to join in the work should assemble at 9 o'clock the next morning on the site we had selected, bringing axes with them. It had been our intention to have a regular detail made—5 from each regiment—and I had been around to the 1st, 4th, 5th and 6th, to find out who was *willing* to engage in the business and report their names to the commanding officers in order that the House of the Lord might go up without grumbling or whiskey. I took this step in consequence of a practice that prevails of dealing out liquor to men who are ordered to perform fatigue duty, which has grown so universal that it is expected as a matter of course. This would not do for us, therefore we undertook to secure the services of such as were interested in the matter and would not need stimulating. But owing to some hindrance at brigade Headquarters, the order for the details could not be issued Tuesday night, although it was promised to be done the next day. We concluded, however, not to wait but to depend on volunteers. We were glad we did so, for at the hour appointed Wednesday morning, more laborers appeared on the ground than we could easily employ. Eastman had the plans all prepared in true scientific fashion and assumed the office of chief engineer and architect, while I, not having like genius, acted as general encourager, and bestowed my muscle on pickaxe, spade, augur and other implements promiscuously. Our Quartermaster Sergeant kindly furnished a wagon and by night a goodly lot of timber had been hauled and ready-dressed for the walls, which were to be constructed on the stockade principle. On Thursday, Friday and Saturday the friends stood by us faithfully and, if everything continues to go as well as hitherto, the canvas roof, furnished by the Christian Commission, will go on Tuesday, and next Sunday we can dedicate. All who pass by seem to regard the undertaking favourably and manifest surprise that the boys go at it with such zeal, unbribed by whiskey. When finished it will be quite an imposing structure. . . . The enterprise was a subject of prayer before it was commenced, and it is fervently hoped that the most blessed results will flow from it. . . . The first two days works made me sore from head to foot, my hands blistered, my back lamed, but the third day I mended of all, and could now keep it up indefinitely without inconvenience. Beside the covering, the Commission will furnish a stove, and with what books and papers we can procure we do not see why it will not become an attractive place to write and read in, as well as sit under preaching in. It is also proposed to use it on occasion for any exercises that may be instructive or innocently amusing. In fact we mean to make the Chapel an institution that the brigade will become attached to and proud of, though choosing before all that God will make it the scene of saints edified and sinners born again. But the chapel may prove to be much more to others than to me. There is a prospect that my connection with it will embrace little more than the labor of its erection. Last night I was startled by the Major's handing me a document which had reached him from the War Department, containing an application to the Dept. by the American Tract Society requesting that I receive sixty days leave of absence for the purpose of aiding the Society and the Sanitary Commission in their joint public efforts to promote the welfare of the Army. I was surprised exceedingly and, to tell the truth, not a little gratified, for the fact was highly complimentary. Perhaps you remember that I wrote how Rev. Mr. Alvord made me propositions to engage in addressing the public etc. on the day we crossed the Rappahannock coming hither, and how I declined them. It now appears that without consulting me he has taken this step to affect the same result. I have concluded to yield, and the Major has returned the document endorsed with his consent. The fact that so many of our men are away and that so many are going, under the provisions of the re-enlistment act, and moreover that the Chapel will permit a consolidation of church-goers, renders it easier for me to absent myself now than at any other time since I came to the regiment. I presume the sixty days leave will come in a few days, but it may not, and therefore you had better not mention the matter out of the family. What kind of a master the Tract Society will make I do not know, but if it don't allow me a few days home at the start, I shall complain. What the exact programme will be I have not been informed, but expect to receive advices by every mail, and will let you know. . . . My love to the girls and all of you. Your aff. Son. Joseph.

> *2nd Regt. Excelsior Brigade. Sunday Night.*
> *Jan. 17th 1864.*

Dear Ned,

The Chapel is done and dedicated. Last night we held a prayer meeting in it, more fully attended than any for several weeks. It was quite damp, but a roaring fire in the fireplace kept it comfortable. At dress-parade in all the regiments yesterday a special order was read announcing service at 2 p.m. and at 6½ p.m. today. The results have been most promising. Eastman preached in the afternoon and I have officiated this evening. On both occasions the place was packed. We felt very thankful and very happy. Maybe you think we can now settle down to our work in better order, but you can't appreciate all the beauties of military life till you have tried it. We had hoped for an uninterrupted season of hard, telling work in that chapel, yet so strong is the force of habit, it did not seriously disturb us when today orders suddenly came that the whole brigade should move camp as soon as possible, a distance of about three miles. Soothing, isn't it? I am sorry enough—principally on account of the faithful friends who have lent such willing hands to help on the enterprise. . . . Perhaps we shall take it to pieces and move it to our new location. We must have a Chapel and if the wheeling is decent, that course of procedure will be easier than to build of fresh materials. For my own part I feel as though today's enjoyment had amply repaid me for the muscular investment I made in the structure. . . .

My sixty days leave has not come yet, nor has the Paymaster. When he does come I shall apply for ten days anyhow. . . . A short letter this time, Ned, as I have other matters to attend to, but just as much love goes with it as with twice the number of pages. Your aff. Bro. Joseph.

P.S. Jas. Lane of Co. B. has been sentenced to be shot on the 29th inst. for desertion. I have been trying hard to get him reprieved, but have little hope of success.

> Twichell received his sixty days' leave and embarked on a speaking tour to benefit the American Tract Society and the Sanitary Commission. The trip took him mainly to upstate and western New York and briefly into Ohio.

Mons. Smith's Office. 98 Broadway, New York.
Tuesday Feb. 9th 1864.

Dear Ed,

I have just returned from Newark where I spent the Sabbath. I had supposed that Syracuse was my appointed place, but on reporting to Brig. Gen. Alvord for instructions I was informed of a change of programme, and was not displeased thereat. The day passed off well. I preached three times and made a speech at a Sanitary Commission last night. Tomorrow or next day I intend to start for the west. Will you be so kind as to forward whatever letters may come for me, up to one week from today, to Buffalo. Make one package of them. It is announced in the papers that our 4th Regt. (2nd Fire Zouaves)° is to arrive here today and I am on the lookout to see it. The whole Fire Department appears to be ready to give their brethren a warm reception. My love to all. . . . Your aff. Bro. Joe.

our 4th Regt. (2nd Fire Zouaves): The colorful Zouave uniform had long been discarded in the Army of the Potomac, but despite its name changes to the Fourth Excelsior and Seventy-third New York Volunteers, this regiment's members still used the name given it in the early days of the war.

Troy—N.Y. Monday night. Feb. 15th 1864.

Dear Ned,

Before I go to bed I must drop you a line to assure you of my welfare and post you concerning my career. Firstly I am well bating a touch of home-sickness.° Camp life is nothing compared to this to make one want to see his Ma, and I never anticipated a sight of home with such greediness [as] I do now the ten days that I hope to spend there and thereabouts between the 10th and 20th of March (proximo).

Last Thursday I came up here from New York expecting to preach in the Presbyterian Church, but owing to some row among the elders I was put off. Then I tried Albany but no one wanted my wares. Thence Saturday morning, in desperation, to Saratoga Springs where I found kind appreciations. Morning in the Baptist church . . . —afternoon before a great congregation in the Presbyterian church—tea and half the evening at Rev. Dr. Beecher's female seminary (30 girls)—eight pages of my speech for the Sanitary Commission in Newark last week Monday night, and a general filling up of the chinks, all day, with hard talking, sent me to bed at midnight an easy prey to the first nap that chanced to come along.

Today, after a sleigh-ride, I came down here. . . . To-morrow I propose to start for the west. . . . I hope to be able to spend my last Sunday at home and shall be willing to expatiate if desired to do so. My love to all. Yours affectionately. Joe.

I am well bating a touch of home-sickness: Twichell is using tanning terminology. "Bating" means soaking a hide in an alkaline solution to remove lime and soften the leather.

In Camp. Sunday night. March 27th 1864.

Dear Mother,

It seems very natural again to sit down in my tent after evening service and write home. Today has been more like a Sunday to me than any for two months. The truth is my business while I was traveling about for the Tract Society had the effect to secularize holy time to a great degree. The drum and fife sounding the church call, the audience of blue-coats, the rude but hearty singing, all was very delightful after so long an absence, and I feel tonight as if I would always like to be a chaplain. My regiment is my home for the present at least—my parish—and I hardly think I can ever love another more. While I have been away, they have had wonderful times here. Such a work of Grace has never been known in the Army. My heart fairly leaped when I went to the meeting Thursday night to hear several, and among them some of my own boys, declare their new found joy in Christ. I felt myself far behind-hand in things spiritual, and could not help thinking that it would have been better for me had I not been away at all. But I hope the best is yet to come. The indications are that many more are on the verge of choosing the better part. . . . Every night the prayer meetings in our Chapel are crowded and such freedom, both in prayer and exhortation, is not often witnessed anywhere. . . . God bless the dear fellows! I do not know how I can ever leave them. They are so glad to have me back and show so many signs of affection that I feel more deeply than ever that I belong to them and they to me.

Saturday I went to Culpepper to see Ned Carrington° and find out what course he would take on the breaking up of his Corps. He is aide to Gen. [John] Newton who, by the order I enclose, is detached from this army, and I was anxious to know whether Ned would go with him. I found him undecided but inclined to follow his general like a loyal friend, also that Gen. N. had been ordered to Cincinnati. So Ned may have a taste of western fighting, but I am very sorry to lose his occasional company. You perceive by the order that our Corps is also broken up° and attached to the 2nd. We hate to part with the old organization, endeared by such glorious associations, but it can't be helped. Hereafter we are the 4th Div., 2nd Corps, and so you must direct your letters. . . .

Mart had everything in order for me against my return. My tent was swept and garnished, a new "barrel" armchair invited to repose, evergreens decked my walls, and the grounds before my door were neatly fenced with green fir boughs. There isn't a snugger place in Christendom. Garryowen was everything I could desire in the way of flesh and spirits. . . . My love to all the house. Your aff. Son. Joseph.

(2nd Excelsior, 4th Div. 2nd Corps. Army of the Potomac)

I went to Culpepper to see Ned Carrington: Carrington remained an aide to General Newton and took part in General William T. Sherman's Atlanta Campaign and March to the Sea. Carrington was killed in a skirmish on the St. Marks River in Florida on 6 March 1865.

You perceive by the order that our Corps is also broken up: In March, after its long and proud history, the depleted Third Corps was dissolved in a reorganization by Grant, who attached the Excelsior Brigade (officially, the Second Brigade of the Fourth Division) to the Second Army Corps. Sickles, deeply involved in his attempts to justify his behavior at Gettysburg before the Congressional Committee on the Conduct of the War, had spoken to Grant trying to dissuade him from dissolving his and Hooker's old corps. Grant, always of single purpose, said no.

Brandy Station, Va. Sunday evening.
April 10th 1864.

Dear Mother, . . .

I received [Sis's] letter and was duly grateful therefor, as I also was for yours of later date. The list of mortality in town surprised and saddened me, though death is a thing with which I have grown familiar. Somehow it seems a much different event at home from what it does here. Sudden as it comes to soldiers, it never seems that a strange thing has happened. Were my Colonel to be killed tomorrow on the picket line, I should be shocked and startled yet not astonished. Much less if it happened in battle. . . .

It has been truly a blessed Sabbath. The morning service at 11 o'clock was very impressively solemn. The brethren were praying when I reached the Chapel. They have a way of dropping in—a few of them—about half-an-hour before the time appointed and going down on their knees to ask a blessing on the Chaplain and his sermon. As others arrive they join in, and so the place and hour are sanctified. The exercises commence, not in coldness, but with the spirit of prayer and worship already alive. It makes the preacher feel strong.

At 2½ o'clock p.m. such of the Division (17 Regts.) as desired to partake of the Communion assembled at the Chapel of the Jersey Brigade, and there enjoyed one of the most sweetly solemn seasons of all their lives. About 100 (a third probably of all the Christians in the Div.—the rest were on duty, or away) took the bread and wine. Seven Chaplains were present. I preached the sermon from John XIV, 19–20.° It would have done the whole Northern Church good to witness the scene. I believe the Lord was there present in a peculiar manner. Every heart was softened. This evening our chapel was crowded and I preached again. I have rarely been so breathlessly listened to, and hope that I spoke God's truth. . . . New cases of conversion or anxious inquiry are made known every day, and Christians are thoroughly awake. The more I think of it, the more doubtful do I feel whether I can leave when my three years expire. Certainly I cannot now decide the matter.

I have been thinking much for several days past of Father. The anniversary of his death is close at hand. He has been gone a year. Can it be? It is more than a year since I saw him alive. That last visit—I can never be thankful enough for it. What a year it has been to him! Let us think of that when the day comes round. . . .

I send you two photographs for our military album. The lady is Miss [Helen L.] Gilson—the Florence Nightingale of our Division—a sweet Christian young lady, whom many a sick and wounded soldier has had reason to bless. She has passed through many hardships with us and borne herself like a true woman. Love to all. Joseph.

John XIV, 19–20: This recounts Christ's words at the Last Supper: "Yet a little while, and the world seeth me no more; but ye see me: because I live, ye shall live also. At that day ye shall know that I am in my father, and ye in me, and I in you."

Brandy Station, Va. Sunday Evening.
April 24th 1864.

Dear Mother,

We have had a week of delightful weather, but the drops that are just beginning to patter on my roof intimate a change of programme. However, it is fair to presume that . . . we are not to be much longer hindered from recommencing those journeys which are marked by more awful tempests than ever clouds produced. The note of preparation sounds on every side. All superfluous persons and baggage have been sent away, the supply trains of food and ammunition are being loaded, the inspectors are busy searching out and remedying all deficiencies—the army is in fighting trim, and a glorious fight, too, I think it will be.

On Friday our Corps (2nd) was reviewed by Gen. Grant. 25,000 men on a wide plain, composed of all three arms of the service, made a grand display. It was inspiring to see such an array of bayonets, cannon and sabres. Everybody felt hopeful at the sight. It isn't best to dwell too much on the probable fate of many a brave fellow who marched proudly by his chief that day. Liberty cannot be defended without war, and war cannot be bloodless. . . . My love to all. God bless you. Joseph.

Brandy Station, Va. May 1st 1864.

Dear Ned,

I hardly expected when I wrote last that tonight would find us still in the same camp. Especially as the splendid weather continued day after day, I began to give up the idea that we could enjoy another Sunday in the Chapel. But though everything seems to be ready, marching orders are not yet issued. They will come, however, before long—soon enough for our taste, since it is not to an easy or pleasant task that we are to be summoned. Ignorant, as we are, of the plan of campaign, we are content to wait till called upon. We are not impatient yet I think the work, when it is indicated, will be performed in finer style than ever before. The general mood of the army appears to me to [be] more proper and promising than at any time hitherto. Boasting is excluded. There is no talk of easy victory. It is conceded that great difficulties are ahead, which it will require great exertion to overcome. Yet there are manifest signs of determination and confidence, such inspire hope. Gen. Burnside with 30,000 or thereabouts° is close at hand, to swell a host already large in numbers. No campaign of the war has excited such intense interest in me as this one now impending. Great issues depend upon it. It will be a battle of giants. God, who sees the end from the beginning, alone reads the result.

But to the journal of the week. . . . During the afternoon of [Tuesday], Patrick McCarty of Co. F., after a short but severe illness aggravated by previous dissipation, died in the regimental hospital. The poor boy (for he was scarcely 20 years old) had been drunk nearly all winter, procuring liquor, by his natural acuteness and address, when no one else could get it—rushing to ruin—crazy after the cause of his wretchedness, yet at times touched with horror at what he was doing. Once he came to my tent to talk with me about it, and cried bitterly and promised to abandon his cups, but the demon was too strong for him. Having re-enlisted, he received 35 days furlough, spent the whole time in debauch, came back bloated and shaking with incipient delirium tremens, fell sick with typhoid pneumonia and died as an old man dies whose constitution is enfeebled by age—the most pitiable instance of life thrown away I ever witnessed.

He sent for me. I found him frightened. He wanted a priest. I went for one and brought him, but myself tried to point the miserable youth to the only Refuge. Wednesday we buried him. At my request, [Lt.] Col. Rafferty had the whole regiment paraded, and I conducted the chief funeral exercises on the color line before we went to the grave. It was a very solemn occasion, for everybody knew McCarty and the cause of his sad end. Such things make me hate liquor and resolve never by countenance, much less by example, to seem to regard it otherwise.

Thursday morning I went to visit Gen. [James C.] Rice of the 5th Corps, near Culpepper. I have lately made his acquaintance through Eastman, who was his classmate in college, and admire him exceedingly. He is a splendid soldier and a very devoted Christian. In the midst of my visit, he suddenly said, "Twichell, let's pray!" and we kneeled down together, after he had read a chapter, and laid our burdens—heart, home and country—on the Lord. It [was] one of the most refreshing experiences of my Chaplaincy. Such a General will fight, and his men will fight. . . . The same afternoon, with Lt. Col. Owen, Chief Q.M. [Quartermaster] on Gen. Warren's Staff, and an old acquaintance of mine, in company with three Culpepper ladies (sweet secessionists), I visited Pony Mountain, our highest signal station which commands a view of our whole army and a large part of the enemy's. . . . Our Surgeon [Edward T.] Perkins is quite sick and I am sitting up with him till 10 o'clock. I fear now the case will terminate. Love to all. Your aff. Bro.

Joseph.

Gen. Burnside with 30,000 or thereabouts: The army was in preparation for the spring campaign, variously called the Wilderness or Overland Campaign.

Grant took his 120,000 men over the Rapidan River on 4 May, hoping to get through the swampy forest known as the Virginia Wilderness before Lee could respond. This was near the spot where the battle of Chancellorsville had been fought the year before. But Lee attacked in the Wilderness on 5–6 May. The forest was so thick that much fighting was confused and hand-to-hand. After two days of this, the horror was increased as forest fires consumed hundreds of wounded, stranded men. The Union lost nearly 18,000 men killed, wounded and missing, out of 100,000 engaged; the South lost about 7,500 of its 60,000 men. Twichell later wrote home to the mother of Vermont Private Joseph H. Eaton, killed in the Wilderness: "I think, Mrs. Eaton, that he received mercy, for I believe he sought rightly. I prayed with him and repeated to him the invitation and promises of our Lord . . . even while I kissed him, he went off into dreams and raved about his comrades and the battle."

Wilderness, Va. Sat. May 7th 1864.

Dear Mother,

Terrible fighting, but rather in our favour so far. I am safe, but hundreds of poor fellows lie dead on the field or groaning about me with the pain of mangled bodies. It is not over yet. God save the Union and bless all the dear folks at home. In great haste. Joseph.

P.S. Col. Rafferty safe yet, but Capt. Nolan mortally wounded.

Despite his agony over the blows struck against his army, Grant continued to move south toward Spotsylvania Courthouse, hoping to outflank Lee. This was a surprising and inspiriting move for the Army of the Potomac, whose generals had tended to withdraw after terrible encounters such as the Wilderness. Lee anticipated Grant's plan and moved south to meet him. Over the next two weeks, they fought a series of battles collectively called Spotsylvania. The most violent day was 12 May, when the federals threw twenty thousand men at a Confederate salient that became known as the Bloody Angle. In the day's ghastly tally of losses, the North lost sixty-eight hundred casualties to the South's five thousand.

Twichell's letters from this period are brief, but he kept a journal of events. "Severe fighting around the Angle," he wrote on 12 May.

"First line of rebel entrenchments carried by surprise. Rode up to the front at about 9 o'clock. Met a stream of ambulances and wounded working to the rear—among them [Lt.] Col. Weygant on his horse, shot [in] the leg." The next day he visited the Angle: "I was astonished at the strength of the captured works, and horrified at the heaps of rebel corpses behind it." On the fourteenth, a rainy day, as he rode along a turnpike turning into mud, Twichell encountered another rebel corpse lying alone by the road. "Found a pioneer [a military engineer likely to have a shovel handy] and buried it. It was inhuman to leave it, and but the decent thing to give it the 'exiqui pulveris.'"

On the eighteenth: "Heavy fighting on the right. Part of our corps advanced but was repulsed with considerable loss. An abattis backed with earthworks arrested what began gloriously and turned back the line. . . . The wounded soon begin to pour in, mostly struck by cannon shot and horribly mangled." Twichell later returned to Fredericksburg with some of the ambulance trains, and said the city had become "one vast hospital—I visited such of our boys as were there."

Twichell rode back to the regiment with an officer friend. "On the way stopped at and entered the deserted residence of Judge Brooke. It was full of signs of wealth and taste within & without, but the straggling vandals had wantonly marred and broken all that was capable of injury. It made my blood boil to see the splendid furniture shattered, and articles of vertu ruined and strewed about the floor."

On 22 May, the army was on the move again, toward Bowling Green, Virginia. Twichell mentions instances of cowardice at sick call, including Captain William H. Ellwood, "who looked quite well, though suspected of not being very anxious to mix in the fray . . . I also saw [Privates] Sam Lawton and John Hawley who were not sick but contemptible shirks."

In Bowling Green, with other officers, Twichell "dropped in to talk with the ladies of the house" whose lawn was being used as headquarters. "The mode of expression used by some of the officers was exceedingly ungentlemanly in them, annoying to the ladies and disgusting to me. . . . I took occasion after they went out to make a sort of apology in behalf of the Army. While I was there a rumor reached the ladies that the husband of the house had been wounded. It created so much perturbation that I escaped."

Over the next week, more battles raged around the North Anna and

Totopotomoy rivers as Lee and Grant continued their gory dance that moved both armies slowly southward. On 27 May, Twichell's twenty-sixth birthday, he exclaimed with unusual fervor:

> How good the Lord has been to (considering his opportunities) the chief of sinners. Twenty-six years old: my youth is well nigh spent—where is the fruit of my time and abilities? May the time past suffice to have wrought my own leisure and pleasure, and the coming days be devoted to diligent service in the vineyard of my indulgent Lord.

"Oh, God! My Father's God; my hope is in Thee!"

Near Spotsylvania C.H. Wilderness, Va. May 11th 1864.

Dear Bro.,

It is not over yet, but I think the Union has the advantage. The fighting has been terrible and almost without cessation. The losses on our side are great, especially in generals—no less than ten of whom are killed or wounded. Gen. Rice, of whom I wrote a week or two since, died yesterday. Capt. Nolan of ours is dead, but the regiment has suffered less than any other of the Brigade.

Yesterday the Division was temporarily attached to the 6th Corps and participated in a general assault at 6 o'clock p.m. and was badly cut up. It seems awful to be here in the midst of this wild country with such scenes of slaughter and carnage occurring daily, but it is God's war and the Truth is being vindicated. I begin to feel, after witnessing the death of so many noble young men, that I will not keep myself back if I am in any way called on to make a sacrifice of my life.

The most splendid devotion to our country is manifested by the most. The troops fight well though they are tired and worn. Just now there is a lull but it is expected that the work will commence again before night.

The wounded are suffering unusually, and there are so many of them that baggage wagons have to be used to transport all but the most severe cases. Such heroic endurance of pain the world never saw. To witness it makes one grow confident that all will be well in the end. I see much to lead me to thanksgiving for the spiritual blessings of the past winter and spring. Some of the brethren are killed, and many are wounded, and I truly believe that nowhere is it possible for religion to be so precious as under the circumstances of war and battle.

I wish all the North could look in here and behold how much is given freely for the national cause. It would give a higher love and a quicker pulse to the public love of country than all the reading and thinking in the world. Love to all. Lt. Col. Weygant is all right so far. Your aff. Bro. Joseph.

Near Spotsylvania C.H. May 15th 1864.

Dear Mother,

I am well and safe, thank God, so far. . . . Affairs here are not yet decided, but we have faith that the result will favour the Union. [Lt.] Col. Weygant was wounded Thursday morning in a charge—only a flesh wound through the leg, but a narrow escape from amputation. I am thankful for him. Horrible scenes, great deeds, noble, noble men! Our Country's darkest and brightest days! Love to all. Joseph.

Near Spotsylvania C.H. May 20th 1864.

Dear Mother, . . .

We are still here confronting the rebel army and fighting more or less every day. Our lists of losses mount up fearfully, but the end justifies the means. Last night, at about an hour before sunset, the enemy tried to seize our main road to Fredericksburg and a severe engagement ensued, resulting in his repulse. Our loss was near 600 killed and wounded, mostly Maine and Massachusetts men. I spent a large part of the night in trying to comfort those noble Yankees, for I felt that they were of my own people, though not of my regiment.

The dead are buried and the ambulances loaded to start for Fredericksburg—but others will soon fill their places. Yesterday a mail came and I received quite a packet of letters, among them one from you. It made me thankful to learn that Ned was all right, so far, for I had been very anxious about him. I cannot now write you long letters, but have kept my journal so as to inform you in future of my adventures, if I live to elaborate it. . . . Love to all. Your aff. Son. Joseph.

On 1 June, after another attempt by Grant to move around Lee's right, the two sides met at a crucial road junction in Virginia called Cold Harbor. An attempt by Grant on 2 June to assault Lee's lines failed. On 3 June, a frontal assault on entrenched Confederates killed or wounded seven thousand Union soldiers and fifteen hundred Confederates. The stubborn Grant ordered a second assault, a similar failure; orders for a third were disobeyed. For three days Grant ignored the cries of the wounded on the field, refusing to allow a truce for both sides to gather their wounded. "No advantage whatever was gained from the heavy loss we sustained," Grant wrote in his memoirs twenty years later. Increasing feeling against Grant's brutal campaign endangered Lincoln's chances for reelection in November.

Frustrated at his failure to destroy Lee's army, yet not willing to withdraw, Grant chose to continue south, cross the James River, and lay siege to the railroad terminus of Petersburg, Virginia. The trench warfare that followed continued almost to the end of the war the following spring. The attacks Twichell refers to in his letter of 19 June are some early attempts to capture the city, attempts that cost more than eleven thousand lives.

Twichell, moving toward the James with his regiment, had come upon one of the places where the Excelsior Brigade had bivouacked during the Peninsula Campaign of 1862. "I thought of the days that we had wall tents and expected to take Richmond as one would pick cherries," he wrote in his journal.

In the field. Near Richmond, Va. June 1st 1864.

Dear Mother,

I have not been able to write to you as often as usual, because we have been without the usual communications. Neither have I had time to write much, and when I have had time, the weather has been so insufferably hot that I have felt fairly disabled from doing anything. . . . I was very thankful to hear good news from home, especially to be assured of Eddy's safety. . . . As I write, the noise of battle is in my ears. I cannot undertake to tell you the news. I do not know what it is myself, but only that the Great Campaign is proceeding amid blood and hardship. The army was never in better spirits, or more confident of success than now. In that respect it improves as the work goes on—an excellent sign.

For the week preceding day before yesterday there was little infantry fighting, but now it has commenced again, and one is as used to the rattling of musketry as to the ticking of a clock at home. Our brigade was somewhat engaged yesterday. The Color Sergeant, brave little Charley Bennett, was killed, and one other. Singularly enough, none were wounded. The other regiments did not fare as well. Several of the Christian brethren are lost to us. Sergt. Major [Benjamin] Whittaker of the 1st—one of our pillars . . . —was instantly killed. The Excelsior Brigade is near its end—the end of a brilliant career. In three weeks the term of service of such as did not re-enlist will expire. I shall then be free. If Richmond falls before that time, and I live, I shall come home. If Richmond has not fallen, and seems about to do so, I shall stay and see it out. My life and health have been preserved mercifully, though both have been endangered. [Lt.] Col. Rafferty has been through everything, yet is unscathed. The Lord has regard to his wife and five young girls. We are now 12 miles from the Confederate Capital—not yet as near as we have been. Gen. Grant has gained a strong point in winning the confidence of his army, and is playing the grand game as if he understood his business. God bless him. The more the war costs, the more imperatively is the nation called upon to support it. Could the great North but see the weary marching columns, and the struggling, bleeding lines of battle, it would open their eyes to the heroism of those who stand in the breach. To look on and see the sacrifice makes one willing to suffer. When I look upon the body of a brave young fellow slain, I feel as if I wanted to die too.

I am glad that Sis has heard from [Lt.] Col. Weygant. If I come home, he must visit us. Perhaps he will in any case. He is a true man.

Last Sunday I was able to hold service with the regiment for the first time since we started. It seemed a precious privilege.

There has been fighting all day. During a lull I visited the regiment, but it broke out again, the enemy charging with a yell, and I had to retire.

I love the boys better than ever, now that I am about to be separated from them. Pardon my scrawl. . . . Love to all. Your aff. Son. Joseph.

> *South Bank of James River, a few miles (8–10) below*
> *Bermuda Hundred—June 15th 1864.*

Dear Mother,

After a very difficult and weary march from our late position near Coal Harbor [Cold Harbor], N.W. of Richmond, the men having been without sleep for 24 hours and on their feet most of the time, we halted at Chas City C.H. night before last, and early yesterday morning crossed the James River in transports at a point about six miles below Harrison's Landing. The march part of the way led through places familiar to many of us, and in one instance I noted the very spot where my tent was pitched overnight in the Spring of '62, but now we are in a new country. What experience will follow our advent here is yet to be unfolded. Yesterday was a day of rest and the most of today and tomorrow will probably be consumed in crossing our trains and artillery, so that we shall start again much refreshed.

Eddy's nice long letter has reached me, a perfect treasure for all the news and talk of home it contained. I was glad to learn from you first, and subsequently from Eddy, that [Lt.] Col. Weygant was at our house and doing well. Salute him in my name. For his sake I would give the present location of our different Corps, if I could, but I know nothing more than that Hancock's troops crossed here. Which way we are going, whether out to the R.R. and Petersburg or up toward Richmond, I have no means of guessing even. Except in point of dust, the weather has favored us for the last week (Army weather takes account of dust).

Some uncertainty still clings about the date of our coming discharge from the service. There is a possibility that we may have to stay till Aug 4th, though I think the probability is that the close of this month will find us en route for home. If times are lively and the result seems near, I shall try to stay and see it. It will go hard, after all, to turn my back on this glorious old Army, and a positive affliction to part with the friends that remain—God bless you all. Your aff. Son. Joseph.

Near Petersburg, Va. Sunday. June 19th 1864.

Dear Ned

I have been up to my elbows in blood all day, and it is a relief now just at night to turn for a few minutes homeward, where there is peace and happiness. Our Division had a terrible time yesterday afternoon charging the rebel lines— all the more terrible because the assault was repulsed. Our Brigade, fortunately, was not engaged, having previously been placed in an advanced position which required to be held as it was. But the rest received an awful fire and, ever since, here at the hospital, we have been full of the saddest business. The First Maine Heavy Artillery, now doing infantry services, a very large Regt. composed of a fine class of young men, was dreadfully cut up. 500 will not much exceed their loss in killed and wounded. The dear, glorious fellows have been writhing and groaning and dying ever since, and my heart aches for them. It is a sorry sight to see them brought one after the other—these Maine boys—and laid on the Surgeon's table. A pile of loyal Maine legs and arms is the token of what the day's work has been. Petersburg seems a hard nut to crack and is costing us heavily. The very morning of our arrival here, at daylight, we were greeted by the severest fire of artillery I ever witnessed. I was exposed to it for quarter of an hour and thought I was killed a dozen times. The regiment has suffered considerably. It has been placed in such exposed situations that three cooks have been severely wounded carrying up provisions. Several of the best men have been killed. It looks as though little would be left to muster out when our term expires. The Sabbath has passed without any distinctive religious exercises, though I had a great mind to go and preach to a thousand Confederate prisoners lying close by, but opportunity did not serve me. . . . If [Lt.] Col. W[eygant] is yet with you, present him my regards. I hope he will never have occasion to take the field again. Love to all. Your aff. Bro. Joseph.

Dear Ned,

It is too hot to admit of much human activity, mental, moral, or physical, and industry is entirely out of the question. For more than three weeks we have been without rain and now the drouth has reached a pitch such as I never witnessed before. Everybody is panting and everything is crisp and withered. The dust lies like ashes several inches thick on all the roads and the fields are baked. The passage of a horse or wagon is denoted by a pillar of dust that hangs suffocating and noxious in the torrid air. Existence is purchased at the price of suffering. I sit here writing with nothing on but shirt and drawers and yet the perspiration rolls off my face though the shade renders it almost dark. We watch for rain "more than they that watch for the morning." Water is so scant that the artillery horses are taken two miles to the rear of the intrenchments to get their daily drink. Mercifully there has been little fighting now for a week, but the few that have been wounded have had a hard time. Yesterday morning I undertook to hold service so early as to avoid the worse of the heat, but though my congregation was assembled before 8 o'clock, [it] was a sweating crowd and the preacher streamed water at every pore. And then the flies—but I forbear further comment lest my temper rise and increase the caloric which already is well nigh unendurable. No body can imagine the hardship through which the army is now passing. Conceive if you can what it must be to march with a soldier's burden—what it must be to work at a great, hot cannon. In addition to the sun's fervor, the torment of fire has been visited upon us. The woods, parched and seasoned, have been flaming on every side, emitting blasts as from an oven and choking volumes of smoke. One's eyes are continually smarting. But our race is about run, thank Heaven. Already the Excelsior Brigade has begun to go home. Parts of the 3rd, 5th and 1st have bidden the Army of the Potomac good bye, and our turn is coming. The prospect now is that the 7th of July will see us marching out of the breastworks to the rear and thence homeward. I am partly glad and partly sad in view of it. We have done our three years work well, yet it is not wholly agreeable to turn our backs on the glorious old army while it is in the midst of its great toils. If I could help the country by staying, I would never stir till the enemy yielded. The sacrifices now being made in these lines of battle are as noble and grand as anything can be.

When I come home, God willing, I shall probably bring Mart to take care of my horse on the way, and he will stay a few days. There is also another of my flock whom I would much like to bring, if he should be discharged from the service, and if you should encourage my project. I speak of little Peter Platz, a

German lad about 14 years old. He is without exception the best boy, naturally, I ever saw, and I have fallen in love with him. He cannot read or write and is very anxious to learn. I have been thinking that he would be just the one to do your chores, help about the house and attend the district school. There isn't a lazy hair in him, he is helpful and very handy. . . . I am so much interested in his welfare that I would do a great deal to get him a good place. If he is properly located for the next year or two, he will be very likely to turn out a fine young man, but if he goes to New York I fear he will fall under bad influences. It is not certain that he will be discharged with us as his time has not yet expired, but application has been made that will perhaps be approved. I do not know that I am treating you fairly to bring my horse home without consulting you, but I think we can settle that. Should I return to the service (as I am already urged to do) I shall want him. If not, I shall turn him over to you to use or sell as you think best. If I should become a pastor, I suppose I cannot keep him on account of his being a stallion, but he has made me a noble beast. . . .

Thursday night we had a precious prayer meeting in the trenches with only a skirmish line between us and the enemy. It was one of the last and I shall treasure its memory. My heart sinks when I think of parting with the boys. It would be harder if I were not going home to those I love best in the world. Your aff. Bro. Joseph.

Near Petersburg, Va. July 3rd 1864.

Dear Mother,

It is not without keen emotion that I sit down to write what is probably my last letter home from the army. I rose this morning at sunrise and breakfasted that I might call the boys together for service while it was yet cool. Nearly all, feeling that it was the last Sunday, came and sat down under the tree I took for a meeting place, and it was a very solemn season. I could not, however, realize that I should never preach to them together again. Tonight there will be a prayer meeting, if nothing prevents, and I doubt if there ever was a more precious hour than it will be. God bless all my boys, and save their souls from death!

It is almost certain that we shall start from the intrenchments on Thursday next. I may not reach home for several days after that as I have considerable business to transact both in Washington and New York, but you can regard me as on the way till I arrive. I am to be disappointed about bringing Mart home with me. It has just transpired that he cannot be discharged till the 21st. I am sorry that this so happens, for I wanted him to take charge of my horse on the journey and would have been glad to have him at our house for a few days. I have contracted a great affection for the honest fellow. He has been very faithful to me. I shall probably get some other of the boys to help me with the horse. I am also to be disappointed about little Peter, the boy I wrote of to Ed. He will not be discharged with us, but may follow before fall. It seems like a dream that we are going to leave the field, and the past three years seem no less like a dream. All its adventures and perils and grand events have a vague unreality attaching to them, as I try to recall the long months that have been made memorable to the country and the world, by them.

There has been no hard fighting, on our part of the lines, for the past week, but there has hardly been an intermission in the cannonade. Rain—we have forgotten that there is every such a thing. We have been parched for a month, though for three days it has been a little cooler than it was. The dust is indescribable.

I hope you are all well and happy as may be. I anticipate a good, long loaf till working weather comes again. What then, I can hardly surmise, but feel sure that God will show the path of duty, if I consult Him rightly. Love to all. Your aff. Son. Joseph.

New York. Sunday. July 17th 1864.

Dear Ned,

We landed in Washington a week ago this morning. There, the interruption of travel by the enemy delayed us° till Friday noon, when we proceeded as far as Baltimore by R.R. and yesterday afternoon embarked (i.e. the regiment did) on a little stern wheel propeller to complete the journey by canal. Dr. Perkins and I were accidentally left behind, by dining too long at a restaurant after seeing our horses and baggage aboard. It was annoying but couldn't be helped, so we took the evening train and reached here this morning early—36 hours probably in advance of the rest—feeling seedy as two old topers from the day's work of tramp, worry and fret followed by the fatiguing night. I repaired at once to Dr. McAllister's quarters at the Ashland House, Cor. 23rd St. and 4th Ave, where a bath, a complete change of underclothing from the Doctor's wardrobe, and a few hours' honest sleep, much revived me. Since then I have been sitting with the Dr. who is in a very feeble health and I fear not long for this world. This evening I intend to go to church somewhere.

The regiment, if nothing happens, will be here tomorrow night. How long it will take us to transact our business I do not know, but I hope to be home next Sabbath at farthest. The journey, owing to the rebel invasion, has been quite eventful. I had a good opportunity to observe Washington in a state of siege. It seemed strange enough to hear bullets whistle within five miles of the

Capitol. Our final victory seems long in coming, but I believe it is decreed and will surely come to pass.

"To doubt would be disloyalty,
To falter would be sin."

Expecting to see you all soon. I am. Your aff. Bro. Joseph.

the interruption of travel by the enemy delayed us: Twichell's travels home were affected by the raid of General Jubal Early toward Washington, one of the last Confederate offensives of the war, while Grant was 150 miles to the south of the capital. The day Twichell arrived in Washington, Early entered Silver Springs, Maryland, on the city's northern outskirts. On the night of the eleventh, Early, seeing Union troops reinforced, decided to give up the assault.

At noon on 22 June 1896, the president and corporators of Yale University climbed the steps to a wooden platform erected between two rows of elm trees on the Old Campus. Before them, ready for unveiling, was a block of red Maine granite supporting a statue of the late president of Yale, Theodore Dwight Woolsey, in mutton-chop whiskers and academic robe, his bronze eyes staring toward Phelps Gate.

One of these men, the Reverend Joseph Hopkins Twichell, the senior member of the corporation, had known Woolsey well. The stern disciplinarian had been president of Yale when Twichell was an undergraduate in the 1850s. One student described Woolsey's classroom as having a "chilly atmosphere of repression." Twichell himself had felt the sting of Woolsey's discipline when he and two classmates were suspended after a student riot. But Woolsey was also a passionate advocate of abolishing slavery. In 1854 he was one of the organizers of a meeting against the Kansas-Nebraska Act. In 1856 Yale undergraduates had helped finance Sharps rifles for antislavery émigrés during the "bleeding Kansas" wars.

Now, as undergraduates began to sing "Integer Vitae," the Reverend Twichell frowned under his mortarboard. His down-turned white moustache gave him a glowering look to begin with, and his deep-set eyes could be severe under his shock of white hair, though at most times he was the most gently humorous of men. Twichell was irked by what the Reverend Newman Smyth had whispered to him as he climbed the steps to the platform: the class of '96, whose commencement was two days away, were to plant their class ivy that afternoon, and they had chosen to plant ivy from the grave of Robert E. Lee.

"I always feel it absurd that a man who fought the devil in the Excelsior brigade should be called a non-combatant," Twichell, referring to himself, told the annual meeting of the Third Corps Union in 1895. Given the extremities of battle, discord among officers, and drunken violence that beset the regiment, he could say that with justification.

Twichell was mustered out of the service with his regiment on 30 July 1864 in New York City. As the war wound down, he was enrolled at Andover Theological Seminary. In February 1865, the Andover students put on a strange patriotic exercise in which they aped their enemies. They made light of the last days of the Confederate government with a satirical performance in which they portrayed members of its congress. In lurid speeches, cabinet officials were ridiculed and someone made a proposal to free and arm the slaves. The high point of the evening was the arrival of General Robert E. Lee—portrayed by Twichell. The local newspaper said Lee "made a dignified, earnest and soldierly speech."

In 1865 Twichell graduated from Andover, was married in November, and in December began his lifelong pastorate at Asylum Hill Congregational Church in Hartford. The public speaking skills he had practiced during his American Tract Society tour remained with him. A New York newspaper reported in May, a month after Appomattox, that he spoke at the Madison Avenue Presbyterian Church, describing the sacrifice of the dead, the mutual support among comrades, and "the value of this fact in our national economy."

The Civil War had indeed been valuable to Hartford's economy. Well-known local industries—Colt's Patent Firearms Manufacturing Company, the Sharps Rifle Company, Pratt and Whitney's machine tool company, and the Phoenix Iron Work—combined with a solid base in banking, insurance, and publishing to make the city rich. Those who had gotten rich with the rise of these industries were now the political leaders of the Republican Party—and Twichell's parishioners.

In October 1868, Twichell met Samuel L. Clemens, already "Mark Twain," who was in Hartford to see his publisher. The minister took him to see the city mission, where Mark Twain met the desperately poor of a city he had at first believed had no poor. Twichell also took the author to a meeting of Twichell's exclusive and patrician Yale senior society, Scroll and Key. These starkly contrasting worlds of poverty and wealth, darkness and light dogged Twain's steps for the rest of his life, as they dogged Twichell's. Throughout Twichell's career the minister kept in mind the interests of the poor even as he remained a friend to the prosperous.

Everywhere Twichell traveled, his journal of forty years shows, he ran into fellow veterans of the Excelsior Brigade, the Third Corps, or the Army of the Potomac. He spoke at dozens of Decoration Day and Memorial Day ceremonies, at meetings of the Grand Army of the Republic and the Third Corps Union. When he wanted an analogy for a point he was making in a sermon, he often went to the Civil War for material. In describing the devious entry of sin into the soul, for example, he used the analogy of Jackson's flanking movement at Chancellorsville that surprised and scattered the Eleventh Corps. He

The one-legged General Sickles arrives at the Gettysburg, Pennsylvania, station in the summer of 1913 for the fiftieth anniversary of the battle. At the side of the ninety-three-year-old general is his housekeeper and reputed mistress, Eleanor Wilmerding. Behind her, in dark suit and hat, is the Reverend Joseph Hopkins Twichell, retired the year before from Asylum Hill Congregational Church in Hartford. (Library of Congress)

also used the career of his beloved general Joseph Hooker (in fact, a man of dubious morality) as a resource. One sermon subject is listed as "the generosity and love of his fellow man displayed by General Joseph Hooker, being used as a parallel to show how the promises of the Gospel to sinful men are redeemed." He named a son after the general.

The war was in his after-dinner speeches too. When he wanted to express modesty at an unasked-for honor or appointment, he told the story of a private who left the famous bayonet charge of the Second Excelsior at Fair Oaks. When Twichell asked him why, the private said, "I hadn't been in there more than three minutes 'fore I see that that wa'n't no place for me." Twain loved these tales, and knowing he could write them down more skillfully than Twichell could, he pillaged them mercilessly. In *A Tramp Abroad*, Twain conveys a Twichell tale of military dentistry during the Second Excelsior's early Maryland encampment. The surgeons found it hard to pull a howling patient's teeth in a medical tent and moved the operation outside, with an audience. The patient kept quiet out of pride—but at every extraction, each of the dozens of onlookers "would clap his hand to his jaw and begin to hop around on one leg and howl with all the lungs he had!"

Twichell's military experience had great attraction for Twain, who had only served briefly in an irregular Confederate company in Missouri. When the Twelfth Annual Reunion of the Army of the Potomac took place in Hartford in 1881, Clemens spoke after William T. Sherman and before General Sickles. He wrote up a spoof menu for the evening's banquet that was studded with fantastic, made-up quotations, one being: "'Give me my choice between New England breakfast-pie and liver and I should take strawberries and cream every time'—John Milton."

Twain and Twichell traveled to Worcester, Massachusetts, in the 1870s to visit Father Joseph B. O'Hagan, S.J., Twichell's old Excelsior Brigade chaplain comrade. The Jesuit was now president of the College of the Holy Cross. The association with O'Hagan and the "rough, wicked men" of his regiment gave Twichell a tolerance and affection for Catholics rare among American Protestant ministers. When O'Hagan died in 1878, Twichell wrote that "as Christian ministers we were continually thrown together in scenes that had the effect to make us forgetful of our differences in religion and mindful only of our sympathies." It was not an untutored ecumenism. There are many clues to his dislike for what he regarded as Roman Catholic superstition. His Civil War scrapbook contains a piece of white cardboard stained with brown blood. It is a prayer to St. Jude for protection, and Twichell (in a note) says he picked it up from a corpse on the battlefield. What clearer proof, he wrote, of Catholicism's superstitious fallacy?

In his own Protestant context, the growing movement for "muscular Christianity" appealed to Twichell with his athletic background and wartime experience. He was a Yale oarsman, his physical strength got him through the terrible wartime marches, and even at forty, when he and Twain traveled in Switzerland in the summer of 1878, he could walk twenty to thirty miles a day through Alpine passes—on days when Twain stayed in the hotel room. In the 1880s and 1890s he gave several sermons on Christian manhood, usually beginning with the tale of meeting a Gettysburg artillery commander at a reunion and realizing that when this middle-aged man had performed brave actions on the field he had been only twenty-two years old. Twichell said the commander personified "the quality and degree of manhood that ever resides in the heart of youth."

For Twichell, this idea combined with the optimistic, Anglo-Saxon-centered evolutionary ideas of the popular philosopher-historian John Fiske to become a vision of "The Coming Man." Twichell's views, like Fiske's, were influenced by Social Darwinism. "In social life," Twichell preached in 1887, "there is a constant conflict of the forces that make for humanity with those that make against it—that lift men up and that keep them down. . . . The consummate feature of true manhood is moral, its aim is what we call character, the ideal is the manhood of Jesus Christ." In a world yet innocent of twentieth-century eugenics and totalitarian efforts to create various forms of the New Man, this kind of evolutionary thinking sounded less sinister than it does today.

Twichell saw no conflict between this idealistic form of social Darwinism and the duty he believed New Englanders had to help others assimilate into American society. In fact, it was a tenet of Fiske's philosophy that the heirs of Puritanism should do this. Sarah Jane Twichell, the "Sis" of his letters, went south after the war to teach ex-slaves. There she married Edward Ware, president of one of the first postwar colleges for blacks, Atlanta University. Twichell's Asylum Hill pulpit was often given over to fundraising for Negro Education or schools for Indians in the West. In 1904, Twichell, by now a trustee of Atlanta University, attended one of the sociological seminars on race organized by the young professor W. E. B. Du Bois.

But Twichell also began communicating with his former Confederate enemies. In 1877 his friend and classmate Robert Stiles broke a long silence, finally responding to a letter when Twichell sent him pictures of his four children. The two men maintained a warm relationship for the rest of their lives. Twichell also developed friendships with ex-Confederate prisoners whom he had comforted in field hospitals. In 1889 he got in touch with William Moffat Grier, the young Southern soldier whose leg had been amputated after the Battle of Williamsburg (see letter of 16 May 1862). Grier was then president of Erskine College in South Carolina. He responded warmly, and Twichell wrote back: "God be thanked for the healings of time!"

But by 1896, when Twichell stood on the platform at the unveiling of President Woolsey's statue, the healings of time concealed deep infection. In an accommodation with Republicans in 1877, the old Confederates had resumed power in the Southern states. By the 1890s, Jim Crow laws and lynchings were becoming commonplace in the South. David Blight says in *Race and Reunion: The Civil War in American Memory* that "by 1897, the sectional reunion was all but complete politically and culturally, and a racial apartheid was steadily becoming the law of the land." In 1896, the United States Supreme Court in *Plessy v. Ferguson* enshrined racial segregation for the next six decades. Nevertheless, two years earlier the spirit of North-South reconciliation had moved a New Haven patent attorney, George D. Seymour. On a visit to the South, he cut a sprig of ivy from the "Lee Vine" growing on the wall of a church in Lexington, Virginia, where the Confederate general is buried. A New Haven nursery rooted it, and Seymour offered it to the Ivy Committee of the Yale class of 1896. The class sought and obtained the permission of Lee's widow to plant the ivy.

As the music of "Integer Vitae" faded, Twichell rose and faced the hundred or so spectators standing in a semicircle and began a flowery and rousing eulogy. He described a meeting with Woolsey in New Haven during the war: "I met him walking up and down on College Street waiting for the second bell; and with what warmth he greeted me and at once began to ply me with questions about the Battle of Gettysburg, which had just been fought, and the Yale men who had borne part in it, and other things at the front, till there was not a second more to spare. It stood revealed in his whole tone and manner that he loved his country with all his hopes and fears."

Instead of going on to speak of Woolsey's preaching ability, Twichell spoke of the statue's forbidding bronze face: "And if I may be pardoned, I must say that if it were possible that face would be averted from the scene, when it shall happen this afternoon—if so be that it shall happen—that an ivy from the grave of Robert Lee, a good man, but the representative of an infamous cause, shall be planted on this campus to climb the walls of ever loyal Yale."

"The utterance of Dr. Twichell came like a clap of thunder from a clear sky," said a New Haven newspaper, reporting on the aftermath. The seniors on the

Ivy Committee huddled, wondering what to do. "You can't change the ivy now," said one: "One third of the class are from the South and it will be a personal insult to them if you do." "But you are insulting the two-thirds of the class from the North," said another. A third proposed a statement that the ivy had been chosen because it was "a good piece of ivy, nothing more." Others rejected this idea "because they thought they would show this respect for a good man and their willingness to put aside the bitterness of sectional feeling." "I wish the committee had selected the ivy from any old place, so that we wouldn't have had this talk," said a pragmatic committee member. It was a reversal of roles, old radicals and young conservatives. "The older members of the audience applauded [Twichell] vigorously and the Seniors kept still and looked a little glum," the *Yale Alumni Weekly* reported.

"The ivy was planted nonetheless," Twichell wrote in his journal. Some greyhaired veterans threatened to tear it up, but the seniors vowed to defend it. The story went out over the Associated Press wire—with Twichell's statement slightly improved for effect—and soon newspapers all over the country were having their say. "Rev. Dr. Joseph Twichell has given the drybones at Yale a healthy stirring up by a strong blast of loyalty," said one clipping in the scrapbook where Twichell carefully preserved mementos of the incident. "I rub my eyes in astonishment," wrote Henry B. Goddard to the *Hartford Times*. "It did not to me seem possible that the manly, noble, muscular Christian that I had known in Hartford could be so ungenerous upon such an occasion." "A serpent's hiss at a great man's grave," said a Georgia paper. Letters poured in to Twichell over the following weeks. "Why is it that sectional bitterness is kept red-hot north—by preachers? Can't you 'draw' by preaching the gospel?" wrote an anonymous correspondent. A Louisiana letter read: "You may know my concern for your words of denunciation of the exponent of a lost cause whose very name is a household synonym of virtue and chivalry in every American home South of Mason and Dixon's line."

Friends and strangers offered support. Leonard W. Bacon, son of a ministerial mentor of Twichell's, wrote: "I take sides with you in the matter of that rebellious ivy . . . it can not be too positively impressed on the ingenuous undergraduate mind that, whatever they may think, we old folks have not yet come to the point of looking upon the Civil War as a football game upon a grand scale."

Twichell's battles with the devil in the Excelsior Brigade and on the Yale platform in no way resembled a football game. He carried these battles on, as he once put it, up to his elbows in blood. In 1911, when the increasingly deaf, seventy-four-year-old Twichell had already announced he would retire from his Hartford pastorate, he was called on to help dedicate a new wing of the Women's Relief Corps Home for Civil War veterans in Cromwell, Connecticut. An account from the *Hartford Times* explains that the home's new hospital rooms would be furnished "by the Rev. Dr. Joseph H. Twichell of Hartford." The story is a surprise. Twichell was not a wealthy man, except in spirit. He was, in fact, occasionally the recipient of financial gifts himself (from Twain and wealthy parishioners).

But the gift turned out to be the act of an old veteran carrying out a promise, and like his Lee ivy speech, it helped bring his Civil War experiences full circle. During the war he had carried thousands of dollars from the soldiers of the Second Excelsior to the Adams Express office where the funds could be safely relayed to the men's families. Sometimes he had received the money from dying soldiers whose families he couldn't locate. Twichell's papers at Yale include carefully kept account books with inked names, dollar amounts, and cross-outs. In some places the only notation is "unidentified dead boy." At the end of the last account book is the receipt for Twichell's $224.28 donation to the Cromwell home—the amount remaining of these funds forty-six years after the war ended. On the eve of a new and more terrible war, he put the money toward relieving the pain of the boys he loved, now grown to be old men.

STEVE COURTNEY

Andrews, Kenneth M. *Nook Farm: Mark Twain's Hartford Circle*. Cambridge, Mass.: Harvard University Press, 1950.

Annual Report of the Adjutant-General of the State of New York for the Year 1901: Registers for the Sixty-ninth, Seventieth, Seventy-first, Seventy-second, Seventy-third and Seventy-fourth Regiments of Infantry. Transmitted to the Legislature January 7, 1902. Albany, N.Y.: J. B. Lyon, 1902.

Atwater, Francis. *History of Southington, Conn*. Meriden, Conn.: Journal Press, 1924.

Blight, David W. *Race and Reunion: The Civil War in American Memory*. Cambridge, Mass.: Belknap Press of the Harvard University Press, 2001.

Bowman, John W., ed. *The Civil War Almanac*. New York: Facts on File, 1982.

Brinsfield, John Wesley, W. C. Davis, Benjamin Maryniak, and James I. Robertson Jr. *Faith in the Fight: Civil War Chaplains*. Mechanicsburg, Pa.: Stackpole Books, 2003.

Casey, Silas. *Infantry Tactics: For the Instruction, Exercise and Manoeuvres of the Soldier, a Company, Line of Skirmishers, Battalion, Brigade, or Corps d'Armée*. New York: D. Van Norstrand, 1862.

Daily Courant, Hartford, Conn., 1861–64.

Derks, Scott, ed. *The Value of a Dollar: Prices and Incomes in the United States, 1860–1999*. Lakeville, Conn.: Universal Reference Publications, 1999.

Dyer, Frederick H. *A Compendium of the War of the Rebellion*. Des Moines, Iowa: Dyer Publishing, 1908.

Foote, Shelby. *The Civil War: A Narrative*. New York: Random House, 1958–74.

Harris, Brayton. *Blue and Gray in Black and White: Newspapers in the Civil War*. Washington: Batsford Brassey, 1999.

Hebert, Walter H. *Fighting Joe Hooker*. Indianapolis: Bobbs-Merrill, 1944.

Keneally, Thomas. *American Scoundrel: The Life of the Notorious Civil War General Dan Sickles*. New York: Nan A. Talese, 2002.

Leech, Margaret. *Reveille in Washington, 1860–65*. New York: Harper and Brothers, 1941.

Lowry, Thomas P. *Tarnished Eagles: The Courts-Martial of Fifty Union Colonels and Lieutenant Colonels*. New York: Stackpole Books, 1997.

McPherson, James M. *Battle Cry of Freedom: The American Civil War*. New York: Oxford University Press, 1988.

Messent, Peter. "Mark Twain, Joseph Twichell and Religion." *Nineteenth-Century Literature* 58.3 (December 2003).

Miller, Nathan. *Theodore Roosevelt: A Life*. New York, William Morrow, 1992.

The New York Times, New York, 1861–64.

Norton, Herman A. *Struggling for Recognition: The United States Army Chaplaincy, 1791–1865*. Washington: Office of the Chief of Chaplains, Department of the Army, 1977.

Osthaus, Carl R. *Freedmen, Philanthropy and Fraud: A History of the Freedman's Savings Bank*. Urbana: University of Illinois Press, 1976.

Pfanz, Harry W. *Gettysburg: The Second Day*. Chapel Hill: University of North Carolina Press, 1987.

Phisterer, Frederick. *New York in the War of the Rebellion, 1861 to 1865*. Albany: J.B. Lyon, 1912.

Robertson, William Glenn. "The Peach Orchard Revisited: Daniel E. Sickles and the Third Corps on July 2, 1863." In *The Second Day at Gettysburg: Essays on Union and Confederate Leadership*, edited by Gary W. Gallagher, 33–56. Kent, Ohio: Kent State University Press, 1993.

Sandburg, Carl. *Abraham Lincoln: The War Years*. New York: Harcourt Brace, 1939.

Sauers, Richard A. *A Caspian Sea of Ink: The Meade-Sickles Controversy*. Baltimore: Butternut and Blue, 1989.

Sears, Stephen W. *To the Gates of Richmond: The Peninsula Campaign*. New York: Ticknor and Fields, 1992.

Silber, Nina. *The Romance of Reunion: Northerners and the South, 1865–1900*. Chapel Hill: University of North Carolina Press, 1993.

Spann, Edward K. *Gotham at War: New York City, 1860–1865*. Wilmington, Del., SR Books, 2002.

Stevenson, James. *History of the Excelsior or Sickles' Brigade*. Paterson, N.J.: Van Derhoven and Holmes, 1863.

Stiles, Robert. *Four Years Under Marse Robert*. Marietta, Ga.: R. Bemis Publishing, 1995 [Reprint of 1904 edition].

Strong, Leah. *Joseph Hopkins Twichell: Mark Twain's Friend and Pastor*. Athens, Ga.: University of Georgia Press, 1966.

Swanberg, W. A. *Sickles the Incredible*. Gettysburg: Stan Clark Military Books, 1991 [reprint of 1956 edition].

Timlow, Rev. Herman R. *Ecclesiastical and Other Sketches of Southington, Conn*. Hartford: Case, Lockwood and Brainard, 1875.

Twichell, Joseph Hopkins. Joseph Hopkins Twichell Papers, Yale Collection of American Literature, Beinecke Rare Book and Manuscript Library, Yale University, New Haven, Connecticut.

Twichell, Ralph Emerson, ed. *Genealogy of the Twitchell Family*. New York: Privately printed, 1929.

The War of the Rebellion: A Compilation of the Official Records of the Union and Confederate Armies. Washington: Government Printing Office, 1880–1901.

Wiley, Bell Irvin. *The Life of Billy Yank: The Common Soldier of the Union*. Indianapolis: Bobbs-Merrill, 1951.

Wilson, James Grant, and John Fiske, eds. *Appleton's Cyclopedia of American Biography*. New York: D. Appleton, 1887–89.

Woodward, Joseph Janvier. *The Medical and Surgical History of the War of the Rebellion, Part II, Volume One: Medical History*. Washington: Government Printing Office, 1879.

WEB SITES

Our work has been eased by the existence of numerous useful Web sites, notably: the Making of America series jointly produced by Cornell University and the University of Michigan (moa.cit.cornell.edu/moa/index.html), which has put the entire official records of the Union and Confederate armies and navies online; the National Park Service's Civil War Soldiers and Sailors System and battle summaries (www.nps.gov); the University of Tennessee's Civil War Generals page (sunsite.utk.edu/civil-war/generals .htm); and Dick Weeks' www.civilwarhome.com collection of biographies.

73, 135, 137, 142, 145, 147, 157, 173; and internal regimental disputes, 84–85, 86, 87, 90, 97, 188; and military duties, 67, 244; and regimental posts, 76, 111–12, 168, 189, 245; and regiment's military role, 55, 282; supports Twichell's religious activities, 60, 83–84; taking of prisoners by, 68, 135, 137; wounding of, 173, 178, 211, 274–75; mentioned, 124, 170, 220, 276, 280, 287. *See also* Excelsior Regiment, Second: internal disputes of

Prince, Henry, 262, 263

Race, 7, 80; African American army servant, theft accusation of, 263; African American regiment, raising of, 272, 273–74; African Americans in Twichell's regiment, 156; African American washerwomen, 162; "colored Ben," 165; Confederacy and use of slave labor, 111, 113; escaped slaves, 102, 108, 160; Hampton Institute, 272; slave hunt in Twichell's regiment, 9, 102–6; slaves cheer Twichell's regiment, 48; Twichell's invitation to join African American regiment, 272, 273–74. *See also* "Joe"; Twichell, Joseph Hopkins: political opinions

Rafferty, Thomas: family of, 305; low spirits of, 215; promotion of, 188–89; recruiting service of, 96; and religion, 84, 146, 215; and temperance, 69; Twichell's liking for, 102, 118, 146, 188, 213; wounding of, 146, 147; mentioned, 113, 192, 201, 207, 220, 275, 276, 280, 299, 300

Rapidan Campaign, 277–85. *See also* Payne's Farm, Va.

Revere, Joseph W., 206, 207, 208

Rice, James C., 299; death of, 302

Richmond, Va.: approach to, 126, 128, 130; Burnside's move toward, 190, 204; as Confederate capital, 107; Confederate losses at, 164; continuing fight for, 285, 304; fighting before, 9, 134, 135, 136, 137, 149, 152; McAllister and Powell in, 167–69; McClellan's plan to capture, 107; price of goods in, 168, 169; Union failure to take, 163, 167; Union retreat from, 159, 160; Union support in, 168; mentioned, 162, 170, 236, 277, 305, 306. *See also* Fair Oaks. Va.; Malvern Hill, Va.; Seven Days' Battles; Stafford, Va.; Yorktown, Va.

Roosevelt, Theodore, 9, 98, 99

Salm Salm, Felix, 223, 224

Sanitary Commission, U.S., 9, 63, 141, 158, 234, 263, 292; Twichell's work for, 294–95. *See also* American Tract Society

Savage's Station, Va., 9, 136, 140, 151, 152, 154, 169

Scott, Winfield S., 48, 50, 75

Seven Days' Battles, 146–47, 148–50, 151–58, 159–60, 176; casualties during, 146, 147, 148, 151, 155, 157, 163–64

Sherman, William T., 296, 314

Shiloh, Tenn., 115

Sickles, Daniel E.: and alcohol, attitude toward, 25–26; and arrest of Patterson, 188; bravery of, 147, 249; celebration ball on accession of, to major generalship, 219–20; and confusion at Oak Grove, Va., 149; and Congress, decision not to run for, 182, 183; death of, 254; and death of aide-de-camp (Palmer), 145; feud of, with Morgan (N.Y. governor), 167, 169; and formation of Excelsior Brigade, 1, 4, 25–26; at Fredericksburg, Va., 200–201; friendship and admiration of Twichell for, and advice to, 9, 82, 188, 249; and Gettysburg, Pa., unauthorized advance toward, 4, 10, 252, 253, 270, 296; and Gettysburg, Pa., wounding at, 4, 10, 249, 252, 253, 254, 313; and "grand supper," 215–16; grievances against, 39, 55; and Lincoln's visit, 226; at Malvern Hill, Va., 157,